The Health

Find out the inside story on:

Paints—which ones are safe, which ones to avoid

Pesticides—natural remedies for ants, mosquitoes, fleas, roaches, and more

Furnishings, floor coverings, and building materials—complete information on which products contain toxic chemicals, and practical alternatives

Air quality—how fatigue, headaches, colds, and other symptoms can be caused by the air in your home, and what to do about it

Ventilation—how to know if your house is *too* airtight

Water—the pros and cons of bottled water, water softeners, home distillation systems, and more

Light—how to avoid winter blahs by making the most of natural and artificial light

Cookware—why stainless-steel, glass, and iron pots and pans are best for your health

Pets—the best ways to protect their well-being and yours

Heating and cooling—how to maintain your system for maximum efficiency and a healthful environment

It's all here, and much more, in one handy reference . . .

The Healthy Home

"*The Healthy Home* gives the most complete picture I've seen. . . . The book provides solutions and tips for improving the indoor health picture and has such helpful features as a healthy-home-inspection checklist."

—*Philadelphia Inquirer*

"A wide-ranging book on every aspect of healthy home living."

—*The Detroit Free Press*

Acknowledgments

Many thanks to Ray Wolf, who believed in me from the beginning; Cheryl Winters Tetreau, my editor, a tireless wordsmith and a real professional; Mary Kay Shanley, for assistance with chapters 10 and 14; Doug Walter, a helpful source of advice on architectural matters; Pat Reeves, for photocopying and typing; Janusz Beer, who answered all my many questions on light and health; Carlton Wagner, who offered his research on the psychology of color; Eileen Bristow, who dutifully typed charts and kept me encouraged; David Strauss, an environmental chemist at New York University, who gave me some basic chemistry lessons and checked facts, as well.

I'd also like to thank the hundreds of health-conscious authors from whose works I have drawn. Special thanks to John Viehman, executive editor of *Rodale's Practical Homeowner* magazine, for permission to use a number of articles.

I have profited from the insights and suggestions of many colleagues and friends who read parts or all of the manuscript. In particular, I appreciate the comments of Bob Flower, who opened his copious files to me, and of Sandra Clark and Alice Mason, who each served as excellent sounding boards. Above all, many thanks to my best friend, Bob, who in ways beyond measure has contributed to this book; and to my parents and my grandparents and their houses, which are homes to me, reference points in memory.

THE HEALTHY HOME:

AN ATTIC-TO-BASEMENT GUIDE TO TOXIN-FREE LIVING

LINDA MASON HUNTER

POCKET BOOKS

New York London Toronto Sydney Tokyo Singapore

Notice

The information in this book has been carefully researched, and all efforts have been made to ensure accuracy. The publisher and author assume no responsibility for any injuries suffered or damages or losses incurred during or as a result of following this information. All information should be carefully studied and clearly understood before taking any action based on the information and advice presented in this book.

---

*We shape our buildings
and afterwards our buildings shape us.*

WINSTON CHURCHILL

For Kim and Scott
Randy and Josie
May all their homes be healthy.

 POCKET BOOKS, a division of Simon & Schuster Inc.
1230 Avenue of the Americas, New York, NY 10020

Copyright © 1989 by Linda Mason Hunter
Cover design copyright © 1990 by Todd Radom

Published by arrangement with Rodale Press

Hunter, Linda Mason.
  The healthy home / Linda Mason Hunter.
    p. cm.
  Includes bibliographical references.
  ISBN 0-671-70819-8 : $9.95
  1. Indoor air pollution—Health aspects. 2. Housing and health.
I. Title.
[RA577.5.H86 1990]
640'.28'9—dc20   90-31090
                                    CIP

First Pocket Books trade paperback printing July 1990

10 9 8 7 6 5 4 3 2 1

POCKET and colophon are registered trademarks of
Simon & Schuster Inc.

Printed in the U.S.A.

Contents

Preface

In the summer of 1986, amid all the papers and paraphernalia that routinely vie for an editor's attention, was a startling report. A five-year study prepared for the U.S. Environmental Protection Agency (EPA) by a scientist at Harvard University found levels of toxic pollutants as much as five times higher *inside* houses than outdoors. And it didn't matter where the samples were taken. Citizens living next to chemical factories in New Jersey or next to smelter plants in Ohio had the same degree of indoor pollution as citizens living in remote, rural areas of North Dakota. The conclusion: Most Americans were living in toxic environments. Among the culprits: paint, plastics, cigarettes, building materials, other consumer products, and tap water.

How did this happen? Home is supposed to be the seat of regeneration, of family, of love, kindness, and nurturance. Now, as we approach the turn of another century, not only is the American family in a state of unprecedented turmoil and change, but the very structure we have always considered essential to the great American dream is an unhealthy place to be.

The EPA report raised only questions. What are these toxins? Are they at least partly responsible for the rising cancer rate? Could they be the cause of the inexplicable mood swings, negativity, and depression that seem to haunt many Americans today?

I wondered if my house was unhealthy and what I should be looking for to find out. How could I treat the causes once I found them?

In digging for answers, I found a few esoteric magazine articles, a lot of scientific studies, and a book or two written for the chemically sensitive. I found nothing to inform the average American of what to look for, what the health effects of some common everyday products are, and what positive steps to take to turn an unhealthy environment into a healthy one. Compounding the problem, information was scattered here and there—no one source pulled all the answers together. Much of the research was disparate, contradictory, and inconclusive. Many of the researchers had vested interests of one sort or another.

That's how this book got its start—to fill a need. I've tried my best to cut through the murk—without, I hope, too much oversimplification. My goal is to add to your knowledge and give you the basics to help you make your home a truly healthy, regenerative place to be.

1

A Synthetic America

Do you live in a healthy home? Chances are you don't. Think about all the things that make up your home environment. For starters, what's in the air you breathe? Many of us routinely sleep in a cloud of synthetics, from formaldehyde in new permanent-press bed sheets to polyurethane-based flame retardant sprayed on mattresses. Unacceptably high levels of radon (an odorless, colorless, radioactive gas) are estimated to contaminate the air in one out of five houses in the United States. Everyday cleaning products like floor wax and furniture polish can create a phenolic haze in the air for days if used without proper ventilation.

How about the water you drink? Do you know where it comes from? How it's treated? And what about safety? Do you have an evacuation plan in case fire breaks out? Are entry doors furnished with good, sturdy dead bolt locks?

All this isn't meant to frighten you. But you should be aware of what the hazards are, where they are located, and how to remedy them. We are living in a dangerous age, a time when crime rates are escalating, common products are often found to be unsafe, and chemical toxins are a regular part of our daily lives. No one knows for sure what these chemicals do to our health, but scientists are discovering that regular exposure over a long period of time may be responsible for the rising rates of cancer, birth defects, and nervous disorders.

Instead of ignoring the dangers, we should recognize them. It's time to take action and make our houses healthy, regenerative places to be.

LIVING IN THE INDUSTRIAL AGE

In the beginning life wasn't easy, but it *was* simple. Human beings lived in caves and hunted and gathered for their food. Nothing mattered but survival. Everything else was secondary.

Then, roughly ten millenia ago, a transition occurred—a mighty agricultural revolution spread slowly through villages and settlements. Cultivating land became a new way of life. Neolithic men and women were on the road to civilization. Shelter changed, too. Instead of caves, families lived in crude houses built with natural, available materials—wood, mud, stone, the hides of animals. Housekeeping consisted of sweeping the floor once a day and whisking the corners for cobwebs.

Somewhere in the mid-1600s humankind experienced another quantum leap forward, moving from the agrarian into the industrial age. Life got much easier and much more complex at the same time. By 1913, the desirable effects of this new evolution were clearly apparent. Science explained many of life's mysteries and cured many ills. There was a spectacular decline in mortality due to changes in sanitation, agriculture, marketing, and general attitudes toward life. By the 1920s, steel mills, auto plants, textile factories, railroads, and food-processing plants brought employment, goods, and services closer to home. For the first time in history, motorized vehicles enabled people to travel with both speed and comfort.

Housing, too, reflected this change. Indoor plumbing replaced privies. Central heating replaced wood and coal stoves. Electricity lengthened productive hours of the day. Hand-cranked washing machines, iceboxes, and gas ovens simplified everyday chores. Carpenters' pattern books (catalogs of popular domestic housing styles) were available to common men and women wanting all the modern conveniences at a price they could afford. Though solidly built, the houses were loose in construction, the buildings often drafty and able to breathe. Natural building materials were used in designs that took advantage of natural ventilation techniques and daylight.

Then, with World War II, a watershed occurred. Instead of solving problems, the noisy contraptions and increasingly fast pace of the 20th century created new kinds of diseases and caused more suffering than they alleviated. Speed of cars, tensions on the job, and poisons in the environment contributed to a general malaise and ill health. As the new appliances and machines became necessities, it became impossible for people to care. Society was reduced to virtual enslavement to the car. Vehicles created more distances than they helped to bridge.

Not only was it the dawn of the nuclear era, but it was also the beginning of the age of synthetic chemicals. In the 40 years following World War II, a virtual explosion of new chemicals found their way into almost every type of industrial and consumer product imaginable. Synthetic fibers were devised in the chemist's laboratory to take the place of cotton, silk, and wool. Plastic replaced wood, glass, and metal. Huge amounts of chemical fertilizers and pesticides were sprayed on the nation's farmlands to enhance yields. Petroleum fueled cars, buses, trains, and airplanes. Birth-control pills promised to control population.

And what about our houses? Instead of wood and stone, building materials are now a unique combination of chemistry and engineering. Plastic, plywood, particleboard, foam insulation, paints, and cleaners are concocted in laboratories, not found in nature. Synthetic chemicals are in our cosmetics and our food. We live among them, breathe them in our air, put them on our skin, and absorb them through the food we eat. Even our water is affected. If it's not contaminated at the source, public water systems inject chlorine and fluoride, and plumbing pipes leach synthetic chemicals and metals into the water that eventually comes out of the tap. To make matters worse, we've insulated, caulked, and weather-stripped to the point where our houses no longer breathe, so toxins hang around inside for days and mix and mingle, creating a witches' brew for us to breathe. As if that weren't enough, our houses are jammed with mechanical and electrical equipment—refrigerators, water heaters, air conditioners, and the like—which alters the natural magnetic field and consumes one-quarter of the nation's electricity.

How does all this affect our health? In the United States today, one person in three has an allergy severe enough to take him or her to a doctor. One person in ten suffers from migraine headaches or high blood pressure. One in five families has a mentally disturbed member. Birth defects are on the rise. One out of every five people will get cancer during his or her lifetime, a 26 percent increase in the last two decades, according to the American Cancer Society. In addition to causing cancer, environmental pollution is suspected to be a major cause of asthma, emphysema, and nervous disorders, and there is speculation that it might also figure into puzzling diseases like Alzheimer's and Parkinson's.

Given all that, can we still argue that the industrial age has relieved our suffering and improved our standard of living? Or is comfort directly related to health? Clearly, humanity is at another crossroads. The long daydream of endless growth, limitless consumption, and irresponsible waste has had a deleterious effect on the environment and on human health. Another 25 years of industrial escalation will see our planet littered with waste, our flimsy houses unable to last even a human lifetime, and our bodies suited only for passivity and indoor living. We will be walking up to our ankles in garbage and drinking only filtered water.

Is this our choice? Or will we choose a genuinely new way of living based on diversified, renewable energy sources? Such a society may, as Alvin Toffler predicts in *The Third Wave* (William Morrow & Co., 1980), turn out to be the first truly humane civilization in recorded history.

The Chemical Menace

Ironically, in the United States today you are far more likely to breathe some of the most debilitating compounds—like methylene chloride, tetrachloroethylene, lead arsenate, or mercury—from pesticides, aerosol sprays, paints, and household cleaners at home. Indoor pollution from radon, household chemicals, pesticides, and other products can reach levels five times higher than in the grimiest air outside.

This development is fairly recent in our history. Since World War II, both the volume and the number of manufactured chemicals have burgeoned, a direct result of research and development of chemical warfare. *One-quarter million* new substances now enter the world *every year*. No one can keep track of what they really are, what they can do to human health, and what they do to the environment. Among them are thousands of chemicals that save lives and improve our standard of living. But among them, too, are chemicals that have caused serious harm and whose effects cannot be judged for years.

No one knows what the health consequences are of breathing a constant stream of these chemicals every day. According to the U.S. National Research Council, no information on toxic effects is available for 79 percent of the more than 48,500 synthetic chemicals listed by the U.S. Environmental Protection Agency (EPA). Fewer than one-fifth have been tested for acute effects, and fewer than one-tenth for chronic, reproductive, or mutagenic effects. Surely, by allowing the production and release of these compounds without understanding their effects, society has set itself up for unpleasant surprises.

HEALTH HAZARDS   One unpleasant side effect of chemical use is cancer, the only major cause of death that has risen consistently since 1900. In a 1980 report to the President, the Toxic Substances Strategy Committee stated that the majority of cancers (80 to 90 percent) are triggered by exposure to hazardous substances in the environment.

But cancer is just one of the most obvious effects of environmental pollutants. Many toxic chemicals we've released into the environment also cause genetic mutations. Mutations are difficult to detect, but scientists say they are almost always harmful and may not be evident for three to four generations. Nervous disorders (like Alzheimer's disease) and respiratory problems are also directly related to environmental pollution.

Scientists agree that the hazard to health posed by a chemical after it enters the environment depends primarily on two factors: (1) its toxicity and (2) the extent of human exposure to it. Here are a few generally accepted scientific facts:

- Some chemicals are immediately toxic. The tiniest amount of some organic compounds found in urethane, for example, invading a single cell causes mutation resulting in cancerous growth. Less toxic chemicals may require a bigger dose to cause such harm.
- Different chemicals have different toxicities. At the same exposure levels, one chemical may produce many more tumors than another. For example, it takes about 100 times more trichloroethylene (TCE) than vinyl chloride in drinking water to produce a similar number of cancers.
- Chemicals react with each other to increase their toxicities.
- Chemicals accumulate in the human body, causing disease. The problem of toxic bioaccumulation is an increasingly serious one. Studies by EPA scientists have found more than 400 chemicals in human body tissue, a fact that troubles doctors.

If you're a young adult who does not smoke, drink alcohol, or take drugs, and if you eat nutritionally, get enough sunlight, and exercise daily, the toxins at home may not affect you. But if you are a child, a pregnant woman, over 60 years old, or if you spend more than 12 hours a day at home, a few chemical toxins in the home can change your life. People who smoke or who suffer from bronchitis, allergies, or heart problems are at high risk, too.

Medical problems caused by environmental hazards in the home are far-reaching. They range from respiratory irritations—stuffy nose, itchy throat, wheezing, shortness of breath—to more serious complaints of ear infection, asthma, and bronchitis. Such subtle symptoms as fatigue, headaches, inattentiveness, and dermatitis are possible reactions to an unhealthy environment.

The most dangerous are chronic, delayed reactions. These result from almost daily exposure, building up over time, and can range from neurological damage (from eating lead paint or drinking lead-contaminated water, for example) to cancer from exposure to radon, asbestos, and chemicals in the air and water.

Acute reactions occur shortly after exposure to high levels of contaminants. They may be just as severe, but they are at least easier to detect, and they signal that something is not agreeing with you. You may develop a rash or headache, for example, soon after bathing or showering in heavily contaminated water.

Some people react more quickly to contaminants than others do. People who wear contact lenses, for example, often are bothered by environmental toxins in the air before anyone else is. Allergic people and those with respiratory problems are often among the first to notice irritating symptoms. But the people who have the most difficulty living in the 20th century are the chemically sensitive. For them, such ubiquitous phenomena as car exhaust, smog, formaldehyde in carpeting and building materials, hydrocarbons in vinyl furniture, perfumes, detergents, and fabric softeners cause severe problems.

Some extremely sensitive people have to struggle to change their lifestyle to reduce exposure to debilitating chemicals. Some must minimize freeway driving because exposure to car exhaust makes them sleepy and confused. Some have to make drastic adjustments, like avoiding gas heat, wearing only natural fibers, staying away from perfumes, cleaning with baking soda rather than commercial soaps. It's a matter of reducing the total toxicity so the immune system has a chance to recover.

A controversial branch of medicine has evolved to treat those people who are acutely sensitive to environmental toxins. Called clinical ecology, this branch of medicine treats allergies and more severe ailments as poisoning. Though clinical ecologists have few friends, acceptance in the scientific community is growing. Arguing in its defense, Al Levin, a prominent San Francisco physician, told *Science* magazine in December 1986 that clinical ecology is only in the early stages of development, as radiation research was in the 1940s. "It took 15 to 20 years for people to realize that ionizing radiation was linked to a higher incidence of cancer," he noted. In time, Levin says, his field will be respected.

One theory about hypersensitivity is that the chemicals that irritate hypersensitive people are poisonous to everyone—but most people never know it. There is growing evidence that the levels of chemicals we used to consider safe are really not. Many scientists agree that for chemicals that may cause cancer or other chronic diseases, the lower the concentration, the lower the risk, but there is no level of exposure so small that the danger of developing the disease is eliminated.

DOESN'T GOVERNMENT PROTECT US?   Why doesn't our government do something to protect us? To be fair, it has tried, but time and time again economic interests win the battle. One federal official put it bluntly when he said, "Today about 4.5 million chemicals are known, 45,000 are in commercial distribution, and it takes a team of scientists, 300 mice, two to three years, and about $300,000 to determine whether a single suspect chemical causes cancer."

State governments, too, are at the mercy of the economic agenda. In 1987 the Texas Air Control Board proposed to ban the sale and use of windshield wiper fluids, air fresheners containing volatile organic compounds (VOCs), and all aerosol products. Manufacturers' economic interests eventually forced the state to back down. In California, the California Air Resources Board proposed to restrict aerosol underarm and hair-care products to try to meet the ozone standard in the Los Angeles and San Francisco Bay areas. Again, the state backed down when presented with the economics of such a ban. According to the May 19, 1988, issue of *Indoor Pollution News*, Albert Pellini, a panelist at the hearings and vice president of Advanced Monobloc Corporation in Pittsburgh, Pennsylvania, decried such state consumer product bans because they could "effectively shut down our industry."

Clearly, living off the fat of big industry is ruining our environment, both inside and outside our homes, and taking our sense of values along with it. Relying on big industry for our daily needs puts hundreds, if not thousands, of miles between us (the consumers) and the producers of the goods we buy. Once we rely on distant industries, neighborly concern for good health is gone. Pollution becomes the price for having a national market. It's an economic issue to big business, rather than an ethical or moral one.

Such a political philosophy confuses the ends with the means. Money is the end—the reason for being—not the means for getting there. This way of thinking obscures the finer details of life, including concern for the individual. The problem, clearly, lies with our 20th century tools for living. Many, from nuclear power plants to synthetic cleansers, are not safe to use. They compromise and exploit humanity. Granted, tools should be efficient, but they should also be safe, productive, and serve humanity—whether they're used in the workplace, in the marketplace, or in our homes.

DEVELOPING A NEW PHILOSOPHY

We are fast discovering that the latest models of fashion, furnishings, food, and fast cars are literally toxic and that living a quality life has little to do with possessions. Instead, it means enjoying good health; nurturing loving relationships; having a regenerative, comfortable place to call home; and spending our daytime hours at tasks that bring satisfaction.

As we enter the 1990s, America is in ecological crisis. We need a society in harmony with its environment, not one that is attempting to dominate it. We need ecological balance. We need to rescale technology to human dimensions. Once we return to natural, low-tox ways of production, ecological balance will begin to be restored and the pollution problems we face today will fade away.

It may seem, in the face of such vast problems, that one lonely voice can't make much of a difference. But you can make a big difference in your little corner of the world—your home. In doing so, you'll not only be improving your own health and well-being, you'll be improving the health of your family and setting an example for others. Your quality of life will improve.

Building Biology

Achieving and maintaining a healthy home requires ecological awareness, a reconciliation between nature and technology. It may seem like a complex journey at first, but it is an attainable goal well worth the effort.

By way of introduction, we can learn from the *Baubiologie* movement currently under way in Germany. *Baubiologie* is a German word meaning architectural biology. It's an essentially utopian concept that strives to bring humanity into harmony with the natural environment. Baubiologists view humans, their clothing, and their dwellings as one living system, comparable to layers of skin. It is essential that all three work in harmony.

The movement grew out of World War II when Germany was devastated by bombings. After the war the country was rebuilt using synthetic construction materials. Over a period of years people living in these new buildings reported suffering from various ailments—depression, insomnia, allergies, circulatory and vascular problems, and cancer. People began to suspect a link between these illnesses and improper sitings of buildings, the use of synthetic materials, and lack of natural light and ventilation.

Baubiologie offers an answer to the 20th century problem of sick buildings. Among its 25 fundamental rules are these:

- Locate a dwelling at a distance from centers of industry and main traffic routes.
- Have dwellings well separated from one another in spacially planned developments amid green areas.
- Use unadulterated building materials of natural origin.
- Use wall, floor, and ceiling materials that allow air diffusion.
- Allow natural self-regulation of indoor humidity.
- Balance heat storage and thermal insulation.
- Emphasize radiant heating and solar energy.
- Construct buildings that smell pleasant or neutral, with no pollution by toxic fumes.
- Choose lighting and colors in accordance with nature.
- Provide adequate protection from noise.
- Preserve natural electrical field conditions.
- Use ergonomic furniture.

Baubiologie advocates holistic living, a philosophy that weaves its way through your whole life. Not only does it emphasize a natural indoor environment, it advocates a nontoxic life-style centered on vegetarian meals made from scratch with foods fresh from the garden and milk fetched from the local farmer, and clothing made of natural fibers colored with vegetable dyes and spun on the family's spinning wheel.

We in the United States may not wish to go that far. Such a drastic change in life-style would be unwelcome and somewhat threatening to many of us. But we can adopt the philosophy of our houses as a third skin, getting rid of the dangers brought about by our industrial mode of living and changing our habits in accordance with our growing ecological awareness.

THE PHYSICAL ENVIRONMENT   It's a sad state of affairs when what we use to build, furnish, and maintain our houses makes us sick. These materials should have a positive influence on the biological functions of the human body, not a negative one. How can you know what is good for you and what is not? Follow two basic rules:

> **Rule 1:** In deciding whether a product should be included in your healthy home, put it through this rugged test:
> (1) Does the product use a renewable resource?
> (2) Can it be disposed of in a safe ecological manner, without polluting the environment?
> (3) Does the product pose a hazard to those who work with it?
> **Rule 2:** In all you do, use *appropriate technology*. Such technologies tend to be inexpensive, readily available to all members of a community, and capable of being produced locally. They are labor intensive rather than energy intensive, are minimally harmful to the environment, and do not violate the humanity of those who use them.

THE EMOTIONAL ENVIRONMENT   The highest purpose of a house is to be a home, to shelter the body and comfort the soul, to serve a person's emotional, as well as physical, needs. This is the concept of *full shelter*. Full shelter promotes well-being, health, and dignity. It is a place that offers comfort when you are tired, inspiration when you are afraid, regeneration when you are defeated. Love itself somehow seems to flow more freely within such a shelter.

To achieve full shelter, we must focus less on packaging and more on nourishment. What good are creature comforts if you have trouble sleeping at night or are always looking for an excuse to be outside? What good is it if everything works efficiently, all the colors match, and the place is luxuriously furnished if the house has no soul? A house with no soul cannot give comfort to yours.

Full shelter is modestly, simply, and honestly done. It has comfortable places for sitting, talking, and sharing. It has a natural identity and function. A house that gives full shelter offers anticipation and appreciation of life. It's a place that shows you have learned to be good to yourself. A house that gives full shelter is home.

The First Step—Commitment

For a quality home life, your house must first be healthy. This book will help you diagnose the dangers and tell you how to fix them. Be careful you don't fall into the trap of expecting to change your whole house overnight. Getting a truly healthy home is, in most cases, a gradual process—a series of little steps that requires time, a change in attitude, and frequently, money.

Cost should not be a big obstacle, however. In most instances, the healthy answer is the simplest one; therefore it's the least expensive. You'll soon discover that though some necessary changes do require a considerable sum (venting a house with unsuitably high radon levels, for instance, can cost more than $1,000), other changes actually cost less than the high-technology mode of doing things. Cleaning products, for example, are much cheaper if you make them yourself, and they're just as effective—sometimes more so. While buying a new, energy-efficient refrigerator requires a cash outlay of about $750 up front, such a purchase can actually save you money in the long run by lowering your electric bills.

In dealing with synthetic chemicals, don't try to get rid of every single toxic molecule. Instead, work at controlling them, minimizing this and minimizing that. Look for safe alternatives, making compromises, if you must, by substituting low-tox products. The lower the concentration, the lower the risk.

Like all big changes, the first step toward creating a healthy home begins with a decision: making the commitment to change. Are you ready for a better tomorrow?

2

Give Your House a Health Audit

As we begin the 1990s, it is obvious that our great industrial age has taken its toll on Americans. We are now exposed to more toxins and dangers at home than anywhere else. The typical American home is in sad shape, indeed. How healthy is your house? To find out, give it a health audit, using the following checklist:

ATTIC

ENERGY EFFICIENCY   (See page 150.)
☐ There is a whole-house fan in the attic, if it is desirable for the climate.

MOISTURE   (See page 148.)
☐ There are no signs of moisture leaking around the chimney, plumbing vents, or skylights or along walls or valleys.

SAFETY   (See page 242.)
☐ There is a nonionizing smoke detector installed here.

VENTILATION   (See page 149.)
☐ There is adequate ventilation—preferably vents in the soffit and in the ridge or vents in the gable ends.

KITCHEN

COOKWARE   (See page 138.)
☐ Cookware is glass, stainless steel, or ceramic.
☐ You do not use aluminum pots and pans or nonstick cookware.
☐ You do not use imported pottery with lead-based paint.

☐ You do not use plastic or Styrofoam drinking glasses.
☐ You use a steamer to cook vegetables.
☐ Food is not stored in plastic containers.

COUNTERTOPS   (See page 138.)
☐ There are heat-resistant surfaces—ceramic tile or stainless steel—next to the oven/range.
☐ All surfaces are hard and smooth with well-sealed joints so moisture and food wastes do not get trapped in the seams.
☐ The total length of the counter is no more than 12 to 15 feet, with no one section less than 4 feet long.
☐ Electrical circuits providing power to the countertops are equipped with ground-fault circuit interrupters (GFCIs).

CUPBOARDS   (See page 139.)
☐ Construction is of solid wood, metal, or exterior-grade plywood.
☐ Any pressed wood is properly sealed at the top and bottom.
☐ There is a locked cupboard for cleaning products.
☐ There is toe space under all cabinets.

FLOORING   (See page 134.)
☐ The floor surface is not too hard—no ceramic tile, brick, or slate.
☐ Any pressed-wood subfloor has been sealed to prevent formaldehyde outgassing.
☐ There is no vinyl flooring.

LIGHTING   (See page 191.)
☐ There is a ceiling light.
☐ Work counters are lit directly from above, preferably with light from under a cabinet, cupboard, or shelf.

MAJOR APPLIANCES   (See page 135.)
☐ Your refrigerator is an energy-efficient model.
☐ You do not have a continuous-cleaning oven; if you have a self-cleaning oven, you do not use its cleaning cycle.
☐ If you have a gas range, it has spark ignition, not a pilot light.
☐ The flame of your gas range is blue tipped, not yellow.
☐ The door of any microwave oven closes tightly.
☐ If the microwave is a countertop model, there are at least 24 inches of adjacent countertop.

SAFETY   (See page 249.)
☐ Your kitchen has a nonionizing smoke detector and a fire extinguisher.
☐ Appliances are unplugged when not in use.
☐ There are no commercial cleaners stored under the sink or in any cabinets or drawers within reach of youngsters or pets.

☐ Pot handles are always turned toward the back of the stove and kept out of the reach of youngsters.
☐ Knives and all potentially dangerous utensils and appliances are kept well out of the reach of youngsters.

VENTILATION   (See page 149.)
☐ There are at least two operable windows, placed on two sides of the room.
☐ If you have a gas range, you have an exhaust fan vented to the outside.

WORK CENTERS   (See page 138.)
☐ You have a preparation and cleanup area centered on the sink.
☐ You have a cooking and serving area centered on the range/oven.
☐ You have a mixing and storing area located close to the refrigerator.

DINING AREA

FLOORING   (See page 133.)
☐ It can take spills without staining.
☐ There is no pressed-wood subflooring, or it has been properly sealed.

TABLE   (See pages 133, 191.)
☐ You have a large table and sturdy chairs, with no protruding nails or rough edges, situated where people can easily walk around them.
☐ There is a soft overhead light hung low over the table.

LIVING AREAS

CEILINGS   (See page 82.)
☐ There is no acoustic ceiling tile containing asbestos.

FLOORING   (See page 133.)
☐ There is no pressed-wood subflooring, or it has been properly sealed.
☐ The floors are made of natural materials—hardwood, slate, ceramic, and so forth.
☐ Any rugs are untreated cotton or wool and have nonslip backings.
☐ Any wall-to-wall carpet has not been treated with pesticides or antistain coatings. The backing is jute.

FURNISHINGS   (See page 132.)
☐ Your furniture is ergonomic—it promotes a natural spinal curve.
☐ There are no particleboard furniture frames, plastic foam fillings, or synthetic upholsteries.
☐ The furniture is solid wood or metal, covered and stuffed with natural, untreated materials.
☐ There are no glued joints in the furniture.

LIGHTING   (See page 190.)
☐ There are two kinds of lighting in each living area: general room lighting and individual task lighting.
☐ Artificial lighting is placed to minimize shadows.
☐ There are no electrical cords running under rugs or carpets.

SAFETY   (See page 242.)
☐ There is a nonionizing smoke detector located here.

WALLS   (See page 108.)
☐ There is no lead paint.
☐ The walls are plaster or solid wood paneling.

WINDOWS   (See pages 116, 133, 182, 266.)
☐ Any recently dry-cleaned curtains and drapes are hung outside for 6 hours before being brought in.
☐ Your window coverings are made of untreated natural materials.
☐ Each room has a window on at least two sides.
☐ There are locks on all windows (here and throughout the house.)

BATHROOM

ELECTRICITY   (See page 248.)
☐ The bathroom circuit is equipped with a GFCI.
☐ There are enough outlets to accommodate your family's use.

FLOORING   (See page 133.)
☐ It is nonslip and easy to clean.
☐ There is no wall-to-wall carpeting.

SAFETY   (See page 235.)
☐ There are a nonionizing smoke detector and a fire extinguisher located here.
☐ The tub or shower floor has rubber, nonskid mats.
☐ There are rails installed at the tub and toilet if elderly people live in the home.
☐ The medicine cabinet is out of reach of youngsters or kept locked.
☐ There are no commercial cleaners under the sink.
☐ If there are small children in the house, razors, soaps, talc, and so forth are kept off the tub sides and out of reach.
☐ Electric razors, blow-dryers, and curling irons are unplugged and put away after use.
☐ There are towels not more than a foot away from the tub, and there is a minimum of 2 feet of towel rack per person.

TOILET   (See page 155.)
☐ You have a water-saving toilet.

TUB/SHOWER   (See pages 61, 93, 155, 193.)
☐ If there is chloroform in your water, you have installed a filter on the shower head.
☐ You keep mold and mildew in check.
☐ You have installed a water-saving shower head.
☐ The bathing area is lit with watertight downlights.
☐ There are no electrical outlets nearby.

VENTILATION   (See page 149.)
☐ There is an exhaust fan vented directly outside using the shortest route possible.
☐ There is an operable window.

WATER   (See page 40.)
☐ If contaminants are present in your water, you have installed a treatment system.

ADULTS' BEDROOM

BED   (See page 139.)
☐ The bed frame does not contain pressed wood or synthetic adhesives.
☐ There are at least 15 inches of standing space along both sides for making the bed.
☐ Your bedding is cotton and/or wool, not foam or other synthetic.
☐ If you use permanent-press sheets, they have been washed several times before being put on the bed.
☐ You do not use an electric blanket or an electrically heated water bed.

CLOSET   (See page 194.)
☐ It has a light inside, mounted at least 18 inches from clothing or other stored items.

COLORS   (See page 199.)
☐ The bedroom is painted a restful, tranquil color.

FURNITURE   (See page 139.)
☐ There is no pressed wood in any bedroom furniture.

LIGHTING   (See page 192.)
☐ There is an overhead light with a switch right inside the door.
☐ Reading lights are placed so you can read in bed.
☐ There is a light switch within reach of the bed.

SAFETY   (See pages 237, 242.)
☐ All small rugs have nonskid backings.
☐ There is a nonionizing smoke detector here.

WINDOWS   (See pages 133, 182, 266.)
☐ Your curtains are of natural fabric and not chemically treated.
☐ There are windows on two sides of the room for good light and ventilation.
☐ Each window has a lock.

CHILDREN'S BEDROOM

FURNITURE   (See pages 139, 140.)
☐ There is no pressed wood in any bedroom furniture.
☐ Babies and small children should not have pillows.

LIGHTING   (See page 192.)
☐ The lights are inside sealed enclosures, like bulkhead lights, for safety.
☐ All the lights have molded plugs.
☐ You have installed special childproof sockets or are using outlet covers.

SAFETY   (See page 242.)
☐ There is a nonionizing smoke detector here.
☐ You have no track lighting here. (Children are known to poke items into the tracks.)

ENTRYWAY

FLOORING   (See page 133.)
☐ It is sturdy and easy to clean and maintain.
☐ There is no pressed-wood flooring or subflooring, or it has been properly sealed.

LIGHTING   (See page 190.)
☐ The entryway and door are well lit.

SAFETY   (See page 242.)
☐ There is a nonionizing smoke detector here.

SECURITY   (See page 262.)
☐ There are dead bolts or other secure locks here and on all first-floor doors.
☐ The door has a wide-angle peephole.

STAIRS

SAFETY   (See pages 243, 245, 251.)
☐ Nothing is ever stored on the steps.
☐ There is a nonionizing smoke detector at the top of the stairs.
☐ You have fire extinguishers at both the top and bottom of the stairs.
☐ There is a light at the top of the stairs, with a switch at both the top and bottom of the stairs.
☐ You have a rail on at least one side of the staircase.
☐ The treads are sturdy and in good shape.

BASEMENT

ELECTRICAL SYSTEM   (See page 152.)
☐ Your wiring has been checked and is adequate and up-to-date.
☐ There is no aluminum wiring.
☐ There are steel conduit or metal-sheathed cable systems.
☐ Old-fashioned porcelain knob and tube wiring has been replaced.
☐ You know which circuits serve which rooms and major appliances in the house and have them listed at the service panel.
☐ A GFCI is on the basement circuit to protect against electrical shock.
☐ Protective plates are on all switches.

HEATING SYSTEMS   (See page 156.)
☐ Your home is heated by a renewable, noncombustible resource—solar gain—with electrical radiant panels as backup.
☐ The filters in a forced-air heating system are cleaned regularly.
☐ You check your gas-fueled appliances annually for leaks.
☐ Each gas-fueled appliance has its own source of combustion air.
☐ The chimney is sound, with no cracks.
☐ The heat has supply and return ducts for each room.
☐ The furnace and other utilities are enclosed in a soundproof room to cut down on noise and air pollution problems.

INSECTICIDES   (See page 119.)
☐ Your house has never been sprayed by an exterminator, or if it has, chlordane (a synthetic chemical used to get rid of termites) was not used.

MOISTURE   (See page 98.)
☐ There is no dampness in wall or slab cracks.
☐ The plumbing pipes do not leak or sweat.
☐ The insulation is not damp.
☐ There are no musty odors or mildew stains.

PLUMBING   (See page 45.)
☐ Your intake pipe is not lead.
☐ You do not have polyvinyl chloride (PVC) or galvanized-iron pipes.

□ There are no recently installed pipes with lead solder.
□ You have had your water tested for lead contamination.
□ The floor drain has been checked for sewer gas entering the house.

SAFETY   (See pages 69, 80, 242.)
□ You have tested for radon and levels are below 4 picocuries per liter of air (pCi/l).
□ There is no asbestos, or it has been encapsulated.
□ There are a nonionizing smoke detector and a fire extinguisher here.

SECURITY   (See page 254.)
□ All basement windows have bars.
□ Any outside hatchway or entry door is equipped with locks.

STORAGE   (See page 251.)
□ If paints or other flammables are stored here, the area is well ventilated and lids are sealed tightly with wax paper to keep fumes from continually leaking.

VENTILATION   (See page 148.)
□ There are operable windows across from each other in each basement room.

YARD

ELECTRICITY   (See page 194.)
□ Lights are placed at the front, side, and rear of the house for security.
□ Any outside receptacles are protected with GFCIs.
□ No heavy electrical wires cross the yard.

GARDENS   (See page 165.)
□ There is no treated lumber near the food gardens.
□ You do not use synthetic pesticides and herbicides.
□ You do not mulch your garden with treated grass clippings.
□ There is a storage shed nearby for garden tools.

GARAGE

ELECTRICITY   (See page 248.)
□ There is a GFCI protecting each outlet.

SAFETY   (See pages 242, 251.)
□ A nonionizing smoke detector and a fire extinguisher are located here.
□ Your electric garage door opener is set so that the door will immediately stop closing if it lightly taps an object.
□ You do not store oily rags, filled gasoline containers, or other combustible material here, where an ignition spark could start a fire.

SECURITY   (See page 254.)
☐ There are bars on the windows and locks on the doors.

STRUCTURE   (See page 90.)
☐ You do not have an attached garage, or if it is attached to the house, the separating wall is as vapor-proof as it can be—no ducts or outlets go from the garage to the house.

HOUSE STRUCTURE

EXTERIOR FINISH   (See page 142.)
☐ There is no preservative-treated wood.
☐ There is no asbestos.
☐ Building materials are biodegradable, and their manufacture did not consume a large amount of energy.

INSULATION   (See page 148.)
☐ There is no urea-formaldehyde foam insulation (UFFI) or asbestos.

INTERIOR FINISH   (See page 173.)
☐ The interior finish materials are lath and plaster, concrete, ceramic, or solid untreated wood.
☐ There is no factory-made parquet or sheet vinyl flooring.

ROOF   (See page 173.)
☐ There are no asbestos shingles.

WINDOWS   (See page 148.)
☐ There is adequate cross ventilation throughout the house.

HOUSE INTERIOR

AIR QUALITY   (See page 64.)
☐ The house is not so airtight it can't breathe.
☐ There is not an attached garage or workshop.
☐ Mold isn't a constant problem in a bathroom or any other area inside the house.
☐ No one smokes in the house.
☐ You do not heat, cook, or dry clothes with kerosene appliances.
☐ The oil furnace, water heater, and any other fossil-fueled appliances are properly vented.

☐ There are no fuel-oil fumes in the basement.

☐ Your house doesn't contain manufactured building products such as particleboard, chipboard, paneling, interior-grade plywood, or hardboard, all of which contain formaldehyde.

☐ There are no new carpets that have been chemically treated.

☐ You never use paints, stains, preservatives, solvents, paint strippers, or finish removers in a room without leaving every window open until the odor is gone, the solvents have evaporated, and the surfaces are dry.

☐ You do not regularly wax floors or furniture or use aerosol cleaners, air fresheners, or insecticides indoors.

☐ The house does not get smoky from a fireplace or wood stove.

3

Site

Where we live does make a difference in our health. Even if we invest ourselves totally in creating a nontoxic home environment, that effort is wasted if we live downstream from a toxic waste dump that is poisoning our water or downwind from an industry that is spoiling our air.

But it's not just air and water. Weather can be conducive to good or ill health, too. Climate is another important consideration. Some people seem to be more productive in a continuously mild climate; others grow hardy with a definite change of seasons. Even the lay of the land has an important bearing on health because it affects the movement of air and dissipation of offending chemical fumes, odors, and smoke. Natural disasters are another consideration—tornadoes, hurricanes, and earthquakes can ruin otherwise ideal places.

These are just a few of the many site-related factors that can single-handedly make a home an unhealthy place to be. It's important to know what these factors are and to evaluate your site for any problems that may exist.

AIR POLLUTION

We breathe 15,000 to 25,000 liters of air a day. Each breath contains ten billion trillion air molecules—or about as many molecules as there are stars in the known universe. Compared with this, we drink at most 2 liters of water a day. Given such figures, air pollution exposure dwarfs exposure from drinking water.

Most of the nation's largest cities—and some rural counties—are still not able to meet the clean air standards set by Congress almost 20 years ago. All told, approximately 80 percent of the nation's more than 210 million people live in urban areas where the air is significantly polluted—by toxic gases and particulate matter, or both—from the combustion of fossil fuels. No one likes to breathe polluted air, but the people who suffer the most are those with heart or respiratory diseases, children, and the elderly. For these people, air quality may very well be the most important aspect to consider when deciding on the best place to live.

The most common chronic respiratory diseases associated with exposures to urban air (according to data from the U.S. Department of Health, Education, and Welfare),are asthma, chronic bronchitis, and emphysema. But air pollution also exacerbates heart disease and may be detrimental to the long-term health of infants and children.

What's in this air we breathe? A partial listing:

- sulfur dioxide and particulates
- ozone
- oxides of nitrogen and hydrocarbons
- carbon monoxide
- toxic fallout
- PCBs
- dioxin and furans
- toxaphene
- radioactivity

Among the harmful ingredients in air outside our homes are sulfur dioxide and particulates, by-products of the combustion of coal, oil, wood, and other fuels, and ozone, produced from hundreds of different sources, including dry cleaners, bakeries, auto body paint shops, household consumer products, and the burning of fossil fuels. Although ozone pollution has been regulated since 1971, there are still 62 areas, mostly major cities, that have not yet attained the national standards for ozone levels.

Los Angeles—Ozone Capital of the World

Year-round sunshine, a car-centered life-style, and a geographical location favorable to air inversions all combine to help Los Angeles violate the ozone standards 140 times a year. Still, this is an improvement over the past. The number of days city air exceeds the recommended level is now down from over 300 in the 1970s to the present 140.

Ozone pollution in Los Angeles is so bad that it can't possibly comply with the ozone standard the U.S. Environmental Protection Agency set for all cities to reach by 1992. A likely scenario is that the city will have to reduce emissions of ozone's key raw materials, volatile organic compound (VOCs), by more than 70 percent to meet the standards of the Clean Air Act. Compliance in some areas could mean restrictions on deodorant sprays and use of gasoline lawn mowers. Already mandatory at Los Angeles gas stations are nozzle controls on gas pumps that catch at least 84 percent of VOCs emitted while cars are filled up.

Oxides of nitrogen and hydrocarbons, the ingredients of smog, are likely to be highest within a few miles of a large power-generating plant or other large industrial polluter. Chemicals in this group damage cells in the lungs and blood vessels. When they get into the stomach, they can produce cancer-causing nitrosamines.

Carbon monoxide is commonly found in significant levels along well-traveled roadways. Other principal sources of carbon monoxide are tobacco smoke, home chimneys, and industrial smokestacks.

Toxic Fallout

Toxic fallout consists of invisible gases and fine particles carrying a startling array of man-made chemicals—compounds such as polychlorinated biphenyls (PCBs), dioxin, toxaphene, and chlordane—that can permanently alter the tiniest mechanisms of a cell. Billions of pounds of synthetic chemicals are released into the air each year, some routinely, from industry and agriculture. Among the worst are polychlorinated biphenyls (PCBs). They were used extensively for more than 30 years in the United States as a heat retardant in electrical capacitors, space heaters, television sets, and other equipment where heat was a factor and the possibility of explosion was a concern. They're also found in hydraulic fluids and lubricants and in some plastics, waterproof adhesives, paints, inks, dyes, and carbonless copy paper. Industries generating the most PCBs are manufacturers of wood pulp, paper, and metals.

Now banned from production, PCBs still sit in electrical capacitors and transformers all across America. High levels of these chemicals are commonly found in the air near large municipal trash incinerators. PCBs are virtually nondegradable and can enter the body through the skin, by inhalation, and through ingestion. They are highly toxic and deadly carcinogens.

Dioxin is thought to be the most dangerous synthetic compound ever concocted in a laboratory. An amount one-hundredth the size of a grain of salt can immediately kill a guinea pig. It was the presence of dioxin in the air, soil, and water that caused a national scandal and mass evacuations at Love Canal, New York, in 1978, and in Times Beach, Missouri, in 1973.

Furans, molecular cousins to dioxin, are almost as hazardous but much more pervasive in the environment. The presence of furans have been detected in the air along Mississippi River towns (particularly in the Midwest, where tons of pesticides are routinely sprayed on cornfields) and in Louisiana, perhaps our nation's most toxic state.

All it takes to form furans and dioxin is heat applied to the right combination of chlorine, hydrogen, carbon, and oxygen. Those ingredients are amply provided in the common garbage burner, especially when fire melts chlorine-impregnated plastic. They can show up in wood-waste boilers, in hazardous-waste incinerators, and in copper and steel manufacturing.

Toxaphene, an insecticide banned in 1982, is known to cause cancer. Levels of toxaphene found in the Great Lakes in the mid-1980s were far above those known to be harmful. Researchers believe the chemicals were blown there in a toxic cloud from southern cotton fields.

Though not a chemical molecule, radioactivity can be found in our air, too. EPA studies of the health effects of radioactive material in the air show that it poses an increased risk of cancer and genetic damage in humans. The greatest risk to large populations is found near large coal-fired power plants on urban sites, near nuclear power plants that regularly vent emissions or have accidents, and around nuclear weapons factories, nuclear waste dumps, and uranium mines.

WATER POLLUTION

We Americans are not accustomed to worrying about our water. We just turn on the tap and there's enough water to take care of whatever task we need it for, from boiling vegetables to bathing to washing the family car. But whether you use chlorinated municipal water or pump your own water from a well, the era when you could take clean tap water for granted is past.

No state or county is immune from water pollution. According to a recent EPA report, 25 states report groundwater contaminated by pesticides; 28 states report contamination by metals; 40 states report contamination from organic chemicals; and 43 states report contamination from inorganic chemicals. Here's a brief rundown of some of the problems:

- According to U.S. and Canadian researchers, the 37 million people who live around the Great Lakes generally have 20 percent higher levels of toxic chemicals in their bodies than other North Americans. One reason: The Great Lakes, which supply fish and water for regional residents, are so contaminated with hazardous chemicals that current pollution control efforts cannot adequately protect human health.
- In 1986, health officials in California discovered that one-fifth of the state's largest drinking-water wells were contaminated at levels above legal safety limits.
- In 1987, authorities in Iowa detected pesticides in at least half the city wells in the state.
- In Newark, New Jersey, 75 percent of the city's water pipes are composed of lead, a heavy metal known to cause mental retardation in children.
- New Orleans may have the distinction of having the worst water in the country. The city draws its water from the Mississippi River, which is the final repository for waste from hundreds of industrial companies that line its banks. Shortly after EPA testing in 1987, the Environmental Defense Fund released a study linking elevated cancer death rates in New Orleans with the presence of organic chemicals in the city's drinking water.
- In San Francisco, asbestos in the water is sometimes found at more than 100 times the acceptable level.
- Tucson, Arizona, one of the cleanest, most picturesque cities in the Southwest, has hardly any heavy industry, yet 3 years ago it was discovered that residents in one area of the city had been drinking

water with dangerously high levels of trichloroethylene (TCE), an industrial solvent; they had been drinking this contaminated water since the 1950s.

These facts are frightening enough, but they're just the tip of the iceberg. Look what's in our immediate future:

■ Nine out of ten toxic chemical dumps are located directly above underground water supplies; many of these are sources of contamination.

■ Two-and-a-half million steel tanks containing fuel for automobiles are buried underground. More than a half million of these are already leaking into groundwater. According to the American Petroleum Institute, 350,000 older tanks will be leaking by the end of the 1980s.

■ Studies in five states have strengthened the evidence for a link between chlorinated drinking water and three types of cancer. About 160 million Americans drink water treated with chlorine.

INDUSTRIAL POLLUTION

Synthetic chemicals, the ones we humans concoct in laboratories in chemical production plants daily all across the country, are polluting our air, soil, and water. In addition to industrial pollution's links to cancer, there has been speculation that pollution caused by synthetic chemicals might also figure into puzzling neurological diseases. Research reported by Canadian scientists suggests that people living near pulp mills and petrochemical facilities have a strikingly high chance of contracting Parkinsons' disease, which afflicts perhaps 1 percent of the world's population (or 50 million people).

The worst industrial states appear to be Louisiana, Texas, and New Jersey. Each is a major chemical producer, and each has severe contamination of both air and water. It cannot be a coincidence that these three states head the list in number of cancer cases. But while New Jersey is making heroic efforts to clean up its environment (every major New Jersey aquifer is affected by chemical contaminants), programs in Texas and Louisiana are at least 10 years behind the times. Louisiana actually courts toxic industry, wooing companies whose business is hazardous disposal and toxic incineration.

Many cancer hot spots are located in areas of chemical manufacture and disposal. A study by the National Cancer Institute showed respiratory and testicular cancers are higher in counties that have some form of petroleum industry. People living within a mile of large chemical plants appear to be 4.5 times as prone to lung cancer as those farther away.

NUCLEAR POLLUTION

Despite the possibility of a nuclear Armageddon and massive destruction that could leave the earth uninhabitable for thousands of years, U.S. bureaucrats have sanctioned the nuclear industry. As a result, about 80 nuclear power plants and 19 nuclear weapons facilities dot the country, putting the life and welfare of every citizen at risk.

Nuclear Power

Since the partial meltdown at Pennsylvania's Three Mile Island nuclear power plant in March 1979, nuclear power has been on its way out in the United States. Though a few more nuclear power plants may begin operating each year for several more years, and such controversial plants as Seabrook (in New Hampshire) may even come on line, the pipeline is nearly empty. All plants under construction were ordered before 1974, and no utility has plans to order another for as far into the future as we can see. Some of the oldest nuclear plants are now being retired.

Still, the psychological and social costs of living near a nuclear power plant are undeniably awful. An increased incidence of childhood leukemia has been reported in the vicinity of two nuclear installations in England. In this country, residents in the Susquehanna River valley immediately around Three Mile Island report increased incidences of cancers and abnormally high rates of birth defects. But no one can say whether the extremely high incidence of cancer is related to the near meltdown in 1979 or to the regular venting of radioactive emissions from the reactor, or both. Health consequences of radiation are cumulative—the more you get over the years, the more likely it is that disease will strike.

Nuclear Weapons

A nuclear bomb is made by mining uranium, enriching it, and putting it into a nuclear reactor where it produces plutonium, which is then turned into a

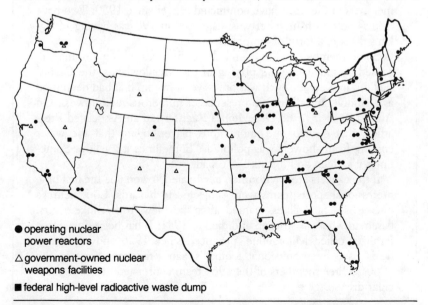

● operating nuclear
   power reactors

△ government-owned nuclear
   weapons facilities

■ federal high-level radioactive waste dump

Nuclear facilities may be too close for comfort. Do you know where the nearest ones to your neighborhood are?

nuclear warhead. In the United States, the process involves more than 90,000 people in 13 states, working at three design laboratories, seven nuclear materials production facilities, seven weapons components and assembly plants, and two test sites. Most of these sites are aging rapidly and becoming even less safe than ever.

According to a February 2, 1987, article in the *Des Moines Register*, the facilities to watch are these:

■ The 32-year-old N Reactor at Hanford, Washington, is the oldest reactor supplying plutonium in the country. It's the same design as the Chernobyl reactor in the USSR, which experienced a meltdown in 1986. Though officials at the U.S. Department of Energy claim the Hanford reactor is perfectly safe, six independent investigations have found it to be otherwise. Even after a $50 million repair job, officials say the N Reactor can operate only until the mid-1990s, when the level of radiation will reach unacceptable limits.

■ Four reactors at the Savannah River Plant are built on an earthquake zone in South Carolina. These reactors have passed their 30-year design lifetime and are thus becoming increasingly prone to leak and vulnerable to a major Chernobyl-like disaster.

Toxic Football?

It's only coincidence, say officials of the New York Giants football team, but team members and some scientists think otherwise. Four members of the team have contracted cancer since 1980. Two have died. The fourth member was diagnosed in 1987 as having Hodgkin's disease, a form of lymphatic cancer.

Some members of the team believe the disease is environmental, caused by practicing and playing in the Meadowlands, the Giants' stadium in New Jersey. It was built over a swamp that had been used as a landfill, and it's in the presence of numerous radio towers. On August 24, 1987, the *Des Moines Register* ran an Associated Press article that quoted one anonymous player saying that the water coming from showers was polluted. "Sometimes it's yellow. Sometimes it's green and it stinks," he said.

If the cancers are environmentally related, it won't be the first time professional sports teams were subjected to hazards. Lou Gehrig's disease is a fatal illness named after the New York Yankees' first baseman who was stricken and died in 1941. It has been linked to a fertilizer called Milorganite, produced since 1926 and applied to fields used by professional football's San Francisco 49ers in the 1960s. Three members of the 1964 team contracted the neuromuscular disease.

■ The 35-year-old Feed Materials Production Center at Fernald, Ohio, supplies uranium for fueling nuclear power reactors. It has dusted the surrounding countryside with 170 tons of poisonous uranium since the early 1950s.

In addition to those in the locations on this list, other large populations are put at risk by the policy of our nuclear weapons industry of shipping nuclear weapons by train. Sometimes called the White Train, this group of trains regularly crisscrosses the country. One travels from the Pantex Plant in Amarillo, Texas, northwest to the Trident Submarine Base at Bangor, Washington. Southeastern routes are followed by trains out of Oklahoma, Kansas, and Missouri to the naval weapons station in Charleston, South Carolina. Another network carries plutonium from the Savannah River Plant in South Carolina to the Rocky Flats Arsenal near Denver. Nuclear shipyards in Connecticut, Mississippi, South Carolina, and Virginia are sites where nuclear loads are shifted and rerouted. Fuel for the nuclear navy travels across the country to and from the National Engineering Laboratory in Idaho. If you live near railroads in any of these areas, you probably live near the route of trains carrying nuclear weapons.

WEATHER, TOPOGRAPHY, AND NATURAL AND MAN-MADE DISASTERS

Air and water quality and proximity to nuclear activity are not the only factors to consider when evaluating the health of a site. You should also take into account the weather, topography, and natural and man-made disasters.

How's the Weather?

Climatic factors are very important to good health. How we feel depends on a myriad of factors—barometric pressure, wind, and whether it's hot or cold, sunny or cloudy, stormy or balmy, humid or dry. Weather affects the brain, nerves, heart, lungs, blood vessels, nasal passages, sinuses, and skin.

Doctors have observed that clear weather, low humidity, and rising pressure bring fewer heart attacks. Heart attacks increase during increasing temperature or steady or failing pressure. Slower reflexes at this time cause more traffic and industrial accidents. Suicides rise. Children, especially, get restless. On a clear, dry day with high pressure and little wind, there is little stress and few heart attacks, and reflexes are fast.

Cold weather brings on attacks of asthma and can cause respiratory diseases, strokes, and heart attacks in people over age 55. Changing weather fronts can cause pain. The *whys* behind these phenomena are still speculative, but researchers continue to probe. Ideal weather for thriving human life is in a relatively limited temperature range—optimally at 77°F.

PREVAILING WINDS Prevailing winds can be pleasant and invigorating, or stressful and annoying. Desert regions are sometimes swept by consistent

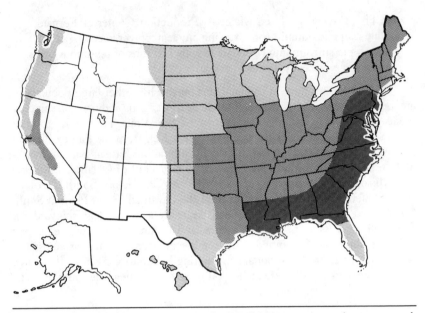

It's not your imagination—the severity of your allergies may vary when you travel. The map is darkest in areas with the greatest potential for causing allergic problems. (*Source:* Copyright © 1979 by Robert A. Shakman. From the book *Where You Live May Be Hazardous to Your Health.* Reprinted with permission of Stein and Day Publishers.)

winds that are intolerable to many people. Coastal sea breezes often bring fog and dampness, especially on the West Coast. Winds can stir up a physical ruckus for allergy sufferers, too. Pollen and fungi spores, which winds can carry as far as 600 miles, can create instant misery in susceptible people.

There is another type of wind that is legendary for its persistence and ill effects. Often dubbed the Devil's Wind, this strong, recurrent wind blows with greater force and from a different direction than the prevailing wind. Examples in this country include the hot, dry Santa Ana winds that bring a touch of madness to southern Californians twice a year, in the spring and in the fall. The winter Chinook carries misery to residents of parts of the Rockies. The summer winds of the Arizona-Mexico desert sweep the ranchers with what the Indians call wind sickness. Nasal allergies and sinus infections flare up. Tempers flare, and crimes and suicides increase.

IONS   Scientists have found that air molecules carry an electrical charges, called ions. Ions affect brain waves, influence moods, and help to explain why rheumatic joints act up before rain, why some animals grow skittish, and why ants block their entrances before storms. The natural ratio is approximately 5 positive ions to 4 negative ones. Ten to 12 hours before an onslaught of Devil's Wind, the ratio of positive to negative ions jumps from a normal 5:4 to up to 132:4. The shift in ion ratio coincides with the onset of nervous and physical symptoms in weather-sensitive persons.

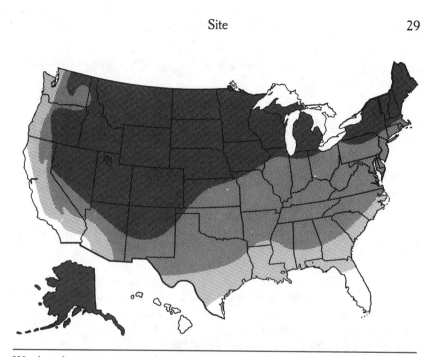

Weather plays an important role in selecting the site of your house. This map is darkest
in areas with the most days each year under 32°F. (*Source:* Copyright © 1979 by
Robert A. Shakman. From the book *Where You Live May Be Hazardous to Your
Health.* Reprinted with permission of Stein and Day Publishers.)

Research has shown that negative air ions are generally good in their
health effects, and positive air ions are bad. In general, too high a level of
positive ions in the air causes a person to feel depressed, fatigued, irritable, and
generally upset. Large numbers of negative ions produce the opposite effect
and make a person feel invigorated, enlivened, and happier. About 25 percent
of the population is sensitive to ion content in the air. Climates that may make
a sensitive person ill include those in sealed office buildings with year-round
climate control, automobiles, electrically heated saunas, and rooms heated
with electric space heaters.

Ion concentration is usually higher in summer than in winter, when the
temperature is elevated, during the day than at night, when the weather is
clear rather than cloudy, and when the moon is full. Mountains and beaches
have higher levels of negative (healthful) ions. Polluted areas have fewer
negative ions.

Altitude and Topography

In locating a house, the ideal site is the highest possible elevation on the
windward side of the community (upstream of prevailing wind currents), away
from all large industry that produces offending emissions. Avoid low-lying
ground, hazardous due to the possibility not only of flooding during wet
seasons but also of atmospheric inversions, a phenomenon that occurs when

heavy particles of air pollution settle in low-lying areas. Atmospheric inversions frequently occur in valleys.

Natural Disasters

Whether it's tornadoes in the nation's midsection, hurricanes on the Gulf and East coasts, or earthquakes on the West Coast, every year natural disasters occur throughout the United States. Fortunately, the possibility of any of these disasters hitting a specific community can be predicted, so you have time to take cover, if necessary.

TORNADO   Spring is tornado season in the South and Midwest. Tornadoes spring from turbulence generated in the collision of fast-moving, warm, moist air. The powerful, swirling winds of a tornado can strike swiftly with deadly force, often wiping out a small community.

HURRICANE   The hurricane belt in the United States is from Texas to Maine. Hurricanes strike this area just about every year, usually in autumn. The heaviest damage is always along the coast; then heavy rainstorms, often with powerful winds, move inland. Rarely does a hurricane strike the West Coast—only one per century has hit Los Angeles.

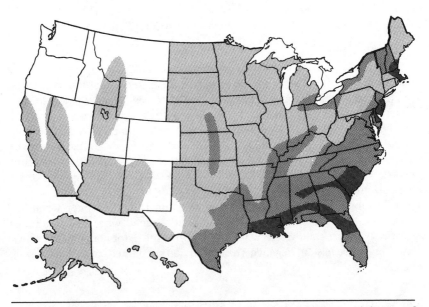

Know the risks of your geographical location, and be prepared for natural disasters if you live in the darkest shaded areas on the map. These are high-risk areas for earthquakes, tornadoes, and hurricanes. (*Source:* Copyright © 1979 by Robert A. Shakman. From the book *Where You Live May Be Hazardous to Your Health*. Reprinted with permission of Stein and Day Publishers.)

EARTHQUAKE   The greatest hazard is along geological fault lines, but all areas in an earthquake region are at risk. Scientists are getting better at predicting earthquakes, although some happen completely unexpectedly.

If you choose to live near a fault, buy a frame house, not a masonry one. Up to a certain point, a frame house can bend and ride out a deforming force, while a brick or stucco house is apt to collapse. Older houses may not measure up to the higher structural standards recently imposed in quake zones. Consult a structural engineer if you're buying or remodeling an older home.

Man-Made Disasters

As if tornadoes, hurricanes, and earthquakes weren't enough to worry about, to ensure a healthy home site you should be on the lookout for areas that harbor the possibility of man-made disasters.

NUCLEAR MELTDOWN   Our country is dotted with about 80 nuclear power plants, recognizable by mammoth concrete cooling towers. These loom over tiny communities and send steam billowing into the air that can be seen for miles. Life seems to change as you get closer to one of these plants. Birds stop singing. The air cackles from high-power lines overhead.

In the case of a meltdown (the worst possible scenario, as happened at Chernobyl, USSR, in 1986), it is generally believed that people living within 10 miles of a nuclear reactor would suffer immediate fatalities. Land would be contaminated within 200 miles downwind of the reactor, and radiation would affect milk from cattle and cause latent cancer deaths within 1,000 miles. These are conservative figures.

TOXIC SPILLS   In light of recent environmental disasters in Bhopal, India, (1984) and the Rhine River in Switzerland (1985), the EPA commissioned a review of toxic spills by industry in this country. The subsequent report documented almost 7,000 accidents between 1980 and early 1985. These accidents caused 138 deaths, 4,717 injuries, and evacuations of more than 200,000 people. And this is only a partial list from selected areas. The real national total is probably at least twice as high. (A copy of the EPA's complete state-by-state listing of accidents and the company index is available for $25. See appendix B.)

TOXIC WASTE DUMPS   There are 10,000 existing municipal landfills in the United States that are designated hazardous waste sites, and more are being added to the list all the time. Most experts agree that, sooner or later, every landfill leaks. And when it does, several toxic compounds are released into the environment—the air, water, soil, and eventually the food chain. Studies have found higher incidences of birth defects and cancer in people living downwind of toxic dumps. And the toxins can contaminate water as far as 65 miles from the actual site.

While incineration may be better in some ways than dumping untreated poisons into the earth, it should never be considered anything but a temporary

Superfund

Where most federal legislation is prospectively aimed at clean air, water, and so forth for the future, the 1980 Comprehensive Environmental Response, Compensation, and Liability Act (called CERCLA or Superfund) is retrospectively aimed at cleaning up waste sites and spills that have already occurred.

The Superfund has been rendered less effective by amendments enacted in 1986. The amendments are four times as long as the original act and will create excessive delays under the Superfund laws.

Municipal landfills make up half of all designated Superfund cleanup sites. U.S. Defense Department properties are among the worst sites on the Superfund list of 200 priorities. The five worst are Rocky Mountain Arsenal in Colorado; Weldon Spring Quarry, a joint U.S. Army/Department of Energy site in Missouri; McClellan Air Force Base, a California installation cited for groundwater contamination; the Naval Air Engineering Center in Lakehurst, New Jersey; and Robins Air Force Base in Georgia.

Though many are not on the Superfund list, there are 10,000 hazardous waste sites posing a serious public health threat and a grand total of 378,000 that eventually will need corrective action.

and highly risky solution to the problem. Many synthetic chemicals break down with heat, then reform—often in more toxic form. Burning releases gases and vapors as well as tiny particulates into the air to be breathed by many people, some of whom live hundreds of miles from the site.

Nuclear waste is another concern. There is clearly *no safe way* to get rid of it. Certainly, burying it is no answer. In Hanford, Washington, site of the Hanford Nuclear Reservation, where much of our radioactive waste has been buried, farmers complain that cropland has been ruined by seepage from government plutonium-processing facilities and a government-operated radioactive waste dump. Other disputes are simmering in South Carolina, Pennsylvania, and New Mexico.

Congress has ordered all states to find methods to handle their own low-level radioactive wastes starting in 1993. These wastes now are being disposed of in sites in South Carolina, Washington, and Nevada.

STATE OF THE USA

The good old USA is not as clean and pristine as it used to be before industry started fouling things up. Here's a regional review of environmental issues.

The Great Lakes: Toxic Sea

This country's five Great Lakes have been called the most valuable inland water body in the world. Today, all 291,080 square miles of these lakes are severely polluted, and have been for the past 25 years. Residents of the area are warned to limit their consumption of fish to one per week, and pregnant women are advised not to drink the water. Frequency of birth defects among farm animals and some waterfowl has risen sharply. Fish-eating birds from the region have increasingly been found to have a deformity called cross-beak syndrome. They suffer from cataracts, and sometimes their heads are so swollen that they cannot open their eyes.

The Northeast: Acid Rain

Rain in most of the country east of the Mississippi has become increasingly acidic, a result of sulfuric pollution from electrical power plants, steel mills, copper smelters, and so forth in the Ohio Basin. It has gotten so bad that hundreds of lakes in the Northeast and Canada can no longer support fish life. About 300 lakes in the northeastern United States will become acidic in the next 50 years unless the pollutants that cause acid rain are reduced, according to a recent EPA study. Many northeastern lakes in jeopardy are clustered in Connecticut, Rhode Island, and southern Massachusetts. Other vulnerable areas are the Adirondack Mountains of New York, where more than 90 lakes are fishless, and the Pocono Mountains of eastern Pennsylvania. Even such central states as Minnesota and Wisconsin may be vulnerable.

The Reading Prong: Hot with Radon

Radon may be a problem in virtually every state, but the Reading Prong is a definite hot spot of contamination. The Reading Prong is a 150-mile geological formation rich in uranium extending through eastern Pennsylvania, northern New Jersey, and parts of New York. Of the 20,000-plus houses tested so far in Pennsylvania, more than 60 percent recorded unsafe levels of the radioactive gas.

The Farm Belt: Poisoned with Pesticides

Purchases of herbicides have risen by 280 percent in the past 2 decades, and most are used in agriculture. What is this doing to our environment? Just take a look at our country's breadbasket, the heartland of the nation, to find out.

In the Midwest, farmers are increasingly dependent on herbicides, which now account for about 60 percent of the pesticides sold. According to recent studies, farmers handling weed killers face a far higher risk of non-Hodgkin's lymphoma. If they are exposed 20 days or more a year, they are 600 percent more prone to serious illness than the general population, according to recent studies.

But it's not just the farmer at risk. Pesticides are polluting the atmosphere. The volume of farm chemicals evaporating directly into the air—not counting what escapes on windblown topsoil—can range from so-called insignificant

The Battle against Pollution:
How Does Your State Rank?

The following, in order of rank, is how the 50 states scored on a scale of 60 possible points in establishing and enforcing environmental protection programs.

State	Points	State	Points
Massachusetts	45	Illinois	29
Wisconsin	45	Montana	29
California	44	Utah	29
New Jersey	44	Indiana	28
Connecticut	43	Georgia	27
New York	42	South Dakota	27
Oregon	42	North Dakota	26
Florida	41	West Virginia	26
North Carolina	40	Arizona	25
Hawaii	38	Idaho	25
Michigan	38	Kansas	25
Minnesota	38	South Carolina	24
New Hampshire	38	Kentucky	23
Rhode Island	37	Missouri	23
Maine	36	New Mexico	22
Vermont	36	Alabama	21
Maryland	35	Alaska	21
Iowa	34	Louisiana	20
Virginia	34	Tennessee	20
Delaware	32	Nevada	19
Washington	32	Oklahoma	19
Nebraska	31	Texas	19
Pennsylvania	31	Arkansas	17
Ohio	30	Mississippi	17
Colorado	29	Wyoming	15

levels to more than half of what is applied. These then ride the winds and settle in fog and rain.

Scientists have found that a toxic fog sometimes hovers over portions of the rural Midwest. It's made up of microscopic water droplets containing pesticides, herbicides, and many other chemicals—sometimes in concentrations thousands of times higher than had been predicted by a widely used law of chemistry. In rain, researchers found levels of the pesticide alachlor that were 600 times higher than those ever recorded for DDT.

The Gulf Coast: Creating a Toxic Cloud

A lion's share of the nation's synthetic compounds is produced in a stretch of land from Mobile, Alabama, to Corpus Christi, Texas. When the outputs of petrochemicals of both Texas and Louisiana are taken together, the two states represent more than half of the nation's production—actually 60 percent. Some of the oil refineries and chemical plants that pock the Gulf Coast are so huge that they have been known to create a phenomenon called the heat-island effect—they produce their own clouds and miniature low-pressure weather systems, all of which can help spread pollutants, according to Michael Brown's book *The Toxic Cloud*.

Because of Earth's rotation, wind generally flows to the east. Therefore, toxins generated by industries on the Gulf Coast are carried on eastward winds, joined in the summer by a warm air mass that pushes north from the Gulf of Mexico, and in the winter by southward forays of arctic air. According to folk wisdom in the area, you can turn loose a molecule of vinyl chloride today in Texas City, on Galveston Bay, and have it over New York City by 8:00 A.M. tomorrow. As much as 20 percent of the air pollution in the Ohio Valley consists of contaminants blown there from factories along the Gulf Coast. The Great Lakes region is particularly vulnerable.

The West: Radioactive Fallout

Among the more poignant stories to come out of the Nevada desert is a story about when John Wayne was filming the epic *The Conqueror*. Filmed in 1955 near an atomic test site, the story told of the conquests of Genghis Khan. The plot called for giant fans to create a dust storm in which the major characters found their way. Twenty-five years later, each of the film's three major stars was dead of cancer—Agnes Moorehead in 1974, Susan Hayward in 1975, and Wayne in 1979.

There are many other sources of radiation throughout the West, most due to uranium mining. By a 1982 tally, Colorado had the largest number of inactive mines with 1,217, followed by Utah, which had 1,093. Mines are also found in Arizona, Alaska, Washington, Idaho, Nevada, Oklahoma, Texas, Pennsylvania, Minnesota, New Jersey, South Dakota, and Oregon.

LOCATION, LOCATION, LOCATION

As any wise realtor knows, the three most important factors in determining the economic value of a house are location, location, and location. The same maxim applies to health. Where a house is located has a lot to do with how healthy it is, especially concerning air and water, inside and out.

When building or locating a house, it's best to take the preventive approach. Assess your house site carefully, following ecologic principles so you won't be disappointed to later discover that something beyond your control is affecting your family's health. If you're planning to stay put, carefully assess where your house is situated. By finding out what's right and what's wrong with your site, you can take steps to remedy any problems that may exist.

How Does Your Location Rate?

To determine how healthy the location of your house is, make a careful, detailed assessment of the environs within a 10-mile radius. Use the following criteria to see how your site stacks up:

Air: Do you live in a city that's troubled with smog? Cities beset with smog are, by nature, unhealthy places to live. Death from respiratory disease is over 50 percent more common in the smoggier parts of Los Angeles, for example, than in sections with relatively cleaner air.

Agriculture: Do you live near chemically polluted farmland? A woodlot or windbreak of fir trees located on the windward side of the house may act as a protective barrier to airborne pollutants. A filter can improve water at the tap. Is there aerial spraying of pesticides and herbicides on crops and forests in your area? If chemical spraying pollutes your air, close windows on that side of the house and work politically to get the spraying stopped.

Altitude: What is the altitude where you live? Living in a hilly terrain can be hard on a weak heart and lungs. To play it safe, if you've had a stroke or heart attack or have chronic respiratory disease, don't move to an altitude above 6,000 feet. People who suffer from migraine headaches also would be wise to avoid high altitude.

Industry: Are there any big industrial plants in your area? If you live near a large industry, find out what goes on there. Are toxic chemicals manufactured or used in manufacture? What chemicals are being emitted from those large smokestacks? How are toxic wastes handled? Learn all you can.

Major transportation routes: Do you live along a major transportation route? Some 4 billion or so tons of hazardous materials are transported each year by rail and truck. Trains carrying such toxic and dangerous products as vinyl chloride, propane gas, and phosphorus trichloride (to name just a few) are making headlines when poor railroad track conditions cause derailments. Of major concern are the routes taken by unmarked trucks and trains transporting highly radioactive nuclear by-products. These pass through virtually every state in the nation.

Railroads and airports: How close do you live to an operating railroad or airport? Both are big noise and air polluters. The ideal site is located more than 5 miles from a railroad line and outside a 20-mile radius of an airport.

Refuse landfills: Where is the nearest landfill? Toxic waste dump? Nuclear waste facility? A healthy home is located several miles upwind of any refuse dump, not within 100 miles of a chemical or nuclear waste facility, and not adjacent to roads along which garbage or incinerated ash is transported.

Topography: Is there a lake or a pond near your house? Or a forest or trees? Living near a body of water can help cleanse the air, but it has to have a large enough surface to allow for dissipation of airborne contaminants. Large areas of trees and bushes can also help filter pollutants.

Traffic arteries: How close do you live to a major interstate highway or freeway? Automobile traffic is the biggest source of nitrogen dioxide, a deadly gas, in the outdoor environment. Studies in New Jersey show that children living within 100 feet of major roadways have higher blood lead levels than those living farther away.

Winds: Which way do the winds blow in your community? Call your local weather bureau to find out. If your house site is located downwind of air-polluting industry, there's a good chance you're breathing bad air at least part of the time. Downwind drift can carry pollution several miles from its source.

NEIGHBORHOOD CONSIDERATIONS What is your neighborhood like? As far as immediate topography is concerned, a quiet street in a built-up part of the community is best. Recently developed subdivisions are often a source of airborne dust and dirt, especially before grass, trees, and shrubs are planted. Rural areas are attractive because you can often have a fresh supply of clean spring water if you dig a deep enough well. Another benefit of rural living is the ability to live organically, growing fruits and vegetables on your land, feasting off uncontaminated meats, and eating unpolluted fish from a nearby farm pond. But these are benefits only if the air and the water are clean.

Do you see chemical trucks in your neighborhood? These are warning signs of a freshly sprayed lawn or house. When an area is chemically sprayed, insects and other pests usually migrate to the nearest "safe" area, and the spray itself may travel from your neighbor's yard to the area surrounding your home.

Does your community permit open leaf burning? This can be a troublesome source of air pollution. Continued exposure to such fumes over a prolonged period of time can cause a sensitivity to develop in even normally healthy individuals.

How is the crime rate? Perhaps establishing a neighborhood crime watch would help. Over 19 million Americans belong to mutual-protection programs that teach neighbors how to look out for each other. Property theft has been reduced by as much as 50 percent in areas with neighborhood watches. (See appendix B.)

YOUR IMMEDIATE SITE Just as important as the city and neighborhood you live in is the immediate site—the land your house sits on and your yard. Here are some considerations to take into account when evaluating your site:

Allergies: Is anyone in your family troubled with allergies? People with allergies can have problems with grasses, weeds, and trees. If allergies are a concern, identify the weeds and trees existing in the area around your house. Dig out the offending ones, if you can (however, this remedy won't do much good if the same weeds are growing on your neighbor's lot upwind of you).

Electricity: Is your house located near high-voltage electric lines, radio or radar towers, microwave relay towers or an electricity-generating plant? If so, you may be living in an electrical stew and not even know it. Recent studies indicate that low-level electromagnetic radiation from these and other sources may pose a significant cancer risk. A study completed in 1986, for example, found a fivefold increase in childhood cancers—particularly leukemia—in homes located within 15 meters (about 50 feet) of primary wires designed to carry very high electric currents, and within 7.5 meters (about 25 feet) of primary wires carrying lower currents. Some researchers advise safe distances of 200 feet from medium-high-voltage lines (50,000 volts) and 500 feet or greater from high-voltage lines (350,000 volts).

Employment: How far is your house from your place of employment? If it's reasonably close you won't have to breathe traffic fumes as you commute every day. You may even be able to walk or ride a bicycle to work.

Insects, vermin, or rodents: If airborne mosquitoes, black bugs, or gnats are the problem, a screened-in porch or patio may be the answer to outdoor living in the summertime. Rodents and vermin can be problems, too. Mechanical means are the best way of getting rid of these unwanted guests. If you have a bad problem—raccoons in the attic, opossums in the cellar—hire an environmental consultant to help in getting rid of them in an ecologically safe manner.

Odors: If there are any suspicious smells, ground fumes may be present from leaky gas lines on an adjacent lot or from the street-line gas pipes. These low-lying gas fumes can seep in through your foundation and contaminate indoor air. In some neighborhoods, emissions from vented clothes dryers can contribute to outdoor air pollution and aggravate allergies. Smoke from wood-burning stoves can also be a problem if you're living downwind of the source, particularly in a valley.

Radon: Have you tested your house or site for radon? No matter where you live, it's important to check your house or potential house site for radon. If your drinking water comes from a well, have it checked for radon contamination, as well.

Water: Where does your water come from? What kinds of pipes transport it? Is it treated? What is in it? Have your water tested. If it's from a well, what kinds of activity in the area are likely to pollute it. Farming? Industry? What is located upstream? Follow the course of the aquifer.

Prescription: A Healthy Home Has ...

... a healthy site. Here's what to look for and what to avoid when choosing your home's location:

■ Try to locate your home outside of an urban area—most of the nation's largest cities cannot meet federal clean air standards.

■ Locate your home as far away as possible from coal-fired and nuclear power plants, as well as nuclear weapons factories, nuclear and toxic waste dumps, uranium mines, and chemical plants.

■ Don't build your home along a nuclear transport route.

■ Be aware that the pristine rural site you've found may be tainted by agricultural chemicals that have been sprayed on crops and/or turned into the ground.

■ If possible, don't locate your home on the Louisiana or Texas gulf, or in New Jersey. All three states are major chemical producers, and all three have severe air and water contamination.

■ If you get your drinking water from a well, have your water tested regularly.

■ If you live in an older home that may have lead pipes or copper pipes with lead solder, have your water tested for lead.

■ Plan for natural ventilation that enters the house from the side farthest from the street so air is free of exhaust fumes.

■ Stay away from home sites located near high-power electric lines or radio or radar towers.

■ Take into account the weather, topography, and natural and man-made disasters at the site you're considering.

■ Don't locate your home near a geological fault line. If you do choose to live near a fault, be sure your house is a frame house (which will bend to some degree) and not a masonry one (which will collapse).

■ The ideal house site has the highest elevation in the area, is upstream of prevailing wind currents, and is away from all large industry that produces offending emissions.

4

Water

For the past 50 years Americans trusted absolutely the water that came out of their taps. Not any more. Not only does much of our tap water taste bad, it's filled with synthetic chemicals that, in large enough doses over a long period of time, can cause cancer, birth defects, and nervous system disorders. People don't always know how to deal with problems and don't always do the right thing, but stories of chemical spills, gasoline contamination, and lead dissolving in water pipes have spurred Americans to take matters into their own hands. Mostly they're doing one of two things: (1) treating water at home with various devices or (2) turning to bottled water.

What's the best answer? Will contaminated water make you sick? What contaminants are the most dangerous? How can you be sure your drinking water is safe?

A HARD LOOK AT THE FACTS

A study released in 1988 by Ralph Nader's Center for Study of Responsive Law in Washington, D.C., shows that much of the nation's drinking water is unsafe. Tests in 38 states have found more than 2,000 toxic chemicals in drinking water since 1974. Nearly 200 of these chemicals are either known or suspected causes of cancer, cell mutations, nervous system disorders, and birth defects. Many of these contaminants are not currently regulated by federal law. At least 1,900 to 2,100 contaminants have never even been tested as to whether or not they cause health problems.

Biologist Walter Hang, who worked on the Nader report, told National Public Radio that some of these contaminants have been detected at potentially dangerous levels of concentration. "The scientific evidence is quite substantial," he said in a March 1988 radio interview. "Unfortunately, it just simply is not being dealt with. Most Americans presume the water is generally safe to drink. What this study shows, for the first time, is that the water in America may not be safe to drink because it is so heavily contaminated with this incredible spectrum of toxic organic chemicals."

Though the U.S. Environmental Protection Agency (EPA) is challenging the Nader report, the agency's data from as far back as 1980 show that as many as one out of three wells tested in this country are contaminated with organic solvents, such as trichloroethylene (TCE), that can cause cancer and birth defects and a whole host of other problems. The EPA also tested for six cancer-causing chemicals in 50 major U.S. drinking water systems and found that every one of them had at least one out of the six contaminants. Such examples of polluted drinking water in this country appear to be endless.

The ones who suffer the most are children. In Woburn, Massachusetts, for example, 26 children were stricken with leukemia in the years from 1968 to 1985. Six of these children lived within a ten-block area. The odds of this happening as a result of mere coincidence are 5,000 to 1. And yet it happened. What did these children have in common? They all drank from the same water system. When a test of the system was finally done, it was found to contain large amounts of industrial chemicals.

It's no surprise that communities in the industrial Northeast have serious problems with groundwater contamination, but that doesn't mean the rest of the country is immune. Pesticides seriously contaminate groundwater in the Midwest. In San Francisco, asbestos is found in the drinking water. Household water in the Southwest has been found to contain high levels of radioactivity from uranium mining. There is no state, no county in America that has not at some time or other experienced problems with drinking water contamination.

What is a community told when the water is found to be contaminated? Generally, officials claim that contaminant levels are too low to cause concern. Don't be so sure! Even though levels are low, they should not be ignored, warns the Natural Resources Defense Council. The EPA's own studies show there are places throughout the country where water contamination is cause for concern.

Since many toxic contaminants cannot be seen or tasted, a community or neighborhood can be drinking contaminated water for years and have no idea there is a problem. The only warning a community may have is when it starts to experience an alarming rate of unusual health problems, and that may take years. What's even worse, when a community does start experiencing such health problems, getting authorities to do something about it can take even longer. People often find they cannot turn to the government for help, because the government itself is the cause of the contamination.

Where Do These Chemicals Come From?

A wide array of industrial and agricultural chemicals has found its way into our groundwater—chemicals from hazardous waste sites, heavy metals and radioactive substances from mining, gasoline and oil from underground storage tanks, pesticides and nitrates from agriculture, salt from road deicing, brine from oil and gas drilling, and bacteria from leaky septic tanks. A nationwide survey was conducted by state water officials in 1987; they found that nearly 1 in every 4 miles of river and one out of every five lakes were being spoiled or

(continued on page 44)

What's in the Water?

Although it is extremely difficult to predict the harm of long-term exposure to low levels of toxic chemicals in drinking water, some effects have been observed in humans and animals. Children, for example, are often more vulnerable because of their lower body weight, growing body organs, and faster respiratory rate. Genetic factors, general health, and life-style (including smoking and diet) can also affect susceptibility to chemicals.

Here's a rundown of the chemicals commonly found in many U.S. water systems and the biological damage each chemical is known to cause:

Inorganic Substances

Arsensic: This chemical causes cancer as well as liver, kidney, blood, and nervous system damage.

Asbestos: There is still some controversy over whether asbestos in drinking water causes cancer, but the U.S. Environmental Protection Agency estimates that drinking water containing 300,000 fibers per liter of water can result in one additional cancer in 100,000 people.

Cadmium: Kidney damage, anemia, pulmonary problems, high blood pressure, possible fetal damage, and cancer are among its effects.

Chromium: Some forms are suspected of causing cancer.

Lead: Its damage includes headaches, anemia, nerve problems, mental retardation and learning disabilities in children, birth defects, and possibly cancer.

Mercury: It causes nervous system and kidney damage. Once mercury enters the food chain, fish and other aquatic animals concentrate mercury in their tissues, and the humans eating these animals receive a greater dose.

Nitrates: They interfere with oxygen metabolism and possibly cause cancer.

Common Organic Contaminants

1,1,1-Tricholorethane (TCA): This causes liver damage, cardiovascular changes, depression of the central nervous system, and possibly cancer and mutations.

1,1-Dichlorethylene: At high levels, it causes liver and kidney damage, central nervous system depression, and possibly mutations; it is also suspected of causing cancer.

1,2-Dicholoroethane: In high concentrations, this chemical causes depression of the central nervous system, liver and kidney damage, gastrointestinal problems, pulmonary effects, and circulatory disturbances and is suspected of causing cancer and mutations.

(continued)

42

What's in the Water—*Continued*

Aldicarb (Temik): It is highly toxic to the nervous system. There has been no evidence of mutagenicity, teratogenicity, or carcinogenicity.

Benzene: Chromosomal damage in both humans and laboratory animals is a hazard of benzene. It affects the blood and the immune system, causing anemia, blood disorders, and leukemia.

Carbon tetrachloride: Effects include cancer and liver, kidney, lung, and nervous system damage.

Chloroform: It causes liver and kidney damage and is suspected of causing cancer.

Dibromochloropropane (DBCP): Its effects include male sterility and cancer.

Dichlorobenzene: This causes liver, kidney, and pulmonary damage. There has been no evidence of mutagenicity or carcinogenicity.

Dioxin: Dioxin is extremely toxic, causing skin disorders, cancer, and mutations.

Ethylene dibromide (EDB): It causes male sterility and cancer. EDB is more potent than DBCP.

Polychlorinated biphenyls (PCBs): Liver damage, skin disorders, gastrointestinal problems, and suspected cancer and mutations are its hazards.

Tetrachlorethylene (PCE): It induces liver and kidney damage and depression of the central nervous system and is suspected of causing cancer.

Trichloroethylene (TCE): In high concentrations, this causes liver and kidney damage, skin problems, and depression of the contractility of the heart and is suspected of causing cancer and mutations.

Vinyl chloride: This causes lung, liver, and kidney damage; pulmonary and cardiovascular effects; gastrointestinal problems; and cancer. It is also suspected of causing mutations.

Biological Pathogens

Viruses and bacteria: A wide range of ailments includes diarrhea, cramps, and nausea, and more serious illnesses such as hepatitis and meningitis. Biological organisms are by far the most common cause of *acute* waterborne illness in this country.

Radiation

Ionizing radiation: Even at low levels, it alters cell structure, which may lead to birth defects, cancer, genetic damage, and sterility.

Reprinted with permission from *Troubled Water* by Jonathan King (Rodale Press, 1985).

threatened by pollutants cascading from farms, mines, and urban areas. Here's a look at some of the major offenders.

TOXIC WASTE DUMPS   Clearly, we've had an "out of sight, out of mind" attitude regarding disposal of hazardous waste in this country. The United States produces up to 290 million tons of hazardous chemical waste each year and dumps it into or onto the land by way of injection wells, pits, ponds, lagoons, and landfills. There are approximately 300,000 toxic waste sites across the United States today.

The EPA admits there is no known way to prevent even the most carefully constructed waste site from leaking and eventually contaminating water supplies. As of October 1988, the EPA had placed 1,000 landfills, impoundments, and other waste sites on its national priority list for cleanup. The Congressional Office of Technology Assessment (OTA) estimates, however, that the number of priority sites could climb to 10,000 and the cost of cleaning them could be as high as $500 billion, roughly $2,000 for every U.S. resident.

LANDFILLS   Americans throw away 6 billion tons of garbage a year, most of which ends up in municipal landfills. Much of this waste includes hazardous substances such as cleaning fluids, home and garden pesticides, and heavy metals. Residue from the accumulation of these substances over the years is now finding its way into our nation's groundwater. In Connecticut alone, 25 of the state's 200 landfills have contaminated drinking water already, and another 35 landfills are considered threats.

There are several hundred thousand active landfills across this vast country of ours. The National Association of Counties puts the total at 360,000. Added to these is an equal or greater number of closed landfills and dumps. Up to 37,000 landfills may be contaminating groundwater, according to a 1985 report by OTA, and the cost of cleaning up the mess could total $229 billion.

UNDERGROUND STORAGE TANKS   Gasoline leaking from underground storage tanks may be responsible for as much as 40 percent of the nation's groundwater contamination. Buried during the late 1950s and early 1960s, there are now more than 2.5 million underground tanks containing gasoline and other petroleum products. Constructed of steel, many of these tanks—perhaps 35 percent, according to EPA estimates—are leaking, presenting a serious threat to our groundwater.

Though new laws in many states require each commercial gas tank to be registered with the state to help officials track down gasoline leaks, that's no help when it comes to contaminated drinking water. A single gallon of leaked gasoline per day is enough to render the groundwater supply for a town of 50,000 people unfit to drink. And it's likely to remain contaminated for hundreds, or even thousands, of years.

PESTICIDE AND FERTILIZER RUNOFF   Pesticide use nearly tripled in the United States in the 20 years between 1965 and 1985. Farmers applied

390,000 tons of pesticides to the nation's agricultural land in 1987. Such routine agricultural practices have contaminated groundwater with 50 to 60 different pesticides in at least 30 states.

No state regulates pesticide runoff, and none has systematically monitored its water supplies for pesticides, so the full extent of contamination is not known. The nation's two most widely used herbicides—alachlor and atrazine—have been among the pesticides most frequently detected. Tests have shown alachlor to cause cancer in laboratory animals, making it a probable human carcinogen. Surveillance efforts in Iowa, which has one of the best monitoring programs in the country, indicate that more than a quarter of Iowans use drinking water contaminated with pesticides.

PLUMBING PIPES   On top of contaminants that leach into drinking water from outside the plumbing system, we've got a pipe system throughout this country that is full of lead, a heavy metal that is extremely dangerous when ingested. The EPA estimates that more than 42 million U.S. residents consume water that contains unsafe levels of lead. That's one out of every five Americans. This excess alone, according to the EPA, may be responsible annually for lower IQ scores for 240,000 children, hypertension for 130,000 males, and pregnancy complications for 680,000 women. Lead gets into drinking water from two major sources: (1) lead pipes, usually connecting the main water pipe to the house, and (2) the lead solder used to connect copper pipes inside the house.

Copper pipes themselves can also be a problem. Water with a low pH (meaning it is more acidic) tends to dissolve heavy metals, like copper. Since water is a solvent, traces of copper get into the water and are then ingested when the water is used for drinking or cooking. Though trace amounts of copper are needed for good health, copper in excess amounts is toxic in the human body.

Old galvanized pipe can be a source of health problems, too. Trace amounts of cadmium are often found in water from these pipes. In the human body, cadmium is known to displace zinc, which we need for good health. Cadmium has been implicated as a possible cause of hypertension, and is suspected of inhibiting the body's immune system and causing various serious illnesses. (See "What's in the Water?" on page 42.)

Plastic pipes can contaminate drinking water, too. Solvent glues used to join sections of polyvinyl chloride (PVC) pipe contain dimethylformamide, a chemical linked to birth defects in lab animals. PVC pipe, as well as polybutylene and polyethylene pipes, may also allow organic chemicals to leach into the water at concentrations higher than recommended federal safety levels. Tests have also detected several other suspected carcinogens in water flowing through plastic pipe, including DEHP, a plasticizer used to make pipe more flexible.

So what kind of pipe is best? Copper pipe with mechanical fittings appears to be the healthiest plumbing system to date. Though it's more costly, it eliminates lead from your water. A more practical answer is copper pipe with lead-free (and antimony-free) solder, available at hardware stores and plumbing supply companies. When using copper pipe, be sure your water has a normal pH, about 7 or so. If pH is low, water will have to be treated to raise the pH so traces of copper won't leach into the water.

WATER TREATMENT PLANTS   As if all this weren't enough, chemicals are routinely added to water as it makes its way through municipal treatment plants. Chlorine is added to kill bacteria. Fluoride is added to prevent dental cavities. How are these chemicals interacting in the human body?

Chlorine is effective in eliminating waterborne diseases, but it is also suspected of causing cancer. Why do municipal systems all over the United States routinely add a suspected carcinogen to our drinking water? It goes back a couple of centuries to a time when some of the worst epidemics in human history were caused by waterborne diseases such as typhoid, cholera, and diphtheria. The advent of chlorination for water disinfection in the early 1900s greatly reduced the incidence of these diseases, but now we're discovering that chlorination seems to spawn new contaminants called trihalomethanes (THMs). They are created when chlorine reacts with organic matter, such as rotting leaves. Chloroform, one of the four major THMs, is known to cause cancer in laboratory animals and is suspected of causing bladder cancer in humans. In a 1975 survey of 80 municipal drinking water supplies, chloroform was found in the tap water of all 80 cities.

Is there cause for alarm? Along with radon in the air, chlorine in drinking water causes the greatest concern to scientists and EPA officials. In June 1988 the National Cancer Institute released the results of a 10,000-person study; it found that people who drink chlorinated surface water for long periods of time have twice the risk of bladder cancer as those who don't drink chlorinated water. The more chlorinated water you drink in a lifetime, the higher the risk. Fortunately, installing a water filter at the tap takes care of the problem.

Fluoride is also added to water at treatment facilities, and has been since the early 1950s, when it was found to significantly reduce dental cavities. A level of 0.7 to 1.2 milligrams of fluoride per liter of drinking water (mg/L) is generally regarded as the optimum balance to reduce dental decay. But in many areas fluoride occurs naturally, so adding it increases the amount to excess levels. Many of us also get fluoride from toothpaste and other sources. Long-term chronic ingestion at higher levels can lead to skeletal fluorosis, which has symptoms resembling those of arthritis, and may produce mottling of teeth, especially in children.

MUNICIPAL WASTE TREATMENT PLANTS   The EPA found in 1988 that three out of every four municipal waste treatment plants have not kept industrial toxic chemicals from polluting tap water. Between 100,000 and 200,000 industries of varying size pump their wastes directly into sewers, where it mingles with the wastes of millions of households and other nontoxic sources. Municipal sewage treatment plants are geared principally to treat human waste and other organic matter so it can be pumped into waterways with minimal environmental impact. Toxic waste from industry, however, remains largely untreated in the process—it is pumped into waterways or trapped in sewage sludge.

IS YOUR WATER SAFE?

There is no such thing as pure water. Water is the universal solvent. It has the ability to dissolve almost anything it comes in contact with. So even the cleanest water contains—in addition to hydrogen and oxygen—minerals, salts, trace metals, and organic matter, most of which are invisible, tasteless, and odorless. Fortunately, many of these are beneficial to health. Good water should contain certain trace minerals, such as iron, zinc, copper, manganese, chromium, cobalt, molybdenum, iodine, and selenium, that are essential to normal body function. Other minerals—such as lead, cadmium, mercury, and arsenic—can be harmful.

We consider water *contaminated* when it contains harmful or objectionable substances. In the last 50 years, particularly since World War II, our water has become highly contaminated with a host of synthetic chemicals. These chemicals can be harmful in small amounts, often in the parts-per-billion (ppb) range. A ppb is a very small quantity, equivalent to 1 second in a 32-year time span. In such small quantities, toxic chemicals usually will not have immediate ill effects, but if consumed over months or years, they may cause serious, irreversible harm.

The health effects of drinking contaminated water depend on the following: (1) the type of contaminant, (2) its concentration, and (3) how long it is consumed. *Acute toxicity* results from exposure to large doses of a toxin over a short period of time. *Chronic toxicity* results from exposure to small doses of a toxin over a longer period of time, but its effects may not be evident for many years. Exposure to toxins from other sources—food, air, and so forth—can contribute to the overall dosage you get in a lifetime.

Though drinking contaminated water is one way for toxic chemicals to enter your body, showers—and to a lesser extent, baths—lead to even greater exposure through inhalation and skin absorption. Twice as much of the chemical can enter the body through the skin as through the intestine, according to research at the University of Pittsburgh. The longer and hotter the shower, the more the chemicals build up in the air. In one study, the levels were four times greater after a shower lasting 10 minutes than for one lasting 5 minutes. Researchers estimate that people could receive from 6 to 100 times more of the chemicals by breathing the air around showers, baths, dishwashers, and washing machines than they would by drinking the water.

No estimate has been made of the health risk posed by inhaling the chemicals, but a joint study by the EPA and the National Academy of Sciences has attributed 200 to 1,000 U.S. cancer deaths each year to inhaling chloroform from water while bathing. Experts advise people taking showers to close the bathroom door and open a window.

Where Does Your Water Come From?

Before you can accurately assess whether or not your water is safe, you need to know where it comes from. There are two main sources: (1) surface water from streams, lakes, and rivers, which accounts for about half of our drinking water supply, and (2) groundwater coming from vast underground networks, called aquifers, lying from a few feet to hundreds of feet below ground. This water moves slowly, perhaps only a few inches a day, through narrow pathways in the ground. Ninety percent of the water in rural areas comes from groundwater.

Surface water is more likely to be contaminated by chemicals from the air—pesticides from fields, contaminants from industrial smokestacks, acid rain, and so on—and by chemicals that are dumped or spilled directly into the water. About half the pollutants that rivers and lakes receive are direct discharges from storm sewers, municipal sewage treatment plants, and industries. Lake Erie gives an excellent example of surface water pollution. The cities of Detroit, Toledo, Lorain, Sandusky, Cleveland, Akron, and Erie all discharge partially treated waste water into this Great Lake. Even though these wastes are partially treated, they are equivalent to the raw wastes of 4.7 million people.

Groundwater, on the other hand, is usually of good quality when in its natural state. Soil overlying an aquifer tends to filter out and break down many potentially harmful substances. The thicker this mantle of soil, the greater its filtering ability. Even so, some of the materials that eventually do reach groundwater can be harmful. These substances may come from obvious

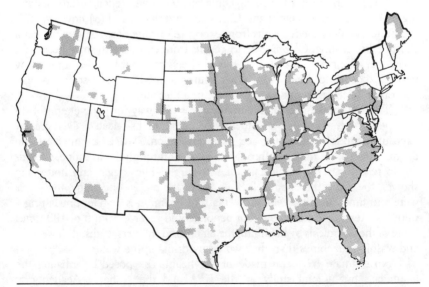

What's in your drinking water? The dark areas on the map indicate contamination of groundwater by nitrates and pesticides. (*Source:* Map © *Harrowsmith* magazine; used by permission.)

sources, such as chemical spills on the ground or leaking underground storage tanks. They may also come from ordinary, everyday activities—such as using caustic chemicals to clean the toilet bowl or spilling oil on the ground while changing the oil in the family car. Practically any activity that goes on aboveground can have an effect on groundwater below.

How much of the nation's groundwater is contaminated? Estimates range from the EPA's 1 percent to as high as 4 percent. Monitoring of groundwater conditions by the states revealed that failing septic tank systems, leaking underground storage tanks, and agricultural activities such as fertilizer applications are leading sources of groundwater pollution. This can be a big problem. In many states that depend on groundwater, and in many of the nation's rural areas, alternative sources of water may not be physically, legally, or economically available. The long-range effects of groundwater pollution are more serious than surface water pollution because it takes many years to flush waste out of an aquifer. Most people who rely on well water simply choose to abandon a contaminated well rather than try to cleanse it.

Is the Government Protecting You?

Many people like to believe that the government is taking care of water quality, but this is not necessarily the case. Although government has taken steps to protect water quality, the individual water user still bears a good deal of the responsibility. To help understand this, you need to understand the distinction between public and private water supplies, and the role of the government in each.

PUBLIC WATER SUPPLY   A public water supply is defined as any water system that has at least 15 service connections or which regularly serves a minimum of 25 people at least 60 days out of the year. This would basically include all city water supplies, rural water districts, and other supplies used by "the public."

Public water systems are controlled by state and federal drinking water regulations that went into effect in 1988. These regulations require routine monitoring and treatment, and that water meet certain minimum quality standards. If the minimum quality standard for a contaminant is exceeded, officials must notify the people served by that system. Notification usually appears in the news media and in the next month's water bill. Although these requirements provide some protection to users, they fall short of ensuring that drinking water is free of contamination. Why? The number of contaminants monitored is small in comparison to the number that may be affecting drinking water. If a contaminant is not specifically tested for, it won't be found, even if it is present in the water. Also, many of these contaminants cannot be removed by the treatment methods currently used. Requirements forcing a public water system to correct a contamination problem are sometimes loosely enforced, allowing continuous violation of some standards.

PRIVATE WATER SUPPLIES   Private water supplies are all water supplies not classified as public. Usually, these are wells used by one or two families. Private supplies are the most common source of water for farms and residents of small towns that do not have a municipal water supply. The quality of drinking water from private supplies is *not* controlled by state or federal regulations. Private supplies are not required to be treated or monitored in any way. The responsibility for providing good-quality drinking water lies with those who use it.

Experts contend that big municipal water systems, with their full-time engineering staffs, are generally safer than smaller systems. But, as you can see, drinking water regulations provide limited protection to water users. Government agencies have taken only partial responsibility for drinking water quality. The rest lies with you, the consumer.

Get It Tested

There are three things you can do to check the quality of your drinking water. First, eyeball it: Pour a glass of water and let it settle for a minute or two. Is the water cloudy? Are there particles settling to the bottom of the glass? Does it have a strange odor or taste? Have you noticed any changes in these qualities over the last few months?

City versus Country Water

City	Country
Unlikely bacterial contamination	Likely chance of bacterial contamination
Chlorine, fluoride treatment	Unlikely contamination with either THMs or fluoride
Regardless of size, all public water systems must be tested for the 30 contaminants listed in the Safe Drinking Water Act	Water quality up to the user
Requirement as of 1988 to test for organics regularly and to try to take them out or switch to an alternate source of water	Likely chance of contamination by synthetic organic chemicals; vulnerability of well water to contamination from leaking septic tanks, dumps, and storage tanks
	Need for radon testing
	Potential well contamination without a concrete liner and a tight cover
	Possible contamination with polychlorinated biphenyls (PCBs) from well pumps made before 1978 (information available from your local EPA office)

Next, if you have your own well, check its location. Is it near any contamination sources such as a septic tank drain field, a feedlot, cropland, a garden, an underground storage tank, or pipelines? Is it located in a depression or pit? How was the well constructed? Is it sealed, cased, grouted, and in good repair? How deep is the well? (Shallow wells are more likely to be polluted.)

Finally, if you're on a public system, contact the city water department and ask to see a copy of the latest test. Ask if water in the system is routinely checked for synthetic chemicals, THMs, pesticides, or metals. Has the supply consistently met drinking water standards for bacteria, nitrates, and other contaminants? What kind of treatment is used? You can then decide whether your water needs further testing.

Often, though, public systems aren't tested for a vast majority of contaminants, so the test results are a bit misleading—officials at the utility say they have met all the drinking water standards so you have good clean water, but you have no assurance this is so, because they have tested only for the 30 contaminants required under EPA law. What about the other 670 identified by EPA? The official doesn't know. You don't know. If you suspect something harmful might be in your water, it's time to get a laboratory analysis.

LABORATORY TESTING   The only way to find out for sure what is in your water is to have it tested by a reputable laboratory. Many local water suppliers will test tap water for contaminants, sometimes without charge. There are also commercial water-testing laboratories. The largest of these, Water Test, provides home testing kits and laboratory analyses that cost from $30 for measuring bacteria levels to $245 for measuring synthetic organics. Other national laboratories have competitive prices. (Check the yellow pages of your telephone book under "Water Quality" or "Laboratories, Testing.")

Make sure the lab you choose is certified and uses EPA methods and quality control procedures. Also, choose a lab whose sole business is water analysis. If they sell water treatment devices, too, there is a conflict of interest. It helps if the lab you choose also offers consultation services to help you interpret test results.

It would be difficult and expensive to test your water for all possible contaminants, so you will need to decide which ones to have the lab test for. Your decision will depend on where you live, where your water comes from, what kind of contaminants you suspect may be affecting your water, and what the tests cost. A basic test will include such things as pH, hardness, alkalinity, minerals and salts, bacteria, total dissolved solids, and so forth. A more complicated test checks levels of lead and other metals, fluoride, and THMs. A still more complex test will show you the levels of organics and synthetic chemicals in your water.

Obtain a copy of your state drinking water standards (which are at least as strict as the federal ones and may include additional standards) from your public health department. If your water comes from a well, request tests for bacteria and nitrates. Whether you're on a public or a private system, if you suspect that any other contaminants might be present, you should test for those, as well. For example, if you live in a mining area, test for iron, manganese, and aluminum; near gas-drilling operations, test for chlorides, sodium, barium, lead, and strontium; in an agricultural area, test for pesticides.

Arrangements for sample collection will vary. A few laboratories will send a trained technician to take the samples, but in most cases the lab will provide sample containers along with instructions as to how you should draw your own tap water samples. If you collect the samples yourself, make sure you follow the lab's instructions exactly. Otherwise, the results may not be reliable.

After the lab has analyzed your water sample, you will receive a report of the test results, usually in parts per billion or parts per million. The lab will give you the federal safety standards so you can compare your levels and see whether your water is safe.

WHAT YOU CAN DO

After testing, you may learn that your drinking water contains one or more contaminants. Such a discovery can be unsettling, even if the level of contamination is within accepted "safe" limits. It is not certain that exposure to the many chemicals found in our household water will cause ill health, but many scientists agree that for chemicals that may cause cancer or other chronic diseases, there is no level of exposure so small that there is no danger of developing disease. Of course, the lower the concentration, the lower the risk. If you do find that your drinking water contains contaminants, there *are* things you can do to improve its quality.

The first step is to try to locate the cause of the contamination and correct it. For example, the mixing, storing, or disposing of chemicals near a well increases the risk of contamination; these activities should be moved to a less vulnerable area. Leaking underground storage tanks can be removed and replaced. A poorly constructed well can be reconstructed or plugged. If lead is a problem, replace the intake pipe if it is lead or replace pipes within the house itself. Removing the contaminating source is the most important step toward water quality. But in many cases, especially if you're on a public system, that is just not possible.

The second step to improving water quality is to treat your drinking water at home.

In-Home Water Treatment

Significant amounts of pollutants can be eliminated from tap water with purifiers available at hardware stores and from retailers who specialize in water treatment devices. None of the purifiers acts on the entire spectrum of contaminants, though, so you should have your water tested before choosing which treatment is right for you. In addition, each of the purifiers must be rigorously maintained so you don't end up with bacteria contaminating your water supply.

None of the point-of-use treatment devices is appropriate for removal of continually high levels of contaminants. Neither do they prevent health problems that may be caused by bathing in water containing high levels of toxic chemicals. For this reason, the best purifiers treat all the water in your house. They cost between $500 and $1,500, and yearly maintenance can be as high as $100. Less expensive units are available for individual faucets.

At present, home treatment devices are not tested or regulated by the government. Advertising claims are often exaggerated and sometimes untrue, making it difficult for the consumer to choose between competing brands. Read labels carefully and consult with a reputable water company before making a sizable investment.

DISINFECTION Disinfection techniques are used to destroy harmful microorganisms in water. The most common technique used is chlorination. Chlorine can also remove some tastes and odors from the water. Since public water systems are required by state law to disinfect their water, individuals on public water systems usually don't need to do this.

Newly constructed or repaired private wells are likely to be contaminated and should be disinfected before being used. This can be done by dousing the well and plumbing system with sodium hypochlorite (common household bleach), a process called shock chlorination.

WATER SOFTENERS Water softeners are probably the most common in-home water treatment system. They remove the minerals (mainly calcium and magnesium) that make water "hard." Hard water requires more soap to produce a satisfying layer of suds. It also leaves rings in bathtubs, water spots on dishes, and scaly deposits on appliances and in water heaters. Hard water can be responsible for dry, itchy skin, particularly in winter. Aside from these nuisances, there is little else to worry about.

Calcium and magnesium are essential nutrients and give mineral water its pleasant taste. A softener replaces these minerals with sodium ions. While the softened water is better for laundering and bathing, the added burden of sodium in drinking water may cause health problems, especially for people who need to be on low-sodium diets. Several studies have shown that people who drink hard water suffer fewer heart attacks and strokes than people who drink soft water.

Softeners can remove small amounts of iron from water. Iron is an essential nutrient, but it can be a nuisance in plumbing fixtures and laundry. Softeners do *not* remove minerals other than calcium, magnesium, and iron. Neither do they remove organic or bacterial contaminants.

It's not difficult to treat your water so that you have softened water for washing and bathing but not for drinking and cooking. Simply rig the drinking water tap to bypass the softener, or install a reverse osmosis device to remove the sodium.

Some public water utilities regularly report that softened water is more prone to lead contamination than hard water is. "That's not true," says Jerry Tone, president of National Testing Labs in Cleveland, Ohio. Water that is *naturally* soft is prone to lead contamination because it is purer and thus attracts other ions. Softened water, on the other hand, is no more prone to lead contamination than hard water is.

ACTIVATED-CARBON FILTERS   This is the least expensive water purification method. It is especially good at removing pesticides, herbicides, industrial solvents, gasoline compounds, radon, and chlorine. Carbon filters are sometimes used by themselves but are also incorporated into distillers and reverse osmosis systems. The use of an activated carbon filter in conjunction with a distiller will, in most cases, increase the filter's organic removal rate to over 90 percent.

Activated-carbon filters remove impurities by passing water through a honeycomb of very small channels in a carbon cartridge. Contaminants stick to the walls of the carbon, while the filtered water passes through. Carbon filters remove many objectionable tastes and odors, sediment, and most organic chemicals, but they are not effective against dissolved minerals such as calcium, magnesium, iron, manganese, nitrates, sulfates, or hydrogen sulfide (the chemical that gives water a rotten-egg taste and odor).

Carbon filters also cannot remove microorganisms from water. They can, in fact, allow bacteria levels to multiply many times over because the wet carbon and trapped organic material provide an ideal breeding ground for bacteria. However, if the incoming water is free of bacteria and the filters are changed frequently, bacteria should not be a problem. Coupling a chlorination system with a carbon filter can be an effective combination because the chlorine will kill microorganisms while the filter removes THMs that may be produced.

There are many kinds of activated-carbon filters on the market. Tests have shown that block filters and granular filters are more effective than powdered filters. There are three types of filter models available: (1) sink-mounted models attached to the faucet, (2) under-the-sink models attached to the cold-water line, and (3) free-standing models that are not connected to the plumbing at all. Generally, the under-the-sink models contain more carbon and are more effective. The cost for filtration units varies from $20 to over $500. Be sure to carefully assess the effectiveness of a filter before purchasing one—the effectiveness of individual brands can vary widely.

How a water filter is used is as important as which brand or model you buy. Here are a few suggestions to help improve a filter's performance:

- Flush out the filter daily.
- Don't filter hot water (it can free trapped chemicals).
- Use a slow flow rate (the carbon will be able to absorb more impurities).
- Filter only water used for drinking, cooking, and bathing.
- Change filters regularly.

DISTILLATION   Nothing beats a distiller for high-quality, consistently almost pure water. Distillers will remove just about any impurity except some toxic chemicals that boil at the same temperature as water. Additional carbon filters are necessary for reliable removal of organics.

In a distillation system, water is heated until it vaporizes. Bacteria, minerals, and other substances are left behind as the water turns to steam. The steam is then recondensed into relatively pure water. Some contaminants, such as chloroform, boil at or below the boiling point of water and can vaporize and be recondensed right along with the water. *Fractional* distillers, however, are able to remedy the chloroform problem.

Distillation is a slow process with daily capacity usually between 2 and 5 gallons. Distillers are difficult to keep clean. The impurities left behind build up and eventually form a scale that can interfere with the unit's efficiency. They also require energy and lots of water (5 gallons of tap water may be needed to produce 1 gallon of distilled water). Another drawback is that the distilled water tastes flat, but most people become accustomed to this or purchase mineral additives to improve the taste.

Distillers cost from around $150 to over $500. All systems must be cleaned and serviced regularly, so it's important to find a dealer who provides a service contract. Choose a glass distiller over a stainless steel one. The latter are known to add traces of aluminum, which has been linked with nervous system diseases and brain disorders.

REVERSE OSMOSIS   A reverse osmosis system is most effective for removing particulates and dissolved solids in soft water but will not remove microorganisms and barely touches volatile chemicals. If you incorporate a carbon filter, the augmented reverse osmosis system can filter lighter pollutants such as formaldehyde, TCE, and other synthetic organics.

Reverse osmosis systems work by passing impure water under pressure through a presediment filter, a cellophanelike membrane, and sometimes also through a carbon filter. The type and placement of the filters needed is determined by the contaminants in the water. As the water passes through the membrane, many of the impurities are left behind. The resulting water is 90 percent free of mineral and biological contaminants.

Reverse osmosis units have several disadvantages. Filters must be changed regularly. Water pretreatment is often necessary. Calcium must be removed by a water softener, and the water must have a pH below 8. Reverse osmosis units are relatively expensive, ranging from about $350 to $1,000.

AERATION   Aeration is a simple and natural way to treat water. Air is bubbled through the water, causing volatile compounds like chloroform to dissipate. It also reduces the concentration of iron, manganese, chlorine, and gases in the water and can improve the flat taste of distilled water.

Aeration has a number of drawbacks. Airborne contaminants can be incorporated into the water, and many substances in water are not volatile enough to be completely removed. Thus it is wise to use aeration along with another form of water treatment.

In-Home Water Treatment Techniques

Contaminant	Reverse Osmosis	Activated Carbon	Distillation	Aeration	Chlorine
Asbestos	■	■			
Bacteria	■		■		■
Inorganic chemicals	■		■		
Lead	■		■		
Nitrates	■		■		
Organic chemicals	■	■	■		
Particulates	■		■		
Pesticides		■	■		
Radon		■		■	
THMs		■		■	
Volatile organic chemicals (VOCs)		■		■	

BOILING   Boiling water for 15 to 20 minutes can destroy small amounts of bacteria or other microorganisms. Boiling can also rid water of volatile chemicals like chloroform. The boiling kettle should be made of glass or stainless steel to minimize contamination. The main disadvantage to boiling is that it will concentrate inorganic impurities such as nitrates, sulfates, and other minerals. Boiled water also tastes flat.

SIMPLE TREATMENTS   If you're not ready to invest in a water purification system, there are some quick and easy remedies you can try:

■ Refrigerating water may improve the flavor.
■ Heavy chlorine tastes and odors will dissipate if the water is kept for several hours in an uncovered pitcher.
■ Use your blender or mixer for several minutes to aerate water and remove chlorine and other volatile chemicals.

Find a New Source of Water

Finding a new source of water is difficult if you're on a public system. The only alternatives you have are to haul in water from some other source or switch to bottled water for drinking. Rural residents, on the other hand, have the option of drilling a new well, making sure it is not located near any potential contamination sources. The quality of the water in the new well should be checked to ensure that it is better than the old supply.

Rural residents may also be able to connect with an existing nearby municipal water supply. Small towns whose residents use individual wells can establish a municipal supply to replace the private wells. Although the cost of such systems can be high, it may be the only viable long-term solution to some water quality problems. Having water hauled in, getting water from a neighbor, or buying bottled water are options that should always be considered temporary solutions.

BOTTLED WATER   In many cases water you buy in a bottle isn't any better than what comes out of the faucet. There's nothing to prevent bottlers from bottling and selling plain old tap water. The seltzer you buy in the grocery store is generally just tap water that's been filtered and carbonated. Bottled water mostly comes from underground and is subject to the same contamination other groundwater is. Several years ago, for instance, both chloroform and benzene were found in bottled water in New York. Though bottled water is required by law to meet the same standards as tap water, the federal government doesn't require that bottled water be tested, nor does the government monitor this water.

If you choose to substitute bottled water for tap water, check with the bottler to find out where the water comes from and what minerals, chemicals, and bacteria may be in it. Buy your water in glass bottles, not plastic. The best kind to buy is distilled spring water, although it will have only trace amounts of the healthful minerals in it. And be prepared to spend 4 or 5 cents per glass— an expensive substitute, considering plain old tap water costs a fraction of a cent per glass.

Dealing with Common Contaminants

The following list will help you assess the risks involved if major contaminants are found in your water and will give you a good idea of measures you can take to get rid of them.

ASBESTOS   *If asbestos is found in your drinking water, a reverse osmosis system or a granulated activated carbon filter should get much of it out.*

Asbestos is one of a small number of naturally occurring substances that are known carcinogens in humans. When found in water, it usually comes from asbestos-cement plumbing pipe installed after World War II. Some 200,000 miles of this pipe are in use across the country today.

Though health risks from drinking asbestos-contaminated water are not known for certain, EPA studies show that where high levels of asbestos exists in drinking water, the cancer rate is above average, especially for cancer of the stomach, kidneys, and abdomen. Cities where high levels of asbestos have been found in the water include Cincinnati, Seattle, San Francisco, and Pensacola, Florida.

The EPA can regulate asbestos levels in drinking water under the federal Clean Water Act, but few towns or cities can afford to replace entire water supply systems. Because acidic water is particularly corrosive, one way to reduce the asbestos in water is to reduce acidity during treatment.

BACTERIA   *Bacteria in water can be treated at home with chlorination or a reverse osmosis system.*

Despite the publicity surrouding toxic chemicals, bacterial contamination remains the most common water quality problem in individual and small systems. These organisms commonly originate in human and animal wastes. They can find their way into groundwater from septic tank drainage, sewage, feedlot manure, or direct drainage of surface runoff into a well. Drinking water contaminated with bacteria can result in a variety of infectious diseases including dysentery, cholera, hepatitis, and typhoid fever. Bacterial contamination can also make infants more susceptible to the toxic effects of nitrates.

Public water systems use a variety of additives to kill bacteria before it reaches the public. Private supplies and small, rural public water supplies, however, are often contaminated with bacteria. If you have a private well, have it tested periodically for bacterial contamination. Your local health department should be willing to do it for you free of charge. When a well is contaminated, it is often because it is located in a depression or pit, is too close to a pollution source, or was not properly sealed.

LEAD   *You can reduce the amount of lead in your tap water with reverse osmosis systems and distillation units. (Carbon, sand, and cartridge filters do not remove lead.)*

Up through the early 1900s, it was common practice in some areas of the country to use lead pipes for interior plumbing. Before 1945, 90 percent of the water service lines running from the street to homes were made of lead. Fortunately, over the years many of these have been replaced with galvanized steel or copper lines. But the solder used to fuse these pipes also contains lead—often as much as 50 percent. Experts regard this lead solder as the major cause of lead contamination of household water today.

Because newly installed solder dissolves easily, new home dwellers or those in older houses with recent repairs are particularly at risk. In these cases, lead levels can remain above the current federal standard of 20 ppb as long as 5 years after installation.

Find out if the connector from the water main to your house is lead. Look at the pipe coming into your house from the outside. This will be the pipe coming into the basement, if you have one. If it is a dull silver color or scratches easily with a key, it is lead. If your house or apartment building was built more than 30 years ago, it is likely to have a lead connector, but some were used more recently, as well.

Two tests will reveal a problem with lead: (1) a blood test, which is relatively painless and inexpensive (a good idea if children live in the home) and (2) a water test by a competent laboratory. The cost of testing ranges widely, though usually it's between $20 and $100. Some utilities will test free of charge, or at least refer you to a reputable laboratory. Your water supplier may be able to offer information or assistance with testing.

Although federal standards limit the amount of lead in water to 20 ppb, independent research and the EPA's own calculations make a strong case for a limit of 10 ppb or less. If tests show that the level of lead in your household water is at this point or higher, it is advisable—especially if there are young children in the home—to reduce the lead level in your tap water as much as possible.

Even if you decide that the risk in your home is so low that it is not worth testing the water, there are still things that can be done to reduce your lead exposure.

First, let the water run from the tap for a few minutes first thing in the morning, or whenever it has been unused for several hours. Let the water get as cold as it can get—this will take anywhere from a few seconds to 2 or more minutes. Doing this will eliminate from the system the water with the highest lead levels. But this must be done with each faucet; taking a shower will not clear out your kitchen tap. Once you have flushed a tap, you might fill one or more glass bottles with water and put them in the refrigerator for later that day.

Second, never use water from the hot tap for drinking or cooking or especially for making baby formula. Heat increases the corrosion of lead substantially, so hot water will generally have much higher lead levels than cold water.

Here are other actions you can take to reduce exposure to lead in your household water:

- If you are served by a public water system, contact your supplier and ask whether the supply system contains lead piping and whether your water is corrosive. If either answer is yes, ask what steps the supplier is taking to deal with the problem of lead contamination. Water mains containing lead pipes can be replaced, as well as those portions of lead service connections that are under the jurisdiction of the supplier. Drinking water can be treated at the plant to make it less corrosive. Cities such as Boston and Seattle have successfully done this for an annual cost of less than a dollar per person.
- If you own a well or another water source, you can treat the water to make it less corrosive. This is easily done by installing a calcite filter in the line between the water source and any lead service connections or lead-soldered pipes. Ask your health or water department for assistance in finding calcite filters.
- Instruct, in writing, any plumber you hire to use only lead-free materials for repairs or in newly installed plumbing.
- You may want to replace connectors between copper and galvanized lines with special connectors that are designed to eliminate the chemical reaction between these two metals. These are called dielectric unions or insulating couplings. They will not only help reduce

---

Lead Solder

Until recently, 50/50 solder (50 percent tin and 50 percent lead) was the most widely used solder for plumbing systems. Because some of this toxic lead can end up in the water, the federal Safe Drinking Water Act Amendment of 1986 banned lead-based solder for potable water supply systems. This applies to all new plumbing installations and all alterations to existing plumbing. Unfortunately, some of the alternatives, like antimony-tin solder, can be even more dangerous than lead. Some scientists believe antimony is potentially even more lethal than mercury. The U.S. Environmental Protection Agency is still working on a study of antimony in drinking water. To find lead-free and antimony-tin–free solder, check your local hardware store or your local plumbing supply company.

---

lead leaching into the water, they will prolong the life of the system by eliminating corrosion between the two metals.

■ Don't use plastic pipe as an alternative to metal pipe. Little is known about leaching of chemicals from these plastics, and there is some concern about the toxicity of gases generated when they burn.

■ It is also a good idea to let the water run a bit before drinking from fountains and taps at work and in school. This water sits unused overnight for even more hours than household water and can have much higher lead levels.

■ Check with your local or state department of health or environment for additional information.

NITRATES   *Getting rid of nitrates is difficult. Generally, a distillation or a reverse osmosis home treatment system will reduce the levels of nitrates in household water.*

Nitrates enter the water through feedlot wastes, failed septic systems, landfills, and garbage dumps, but by far the main source of contamination is through nitrogen fertilizers. Use of chemical fertilizers in this country has increased more than 600 percent since 1950. And, according to U. S. Department of Agriculture estimates, plants take up little more than a third of it. The remainder either runs off the land into surface waters or filters down through the ground to the water table.

Nationally, more than 500,000 households are drinking water that contains potentially unsafe levels of nitrates. The situation is particularly serious in midwestern states that rely on agriculture as the main industry and in California, where nitrates are the major polluter of groundwater.

Nitrates affect the human body in two ways. Once ingested, they may be converted to cancer-causing chemicals called nitrosamines. Several studies have linked nitrates to a high incidence of stomach cancer and non-Hodgkin's lymphoma, although evidence is far from conclusive. In infants, the presence of nitrates is known to cause blue baby syndrome, a rare blood disorder that causes respiratory distress from lack of oxygen.

Municipal water systems regularly test and filter for nitrates in water. Many small towns and private wells, however, do not. For them, dealing with elevated nitrates in water is difficult. Nitrate levels tend to fluctuate depending on the time of year, so tests need to be taken periodically. Boiling is not effective in removing nitrates. Filtering them is expensive. Once a water system is contaminated with nitrates, drilling a new well is usually the only realistic alternative.

SYNTHETIC ORGANIC CHEMICALS   *If organics are found in unsafe concentrations in your drinking water, an activated-carbon filter can usually clear up the problem. Though they can't get everything, they are effective at filtering out more than 200 man-made contaminants.*

All organic substances contain carbon in combination with other elements such as oxygen or hydrogen. They include pesticides, volatile organic compounds (VOCs), THMs, and petroleum products. The concentration of organic chemicals in drinking water is usually too low to produce acute toxic effects, so chronic toxicity is the main concern. Certain doses over a long period of time are known to cause cancer and have adverse effects on the central nervous system, liver, kidney, and cardiovascular system. Residents of communities where water has been contaminated by VOCs have suffered a range of health effects from skin rashes to terminal illnesses. High rates of miscarriages and birth defects have also been observed.

Tests have shown that TCE—a VOC that is widely used as an industrial solvent—causes cancer of the liver and kidneys in animals. One cup of TCE can contaminate 3 million gallons of water. Benzene is another solvent for which there is strong evidence of carcinogenicity. The EPA has not yet established mandatory standards for VOCs.

Public systems have to treat the water if organics are found, but they're required to test for only a small fraction of organics. The only way to find out for certain if organics contaminate your drinking water is to test for them yourself. These tests are more expensive than tests for other contaminants, such as radon and lead. Cost is one reason why neither government nor private agencies have launched massive programs to detect all organics in water.

PESTICIDES   *Installing a granulated activated-carbon filter or a distillation system can usually filter out most pesticide compounds from household water.*

Municipal water systems are required to test periodically for pesticides and to provide treatment or alternate supply sources if residue problems arise. Private wells, however, are generally not tested unless the well owner requests such analysis. A 1984 EPA study of rural water conditions reported that 63 percent of rural drinking water supplies contained excessive amounts of pesticides and other contaminants.

If you get your drinking water from a private well, you can reduce the chance of contaminating your water supply by following these EPA guidelines:

- Be cautious about using pesticides and other chemicals on your property, especially if the well is shallow or is not tightly constructed. Check with your EPA regional office or county cooperative extension service before using a pesticide outdoors, to determine whether it is known or suspected to leach into groundwater. Never use or mix a pesticide near your wellhead.
- To avoid contamination problems of surface wells, be sure your well extends downward to aquifers that are below, and isolated from, surface aquifers, and be sure the well shaft is tightly sealed. If you have questions about pesticide or other chemical residues in your well water, contact your state or county health department.
- If your well water is analyzed and found to contain pesticide residue levels above established or recommended health standards, you may wish to use an alternate water source, such as bottled water, for drinking and cooking.

RADON   *A reverse osmosis water purifier can usually clear up a radon problem, but granulated activated carbon is more economical.*

If you live in an area with elevated levels of radon, it is possible for the radioactive gas to contaminate your household water. This usually happens when the water passes through radium-containing deposits of granite or other radioactive materials, as it does in Arkansas, California, Florida, Georgia, Massachusetts, North Carolina, Oklahoma, Pennsylvania, Texas, Utah, Virginia, and much of the eastern United States and Canada.

Radon in water has been linked to leukemia as well as bone cancer. But radon is more likely to affect people through the air they breathe than through the water they drink, so the main cause of concern is release of radon into the air from activities such as showering, bathing, and washing.

Individual wells and small town systems present the greatest concern; water from municipal systems releases most of its radon before it reaches individual houses. Some private and public testing labs will analyze a sample of your water for radon, usually for less than $50. Well water detectors are available for $22. Contact your local public health department for more information.

If levels higher than 20,000 picocuries of radon per liter of water (pCi/L) (the minimum federal standard) are found in your well water, consider purchasing radon removal equipment. The entire household water supply should be treated. A reverse osmosis water purifier can usually clear up the problem, but granulated activated carbon is more economical. Residential reverse osmosis systems usually range between $350 and $1,000 for devices of 1 to 3 cubic feet, and installation cost is approximately $50 to $100. On the other hand, granulated activated-carbon systems cost from $20 to about $500.

THMs   *To rid water of chlorine, boil it for 2 or 3 minutes or let it stand overnight. Or install an activated carbon filter.*

Chlorine is added to municipal water systems in this country to kill bacteria. But something else happens in the process. When chlorine reacts with organic matter—rotted leaves and so forth—methane gas is given off. This then reacts to form trihalomethanes, or THMs, which are suspected of being carcinogenic. The EPA has set 100 ppb as the maximum level of contamination for THMs in water. In Germany and Switzerland, however, the level is 25 ppb, and a proposal by the European Economic Council would set a limit of 1 ppb.

"No city water system in the United States could pass that rigid standard," said Jerry Tone, president of National Testing Labs in Cleveland, Ohio. Water in smaller towns is not monitored or treated as well as it is in big cities, he said, so levels of THMs in those systems are often more than 100 ppb. In city systems, the longer the water sits in a pipe, the higher the THM content may be. So if you're at the tail end of a city plumbing system, water coming out of your faucet is likely to carry a higher level of THMs than is water closer to the treatment plant.

No system serving fewer than 10,000 people is ever required to meet or even test for the standard of 100 ppb THMs. Small systems generally cannot afford to.

Prescription: A Healthy Home Has ...

... the healthiest possible drinking water. Technology does exist that could eliminate 87 to 100 percent of the contamination in public water systems, according to a 1988 study by Ralph Nader's Center for Study of Responsive Law in Washington, D.C. Granulated activated carbon has been found to filter out much of the contamination. This is already being used in a few public water systems in the United States.

Bottled water often has some of the same contaminants found in public water systems. And home filtration systems are not standardized, so quality varies. There are several things you can do:

■ Find out what is in your water supply—have it analyzed and compared to all of the Safe Drinking Water Act limits by an independent certified testing laboratory.

■ If the analysis shows you have a problem, seek the help of a reputable water treatment specialist. Follow the specialist's advice, and maintain the equipment according to instructions.

■ Have your drinking water retested after installation of water treatment equipment to be sure it is performing as advertised. If your problem is a serious one, have an analysis performed at least once a year, just to be sure no changes have occurred.

5

Indoor Air Quality

Soon after Sue and Ed Maschak bought their new house in western Pennsylvania in 1977, Sue began experiencing a nagging cough. At first she thought it was just a winter ailment. But winter came and went, and the cough persisted. Sue also noticed that other family members seemed more irritable and depressed since they'd moved, and they had more headaches and sleeping problems than usual.

"It was especially terrible because I thought the problems with the kids might be psychological," Sue told *Practical Homeowner* magazine. "I thought that we might be doing something wrong." Finally, in 1986, the Maschaks learned that there was nothing wrong with *them*; the problem was their house. Their indoor air was contaminated with chemical toxins, given off by the building materials and bottled up inside the tight house.

The Maschaks are among a growing number of victims of what is being called sick house syndrome, a potentially crippling reaction to the multitude of chemicals found in most houses today. It used to be that only a few allergic and chemically sensitive people suffered from the malady. But now, as we build tighter houses using more man-made materials, many people who were never affected before are, like the Maschaks, discovering that their houses are making them ill.

Why is this problem occurring, and why now? A deadly combination of two modern phenomena has brought the problem of indoor air pollution to a head. The first, and by far the most important, is the sheer volume of chemicals used in our society. An estimated 1,500 hazardous compounds in 3,000 products eventually find their way into American houses. Such things as carpet that does not stain, wallpaper that does not harbor mold, furniture made of pressed wood, and synthetic cleaning products all emit vapors into the air that mix and combine to form a chemical mélange we breathe each day. It's not clean and it's not healthy.

The second is our quest for energy efficiency. Such things as air-lock entries, walls and attics packed with insulation, tightly caulked windows, and even windows that do not open greatly reduce the number of times stale indoor air is exchanged with fresh outdoor air. The same tightening and insulating measures that enable our houses to store heat efficiently also trap pollutants inside while adding new toxins to the air from caulks, adhesives, and insulation. The tighter the house, the worse the problem.

So, what we have now in the typical American house is a dichotomy—it's never been better as far as comfort and ease of maintenance are concerned, but such technology comes with a price: a significant reduction in the quality of indoor air. The good news is that the environment indoors is under our control—unlike the outdoor environment. We *can* clean up indoor air once we know what the problems are and what we can do about them. Cleaning up indoor air without sacrificing either comfort or ease of maintenance is the challenge American homeowners are facing today.

STATE OF THE AIR

As many as 20 to 150 hazardous chemicals in concentrations 10 to 40 times those outdoors can be found in the typical American home. Often these pollutants reach levels indoors that would be illegal outdoors. Yet we spend 90 percent of our lives inside—and more than half of that time in our homes—breathing this air. The problem is so critical that officials at the U.S. Environmental Protection Agency (EPA) have called indoor air quality "the most significant environmental issue we have to face now and into the next decade."

People who live in polluted houses suffer from such common symptoms as headache, fatigue, cough, nausea, sensitive mucous membranes, irritable noses, trouble with contact lenses, and upper respiratory problems. But that's just short-term. Studies show that your risk of getting cancer from exposure to chemicals in the water, paint stripper, and other solvents found in your home is greater than your risk from exposure to the same chemicals in a hazardous waste site. The EPA estimates that indoor air pollutants cause as many as 6,000 cancer deaths each year and that radon causes an additional 20,000. And cancer is just one insidious outcome of exposure to synthetic chemicals. It is now thought that people who have low-level, repeated contact with certain common household chemicals may gradually develop subtle brain and nerve impairments, as well.

There are many potential contributors to indoor air pollution. Pesticides and fungicides, for example, can be found in everything from carpeting to wood preservatives to wallpaper adhesive. Fumes from solvents used in paints, sealants, and varnishes are also harmful, especially with high indoor temperatures. (For more on these and other household chemicals, see chapter 6.) Carbon monoxide from gas stoves and wood stoves can reach dangerous levels inside. Organic compounds, like methylene chloride (found in many aerosols), present a more serious health hazard than urea-formaldehyde foam insulation,

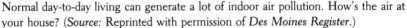

Normal day-to-day living can generate a lot of indoor air pollution. How's the air at your house? (*Source:* Reprinted with permission of *Des Moines Register.*)

which got a lot of press in the early 1980s. Bacteria can be found in many heating, cooling, and dehumidfying systems. By far the most ubiquitous chemical in modern houses is formaldehyde—more than 6 billion pounds of the stuff is used each year in this country. It's found mostly in pressed-wood products such as plywood, particleboard, and medium-density fiberboard (MDF, the worst of the bunch). Pressed wood is often used to build countertops, kitchen cabinets, subflooring, and furniture. It's even found in stereo speakers.

Who's at Risk?

While scientists differ over safe minimum levels of various pollutants, individuals who have allergies or weakened immune systems may feel the effects

---

Is Air Pollution Getting You Down?

If someone in your house suffers from persistent headaches, prolonged colds, coughs, sore throats, repeated intestinal upsets, feelings
of lethargy, or other chronic and medically inexplicable ailments, the
villain may be your house. How do you know if your symptoms are
caused by indoor air pollution? Ask yourself these questions:

- Do you have a runny nose?
- Do symptoms go away when you leave the house and recur when
you come back home?
- Is more than one family member symptomatic, especially those
who spend the most time at home?
- Do symptoms diminish when windows and doors are opened?
- Do symptoms get worse when the heat is turned on or when the
humidity goes up?
- Did you start feeling bad when you moved into a new house,
remodeled your house, got new furnishings or draperies, sprayed
with pesticides, or changed your activity level?
- Did symptoms develop after energy conservation work was done
on your house?
- Do symptoms become most severe during warm, humid weather,
or when the house is tightly sealed in cold weather?

---

from relatively small doses. Others at high risk include young children, pregnant women, the elderly, and anyone with a pre-existing illness such as
asthma, emphysema, chronic bronchitis, lung disease, angina or other heart
problems, or vascular diseases. Symptomatic people are usually those who
spend from 75 to 85 percent of their time inside the house—housewives,
young children, retired people, those working at home. But everyone who
consistently breathes synthetic chemicals is at risk. The more we are exposed
to chemical toxins, the more likely a sensitivity will develop.

How do you know if your house is so airtight it's unhealthy? First, are
there any detectable odors? If you can smell yesterday's breakfast when you
walk into the house, there's a pollution problem. Second, how do you and
others living in the house feel? Sneezing, wheezing, headaches, nausea,
irritability, forgetfulness, and a general vague malaise are common complaints.
In many cases, people have been feeling bad for so long they don't remember
what it's like to feel well.

Tight Houses Pose a Problem

How sick a house is may vary from season to season and day to day, depending
on the weather. Rainy, humid weather encourages the growth of germs that

promote illness. Very hot or very cold weather can also affect your home's healthiness.

How "tight" a house is greatly affects indoor air quality, too. The threat of indoor air pollution is most serious in superinsulated houses, where tightly closed windows and double-insulated walls and ceilings keep heat in at the cost of fresh air. Pollutants can be trapped inside these houses for days, gradually building up to dangerous levels. Though indoor air pollution is not necessarily absent from old, uninsulated houses, it is less of a problem.

How bad the problem becomes is generally a matter of how well the house can breathe. In a drafty, old house in winter, warm air will be replaced naturally by fresh, cold outdoor air once every hour or so, sometimes less, through cracks, holes, and leaky windows. But a new house designed and built for energy efficiency will exchange its air volume as seldom as twice a day.

Tightening a house will not cause a pollution problem, but it can aggravate an existing one. If a home already has high pollutant levels, house-tightening measures will slightly increase the risk of health problems. New extra-tight buildings can maintain good indoor air quality if pollution sources are minimized and if adequate ventilation is supplied mechanically.

Heat and Humidity Have an Effect

Tight houses aren't the only reason for poor indoor air quality. Heat and humidity also have a lot to do with how bad indoor air pollution becomes.

High heat levels release toxic vapors in paints, metals, and building materials. High humidity also accelerates the release of formaldehyde. Such toxic *outgassing* is dramatized by research showing that toxic smoke from synthetic materials, not fire itself, is the cause of 80 percent of fire-related deaths. Fumes capable of causing a multitude of subtle physical and mental symptoms are also released at much lower, or even normal, room temperatures. They come from synthetic materials in carpets, adhesives, upholstery, pressed wood, and other sources.

Achieving the Right Balance

You *can* have energy efficiency and good indoor air quality, too. You just have to achieve a balance. In St. Paul, Minnesota, environmental scientists did just that with a house that had been retrofitted to reduce energy consumption by 50 percent. The only problem was that the occupants were complaining about bad odors and various discomforts from stale air.

Not surprisingly, the scientist in charge of the investigation found that several pollutants were being trapped by the tight-house improvements. In his report he wrote, "The effect is similar to placing a house in a giant plastic bag. A key indicator was the nearly constant formation of condensation on the windows."

Modifications to the house included reducing relative humidity, adding return air ducts, relocating an exterior air intake for the house's air-to-air heat exchanger away from nearby car exhaust, and replacing the kitchen range hood with an electronic air cleaner. The air quality was improved without sacrificing energy efficiency.

THE POLLUTANTS

In large measure, it wasn't until scientists began to better understand the adverse health effects of three indoor air pollutants—asbestos, formaldehyde, and radon—that they began to be concerned about indoor air quality in general. Asbestos surfaced as a significant problem in the 1960s, formaldehyde in the 1970s, and radon in the 1980s.

At this time, the known indoor air pollutants of primary public health concern, according to the EPA, are the following:

Radon: By far the most serious air pollutant, it is a naturally occurring radioactive gas found in geological zones in soil, rock, and groundwater.

Tobacco smoke: Smoking aggravates the health hazards of nearly every indoor pollutant.

Asbestos: This substance becomes a hazard when aging plaster, pipe insulation, or tiles containing the fiber begin to crumble.

Formaldehyde: Pressed-wood products such as particleboard, plywood, and fiberboard use formaldehyde as a binder, or glue.

Volatile organics and chlorocarbons: These are present in many synthetic household cleaning, repair, and hobby products, especially aerosols. For more detailed information on VOCs, see chapter 6.

Combustion by-products: Nitrogen dioxide and carbon monoxide may be emitted from unvented, poorly vented, or malfunctioning gas and oil stoves, furnaces, and water heaters and from damaged chimneys.

Biological pollutants: Bacteria and other infectious agents become airborne when people sneeze or cough or are released from dirty air-conditioning or air-cleaning devices.

RADON: PUBLIC ENEMY NUMBER ONE

When it comes to having a safe and healthy home, radon is public enemy number one. It doesn't matter if you've carefully eliminated all other pollutants, installed expensive air or water filters, and have smoke detectors and fire extinguishers in all the right places—if radon levels are unacceptably high, your house is seriously unhealthy.

Radon—an odorless, colorless, naturally occurring radioactive gas—can accumulate in your home. It is estimated to cause from 5,000 to 20,000 cases of lung cancer each year, second only to cigarette smoking, according to the EPA. The EPA also estimates that as many as one out of five houses has radon levels above the recommended action level of 4 picocuries per liter of air (pCi/l).

Researchers at the EPA and other institutions have learned quite a bit about indoor radon in the past 3 years. Here is a short update of what you, the homeowner, should know.

The Threat

Though radon is a serious health threat to a large number of people, not only is dealing with that threat possible, it is often inexpensive—comparable in cost to dealing with termites. "Radon is the most controllable environmental hazard we face today," according to Richard Jordan, editor of *Radon Digest* and president of Radon Environmental Services in Indiana.

SETTING GUIDELINES   Although the EPA has set a recommended level for remedial action at 4 pCi/l of air, studies show that four to five people out of every 100 exposed to that level during their lifetimes will die of radon-induced lung cancer. The EPA's "safe" action level is equivalent to receiving 200 chest X rays per year! The American Society of Heating, Refrigeration, and Air-Conditioning Engineers (ASHRAE), which sets standards for indoor air quality, has recommended a 2 pCi/l guideline, which may be more realistic.

Since mid-1987, Congress and the EPA have been debating whether health standards (rather than action guidelines) for radon should be issued by the federal government. An EPA official has said that issuing health standards would "unduly scare the American people" because there is "no safe level for radon exposure."

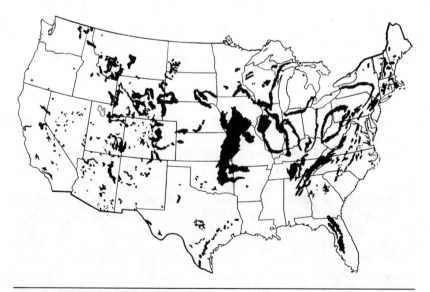

Radon isn't a problem just for residents of the Northeast. The dark areas of the map show that potentially high radon levels are scattered across the country. (Map courtesy of U.S. Environmental Protection Agency.)

WHERE RADON IS FOUND   Radon may be a problem in virtually every state. The EPA estimates that, nationally, 8 to 12 percent of all houses are above the 4 pCi/l action level, but on a regional basis the percentage is, in some cases, much higher.

In a ten-state study completed in 1987, 21 percent of the homes surveyed contained more radon than the 4 pCi/l recommended level—that's about one in five houses—and 1 percent exceeded 10 pCi/l. Radon levels varied significantly among, and even within, the states. In fact, the two states with the lowest overall average radon levels—Alabama and Michigan—recorded the two highest individual readings: 180 and 162 pCi/l, respectively.

HOW RADON ENTERS THE HOUSE   Radon is present in all soil to some degree. Basements often act as chimneys, particularly in wintertime, pulling radon in from areas of high pressure to areas of low pressure. The use of exhaust fans, combustion appliances, and clothes dryers that draw air out of the house; the presence of open fireplaces; the inside and outside temperature differences; and the velocity of wind around the house will all influence the degree of basement depressurization that will exist. If there's a large enough pressure differential, the house can literally suck in the gas through dirt floors, cracks in the foundation, floor drains, sump pits, joints, and tiny cracks or pores in hollow block basement walls. This is called the *stack* effect. In places with very permeable or porous soil, houses can pull radon from distances of up to 40 feet.

A 1988 study at the University of Pittsburgh found the following:

■ Radon levels measured 60 percent higher in winter and 40 percent higher in the spring and fall, compared with measurements taken in the summer.
■ Basements averaged 2.5 times higher radon levels than the rest of the house.
■ Well-weatherized houses tested about 40 percent higher than poorly weatherized houses.
■ Simply ventilating with open windows reduced radon levels by a factor of about 2.5.

RADON IN WATER   It is possible for radon to enter the water and be released into a house when the water is used, particularly through activities that spray or agitate heated water (taking showers and using dishwashers and clothes washers). Well water presents the greatest concern. Water from municipal systems releases most of its radon before it reaches individual houses.

At this time, radon in household water is not considered to be a big concern because the water's radon levels must be very high to significantly influence the overall radon level in indoor air. As a rule of thumb, 10,000 pCi/l of the incoming household water can produce 1 pCi/l of indoor air. If radon is found in your water, a carbon filter can clear up the problem.

Testing for Radon

To protect consumers against possible fraud, the EPA tests radon detectors to make sure the monitors being sold provide accurate readings. The EPA also publishes a list of the companies that have passed its radon measurement proficiency program. To get a copy of the current listing, write to your regional EPA or state radiation office.

As a first step, the EPA recommends a closed-house screening test with a carbon monitor (these cost between $10 and $25) placed in the lowest livable level of your home. If radon levels are between 4 and 20 pCi/l, a follow-up, longer-term test with an alpha track detector ($25 to $50) is recommended. If, after both tests, radon levels in your house are higher than 4 pCi/l, it's best to hire a professional diagnostic service to find out where the radon is most likely coming from. Though more expensive (anywhere from $100 to $400), these diagnostic tests can help to identify the best remediation method to use. They may include flux measurements through walls and floors with an electret (a Teflon disc that is electrostatically charged), monitoring with low-level gamma radiation detectors, visual checking by trained radiation protection technicians, and drilling of small holes in the slab. These measurements should be made in the most lived-in room of the house. If your house has more than one floor, you may wish to take measurements on each floor.

Check with your local board of health or state radiation protection office for information on radon measurement and diagnostic services.

Reducing Exposure to Radon

There are two approaches to reducing exposure to radon: (1) prevent radon from entering the house in the first place and (2) remove radon after it is in the house. Understandably, the first approach is the most desirable, especially if it can be done in a manner that does not require maintenance or checks.

PREVENTION   The most effective measures for preventing radon from entering your house are these:

- Seal cracks in the foundation floor and walls with good-quality caulks or other sealants.
- Cover and seal other openings in the foundation, such as floor drains, sump pits, and the spaces around utility penetrations.
- Ventilate crawl spaces and isolate them from adjacent basements.
- Seal tops of hollow concrete block foundations.
- Exhaust soil gas from beneath slabs either directly through a pipe inserted into the slab or through a covered sump that is tied into a drain tile loop around the foundation footing.
- Cover exposed earth inside or under the residence with concrete or a tightly sealed polymeric vapor barrier.

In a home under construction, all of the techniques listed above can be built in at low additional cost. Your new home will then be radon resistant, and any postconstruction radon removal that may be needed will also be less expensive.

REMOVAL   Methods for removing radon once it's in the house vary, depending on type of construction, where the radon is coming from, and how high the levels are. A few tried-and-true techniques include these:

- Open basement windows. This can be effective as long as it's not too cold outside and radon levels are low to begin with. Fans can be used to blow outside air through the basement and out windows. These should not be exhaust fans, though, since they lower the air pressure in the basement, thus sucking in more radon.
- Install an active (fan-driven) subslab ventilation system when average annual radon levels are above 20 pCi/l. This is the method of choice for most radon contractors today. Such a system usually costs from $500 to $2,500 (depending on the number of suction points and vent pipe routing problems) and can eliminate as much as 99 percent of the radon in a house. Subslab suction takes two forms: (1) a fan-driven ventilation system that sucks radon from beneath the basement floor through one or more suction points, carries it through pipes to the attic, and exhausts it through the roof to the outdoors, and (2) fan-driven suction on drain tile loops (4-inch perforated pipe) installed just inside or outside the foundation footing. These loops often terminate in a sump that can be covered and then used as the suction point. If drain tile loops vent to daylight, you can tap into the loop outside the house and apply fan-driven suction directly on the loop.
- Avoid the use of a heat-recovery ventilator (HRV, or air-to-air heat exchanger) as a stand-alone measure where radon levels are higher than 10 pCi/l. Even with lower levels, HRVs have serious drawbacks. They can cost up to $2,500 installed, and intake and outlet vents must be well balanced or the house can become depressurized and draw in even more radon.

Always follow up any radon mitigation efforts with another test to determine how much the level of radon has been reduced. Some states provide this service. If radon levels have not been satisfactorily lowered, additional mitigation steps may be taken, and the testing process repeated.

USING CONTRACTORS   Many radon remedies are beyond the skills of typical do-it-yourselfers. For complex remedies, it's best to hire a professional contractor who is experienced in radon reduction procedures. The best contractors will guarantee a reduction in radon levels to below 4 pCi/l. "It's not only possible, it's common," says Richard Jordan. "Every day, we obtain levels below 1 pCi/l."

Many states provide a list of qualified contractors, and some states now have certification programs for radon measurement and mitigation. Check with your state's radiological health department or the regional EPA office.

Reducing Risk

Short of eliminating the problem altogether, there are several things you can do to reduce your risk of radon exposure:

Stop smoking. Cigarette smokers routinely exposed to radon *double* their risk of dying from lung cancer.

Avoid living and sleeping in the basement. Distribution of radon throughout the house is not uniform. In general, those living areas closest to the source of radon entry have the highest levels of the gas. In most cases, the area of highest contamination is the basement, although heating and air-conditioning systems can quickly spread radon to other parts of the building.

Ventilate the house, including crawl spaces. Proper ventilation techniques have been known to reduce radon concentrations by 30 to 90 percent, depending on the time of year. When ventilating, open all the windows in the house and all the vents in a crawl space, not just those on one side, to allow pressure differences to equalize.

For more detailed information about radon, ask your state environment office or the EPA for the following free booklets: "A Citizen's Guide to Radon: What Is It and What to Do about It," "Radon Reduction Methods: A Homeowner's Guide," "Radon Reduction Techniques for Detached Houses, Technical Guidance," and "Radon Reduction in New Construction, an Interim Guide."

TOBACCO SMOKE

During any 5-year period more Americans now die from smoking than from all the wars the United States has ever fought, from the American Revolution to Vietnam. Though the health effects of smoking have been known for decades, people continue to smoke and to expose innocent nonsmokers who just happen to be sharing their air.

Once indoor air is polluted with smoke, it takes a while for it to be free of noxious vapors. Smoke odors cling to walls, furnishings, draperies, clothing, and other materials where it is released slowly, for days or weeks. Even where there is good ventilation, smoke odors may persist and contaminate the air.

Tobacco smoke not only harms the smoker, it's bad for anyone who breathes smoke-polluted air. The most irritating smoke comes directly from the burning end of the cigarette. This side-stream smoke has higher concentrations of noxious compounds than smoke inhaled by the smoker, plus it pollutes the air continuously.

Some studies suggest that passive smokers (nonsmokers exposed to smoke-polluted air) have twice the risk of suffering chronic lung cancer as do people who are not exposed to secondhand smoke. An EPA scientist calculated that from 500 to 5,000 deaths occur annually in this country from passive smoking. The National Council for Clean Indoor Air goes even further, saying that involuntary exposure to tobacco smoke may lead to as many as 46,000 deaths a year.

As is the case with other pollutants, children are especially at risk. Respiratory illnesses happen twice as often to young children whose parents smoke at home, compared with those with nonsmoking parents. Recent studies show that children who live with parents who smoke are at higher risk of dying of leukemia, both as children and as adults. One major study discovered that babies of parents who smoke at home have a higher incidence of bronchitis and pneumonia in their first year than babies with nonsmoking parents. In addition, parents who smoke at home can aggravate symptoms in some children with asthma and even trigger asthma attacks.

The solution to curbing this indoor air pollutant is a simple one: Don't smoke and don't allow others to smoke in your healthy home. If that rule is too strict for you, limit smoking to a single, well-ventilated room, and don't allow smoking around children.

FORMALDEHYDE

Formaldehyde has been used in construction and manufacturing for more than 100 years, but only in the last decade have studies linked the gas to nasal cancer in laboratory animals. Living with formaldehyde fumes on a daily basis can make you miserable. Low levels of formaldehyde can cause chronic respiratory problems, dizziness, rashes, lethargy, and nausea.

Today, 6 billion pounds of formaldehyde are used in the United States each year. It's found in practically every American home—in drapes, upholstery, some foam insulations, adhesives used in carpeting and wallpaper, milk cartons, car bodies, household disinfectants, permanent-press clothing, and paper towels, to name only a few common products. But the major source of formaldehyde contamination is pressed-wood products, in which it is used as a binder. As much as 10 percent of the average sheet of particleboard, medium-density fiberboard, or hardwood plywood may be formaldehyde.

"This is a wood products problem," says Thad Godish, director of the Indiana Air Quality Research Lab. "Though urea-formaldehyde foam insulation has gotten a lot of coverage, its use is minuscule compared with the formaldehyde in pressed and veneered wood." Godish adds that of all the houses he has tested, none has tested negative for formaldehyde.

The EPA classifies formaldehyde as a potential human carcinogen, but it can make you very sick years before cancer has time to develop. Formaldehyde is a problem because of outgassing. When urea-formaldehyde resin is mixed, excess formaldehyde is used in the mixture to speed up the curing time. This free formaldehyde never forms a chemical bond; it simply sits in the tiny nooks and crannies of particle board, fiberboard, and plywood. Most other consumer products containing formaldehyde do not release free formaldehyde, so they aren't as much of a problem.

Outgassing is at its highest level when the material is new, but materials continue to emit vapors for years. Even in small amounts undetectable to the senses—less than one part formaldehyde per million parts of air—the gas can cause minor eye, nose, and throat irritations; shortness of breath; headaches; nausea; and lethargy. Though you don't die from breathing the fumes, your quality of life is not what it should be and your potential is definitely diminished.

The EPA has set an acceptable level of formaldehyde in indoor air at 0.1 ppm (parts per million), but new studies done in Canada show formaldehyde-related symptoms at concentrations as low as 0.05 ppm. Thad Godish says the U.S. level is at least ten times higher than it should be, citing the fact that Canada has a target level of 0.05 ppm, with action recommended when formaldehyde levels reach 0.1 ppm. "I think the Canadian figures are more on target," he says. "When I get into a house with formaldehyde levels higher than 0.1 ppm, I can feel it. Somewhere in that neighborhood there is a threshold."

Urea-Formaldehyde Foam Insulation

It seemed like a good idea at the time. In the mid-1970s and early 1980s, with the cost of heating fuel skyrocketing, American home-owners by the thousands insulated their houses with urea-formaldehyde foam (UFFI). Made by mixing urea-formaldehyde resin with a foaming agent and an acid catalyst under pressure, the insulation was easily blown into the walls of buildings where it hardened within minutes and cured and dried within days. It worked and it was not expensive—in short, it seemed ideal.

Approximately 170,000 houses were insulated with UFFI in 1977, its peak production year, and about 150,000 additional houses were retrofitted with it annually after that until it was discovered that, in an overwhelming number of cases, the formaldehyde was leaching from the product into the air inside the houses, often causing acute illness.

In 1982, the Consumer Product Safety Commission banned use of the foam as being a health threat. That ban was subsequently overturned in federal court after manufacturers sued. Still, many experts believe a house insulated with UFFI poses a health threat from formaldehyde offgassing as long as 10 years after the insulation is installed. Few houses have installed UFFI since the scare of 1982, and little of the insulation has been produced since then.

If your house is insulated with UFFI, you should have it tested to see if your indoor air contains dangerous levels of formaldehyde. If tests show formaldehyde levels above 0.05 parts per million, try to lower them by caulking or sealing all cracks around baseboards and ceilings that might allow fumes to escape. Only extreme or lingering cases of high emission levels or adverse health reactions necessitate the costly measure of ripping out your walls and physically removing the foam insulation.

WHERE TO FIND PRESSED WOOD IN YOUR HOME   Pressed wood can be found in every room of the typical American house. Here's where you should look for it:

Subflooring: Plywood and particleboard are used as subflooring in millions of houses because they're cheap and they make a good base for laying a flat carpet. When used in this manner, pressed wood presents the worst formaldehyde problem because it covers such a large area. Homes with particleboard subflooring, even 2 to 5 years after installation, will have levels of formaldehyde in the range of 0.06 to 0.30 ppm, with peak levels in the range of 0.20 to 0.30 ppm.

Countertops: Particleboard and fiberboard are also used for countertops. Covering the product with plastic laminate, as is done in most applications, seals in the formaldehyde fumes, but only if the pressed wood is also sealed underneath, an often neglected spot.

Cabinets: Kitchen cabinets are another likely place to find pressed wood. When you open up pressed-wood cabinets, the sweet smell of formaldehyde can be overwhelming.

Paneling: Commercial paneling usually consists of three plies of wood veneer glued together with urea-formaldehyde resin. Since this product has a high ratio of formaldehyde to urea, the outgassing is potent. How concentrated formaldehyde becomes in the air depends on the surface-to-volume ratio (surface of wood to room volume).

Furniture: More than 90 percent of the furniture made and sold in America today is built with pressed wood. Such furniture is usually composed of plywood glued to a wood core containing formaldehyde resin. What's more, formaldehyde glues are used instead of nails or joinery. The potency of formaldehyde outgassing in a piece of furniture depends on its core. The most potent core wood is medium-density fiberboard.

"Usually, furniture doesn't present much of a problem unless a lot of it is put in a small space," Godish says. "A new bedroom suite in a standard-size bedroom, for example, puts as much formaldehyde into the air as would urea-formaldehyde foam insulation in the walls."

SYMPTOMS   As many as 10 to 20 million Americans a day have symptoms from formaldehyde outgassing and don't know it. Many of them live in mobile homes, which are notorious for their high formaldehyde content. "At least half the mobile homes in America today have formaldehyde levels that cause symptoms," says Godish. "It's at two to five times the maximum level found in a house insulated with urea-formaldehyde foam. The more time spent inside mobile homes, the greater the risk. An 18-year-old mobile home can still have formaldehyde levels over 0.1."

In its risk analysis, the EPA estimated that as many as 2 out of every 10,000 persons who have lived in mobile homes for more than 10 years will probably develop cancer. More than three million mobile homes are currently in use in the United States.

New houses are also suspect for high formaldehyde levels. If you live in an older home that has not been remodeled or retrofitted with urea-formaldehyde foam insulation, the levels of formaldehyde emissions are probably not significant, because formaldehyde seeps out quickly at first and more slowly later on. New furniture or renovations to your house, such as new kitchen cabinets or paneling, may pose a problem, though.

Classic symptoms of low-level formaldehyde poisoning are runny nose, sore throat, difficulty sleeping, headache, fatigue, difficulty breathing, sinus irritation, eye irritation, chest pain, frequent nausea, bronchitis, and/or menstrual and gynecological problems—many of which may occur at exposure levels as low as 0.05 ppm. Symptoms appear most often in the heating season, particularly at the beginning, when the house is closed up. When windows are opened, symptoms diminish. The most likely person to have symptoms is the one who is home all the time; however, multiple family members often have the same symptoms.

TESTING FOR FORMALDEHYDE   The only way to tell for sure if your house has high levels of formaldehyde is to test for it. Though you can do this yourself with inexpensive monitors, they aren't reliable indicators of how much formaldehyde is in your house. To get an accurate reading, have your house tested by your local, county, or state health department, or hire a private testing agency.

Some states provide formaldehyde testing free of charge if you have serious problems and your doctor makes a formal request. Hiring a private testing agency generally costs anywhere from $200 to $300. With a doctor's prescription, you may be able to deduct the expense from your income taxes. To find an independent laboratory, consult the yellow pages of your phone book under "Laboratories." If you have any questions or need help locating a laboratory in your area, call or write the Consumer Product Safety Commission, Washington, DC 20207; (301) 492-6800.

Regardless of which monitoring procedure is used, remember that the results you get report only the air level of formaldehyde during the monitoring period. Formaldehyde levels vary from day to day, but particularly with the seasons. Therefore, for a peak reading, it's best to monitor in the winter with the house closed up and the heat turned on. And be sure to record the temperature and humidity at the time of testing.

If you have health problems that may be due to high levels of formaldehyde, increase ventilation as much as possible and consider reducing the contamination by using one of the six basic approaches listed below:

Remove the source. This is the most effective but, in the case of subflooring or insulation, may be expensive. Paneling, furniture, or carpeting can be removed and replaced with natural materials.

Treat the source. Formaldehyde vapors from urea-formaldehyde foam insulation can be reduced by covering walls with vinyl wall coverings and vapor barrier paint (such as Glidden Insul-Aid), sealing cracks in walls, and putting gaskets in electrical outlets. Paneling, plywood, and particleboard can be covered with urethane, varnish, shellac, or special sealers.

Thad Godish recommends removing a particleboard subfloor. If that is impossible, he recommends taking up the carpet and sealing the wood, preferably with Valspar formaldehyde sealer. One coat on the top surface should reduce formaldehyde levels from this source by 85 percent, he says. As a second choice, he recommends two coats of nitrocellulose-based varnish.

Purify the air. Chemical filter systems can be used to reduce contaminants in the air. However, these may be costly and they require constant monitoring. A cheaper alternative is to buy some houseplants. Research by the U.S. National Aeronautics and Space Administration (NASA) has shown that the leaves of philodendrons, spider plants, and other common houseplants absorb formaldehyde. Dr. Bill Wolverton, senior research scientist at NASA, told *Practical Homeowner* magazine (September 1987) that about 15 to 20 such plants should completely remove the formaldehyde from an 1,800-square-foot house.

Ventilate. Increasing ventilation is an easy solution, but this allows heat to escape, as well. Heat-recovery ventilators (HRV, or air-to-air heat exchangers) are helpful in summertime. Though they're not as good in winter, they may be the cheapest answer to reducing formaldehyde levels in a foam-insulated house, says Godish.

Avoid formaldehyde products. One way to start cutting down on the amount of formaldehyde floating around in your house is to avoid medium-density fiberboard in your next furniture purchase or construction project. MDF is about three times more potent than particleboard. The fiberboard is commonly used as a core material underneath plywood or veneers in cabinets and furniture. It's most often seen in 5/8-inch-thick sheets and looks like a thick hardboard. It should be labeled in this rough form at the lumberyard (and come with a health warning stamped on the wood), but you may have to ask to find out if it was used in cabinets or furniture you're considering buying.

Exterior-grade plywood is best for construction projects, even for indoor finish work. It contains phenol-formaldehyde resin, which is more stable than the urea-formaldehyde used in some indoor grades.

Read labels to discover formaldehyde content in common products. Swedish Glitsa, for example, a popular finish for hardwood floors, has notoriously high levels of formaldehyde in it, according to Godish.

Control indoor climate. Maximum formaldehyde levels occur under warm, humid conditions, particularly when the residence is closed. Therefore, controlling the climate indoors is helpful in reducing formaldehyde levels. This also helps diminish outgassing from other pollutants, such as pesticides in carpet and solvents in varnish.

The higher the indoor temperature, the higher the formaldehyde concentration in indoor air. As a general rule, when temperatures are between 68° to 86°F, a temperature increase of 10°F will result in an approximate twofold increase in formaldehyde levels. Conversely, a decrease of 10°F will result in a 50 percent reduction in levels.

Less significant, but nevertheless important, is the effect of humidity. Symptoms are most severe when humidity levels are 50 percent or greater. When humidity is less than 35 percent, symptoms diminish in severity. An increase in relative humidity from 30 to 70 percent can be expected to result in an approximate 40 percent increase in formaldehyde levels.

ASBESTOS AND OTHER MINERAL FIBERS

Tiny man-made mineral fibers used in some building materials can escape into the air, particularly if the material is loose, damaged, or decayed. When this happens, people who breathe the fibers are at risk of developing severe lung disease. Once inhaled, the long, thin, sharp fibers, so foreign to the human body, take a long time to dissolve or, in the case of asbestos, do not dissolve at all. Instead, they become permanently embedded in the body, causing cancer and other diseases from 15 to 30 years after exposure. The worst offender is asbestos, but fiberglass and mineral wool are suspected by some to pose a similar hazard.

Asbestos

If you live in a house that was built or remodeled between 1900 and the early 1970s, it's highly probable that you're living with asbestos, a highly carcinogenic building material. Once thought to be a miracle mineral, this fibrous material has been used to insulate walls and heating pipes, to soundproof rooms, to fireproof walls and fireplaces, to strengthen vinyl floors and joint compounds, and to give many paints their texture. Asbestos use reached its peak in the 1970s.

We now know asbestos is no miracle. It's known to cause cancer of the lung, stomach, and chest lining as well as asbestosis, a lung disease that is usually fatal. Smoking aggravates the disease. According to the American Lung Association, prolonged exposure to asbestos almost doubles the likelihood that a smoker will develop lung cancer.

It takes 15 to 30 years for cancer to develop from asbestos exposure. Because of this time lapse and the ubiquitous nature of asbestos, an estimated 20,000 people will die each year for the next 40 years from asbestos exposure. There is no effective treatment and no safe level of exposure.

Asbestos poses a health hazard only if fibers are released into the air. But this can happen easily. Fraying pipe insulation, for example, found in the basements of many older houses, releases the microscopic fibers. So does any cracked or disintegrating fireproofing board, often found behind radiators in steam-heated houses and apartments. Even pulling up old linoleum or replacing roofing shingles can make asbestos crack and release tiny particles into the air. Once released, asbestos fibers hang suspended in the air, some for more than 20 hours—or longer, if fans or air conditioners disturb air flow. If not properly removed, these nonbiodegradable fibers can pollute the air in a home for the lifetime of the house, becoming airborne whenever dust is stirred up.

If asbestos at your house has been damaged so that it's getting into the air and can be inhaled, it should be either removed or contained. Never attempt to tear out asbestos-containing material yourself; the danger from exposure during its removal is much greater than from the low level of exposure you face from damaged but undisturbed material. An ordinary dust mask is practically worthless as protection.

Since the 1970s, the federal government has prohibited the use of asbestos in patching compounds and artificial fireplace logs, and it is consider- ing a ban and phase-out rule on asbestos in all consumer products. Any asbestos-containing product manufactured after December 1986 is required to be labeled as such. Because it's widely known to be a health hazard, asbestos is not used much anymore. But it remains in nearly one-quarter of existing American houses and apartment buildings, and as late as 1979, 600,000 tons were used in the United States. Here's where you're likely to find it:

> **Hot water and steam pipes:** In some older houses, hot water and steam pipes may be covered with an asbestos-containing material to reduce heat loss. Manufactured from 1920 to 1972, this insulation was usually preformed in half-rounds, then wet-gauzed in place. Pipes were also wrapped in asbestos-paper tape. Look for this whitish material on pipes in the basement.
>
> **Ducts and furnaces:** During the 1940s and 1950s, these were frequently insulated with asbestos-impregnated papers. The chalk-colored insulation was applied as flat sheets as thin as $1/16$ inch or as corrugated versions. As these age, asbestos fibers may be released into the ventilation system. Asbestos cement was the material of choice for heating ducts built into concrete slab floors in houses constructed between the 1950s and late 1970s.
>
> **Asbestos boiler wraps:** Typically made of chalky blocks about 2 inches thick, asbestos wraps were fastened to boilers by wires or metal lath and then coated with plaster-saturated canvas. They tend to disintegrate rapidly in humid environments or when soaked with water. This type of product wasn't banned by the EPA until 1975.
>
> **Vinyl flooring:** Vinyl floor tiles and sheet flooring often contain asbestos to strengthen the flooring and help it resist wear. While asbestos fibers normally can't escape from the surface, tearing, cut- ting, or sanding can release asbestos. Some mastics and felts found below the vinyl have a high asbestos content as well. While asbestos is not banned from use in flooring tile, manufacturers say they have not used it since 1979.
>
> **Decorative coating:** Walls and ceilings may have a fluffy, asbestos-containing coating that was sprayed or troweled on and used for thermal, acoustic, or decorative purposes. This was especially popular

during the late 1960s and early 1970s and is found most often in hallways and entries (and in schools and public buildings—particularly in earthquake zones, where the material was used to hide cracks). The EPA says it is *extremely important* that a trained asbestos-removal contractor remove it before you remodel. These coatings are no longer in use.

Insulation: Wall, ceiling, and attic insulation in houses constructed between 1930 and 1950 may contain insulation made with asbestos. This is often found inside the structure, sandwiched between plaster walls and the framing. A trained asbestos-removal contractor should always be used during renovation or remodeling when this type of asbestos is found.

Roofing and siding: Asbestos cement used to be a popular material for roofing shingles (1940s through 1960s) and siding (1930s through 1970s). Asbestos-containing roof shingles are usually grey and often bear brownish white streaks along areas where water drains more slowly. You can recognize them by the pinging sound a pebble makes when it hits the surface. Asbestos-cement shingles used as siding might be any color. These have a propensity to crack and chip along their edges. These products are still in use.

Though the hazard is greater for people working with the material during either patching or renovation, there is also danger to the house's inhabitants. These shingles can shed asbestos fibers during the natural course of weathering; when they do, fibers can enter the indoor environment through open doors and windows.

Joint compound and textured paint: Joint compound made before 1977, used to tape joints on wallboard and fill holes in plaster, contains as much as 12 to 15 percent asbestos. Textured paints made before 1978 may also contain asbestos. If the material is in good condition, it is best to leave it alone. Sanding and scraping will release asbestos fibers. In 1977, the Consumer Product Safety Commission banned patching compounds containing asbestos because they presented an unreasonable carcinogenic risk to consumers.

Fireproof board: When wood-burning stoves and oil, coal, or wood furnaces were installed in the past, asbestos-containing cement sheets and millboard were frequently used as a fireproofing material to protect the floor and walls around them. It is quite brittle and easily broken. You can recognize it by its gray color and the size of the sheets, usually ¼ to ¾ inch thick, resembling plasterboard. Avoid scraping, sanding, drilling, or sawing these materials. These products are still being manufactured.

Acoustic ceiling tiles: Asbestos is found in acoustic tile, the kind you often see in basement recreation rooms. Asbestos in this product is usually a brownish material. When renovating, don't plan on adding ceiling tile unless you're sure it is asbestos free. Ask the manufacturer, and don't stop pestering for information until you're satisfied.

Door gaskets: Some door gaskets in furnaces, ovens, and wood and coal stoves may contain asbestos. Handle this material as little as possible.

Appliances: Asbestos lurks in home appliances such as toasters, broilers, slow cookers, waffle irons, dishwashers, refrigerators, ovens, ranges, clothes dryers, and electric blankets. Products manufactured after December 1986 must be labeled if they contain asbestos, so *read labels* when shopping for new appliances. If you want more information, contact the manufacturer, or write the Consumer Product Safety Commission.

Fabric: Asbestos is sometimes woven into yarn, cloth, and other textiles used to manufacture fire-resistant curtains, blankets, gloves, protective clothing, electrical insulation, thermal insulation, and packing seals.

Children's play items: Asbestos has even been found in some play sand sold for children's sandboxes, and in papier-mâché mixes. According to the August 1988 issue of *Health Letter,* two brands of sand sold for children's sandboxes contain tremolite, one of the most dangerous components of asbestos. The two brands are Kiddies FunSand, made by Quickrete Company, and Basins brand play sand.

Brake linings: Another source of asbestos is brake linings in cars, trucks, and buses. As a vehicle ages, asbestos wears off and is released into the air. If you live near a busy street, it's best to leave windows on the street side of the house closed, particularly during dry, windy periods.

DEALING WITH ASBESTOS IN YOUR HOUSE   Always be cautious around suspected asbestos-containing materials in your house. Look for areas where asbestos has become damaged by water, dented, corroded, blistered, or otherwise changed in a fashion likely to release fibers into the air. If you find damaged asbestos, don't disturb it. Before doing anything else, determine if it really is asbestos.

An experienced remodeling contractor can pinpoint asbestos-containing materials in your home. For a free copy of EPA-certified asbestos-detection agencies, write to Asbestos List, U.S. Consumer Product Safety Commission, Washington, DC 20207.

In some cases you may want to have the material analyzed by a laboratory. An analysis might be useful if you are preparing a major renovation that will expose materials contained behind a wall or other barrier. A state health agency or your local environmental protection agency should be able to take a sample for you and have it analyzed. Or call the EPA's Toxic Substances Control Hotline at (202) 554-1404 for information on sampling and to locate a laboratory near you. Testing costs $30 to $50 per sample and ordinarily takes less than a week.

If the sample tests positive, you have three options for solving the problem: (1) removing the asbestos (considered by experts to be the only permanent solution), (2) encapsulating the asbestos (the asbestos is sprayed with a sealant that bonds the fibers together, preventing further escape of the fibers into the air), or (3) erecting a barrier to seal off the asbestos (airtight walls and ceilings are constructed around the asbestos-containing surfaces).

You must make a judgment based on what you can afford for sampling and removal of asbestos. In many cases, the application of a sealer to contain the material provides the best protection from health risks at the most reasonable cost. For example, taping and painting rotting insulation around your steam heating pipes will end the potential for air contamination in many cases. In instances where the asbestos-containing material shows no signs of deterioration, the best solution is to do nothing and avoid cutting or sanding the material. Make your decision based on the information supplied by an experienced contractor or on laboratory results.

Do not attempt to remove asbestos yourself. If you can, leave the asbestos-containing product in place. If you're redoing a vinyl-asbestos kitchen floor, for example, don't take out the old layer—cover it up instead. Dings on asbestos siding can be painted to retard fiber release. When it comes to re-siding your house, cover up any asbestos shingles in place. The worst thing you can do is sand or cut asbestos shingles or flooring; that will release countless small fibers into the air.

If you have asbestos pipe insulation and its covering is slightly frayed or has small punctures, don't remove it—repair it. You may be able to do the job yourself, with the proper precautions. Wear protective gloves, hat, and long clothing or a disposable plastic suit. The EPA recommends first wetting the insulation with a soapy water mist (about a teaspoon of soap per quart of water), then wrapping the pipes with a good-quality, wide duct tape, and then painting with a coat of latex paint. If there's a lot of pipe, it's wise to invest in an asbestos-approved respirator. Then, wash your work clothes separately from the rest of the laundry, or throw them away.

If the pipe or boiler insulation is badly damaged or needs to be removed, hire a professional asbestos abatement crew to handle the project. Don't be surprised if workers treat the material like radioactive waste. They'll wear disposable uniforms and respirators, enclose rooms in plastic sheeting, and use special negative-air-pressure vacuums.

Because of the precautions and risks, professional removal is expensive. Most companies charge between $15 and $35 per linear foot to remove asbestos pipe insulation and between $10 and $35 per square foot to scrape asbestos-containing paint from walls. Even a small job can cost $1,000, and larger projects can run as high as $10,000. (In some cases the cost of asbestos abatement can be considered a home improvement, reducing taxes on capital gains when the house is sold. Check with an accountant or tax attorney for details.)

Before hiring an abatement firm, check its credentials carefully with former customers and local health agencies. Improper asbestos removal can unleash a monster far worse than the one that existed before. It's also a good idea to get air samples so you'll know how much asbestos is floating around inside your home both before and after removal. Make sure any remodeling contractors you hire understand the problems associated with asbestos, especially if they'll be renovating a kitchen or basement. One Colorado couple learned these lessons the hard way when their contractor used a power sander on the felt-and-mastic residue below a linoleum floor he had removed, not realizing it contained asbestos. The fibers that were released contaminated the house so badly, the owners were forced to abandon it.

Until more is known about the health effects of long-term and short-term exposure to asbestos, the safest plan is to avoid it when you can, and proceed carefully when you can't. And if you have *any* questions about how to handle specific asbestos problems, get them answered by the EPA or local health officials before proceeding.

The Fiberglass Furor

Is fiberglass insulation as potentially hazardous as asbestos? While data aren't definitive, the product (along with mineral wool and ceramic-based fibers) has scientists concerned.

Glass fiber and some other insulation products have long been known to cause skin rashes and respiratory irritation. But such materials and asbestos, several scientists say, also share a potentially fatal trait: All contain masses of small, inhalable fibers that can lodge in human lungs. Size, not chemistry, seems to be the most important factor. Fibers that are thin, long, and durable are the most suspect. The ratio of length to diameter in suspicious fibers is 3:1. "Fibers with these dimensions are probably equally carcinogenic," says Dr. David Groth, a scientific researcher with the National Institute for Occupational Safety and Health.

Though most fiberglass fibers are too large to be inhaled, manufacturers have begun increasing their fine-fiber output, largely for blown-in insulation. Fine fibers provide greater insulation than larger-sized fibers do, and at lower cost. They also aren't as itchy. CertainTeed Corporation's InsulSafe III has the distinction of being the fiberglass insulation product with the smallest fibers, but all fiberglass products have some small particles.

Makers of the materials under scrutiny all defend their products' safety. And researchers believe that most currently used insulating products don't appear to threaten homeowners and are less toxic than asbestos. The fact that fiberglass, unlike asbestos, seems to dissolve in animal tissue makes it appear to be less of a hazard, although the rate of dissolution is only 10 percent per year, or less.

If there is a danger, it is mainly to plant workers and installers of the material. However, homeowners can be placed at risk during remodeling when an exterior wall is disturbed, or when they're crawling around in an attic or crawl space with fiberglass batts dangling from the ceiling joists, or if fiberglass insulation somehow manages to contaminate the ventilation system.

Future U.S. regulatory action on fiberglass and other insulating fibers is likely. Currently, these are regulated as so-called nuisance, or nonhazardous, dusts. Both industry and academic institutions are involved in new studies of insulation fiber safety. In the meantime, anyone working with the material should wear a full-face, powered or supplied-air respirator. Families with small children should block access to attic and basement crawl spaces, where loose fiberglass and mineral wool insulation is often found.

COMBUSTION BY-PRODUCTS

Every time something is burned—from oil in the furnace to a steak on the grill—combustion by-products are given off. These are a combination of deadly gases and tiny particulates that can easily be inhaled. Wood stoves, fireplaces, candles, kerosene heaters and lamps, cigarettes, and gas ranges are all sources of combustion products. The gaseous contaminants are nitrogen dioxide, nitric oxide, carbon monoxide, carbon dioxide, and sulfur dioxide. If these build up in your house, they can cause chronic bronchitis, headaches, dizziness, nausea, fatigue—even death.

Carbon monoxide is one of the most immediately hazardous pollutants. Carbon monoxide poisoning accounts for one-half of the fatal poisonings in the United States each year. Dangerous exposure may occur before one is aware of the problem, and chronic exposure can have serious effects. Faulty gas appliances alone account for 300 carbon monoxide deaths a year. Poorly ventilated kitchens and rooms over or next to garages top the list of sites that can have dangerously high levels of this gas.

Even though you can't see, smell, or taste carbon monoxide, there are clues to its presence:

- stuffy, stale, or smelly air that never clears
- high humidity, often showing up as condensation on windows
- no chimney draft
- a hot draft from the chimney into your home

In most houses, pollution from combustion appliances is not a serious problem as long as the appliances are properly installed, vented, and serviced regularly. (Avoid using kerosene heaters and lamps—they don't belong in a healthy home.) However, new superinsulated houses and sensitive people are another story. In these cases, special measures to control pollution are a must. Perhaps an all-electric house is the answer, or installation of a monitoring device, such as a carbon monoxide detector that sounds an alarm when levels of the gas get too high (costing anywhere from $25 to $250; see appendix A).

Gas Furnaces and Appliances

In most houses, externally vented central furnaces fueled with natural gas pose no indoor pollution problem when properly designed and maintained. However, if there is a faulty exhaust system (like a blocked flue), or if there are cracks and leaks in the pipes or improper adjustment of the burner, or if there is lower air pressure inside the building than outside, the furnace can create serious indoor air pollution. If you suspect incomplete combustion or leakage in a gas furnace or other appliance, call your utility company or a heating contractor who can test carbon monoxide levels. Here are some things you can do to ensure gas furnace safety:

■ If you have an older gas furnace, install a supplementary induced-draft fan that reduces the possibility of backdrafting. There are also automatic shutoff devices that turn off the furnace if it begins to backdraft. You may want to think about buying a new, energy-efficient furnace.

■ If you're installing a new gas furnace, choose one of the more efficient models that uses an induced-draft system or brings outside air directly into the combustion chamber.

■ Have your furnace inspected and your chimney cleared of debris in the fall before starting up the heating system. Among things to look for are holes or open joints in the metal pipe and such obstructions as birds' nests, heavy accumulations of soot, or even pieces of masonry that have broken loose in the chimney flue.

■ Have a separate flue for each combustion device. Many chimneys are partially blocked because the pipe from a wood or coal stove has been brought into the same flue that vents the furnace. This dangerous arrangement could send gases from both furnace and stove into the house.

Gas ranges were once associated with indoor pollution, but more recent studies indicate that, if a range is properly operating, the pollution emissions are minimal. Pilot lights are usually the highest source of emissions, but newer gas ranges solve that problem—they come equipped with a device for electrical ignition called spark ignition. According to the Gas Research Institute, spark ignition cuts fuel consumption—and the amount of combustion gases released—by one-third. Here are some other ways to make sure you use your gas range safely:

■ Check the color of the gas flame. A yellow-tipped flame, instead of a blue flame, indicates that a gas range is not burning properly and should be adjusted.

■ Install an exhaust hood vented to the outside, and *use* it whenever you cook. This will remove 60 to 87 percent of the pollutants from a gas range. An unvented, recirculating range hood is practically useless. Outdoor ventilation systems for a gas range cost between $200 and $800, depending on how far the appliance is from an exterior wall.

■ Keep the kitchen otherwise ventilated. If nothing else, at least install an exhaust fan in the window.

■ Never use the gas range as a device for heating the kitchen in cold months.

■ Study energy-use labels when purchasing a gas range. The newer, high-efficiency models burn better and give off fewer emissions.

Gas dryers should always be properly vented directly outside. Energy

A Case of Carbon Monoxide Poisoning

Fran Lucas didn't know what was happening to her. The normally energetic, middle-aged woman had been healthy all her life. Then, suddenly, she began having horrible headaches, her speech was slurred, she experienced shortness of breath, and she often blanked out. "Some days I would feel better. Then, inexplicably, I'd be worse again," she explained. "Sometimes I felt as if there just wasn't any air, so I'd crack a few windows. I'd feel better then." Better maybe, but not well.

Fran's troubles began in the fall of 1986, about the time the furnace started running in the sprawling, four-bedroom, ranch-style house at the edge of the fairgrounds in Des Moines, Iowa. Built in 1967 as an all-gas show home, the big house had been recently insulated and re-sided, and the windows had been tightly caulked.

Since Fran works from her home, she spends the better part of every day there. When she started complaining of headaches, neither she nor her husband thought the cause could be environmental. Her husband, Marion, felt fine but he didn't spend nearly as much time inside the house as Fran did.

About the time the philodendrons started dying, Fran's health worsened: She complained of chest pains. Her face was perpetually white. She was often confused. Her eyes had a strange, uncustomary blank stare. By now Marion was really frightened. "She kept getting worse and worse. We thought it might have been a massive heart attack," he said.

After a week-long stay in the hospital, Fran felt better, even though her doctors could not find a cause for her illness. Fran returned home, only to be bedridden with illness again two weeks later. Ultimately, it drove the couple out of their home. They stayed away for two months. Meanwhile, a team of house inspectors combed the house for any signs of toxins or gas leaks.

What they found was a form of *reverse stacking*. The clue was three chimney flues spaced closely together on the roof. Since the house had been tightened up for energy efficiency, there was a shortage of air for the gas combustion furnace. When the furnace kicked on, it couldn't get the air it needed from the tightened-up basement, so it drew air from the living spaces in the house. It began sucking air down the fireplace chimney. Unfortunately, when the wind was just right, that sucked-in air was badly contaminated with carbon monoxide exhausted from the furnace through an adjacent flue on the roof. This polluted air spilled into the living room and kitchen through the fireplace opening, contaminating air inside the house, especially in those two rooms. *(continued)*

A Case of Carbon Monoxide Poisoning—*Continued*

This is exactly where Fran spent most of her time during the day. When illness overcame her, she would lie down on the couch, only to become worse. "After we discovered what was wrong, we learned that carbon monoxide is a heavy gas—it hangs close to the floor. So by lying on the couch I was actually breathing more fumes," she explained.

Fran is lucky. The house is now fixed and her health has returned. The family dog didn't fare as well. Muscles in the young Doberman are permanently destroyed from chronic exposure to the gas. "Because he lived so close to the floor, he got bigger doses," Fran explained.

It took 120 days to work out a solution to the Lucas' gas problem. They now have two new furnaces in the basement, both designed to draw combustion air from outside the house. A small fan forces combustion gases out the chimney. Carbon monoxide detectors are placed strategically inside the house, and the furnace flues have been relocated so they aren't so close to the fireplace chimney.

conservation devices that allow the hot-air exhaust from the dryer to blow directly into the room should never be used with gas dryers.

Wood Stoves and Fireplaces

Loose stovepipe joints and leaky door gaskets on wood stoves can allow significant emissions of pollutants to escape indoors. A chimney that is too short will allow smoke from outside to reenter at windows, doors, or air vents. However, with recent innovations—like the secondary combustion chamber and the catalytic converter—wood stove emissions are less of a problem than they once were. In a study of 20 southern Wisconsin homes where wood was the primary or partial heating fuel, it was found that a house with an attached garage, a gas range, or a cigarette-smoking occupant was likely to have more indoor air quality problems than a home heated by a wood stove or furnace. To ensure that your wood stove is doing its job cleanly, take these precautions:

- When purchasing a wood stove, buy one with a secondary combustion chamber and/or a catalytic converter to reduce emission of hydrocarbons.
- Periodically check gaskets and joints of the stove to make sure they are tight.
- Make sure your wood stove is carefully installed and all exhaust pathways are periodically inspected for possible air leakage. A proper draft will help to exhaust combustion products efficiently.
- Have your wood stove cleaned annually to ensure a proper draft.

Most of the pollutants from a fire in a fireplace enter the room through cracks in a stovepipe or by downdrafts or spillage of wood from the fireplace. The rest goes up the chimney or flue. Organic compounds and particulates pose the greatest health risk, based on the large number of carcinogens involved and the fact that almost all the particulates are small enough to be easily inhaled. Use your fireplace wisely by following these steps:

■ Open the fireplace damper before lighting a fire, and keep it open until the ashes are cool.

■ Do not burn coated-stock paper or colored-print paper such as magazines and newspaper comics. Arsenic vapor and volatile organic chemicals in the inks can cause acute respiratory problems in poorly ventilated rooms.

■ Don't use synthetic fireplace logs. These are basically made of wood pulp and chips bound with highly flammable resins and alcohols and imbued with chemicals that give off bright colors when burned. Traces of these chemicals persist in the air and cling to drapes, carpeting, and upholstery.

■ Install a fresh-air duct directly to the firebox, and close the fireplace opening itself with glass doors. This will alleviate pollutants and make your fireplace much more energy efficient.

Coal Stoves

Coal stoves emit high levels of sulfur dioxide, a pollutant best known for its connection with acid rain. Sulfur dioxide is also associated with the deadly industrial smogs that blighted many parts of England 500 years ago. The owner of a healthy home avoids burning coal.

Attached Garages

A car running in an attached garage can cause significant pollution, allowing lead, organic vapors, carbon monoxide and nitrogen dioxide to enter the house. To keep this from happening, *do not start your car or other combustion engines in a closed garage*. Attached garages should be well isolated from living spaces, and air-handling ducts should not pass between them. The truly healthy home has an unattached garage.

Spilling and Backdrafting

Anything that relies on a natural draft to exhaust combustion products (fireplace, stove, gas furnace, or water heater) is subject to backdrafting under certain conditions. When this occurs, combustion products spill into the living space instead of going out the chimney. The chances that backdrafting will occur are increased by chimney blockage or deterioration, tight house construction, competition with other exhaust points (kitchen fan, bath exhaust, dryer, and so forth), weather conditions, or a combination of these.

If the problem is backdrafting of a wood stove or fireplace, it's usually easy to see or smell the smoke. Most of these pollutants, however, are invisible and odorless. It is difficult to test for low levels or for intermittent spillage from furnaces or water heaters. Testing for carbon monoxide may be advisable if anyone in your home is experiencing headaches; irritation of the eyes, nose, and throat; and other respiratory difficulties.

REVERSE STACKING Reverse stacking—a form of spilling—is a common occurrence and one you should watch out for. Reverse stacking occurs when two or more combustion appliances share the same combustion air source, such as when a gas furnace and a gas water heater are both located in a basement room. A reverse stack condition may occur when one device is operating and the other is not.

A typical scenario is this: When the burner of the gas furnace turns on to supply heat to the house, it begins drawing air to burn. It doesn't care where the air comes from. Usually the air comes from the basement or living space. Replacement air comes in through a collection of cracks and openings in the lower part of the house. If there are fewer cracks and crevices because they've been sealed to save energy, the furnace burner will draw air from somewhere else. If the house is tight enough, it may begin pulling air down the stack of the appliance that is not operating, in this case the water heater, and the combustion pollutants in that stack will be spilled into the indoor space.

How can you solve the problem? Control air movement in the house. A common solution is to duct outside air directly to the fuel-burning appliance. If you are considering a new furnace, be sure to buy one that is either a sealed-combustion or an induced-draft unit. Sealed-combustion furnaces draw air from outside the house and do not use house air. Induced-draft furnaces use a small fan to force combustion gases out the chimney. This guarantees there will be a proper draft or the furnace burner will not operate.

BIOLOGICAL POLLUTANTS

Some 40 million Americans suffer from allergies—that's one out of every six Americans. Whether it's from something as common as house dust, as seasonal as pollen, or as slimy as mildew, when these people are exposed, they suffer from runny nose, watery eyes, itchy hives, coughing, wheezing, sneezing, headache, and/or lethargy. And the problem is getting worse, experts believe, because air pollutants have increased alarmingly in the past few years.

It is estimated that 40 percent of the population 30 to 40 years old is genetically predisposed to allergic diseases. And persons not predisposed can develop asthma and rhinitis (inflammation of the nose) when exposure is heavy. Children, especially those under 4 years old, seem to be more susceptible than adults. And they're more allergic to common substances.

The most frequently encountered indoor allergens—dust, mold, and animal dander (small scales from feathers or hair)—pollute the air. But bacteria, too, contaminate the air in many houses, often through the heating and air-conditioning systems. Since people spend more than 20 hours per day indoors, it's important to identify the substances that are causing problems, then take remedial efforts to get rid of them.

Dust Mites

You can't see them—they're far too small to be visible to the naked eye. But they're probably in your house, no matter how spotlessly clean you keep it. And they aren't healthy. Dust mites (actually their feces) are the single most common allergen that people inhale in their homes. They feast on skin flakes that we shed all the time, so food is constantly available to them.

The fecal pellets of dust mites are so light, they stay in the air for a good 10 minutes after they're disturbed. The membrane that covers the outside of the pellet is strong—it does not break down quickly—which means the pellets keep their allergy-causing potential for months. Just moving a pillow or walking across a carpet is enough to stir them up into the air.

Mite colonies thrive at 70 percent humidity, so they tend to hit their peak in late summer, around August and September. When the home heating system comes on, their numbers drop off. The colonies hit their lowest point in January and start to rise again in spring, when the heat goes off and the humidity goes up. Mites proliferate in climates where the winters are humid and mild, such as along the West Coast of the United States and along the Mediterranean. Since humidity decreases with increasing height above sea level, dust mites are less common at high altitudes.

The bed is the primary breeding ground for dust mites. They're commonly found in mattresses and bedding due to moisture and skin flakes from the sleeper. Mites also breed in carpets because the cool floor creates higher humidity. They are more common on the ground floor than on upper stories.

To control dust mites, control the humidity in your home. Air conditioning is a good way to do this. If you live in a very warm, moist climate you may also need a dehumidifier. Be sure to empty it regularly, though, because bacteria and mold can breed in the standing water, causing more air pollution problems.

Rid your carpet of dead mites and their fecal pellets by vacuuming. If any member of your household is allergic, don't use the conventional air-bag-equipped vacuum that vents dust out the exhaust hatch. This will just send the mites back into the air again. The best cleaner to use is a central vacuum-cleaning system (vented away from the living area), a water-based vacuum, or one specially designed for people with allergies (see appendix A). If you're allergic, wear a dust mask while vacuuming and use a silicone-treated cloth to dust.

Since mite count is almost always highest in the bedroom, this is the best room in the house *not* to have carpeting in. Get live mites out of your bedding by washing it with *hot* water—cold water and detergents won't harm them. Vacuum the mattress and box spring frequently. Get rid of feather pillows and down comforters, too. Dacron and other synthetics are the best materials for pillows if you're prone to allergic reactions.

Mites are fond of furniture, as well. So if you're allergic, avoid upholstery with deep, sculpted fabric. Hardwood and cane furniture are best, followed by "nonfabrics," like leather.

Mold and Mildew

No one likes mold and mildew. Even if you aren't allergic to it (and 29 percent of the general population is), mold is dirty, slimy, smelly, and just plain unhealthy. It's not good for the house, either. Mold grows because of excess humidity, which can get into the wood substructure and eventually cause rot and decay.

Mold thrives in damp, warm, dark, poorly ventilated places. An exceptionally rainy summer is likely to promote a bumper crop of mold. Look for it blooming on basement walls, in closed-up closets, in musty bathroom crevices, behind wallpaper, on rotting vegetables, and in sweaty running shoes. During hot, muggy weather mold may form on books, on stacked magazines, in the clothes hamper, and on bathroom towels. Mold dies with frost, so it's usually not a problem in winter unless your basement is damp.

Once the bloom of mold and mildew appears, it quickly matures and sends spores floating throughout the house to be breathed by every member of the family. For people who are sensitive to the fungus, exposure to even a tiny amount causes discomfort—headache, irritation of the eyes and nose, sneezing and wheezing, skin rash, and nausea. The more of the stuff you breathe, the more allergic you become.

Anyone with a stuffy nose or other nasal trouble (allergic or not) is at a higher risk of developing respiratory problems if exposed to mold. Once these people develop a respiratory problem caused by mold, they are sensitive to molds forever. Even if you're perfectly healthy, you aren't safe from the fusty fungi. Anyone who consistently breathes mold spores can develop a sensitivity.

Getting rid of the fungus requires a combination of repair and preventive maintenance. First, check the house for leaks and damp spots that could harbor mold. Seal all walls and patch all cracks. The sooner they are dried out, the better. If an area is dry, you will not have mold.

Then, increase air circulation to get rid of excess humidity. Remove as much moisture as possible at the point of production. Install ventilation fans in baths, kitchens, and laundry areas—anywhere you use lots of water. The rule of thumb is 1 square foot of vent per 30 square feet of floor area.

If mold is a bad problem and you're willing to pay higher electric bills to get rid of it, install an air conditioner. (See information on air conditioners on page 95.) If you don't want to go to that expense, get a dehumidifier (an especially good solution for a damp basement). Dr. Alfred V. Zamm, clinical ecologist and author of *Why Your House May Endanger Your Health* (Simon and Schuster, 1980), recommends buying the largest capacity dehumidifier possible, preferably one that automatically turns off when humidity reaches a certain level.

Empty the dehumidifier regularly, as well as any other appliance that harbors water, such as a vaporizer, humidifier, air conditioner, or refrigerator. Standing water can quickly become a breeding place for mold and bacteria.

Installing a whole-house fan is also an effective way to increase ventilation. You can do this yourself, or call a heating-and-cooling contractor to do it.

Once mold and mildew form, the best way to get rid of them is with a nontoxic cleaner. Avoid commercial products for a truly healthy house. Most contain phenol, kerosene, pentachlorophenol, or formaldehyde—substances that, over time, cause more serious problems than the mold and mildew they were meant to correct. Instead, mix a combination of vinegar and borax in a spray bottle and spray it on moldy surfaces. Once dampened, the mold usually wipes right off. For more stubborn stains, apply the vinegar-borax solution and scrub heartily with a vegetable brush. If that doesn't work, try using bleach—but only as a last resort. (Always wear rubber gloves when using these solutions.)

If mold forms on structural beams in the house, get rid of it by scrubbing with a solution of chlorine bleach and trisodium phosphate (TSP), available in paint and hardware stores. Add 1 quart chlorine bleach to 1 cup TSP dissolved in 3 quarts warm water. Wear rubber gloves and goggles. Sponge the liquid onto the stained areas; then scrub with a brush and rinse with clean water. Dry with a cloth and allow the wood to dry completely. If this doesn't do the trick, try oxalic acid, a stronger bleach, available at paint stores. Mix it in the same proportions with water and TSP, and apply it in the same way.

To keep mold from forming in the first place, get a bottle of Zephiran concentrate (harmful if swallowed), a mild disinfectant and excellent mold inhibitor available at most drugstores. Mix an ounce of this to a gallon of distilled water, and you'll have a good, nontoxic fungicide and general germicide available whenever you need it. Use this to wipe down any hard-to-clean moldy surfaces.

Borax is a good natural deodorant and antimold agent, too. It's available in the cleaning products section of your supermarket. Sprinkle it in corners and other areas where mold and mildew are likely to form. Don't let children or pets get into it, though; borax is harmful if swallowed.

Get practical help with moisture, mildew, condensation, and other unpleasant by-products of summer heat and humidity by contacting the Conservation and Renewable Energy Inquiry and Referral Service, Box 8900, Silver Spring, MD 20907; 1-800-523-2929. Ask for their booklets on moisture control.

Bacteria and Viruses

Airborne bacteria and viruses are frequently found in indoor air and may represent a significant health threat. These microorganisms can carry infectious diseases such as influenza, Legionnaires' disease, tuberculosis, measles, chicken pox, and rubella.

Most bacteria and viruses are generated by people, through coughing, sneezing, and breathing. However, a complex mixture of amoebas, bacteria, molds, and fungi can breed in water reservoirs in humidifiers, air conditioners, and vaporizers. These appliances provide ideal conditions not only for breeding bacteria, but also for dispensing the tiny microbes in the air throughout the house. Some researchers believe that bacterial contamination of these appliances approaches 100 percent.

Humidifiers are perhaps the worst culprits. Molds and bacteria growing in humidifiers are the source of "humidifier lung," a condition many office and factory workers get from air contamination at work. Symptoms are fever, chills, headaches, chest tightness, and breathing difficulty. At home, humidifiers are used mainly in winter to add moisture to dry, heated air. Since an arid climate dries up delicate mucous membranes in the nose and throat, leaving one more susceptible to cold and flu viruses, it makes sense that adding moisture to the air will correct the problem. But if the appliance is not regularly emptied, cleaned, and disinfected, it will disseminate a plethora of bacteria into the air, affecting everyone living in the house.

Though not as efficient a breeding ground as the humidifier, the air conditioner, with its cool, wet coils, is another likely source of bacteria and molds. When the contaminated appliance is turned on, thousands of spores and microbes are blown from these surfaces into the room and throughout the house.

Another common culprit is the vaporizer, used when people (particularly children) suffer from deep congestion and breathing difficulties. If not emptied and cleaned daily, the vaporizer will spew out millions of spores and germs with its fine mist, aggravating illness instead of shortening it. The problem worsens when a commercial antimold chemical, bleach, or chlorine is added to the water, further contaminating it. Here's how to head off mold and bacteria problems with appliances:

Air conditioner: Prevent problems by servicing and repairing your air conditioner frequently, cleaning the coils, replacing the filter, and checking for visible mold and bacterial growth. If you have a central unit, clean the coils every month or two with Ivory soap and water, followed by a solution of eight parts water to one part vinegar.

With all air conditioners, the key to adequate drainage is the drain pipe. It should *always* be dripping water when the air conditioner is on. If it's not, the drain is probably backed up, meaning there's a good chance there is standing water in the system. If you have a window unit, make sure it is tilted so that it drains properly.

Humidifier: Keeping the appliance clean and mold free will reduce contamination but probably won't eliminate it completely. If you must have a humidifier in your home, buy the ultrasonic kind. According to research done by the Consumers Union, ultrasonic humidifiers disseminate far fewer mold spores and bacteria than the more common and less expensive type of humidifier. If you have the old-fashioned, cool-mist kind, clean it regularly with a strong solution of vinegar and water. When you use it, start it with *hot* water, which contains fewer microorganisms. And remember, empty the pan often.

Getting Rid of Pollutants

Getting rid of indoor pollutants doesn't have to be an expensive, time-consuming project. In most cases, solutions are simple and involve a combination of two procedures: (1) control or removal of the source and (2) ventilation. Here are six basic methods for dealing with indoor air pollutants:

1. Remove the source. (Get rid of that kerosene heater.)
2. Isolate the source. (Encapsulate asbestos.)
3. Provide localized ventilation. (Install a range hood or a bathroom exhaust fan.)
4. Provide whole-house ventilation. (Open windows; install a whole-house fan or a heat-recovery ventilator [HRV].)
5. Regulate humidity. (Between 30 and 50 percent in winter and 40 and 60 percent in summer, depending on the part of the country in which you live, is best for the health of the house and its occupants.)
6. Purify the air. (Get plants, especially spider plants. Studies show that plants filter house air, much as they do in greenhouses.)

Chances are that applying just one of these methods won't do a lot of good. A balanced combination—a little of this, little of that—is probably what's needed in most cases to clear the air.

Vaporizer: When using a vaporizer, put hot water in it to begin with; never allow the water to stand for long periods of time; and empty, clean, and disinfect the vaporizer with hot water and vinegar at least once a day.

If you have a crawl space underneath your house, make sure it is ventilated all year round. If anyone at your house is sensitive to mold, cover the ground and the floor joists above the crawl space with a poly barrier.

Molds and bacteria flourish in poorly maintained heating ducts and ventilation systems. When this happens, severe health problems can be transmitted throughout an entire building. Legionnaires' disease is one of the more serious examples of what can happen in a situation of cultivated pollution. Prevent this from happening in your house by following good ventilation practices. Air out your home frequently, and keep the heating system clean and in good order.

Pollen, Pets, and Pests

Pollen, animal dander, and insect antigens all create allergies for many people. Pollen enters from outside the house, usually through open windows or when you bring in cut flowers. To control the pollen count in your house, keep windows closed in late evening and between 4 A.M. and 10 A.M. spring through fall. This is when pollen activity is the greatest. Pollen count is highest in the country. The seashore and high mountains have the least pollen.

An allergy to pets can develop at any time, even if the same pet has lived with you for years. Cats are the worst offenders, with dogs running a close second. But other pets—mice, guinea pigs, gerbils, hamsters, and birds (especially pigeons)— also shed dander.

Unfortunately, the best antidote for a pet allergy is to give the animal away or banish it to the great outdoors. If a strong emotional attachment makes such action impossible, at least take some precautions. Make some rooms in the house off limits to the pet, especially bedrooms. Brush the pet outside of the house. Or, try vacuuming your pet (a procedure that works better with dogs than with cats)— many pets love it. Reducing the level of allergens often reduces the symptoms and their severity. But removing the pet doesn't always relieve symptoms. Animal dander and other pet residue can linger in carpets or house dust for several months after the animal is gone.

Insect antigens are highly allergenic. The cockroach (actually its feces) is particularly bad and is a frequent cause of asthma. To get rid of cockroaches, mix 2 tablespoons flour, 1 teaspoon cocoa, and 1 teaspoon borax and then sprinkle this mixture where roaches have been found, but out of reach of children and pets. (See chapter 6 for more nontoxic solutions.)

IF ALL ELSE FAILS   The list of allergenic substances is endless, ranging from insecticides, cigarette smoke, plaster, newsprint, and glue to microscopic particles of linen and wool in common household dust. For allergy sufferers, the best line of defense is to avoid contact with these substances. This means keeping a spotless house and storing chemicals away from the living area. For maximum air filtration at home, you might want to get a HEPA, or high-efficiency particulate air filter. If all else fails, medication or allergy shots may give temporary or lasting relief.

MOISTURE AND HUMIDITY

Moisture can be a problem in a house because it requires a delicate balance. *Too little* moisture, and the air feels dry. People experience more respiratory problems and coughs, and their noses and mouths dry out. Asthma becomes more of a problem, and bacteria and viruses flourish. *Too much* moisture, though, is no better. Bacteria and viruses thrive in high humidity, as do fungi and dust mites. Moisture encourages the growth of mold and mildew. It also contributes to certain chemical reactions, such as the release of formaldehyde gas from building materials. Structural problems caused by excess moisture include rotted roofs, deteriorated walls (framing and drywall), and mildew damage. The right balance—for the health of the occupants as well as the health of the house—is humidity in the 40 to 60 percent range. Relative humidity is measured by a device called a hygrometer. It can be as simple as the kind sold in hardware stores (usually in combination with a thermometer) or as sophisticated as an electronic unit with attachments for testing the moisture content of various materials. The hardware store model, available for less than $10, is fine for home use where extreme accuracy isn't needed. For greater accuracy, speed, and portability, an electronic hygrometer will cost $500 to $1,000.

The amount of moisture in indoor air depends on how much is produced and how much ventilation takes place to eliminate or dilute it. Most moisture is produced by the occupants themselves and their activities (cooking, bathing, breathing, and so on). The average family of four produces about 6 gallons of water per day. Houseplants add to this total, as do firewood stored inside, humidifiers, and vaporizers. The structure itself can also be a major source of moisture, particularly if it is built over a dirt-floored crawl space.

Houses that are somewhat "leaky" or drafty may have a problem of *too little* moisture in winter. Low relative humidity indoors is caused when warm, moist indoor air leaks out and is replaced by cold, dry outdoor air. On the other hand, if you tighten up your house to reduce heat loss, you're likely to have too much moisture inside.

As with most pollutants, removing the source is the best solution to removing moisture from the air. Here are some suggestions:

■ Store firewood outside and limit the number of houseplants. Often, this is all that is needed to reduce moisture content in indoor air.
■ Spread a sheet of 6-mil polyethylene over a dirt-floor crawl space. This can dramatically reduce the amount of moisture evaporating into house air.
■ Cover pans when cooking.
■ Ventilate right at the source to deal with moisture from cooking and bathing. Bathroom fans and vented range exhaust hoods are extremely useful. These should always be vented *to the outside*, not simply into the attic. Recirculating (unvented) exhaust hoods are virtually useless. Some whole-house ventilation systems include dehumidification. Portable dehumidifiers may be useful in certain spots, but they are costly to operate and are not a long-range solution.

Remember to clean and drain dehumidifiers once a week and to have air-conditioning units serviced and their filters cleaned every spring. To *add* moisture to the air, you can use a portable humidifier or vaporizer, or a whole-house humidifier attached to the furnace.

IS YOUR BASEMENT DAMP?   If your basement is often damp, check the downspout. There's a good chance it is depositing water too near the foundation. The solution to this is simple—just extend the leader spout to carry rainwater farther away and downhill from the house.

Another cause may be that surface water is running downhill into the basement. In this case, berm the earth around the foundation wall and incline it away from the house. Sometimes, however, the problem is more complicated—a high water table or an underground creek or river. These require a sump pump to solve the problem. In any case, repair any cracked or defective mortar in the foundation wall.

If simple cures fail to remedy the dampness, the most cost-effective solution may be to build a new frame wall around the inside of the entire room. Insulate the new wall, and install a polyethylene vapor barrier. Make sure the bottom sill plate of the wall is of rot-resistant material (such as redwood or cedar), and cut through the foundation in several places to ventilate the cavity between new and old walls.

A better solution, but a much more expensive one, is to excavate the entire perimeter of the house down to the footings. This is a radical step, indeed, involving a lot of hard labor and disruption to existing landscaping. But the justification is simple: Most older foundations have little or no damp-proofing applied to them. After excavation, clean the exposed foundation wall and apply a thick coating of waterproofing, such as coal tar, asphalt, betonite (sold in sandwiches between cardboard sheets), or a product like Owens Corning's Tuf-N-Dri. Then insulate the exterior wall before backfilling.

PLASTICIZERS

Plasticizers are additives that make plastic products flexible. Sometimes you can identify them by their "plastic smell." They're found in plastic wrap, some car seats, vinyl sheet flooring, and vinyl shower curtains. Most people experience eye irritations to some degree from plasticizer vapors in the air.

Soft plastics present a greater hazard than hard plastics do. The reason is that soft plastics are chemically unstable—they outgas into the air, whereas hard plastics are chemically inert. So plastic soda bottles or liquor bottles, for instance, may release vinyl chloride compounds into the liquids contained within them. Similarly, any pliable plastic will release invisible, toxic vapors into the air, particularly when the plastic is heated.

The problem becomes acute in a small space, such as inside an automobile with soft plastic seats, especially when the car is new. Vinyl chloride is what gives a car that "new car smell." In some of these cases, you can even taste residues of vinyl chloride in your mouth or see a dull film of the substance on the windshield. This occurs frequently when the car sits in direct sunshine with the windows rolled up. Breathing air polluted with vinyl chloride fumes can make you miserable. It's been known to cause migraines and upset stomachs and to change a cheerful day into an irritable one.

PCBs

Polychlorinated biphenyls (PCBs) are oily substances that are known carcinogens. Where are PCBs likely to be found in a house? In pre-1978 fluorescent fixtures with capacitors in their ballasts, according to Ellen Greenfield, author of *House Dangerous* (Vintage Books, 1987). Outrageously high concentrations of PCBs have been found in kitchens and bathrooms with PCB-filled fluorescent light ballasts. Removal of these ballasts caused the levels to drop dramatically within 2 months.

In your home, be on the lookout for any liquid (usually black and oily) dripping from an overhead fluorescent fixture—it's probably coming from the ballast and may be PCB. In such a case, have an electrician replace the ballast. Clean up the spills with soapy water on paper towels, using a polyethylene bag over your hand as a glove. Even if old fluorescent fixtures appear to be all right, it's best to replace them with new, preferably incandescent, lighting.

ELECTROMAGNETIC RADIATION

As if all these hazards weren't bad enough, it appears likely that something as common and ubiquitous as electricity—the power source that courses through the walls of nearly every American home—may be a health threat. It's a controversial subject, and more studies need to be done. But the results of current research show cause for concern.

The landmark study concerning electromagnetic radiation (emr) was done at the University of Colorado in 1979, where researchers found more cancer cases than would have been expected among children in the Denver area living near power distribution lines. More recent studies confirm those findings. The intensity of emr produced by ordinary utility lines strung along a street clearly seems to increase the risk of leukemia in children living nearby.

In 1984, the same University of Colorado researchers noted an above-normal rate of miscarriage among some 1,700 pregnant women who used electric blankets. Three-fourths of the miscarriages occurred in September through January—months when electric blankets would be used.

The problem centers on extremely low frequency (ELF) waves, nonionizing electromagnetic radiation that most closely resembles the body's own micropulsations. It's an invisible form of energy generated by high-voltage, alternating-current (AC) power lines and a you-name-it list of modern devices: computer video display terminals (VDTs), microwave ovens, hair dryers, TV and radio transmitters, radar, and the previously mentioned electric blankets.

It's true that no definite link has been discovered between this kind of radiation and cancer. Whether magnetic fields actually affect cell development is a controversial subject. But a growing body of research has raised disturbing questions, and many scientists believe a link does exist.

"There's no definite proof of carcinogenicity, but there's enough in the way of statistical evidence to arouse concern," says Baylor University cancer specialist Harris Busch in an August 1986 article in *American Health* magazine. "You have to remember that 50 years ago there was no definitive proof of the carcinogenicity of cigarettes."

PROTECT YOURSELF   Be leery of new products on the market purportedly designed to protect against emr. There are a number of hoaxes out there that will do absolutely no good at all. You can minimize exposure to emr by heeding the following advice:

■ When using a VDT, screen the front of it with a grounded conductive micromesh filter, designed to weaken low levels of radiation coming from the screen.

- Because there is some evidence that radiation from a VDT can harm developing fetuses, it's probably best, until more is known, to not use a VDT if you are pregnant. If using a VDT is part of your job, request assignment to a non-VDT job until the baby is born. (It is thought that different computer brands produce differing biological changes. So just because your neighbor worked at a VDT every day during her pregnancy and still gave birth to a healthy baby doesn't mean that everyone else will.)
- If your computer has a detachable keyboard, try using it several feet away from the screen.
- After every 2 hours, take a 15-minute "break" away from the VDT, and restrict VDT use to 50 percent of the working day.
- Have an eye exam before starting to use a VDT, and annually after that.
- Don't use an electric blanket, especially if you are pregnant.
- If you have a microwave oven, make sure the door closes properly and the seals around the door aren't damaged. Never operate the oven when an object is trapped in the door—even something as seemingly insignificant as a piece of paper toweling. And keep seals clean.
- Avoid standing in front of a microwave oven while it's on.
- Electrical cords can be a source of trouble for some sensitive people. Move the cords as far from your sleeping area as possible. You can also purchase armored cable that encloses the wires in a metal sheath.
- If you have an ionizing smoke detector, send it back to the manufacturer.
- While watching television, don't sit up close to the set. Distance diminishes the strength of emr.
- Remove any electrical appliances from around the beds in your home. This includes radios and clocks.

Researchers are currently evaluating different types of home heating systems, looking for possible heating-related causes of illness and disease. Meanwhile, Nancy Wertheimer, a scientist studying epidemic diseases at the University of Colorado Medical Center, believes that exposure to ELF fields does not pose a very big risk for the individual but that from a public health viewpoint there may be need to worry. "The early warning is out," she told *Science News* (February 14, 1987), "which is what the epidemiologist is supposed to do."

TESTING FOR INDOOR POLLUTION

There are lots of little ways to test for indoor air pollution. Smell is the best indicator. It's important to finely hone your sense of smell so you can detect some vapors and gases in the early stages. Visual tests are another way. Many respirable particles are large enough to be visible—just stand in front of a window and watch the play of sunlight as it streams inside. In a few cases, taste is an indicator. Vinyl chloride, for example—that soft plastic in car seats—emits a plastic fume when it is heated that, in a closed-up car, can pollute the air so badly that people report actually tasting it.

Beyond these sense indicators, testing with a reputable air pollution monitoring device is the only absolutely certain way to tell if your house is polluted. Special sensors monitor houses and buildings for radon, formaldehyde, and nitrogen dioxide. These sensors hang in a house or office for a number of days or weeks and are then removed for analysis. The tests are relatively inexpensive, running about $30 to $40 per measurement. New monitors are also under development by the U.S. Department of Energy to measure carbon monoxide and water (for humidity) in the air.

As yet, there is not a passive monitor to test for volatile organic chemicals such as cancer-causing benzene, which often contaminates houses and offices. Nor is there a good passive monitor for allergy-causing substances, such as dust mites, or for the many microscopic organisms, such as fungi, which can cause disease. (See appendix A for air pollution monitors currently available.)

In just the last two years, pollution control has mushroomed into a billion-dollar-a-year business with its share of charlatans and phony pollution detection devices. Don't get caught with your guard down. In most states, lists of qualified companies can be obtained from either the environmental protection or the health department.

The air pollution problem is getting so bad, there's a good chance houses will have to be tested in the future before they can be sold. And testers will need to be licensed or certified. The five air pollutants which will probably be tested for, according to experts, are radon, formaldehyde, asbestos, carbon monoxide, and moisture.

Prescription: A Healthy Home Has . . .

. . . taken precautions against indoor air pollution. Here are a few guidelines:

■ If there are high radon levels in your area, test radon levels in your home. If levels are high, call in a professional to retest and offer advice.

■ Don't smoke or allow smoking in your healthy home. Smoking aggravates the health hazards of nearly every indoor pollutant. Reduce smoke by using an air cleaner or by opening a window and using an exhaust fan.

■ Look for, and buy, materials that contain little or no formaldehyde. Never buy a product containing medium-density fiberboard. This contains extremely high levels of formaldehyde.   *(continued)*

Prescription: A Healthy Home Has . . .—*Continued*

- Reduce formaldehyde by increasing ventilation, by using an appropriate air cleaner or heat exchanger, or by covering sources of the gas with appropriate coatings and sealers.
- Check around furnace ducts and other areas for asbestos insulation. Cover exposed asbestos in plastic and/or duct tape to provide an airtight seal rather than remove it. If the asbestos is flaking, don't remove it yourself; hire a certified contractor to remove it.
- See that your gas range is fitted with a hood fan that vents pollutants to the outside. If that's not possible, keep a window open and use an exhaust fan while cooking.
- Make sure gas and oil heating equipment and the water heater are operating correctly, so deadly carbon monoxide fumes don't leak into your house. Have your gas or oil company regularly inspect your gas furnace, water heater, and clothes dryer.
- If possible, convert your gas appliances from using pilot lights to using spark ignition.
- Never use the oven or burners of a gas stove to heat your home.
- Use an exhaust fan in the bathroom to vent excess moisture.
- If you have a humidifier attached to your furnace, periodically clean it so bacteria won't grow and become airborne.
- Make sure wood stoves and space heaters are vented to the outside and are crack free.
- Open the fireplace damper before lighting a fire, and keep it open until the ashes are cool.
- Don't use a microwave oven if the door does not close tightly.
- Keep filters in air cleaners, humidifiers, and dehumidifiers clean. A dirty filter may become a breeding ground for bacteria.
- If you think a product is dangerous, keep it out of the house. Store paint thinner, gas, and other volatile solvents outside the house, and keep container lids tightly closed.
- When tightening your house for energy efficiency, check to make sure it's not *too* tight and that you have adequate ventilation.
- Use an exhaust fan to push fumes or other pollutants out of the house when you paint a room, refinish furniture, or engage in hobbies that require chemicals.
- When in doubt, vent it out.

Once you have eliminated the worst of the household polluters, maintaining a relatively healthy environment is mostly a matter of awareness, keeping in mind the environmental villains over which you have the most control. Using good old common sense will help ensure that home, sweet home is also a healthy home.

6

Hazardous Household Products

There's a source of indoor pollution that's found in nearly every house and apartment in America: that giant cache of household products used to polish, paint, open drains, disinfect, deodorize, control dandruff, shave beards, repel insects, and otherwise take care of the daily needs of house and body. Such chemicals pollute indoor air with vapors and fumes that hang around for days, especially if the house is poorly ventilated.

Chemicals contained in some of these products have been found to be neurotoxic, meaning they disrupt brain and nerve functions. Others are suspected of causing cancer and birth defects. Still others cause respiratory ailments and eye, nose, and skin irritation. A vast majority of them, when contained in the air we breathe, have a wide range of psychological effects. We may feel sluggish, dizzy, nauseated, confused, depressed, or headachy.

Though small doses of these substances probably won't harm you, no one knows about the combined, long-range effect. We may ultimately find that many "inexplicable" neurological diseases are the result of exposure to toxic chemicals. As Dr. David Straus, an environmental chemist at State University of New York in New Paltz, explains, "Although the person who, every few days, breathes chlorinated solvents from paint thinners and spot removers probably won't die from them, when linked with the hundreds of other chemicals that daily assault his or her system, the solvents might very well push such a person over the edge into episodes of unexplained depression."

THE CHEMICAL HOME

Besides being strong pollutants, many common household products contain petrochemicals and other nonbiodegradable ingredients and come in nonreusable containers requiring vast amounts of energy to manufacture. So, not only do they depress us physically, they threaten the global environment as well.

Oven cleaners, air fresheners and disinfectants, furniture and floor polishes, fabric cleaners and stain repellents, drain cleaners, and bleaches all contain an astonishing array of organic compounds, solvents, and toxic chemicals that pollute indoor air. In many cases, ingredients are not listed on the label, leaving the consumer completely unaware of what is in them. Once used, these chemicals evaporate over time, severely contaminating indoor air.

Here's a partial list of noxious household products found in the typical home:

Aerosol sprays and paint strippers: These may contain methylene chloride, a suspected carcinogen.

Ammonia: This is a powerful toxicant; if mixed with chlorine bleach, it produces deadly chlorine gas.

Carpet shampoo: It contains a respiratory irritant. Outbreaks of flulike symptoms have frequently been reported after carpet cleaning in day care centers, schools, offices, and motels.

Drain, toilet, and oven cleaners: These contain sodium hydroxide (lye), a powerful toxin and mucous membrane irritant.

Glue, liquid spot remover, paint, and varnish: They frequently contain toluene, a toxin that can cause fatigue, muscle weakness, and confusion. When vapors are inhaled, they cause central nervous system depression, psychosis, and liver and kidney damage.

Laundry detergents: These may contain liver-damaging chemicals, and bleaches that irritate both the lungs and skin.

Many household chemicals are high in organic compounds. These organic chemicals have carbon as a major constituent of their makeup and include halocarbons and hydrocarbons found in petroleum distillates (which make some products flammable). Organic chemicals are linked to cancer and respiratory ailments as well as to nausea and dizziness. High levels of organic compounds are found in aerosols, cleansers, polishes, plastics, paints, varnishes, furnishings, pressed-wood products, and pesticides, among others.

The best way to minimize exposure to toxic household chemicals is to use safer alternatives: latex paints that do not contain petrochemicals; baking soda, borax, and other old-fashioned cleaners; pyrethrins and other nontoxic pesticides. When using noxious products, make sure there is plenty of ventilation—open windows and turn on exhaust fans. Store products where they won't evaporate and pollute the air inside your house.

Solvents

Solvents are a class of organic chemicals often found in paints and paint products such as thinners and strippers. They are also found in stains, caulks, adhesives, and glues. Volatile solvents evaporate easily, polluting the air for days at a time. When you strip furniture or paint a room without plenty of

Methylene Chloride: The Worst Offender

A recognized villain in commonly used consumer products is methylene chloride, a chemical solvent listed by the government as a probable human carcinogen. Methylene chloride (along with a series of halogenated methanes and ethanes, which are also thought to be carcinogenic) is encountered by millions of Americans each day in products ranging from paint strippers and paint thinners to aerosol sprays (paints, hair spray, antiperspirants, room deodorizers, shoe polish), to cosmetics and decaffeinated coffee.

In 1985, results of a 5-year, $1 million dollar study by the National Toxicology Program, a scientific unit of the U.S. Department of Health and Human Services, concluded that methylene chloride caused tumors at a statistically significant rate in at least two animal species. That is the definition of a carcinogen applied by government agencies. The substance is so bad, staff scientists at the Consumer Product Safety Commission (CPSC) say that with the way people use products containing methylene chloride, the chemical poses "one of the highest cancer risks ever calculated for a consumer product." Even stripping one piece of furniture per year can put a person in the high-risk category, according to CPSC.

"There is clear evidence that methylene chloride is an animal carcinogen and has adverse health consequences for humans," says Mary Ellen Fise, product safety director for the Consumer Federation of America. Seconding that opinion is Dr. James Cone, chief of the Occupational Health Clinic at San Francisco General Hospital. Dr. Cone suspects that most chlorinated hydrocarbons, one of which is methylene chloride, will eventually be found to be carcinogenic. Chlorinated hydrocarbons are found in a whole array of household products, from paint thinner to hair spray.

Manufacturers sell more than 628 million pounds of methylene chloride a year. Industry experts estimate annual sales to be worth more than $150 million. And until July 1988, the substance wasn't even listed on product labels! The only way to avoid it was to avoid products suspected of containing it.

The CPSC moved in March 1986 to designate methylene chloride a hazardous substance. Starting in 1988, products containing methylene chloride were required to list the ingredient on the label. Actually banning the substance could take years. Until then, consumer beware.

ventilation, household levels of solvent fumes can skyrocket to 10 or even 100 times the levels seen in occupational settings. These chemicals tend to depress brain function and cause slow reflexes, loss of alertness, confusion, and other debilitating behavioral changes.

Oil-based paints generally contain more solvent than latex paints, but even many latex paints contain between 5 and 15 percent solvent. Plus, the mercury added to some latex paints can remain in the air, at five times the level considered safe, for up to a week after painting.

It's important to remember that solvents can be dangerous. When working with them, take these precautions:

- Follow the directions on the can.
- Work in a well-ventilated area, and wear a respirator, if possible.
- Wear goggles to protect your eyes.
- Protect your skin. Wear gloves and long-sleeved clothing. Don't use solvents to clean your skin.
- Keep a bucket of warm water nearby for flushing your skin in case you accidentally splash solvent on yourself.
- Never use solvents near flames or electrical circuits.
- Don't store solvents. Stored solvents are considered toxic waste—as well as a fire hazard. (Call your local waste disposal agency for disposal instructions.)

Another often-overlooked source of indoor pollution is dry-cleaned clothes. Tetrachloroethylene (PCE), the most common dry-cleaning solvent, can fill a house with vapors for a week or more after clothes are brought back from the cleaner. If you have items dry-cleaned, air them outdoors for at least 6 hours before bringing them inside.

Aerosol Sprays, Air Fresheners, and Disinfectants

The Consumer Federation of America estimates that the average home has 45 aerosol spray products. These generally contain three sets of ingredients—the propellant, the active ingredient, and miscellaneous additives. Propellants are usually flammable hydrocarbons—propane, nitrous oxide, and methylene chloride, which are both neurotoxic and carcinogenic. Methylene chloride, once inhaled, is converted to carbon monoxide in the blood. As if these dangers weren't bad enough, propellant gas from aerosol sprays remains airborne permanently, scattering the product in a fine, easily breathable mist.

Paradichlorobenzene, which has recently been found to be a potent carcinogen in animals, is found in solid and aerosol air fresheners. In addition, a few air fresheners contain chemicals that diminish the ability to smell. Not only does this destroy our ability to detect spoiled food, smoldering electrical fires, and other odoriferous hazards, it diminishes our ability to tell when the air we are breathing is polluted.

Pick up any household disinfectant, and chances are the label will list either phenol or cresol, two powerful and closely related compounds. Both are found in a number of products for disinfecting, deodorizing, and sanitizing.

Phenol can temporarily deactivate the sensory nerve endings, which is why contact with it often causes little or no pain. Cresol attacks the liver, kidneys, spleen, pancreas, and central nervous system.

Commercial disinfectants should never be used in a healthy home. Even with heavy cross ventilation, it can take more than a year to completely eliminate the unhealthful effect of one spraying of 2 ½ ounces of a widely promoted disinfectant, according to Francis Silver, writing in *Household Environment and Chronic Illness* (Charles C. Thomas, 1980).

Pesticides

There are about 50,000 pesticides on the market today, and greater quantities are used in the house and yard than on our nation's farmlands. Pesticides pose a particular problem because they are sold without adequate safety testing for cancer, birth defect potentials, and other possible health effects.

Among the worst, and most frequently used, pesticides are yellow strips that hang around the house, saturating the air for weeks until the chemicals are completely evaporated, when it's time to buy another strip. Just one of the seriously harmful ingredients is dichlorvos, which is, according to the U.S. Environmental Protectin Agency (EPA), a probable human carcinogen. A person who lives every day of his or her life in a house with one of these pest strips has a 1 in 100 chance of getting cancer. The strip is also under investigation for possible oncogenic, mutagenic, teratogenic, fetotoxic, and neurotoxic effects. Dichlorvos is also present in some flea collars, roach sprays, and flea bombs.

Instead of commercial pesticides, the best remedies for unwanted pests are proven old remedies. (See Natural Remedies on page 121.) Whenever using pesticides, watch where they are placed. Those in the basement can be dispersed throughout the house by forced-air heating systems; those near air conditioners can also be dispersed throughout the house.

Testing for pesticides is expensive and is recommended only if you suspect that high levels may be present. To locate a commercial laboratory qualified to test your indoor air for traces of pesticides, call the National Pesticides Telecommunications Network at 1-800-858-7378. If you have questions about pesticides, write to the National Coalition against the Misuse of Pesticides, 530 7th Street, SE, Washington, DC 20003.

Lead Paint

Your old house may have delightful character and charm, but there's a good chance it also contains lead paint on walls and woodwork, inside and out. As that paint peels, chips, and flakes, it can pose a health hazard. Tiny flakes, some smaller than you can see, become airborne, where they can be breathed by anyone in the house.

Lead serves no useful purpose in the body. In large amounts it results in lead poisoning. Small children and unborn babies are the most vulnerable.

The consequences can be brain damage, stunted growth, hearing loss, and blood and kidney disease. For adults, especially males, even relatively low lead levels can cause a significant increase in blood pressure. At very high levels, lead poisoning can be fatal.

Before 1950, lead oxide and other lead compounds were added to interior and exterior house paint to make it shinier, to fix colors, and to make it last longer. In those days, the better the paint, the more lead it had. Though lead levels in paint were lowered in the 1950s and latex paint became more common, lead-based paint was still valued for its durability. Lead compounds continued to find their way into paint until 1976, when the U.S. Consumer Product Safety Commission reduced the amount of lead in paint sold for use in homes to 0.06 percent.

In the United States alone, it's estimated that 40 million houses built before 1950 and 20 percent of those built between 1960 and 1975 are potential sources of heavily leaded paint. Some of that old paint may be more than 50 percent lead! If your house is more than 40 years old, layer upon layer of the paint may be on the walls, windows, stairs, porches, and doors.

REMOVING LEAD PAINT   There are ways to identify lead-based paint. As it weathers, it forms fine, irregular cracks that give lead-based paint the checked appearance of a dried mud puddle. If loose, the paint comes off in small, brittle pieces.

If you're in doubt about whether the paint in your house is leaded or not, have a sample tested. Call your local board of health or a private home inspection service to find out what the testing options are in your area. Since lead can leach out of paint and be washed into the soil around a home, you should also have the soil tested if lead paint on the exterior of your house is cracking and flaking. Contact your state agricultural extension service office for details.

If you discover a lead paint problem, first clean up all sources of loose paint, especially in a child's environment. Next, remove the paint or cover it. But take precautions! Removing the paint is often more dangerous than living with it.

A combination of chemicals and scraping appears to be the best method of removing the paint. When scraping, be sure to use a blade that is kept sharp. When using chemicals, wear a respirator certified by the U.S. Occupational Safety and Health Administration (OSHA) for this purpose. Replace the filters according to the directions that come with the respirator.

Don't use heat guns, power sanders, blowtorches, or sandblasters on lead paint. Heat guns and blowtorches vaporize the lead, which is then easily inhaled. Sanders create dust, and sandblasting explodes the paint into a cloud of tiny particles.

Beware of peeling *exterior* paint and lead that has leached into the soil outside of the house. Plan play areas and gardens away from painted structures and busy roads. Once soil is contaminated, lead remains for more than 2,000 years unless the soil is dug up and safely disposed of. Generally, most lead is in the top ½ inch of soil. Unless the soil has been tilled or turned over for a garden, removing that layer and replacing it with uncontaminated topsoil will probably get rid of the lead hazard.

If you remove lead paint outdoors, be cautious! Don't attempt it on a windy day, and put down drop cloths to catch flakes and dust. Close windows and remove all toys from the area. Lead dust settling on soil, shrubbery, and surrounding grass can be a hazard to children and pets playing in the area. Here are some other tips for safe lead paint removal:

- Make sure children, pregnant and nursing women, pets, and anyone not involved in the renovation are clear of the job site. If this isn't possible, isolate the area by taping doors shut or sealing the area with plastic drop cloths.
- Remove all belongings from the room. Seal permanent fixtures and carpeting securely with plastic sheeting and tape. Fine lead dust is almost impossible to remove from carpets and furniture upholstery.
- Ventilate the space during both removal and cleanup. Opening windows is not sufficient. Neither is relying on an air conditioner—air conditioners recycle air instead of replacing it. According to the Center for Occupational Hazards, a window exhaust fan or other forced-air exhaust system is needed to maintain the necessary flow of 10 to 15 room air changes per hour. Make sure the exhaust is filtered and discharges to the outside.
- Wear protective clothing, including goggles, gloves, head and shoe covers, and a respirator.
- Don't smoke, eat, drink or keep food or cigarettes in the work area.
- If you leave the work area and expect to return that day, change to clean clothes and shoes. When you return, change back into your work clothes.
- At the end of each day, wash the respirator face piece and store it in a clean, dust-free place. Clean the renovation area with an industrial vacuum. (The family vacuum should *not* be used.) Bag paint chips and debris, and wet-mop all exposed areas with a high-phosphate detergent, such as trisodium phosphate (TSP).
- Keep your work clothes in a plastic bag until you're ready to use them again. Throw them away at the end of the job, or wash them separately.
- When the removal is complete, vacuum and shampoo the carpet thoroughly. (Don't sweep—it stirs up dust.) When work is finished outside, collect chips and vacuum visible dust and debris with an industrial vacuum cleaner. Hose down everything children come into contact with—yards, sidewalks, driveways, play equipment, cars, porches, riding toys.
- Contact your local board of health for information about proper disposal of leaded debris.

RECIPES FOR NATURAL CLEANERS

Though you can't create a 100 percent nontoxic environment in today's world, you can take steps toward minimizing the toxins you have in your home. The best place to start is with cleaning products—oven cleaners, furniture polish, disinfectants. Box them and store them in the garage until you can dispose of them properly.

Replace those smelly, unhealthy synthetic chemicals with natural products. They are cheaper and just as effective. You can make low-tox, no-tox cleaners with ingredients you probably already have in your kitchen. The big five ingredients you'll need are borax, distilled white vinegar, baking soda, salt, and one or two lemons. All these are low-tox substances. Borax, a mineral mined from the earth, and Bon Ami cleanser, available at supermarkets, are nonchlorinated, ecologically safe cleansers.

If you want more options for recipes, get some cornstarch and washing soda (available at the grocery store). On the few occasions you need a heavy-duty cleaner, use TSP (trisodium phosphate), available at hardware stores. TSP is moderately toxic if ingested and is a minor skin irritant. It does not produce toxic fumes, but it does pollute our waterways with phosphates, so use TSP only when absolutely necessary, and always wear rubber or vinyl gloves. Some brands of cleaner identified as TSP are actually sodium metasilicate. They may not work as well as TSP, and they present their own health hazards.

Most of these cleaners work best when freshly mixed. If you do store some of them, tighten the lids and put them in a locked cabinet where young children and pets cannot find them.

Window Cleaner 1

2 teaspoons white vinegar
1 quart warm water

Mix them well. Use a natural linen towel or other soft cloth to clean.

Window Cleaner 2

½ cup cornstarch
2 quarts warm water

Mix them well and apply with a sponge, then wipe windows dry with absorbent cloth or old towels.

This solution is great for car windows and bathroom mirrors. It leaves them shiny and streak free. (Never wash windows when the sun is shining directly on them. This causes the cleaner to dry too quickly, creating unwanted streaks.)

General Cleaner and Disinfectant 1

½ cup borax
1 gallon warm water

Dissolve borax in water and apply with a sponge.

General Cleaner and Disinfectant 2

½ cup household ammonia
½ cup washing soda
1 gallon medium-warm water

Mix the ingredients in a pail. After washing, rinse with clear water.

Store in clean bottle and use as needed.

Drain Opener 1

½ cup baking soda
1 cup vinegar
boiling water

Dissolve baking soda and vinegar in boiling water, and pour the solution down the drain. Continue to flush with hot tap water until the clog breaks.

Drain Opener 2

½ cup salt
boiling water

Pour salt down the drain, followed by boiling water; flush with hot tap water.

Scouring Powder

Sprinkle borax, baking powder, or dry table salt on a damp sponge; scour and rinse.

Oven Cleaner 1

Let the oven cool, then sprinkle salt on the spill right away. Let it cool for a few more minutes, then scrape the spill away and wash the area clean.

Oven Cleaner 2

Use baking soda for scouring.

Dishwasher Soap

1 part borax
1 part washing soda

Mix the two and use the mixture in dishwasher in place of commercial detergent. If you live in a hard-water area, you may have to adjust the proportions to avoid formation of soap film on the dishes.

Garbage-Disposal Freshener

Grind a used lemon or orange in the disposal.

Toilet Bowl Cleaner

baking soda
vinegar

Sprinkle some baking soda into the bowl. Drizzle with vinegar; scour with a toilet brush.

This not only cleans, it deodorizes, as well.

Mildew Remover

½ cup vinegar
½ cup borax
warm water

Dissolve vinegar and borax in water. Mix them fresh for each use.

Spot Remover
for Blood, Chocolate, Coffee

¼ cup borax
2 cups cold water

Dissolve borax in water. Sponge it on and let it sit until it dries, or soak the fabric in the solution before washing it in soap and cold water.

This works well for blood, chocolate, coffee, mildew, mud, and urine.

Spot Remover for Grease

Rub a grease spot with damp cloth dipped in borax.

Or apply a paste of cornstarch and water; let it dry and brush it off.

Sprinkling fuller's earth (available at drugstores) on the spot will absorb grease in 15 minutes to 2 hours.

Spot Remover for Ink

If the stain has set on white fabric, wet the fabric with cold water and apply a paste of cream of tartar and lemon juice. Let it sit 1 hour, and wash as usual.

Spot Remover for Scorch Marks

To remove a scorch mark from white linen, cut a raw onion and rub its flat side on the scorched area until the onion juice is absorbed by the cloth. Let it set, then soak it in cold water for a few hours.

Spot Remover for Wine

To remove red wine, dab out excess moisture with an absorbent cloth and sprinkle salt on the stain. Let it sit several hours. When it's dry, brush or vacuum it away.

Or clean the stain immediately with club soda.

Basin, Tub, and Tile Cleaner

Rub the area to be cleaned with half a lemon dipped in borax. Rinse, and dry with a soft cloth.

Appliance Cleaner

Dry baking soda will shine up small appliances, such as toasters. It even removes bread wrappers that have been burned onto the toaster.

Ceramic Tile Cleaner 1

¼ cup vinegar
1 gallon water

Mix them well. This removes most dirt without scrubbing and doesn't leave a film.

Ceramic Tile Cleaner 2

1 tablespoon TSP
½ gallon water

Dissolve TSP in water. Store the solution in a glass container until you're ready to use it. Moisten a sponge with the cleaner and wipe. (Wear rubber or vinyl gloves.)

Laundry Detergents

Detergents were designed to clean synthetic fibers. Natural fibers can be cleaned quite adequately with natural substances. Use borax, baking soda, washing soda, or natural soap. Grate pure bar soap, such as Ivory, add water, and liquefy in a blender. Store in a tight glass container.

Helpful Hint: A drop or two of vinegar in the laundry water can help prevent colors from fading.

Laundry Starch

1 tablespoon cornstarch
1 pint cold water

Dissolve cornstarch in water. Place the solution in a spray bottle. Shake it before using.

Bleach

¼ to 1 cup sodium hexametaphosphate*
5 gallons water

Add sodium hexametaphosphate to water. Proportions vary depending on water hardness. To prevent a dull film from forming, the solution should feel slippery between your fingers.

*Sodium hexametaphosphate must be specially ordered. Look in the yellow pages of the phone book for a local chemical supply house.

Shoe Polish

Add a shine to shoe leather by polishing it with the inside of a banana peel; then buff.

Silver Polish

Clean silver with toothpaste and warm water, using an old, soft-bristled toothbrush on stains.

To magnetize tarnish away, soak silver in salted water in an aluminum container; then wipe it clean.

Copper Cleaner

Combine vinegar and salt. Apply the mixture to copper surfaces with a rag, and rub clean.

Furniture Polish 1

2 parts olive or vegetable oil
1 part lemon juice

Mix olive or vegetable oil with lemon juice. Apply the mixture to furniture with a soft cloth, and wipe it dry.

Furniture Polish 2

Use a soft cloth and wipe with a little bit of mayonnaise.

Or rub furniture with a cloth dipped in cool tea.

CLEANING HOUSE

A hundred years ago, our great-great-grandparents reserved one week twice a year—in the spring and in the fall—to thoroughly clean the house. In preparation, they cooked and baked enough food to last the week, cleverly concocted a few simple homemade cleansers, and hard-heartedly got rid of everything in the house that was no longer useful. At the close of the week they found time to black the stove, paint the rain barrel, and oil the woodwork.

Back then, such cleaning was an annual ritual, a labor-intensive week that ended with the satisfaction of having a clean and healthy house. Today, while the ritual remains, the process for accomplishing the task has changed considerably. Where our great, great grandparents spent a week thoroughly cleaning every corner of the house, top to bottom, we spend as little time as possible and rely on synthetic chemicals to make the job go faster. Not only is it making us sick, it's not getting our houses clean. Clearly, it's time for change.

Celebrate the start of your healthy home program by giving your house a thorough cleaning—top to bottom—with natural cleansers. Start with one room. Open the windows, put on some music, and enjoy yourself.

In preparation for thorough cleaning, *Household Discoveries and Mrs. Curtis' Cookbook*, the bible for practical housekeepers at the turn of the last century, offers this timeless bit of advice: "Have nothing in your house that you do not know to be useful or believe to be beautiful. Destroy with a hard heart every useless thing. The art of successful living consists in getting along with as few articles as possible, rather than in accumulating many different pieces. Remember that every additional one is an additional care."

Even if you hire a cleaning service, make sure the products it uses don't pollute your air with toxins. Mix a few natural cleaning products and have them ready the next time you or anyone else cleans house. (*Source*: Reprinted with permission of *Des Moines Register*.)

First, the Basement

A good rule in house cleaning is to first clean the cellar, because it is the most difficult and often the most neglected part of the house. Afterwards, begin with the attic and work down.

Damp, cluttered basements are ripe places for mold to breed. Prevent this from happening by going through your basement and throwing away everything you have no use for. Are there any clothes in the laundry room that were washed and not thoroughly dried or any that were stored slightly damp? They're good breeding grounds for mold and mildew. Either air them out and wash them again, or throw them away. What about sleeping bags? They can harbor mold, too. Be sure they are aired out thoroughly after each use. While you're at it, throw out old carpets, cast-off furniture, dingy pillows, and broken toys—anything you're not going to use anymore. This reduces the number of surfaces mold can grow on.

Old-fashioned basements, particularly those having dirt floors, are places molds love to haunt. Check potato and coal bins, jam shelves, sheds, cellars, and crawl spaces. If you store fruits or vegetables in the basement for the winter, check them frequently for mold. Potatoes, carrots, and other root vegetables begin to mold soon after they are taken from the ground. Protect filled canning jars from mold by wiping the outsides with white vinegar.

Clean One Room at a Time

Thoroughly clean one room at a time, settling it as you go. The following steps compose a good ritual to follow each time you clean.

LAUNDER CURTAINS   When cleaning a room, first remove the curtains. Launder, fold, and store them before actual cleaning begins. That way they will be out of the way and ready to be put up when wall washing and general cleaning are finished.

Dry-cleaning curtains or drapes (or anything else for that matter) is not recommended unless you air them out before hanging. Avoid dry cleaning by washing curtains in cold water, then take them to a professional dry cleaner for pressing. If you do dry clean, remove the items from their polyethylene wrapping as soon as possible and air them out in a place with good ventilation (preferably outdoors) for at least 6 hours so you won't breathe fumes from the solvents used.

MOVE FURNITURE   Move all furniture to the center of the room so you can reach the corners. Working from the ceiling down to the floor, sweep cobwebs out of all corners and wipe all surfaces with a damp rag. Don't forget light fixtures, moldings, and door and window tops. Open the windows to get rid of dust.

WASH WALLS   Wash painted wood with 1 teaspoon washing soda in a gallon of hot water. Rinse with clear water.

To remove a wall stain, make a paste of water and cornstarch. Cover the stain with the paste, and let it sit for 1 hour. Brush off the powder, and repeat if necessary.

A paste of borax and water makes a good wallpaper cleaner. Apply it to the spot, and let it sit for a few minutes. Brush it off with a soft cloth, and repeat if necessary. Or sprinkle baking soda on a damp cloth and rub it onto the spot, then rub lightly with fine steel wool.

MOP FLOORS   Mop vinyl floors with 1 cup white vinegar mixed with 2 gallons of water to remove dull, greasy film. Polish with club soda.

Painted or finished wood floors can be washed with a rag dampened in a mixture of 1 teaspoon washing soda and 1 gallon of hot water. Rinse with clear water.

Avoid frequent waxing of floors. Odors from commercial floor waxes hang around for months, polluting the air with such solvents as morphline, isopropyl alcohol, turpentine, mineral spirits, perfume, wood preservative, and naphtha. The wood preservative might well be the most toxic; most are easily absorbed through skin. Instead, get a *waxless* floor covering—there are many currently on the market. Once or twice a year, wax hardwood floors with paste wax, instead of liquid wax, and open the windows while doing it. Although paste wax is still quite toxic, the fumes dissipate quickly.

CLEAN CARPETS   Steam cleaning is the best way to clean a carpet. To remove carpet stains that don't succumb to steam cleaning, mix ½ cup mild liquid dishwashing detergent and 1 pint of boiling water. Let the mixture cool until it forms a jelly, then whip it into a stiff foam with a beater. Apply it with a damp cloth or sponge to a small section of carpet and rub gently. Wipe with a clean cloth, and allow the carpet to dry.

Or blend equal amounts of salt and baking soda. Add several drops of white vinegar to each 8 ounces of the dry mixture. Stir in sufficient water to form a paste. Spread the paste on the soiled area, and let it dry completely. Then brush away the powdery cleanser along with the dirt. For stubborn stains, gently scrub when the cleanser is first applied. Test a tiny area for colorfastness before applying the cleanser to a larger area.

CLEAN FURNITURE   Clean wood furniture with a slightly damp rag that has been dipped in soap and water. Then remove soap residue with a clean damp rag, and dry with a soft cloth. Clean unfinished wood furniture with mineral oil.

Vacuum upholstered furniture well at least once a week; don't just beat the dust out of it.

CLEAN THE FIREPLACE   Clean the tiles around your fireplace with full-strength white vinegar or 1 cup washing soda dissolved in 2 gallons of hot water. Rinse with clear water.

Clean soot and smoke stains from fireplace brick with a solution of 1 gallon hot water and 1 cup washing soda. Scrub the bricks with a brush, and wipe clean with a paper towel.

Clean the flue by throwing a handful of salt into a blazing fire. The flame will turn yellow and the combination will help clean out excess soot.

FRESHEN THE AIR   Most synthetic air fresheners do nothing to freshen the air. They only add more pollutants in an attempt to mask or cover up the offensive odor. Some work by emitting compounds that inhibit our sense of smell. Instead of using phony synthetic smells, ventilate the house frequently by opening windows throughout the house at least once a day for a short period of time. If you must use an air freshener, make it a natural one.

A good natural deodorizer for dissipating offensive odors consists of a mixture of 4 teaspoons baking soda in 4 cups of water. Fill a convenient-sized spray bottle, and spray the solution in a fine mist. Or wrap cloves and cinnamon in cheesecloth, and boil them in water. Leave herbal bouquets standing in open dishes for a fragrant smell.

PESTICIDES

Rachel Carson startled the world 25 years ago with dire warnings about pesticides in her landmark book, *Silent Spring* (Houghton Mifflin, 1962). Today, some of the compounds she rallied against, such as dichloro-diphenyl-trichloro-ethane (DDT) and other chlorinated hydrocarbons, have been yanked from the market. But pesticide use in the United States has more than doubled since the early 1960s. The amount of active pesticide ingredients manufactured in this country rose from slightly less than 25 million pounds in 1947 to over 140 billion in 1985.

The United States accounts for 30 percent of the $5 billion annual worldwide pesticide sales. Nine out of ten American households use pesticides. American consumers spend about $630 million a year on over-the-counter pesticides. Even that is small change compared with the $2.5 billion a year spent for professional pest control.

Despite such heavy use, there is little scientific data on how these chemicals affect us. Until 1978, the EPA did not require rigorous tests to register pesticides, and it has not reevaluated many of the substances that were on the market before then. Consequently, we have adequate data to assess the human health hazards for only 10 percent of the pesticides used in the United States. Approximately 90 percent of the pesticides used every day have not been adequately examined for their ability to cause cancer, genetic mutations, or birth defects.

To date, there are over 1,400 different active pesticide ingredients used in over 50,000 formulations. Such chemicals include rat poisons, the germicides used in household disinfectants and cleaning products, wood preservatives, and the antimildew chemicals used to treat wallpaper and carpeting. Of these, 60 percent of the herbicides, 30 percent of the insecticides, and 90 percent of the fungicides used in this country cause cancer, according to a 1987 study by a panel of experts from the U.S. National Academy of Sciences.

So the mere fact that a pesticide has been approved for use by the EPA does not guarantee that it is safe, even if used as directed. The information on pesticide toxicity is simply too limited. Consumers must learn to be aware of pesticide hazards to protect themselves, their families and pets, and their neighborhoods and environments.

Health Effects

Pesticides are designed to attack living cells and organisms. The suffix *cide* comes from a Latin word meaning "to kill." Because humans, pets, and wildlife are made up of living cells, they can be dangerously harmed by pesticides. In *Silent Spring*, Rachel Carson graphically describes the effect of modern pesticides:

> In being manmade—by ingenious laboratory manipulation of the molecules, substituting atoms, altering their arrangement—they differ sharply from the simpler insecticides of pre-war days. These were derived from naturally occurring minerals and plant products—compounds of arsenic, copper, lead, manganese, zinc, and other minerals, pyrethrum from the dried flowers of chrysanthemums, nicotine sulphate from some of the relatives of tobacco, and rotenone from leguminous plants of the East Indies.
>
> What sets the new synthetic insecticides apart is their enormous biological potency. They have immense power not merely to poison but to enter into the most vital processes of the body and change them in sinister and often deadly ways. Thus, as we shall see, they destroy the very enzymes whose function is to protect the body from harm, they block the oxidation processes from which the body receives its energy, they prevent the normal functioning of various organs, and they may initiate in certain cells the slow and irreversible change that leads to malignancy.*

Pesticides are stored in body fat and can accumulate to toxic levels, causing cancer and other illnesses. Even small amounts inhaled through the air can attack the central nervous system, causing depression, irritability, impaired thinking, and communication and memory disorders. What's more, when pesticides are combined, they are even more toxic.

Since pesticides are specially formulated to kill over an extended period of time, they are made to resist natural decomposition processes. When sprayed indoors, protected from sun and wind, they are even more long lasting. Pesticides can remain actively airborne indoors for days or weeks—some last as long as 20 years!

Innocent victims of our ignorance are children. Since their bodies are smaller, it takes only a small amount of pesticide to cause harm. And it happens frequently. According to the June 14, 1987, issue of *Family Practice News*, a doctor in San Diego discovered than many common insect repellents have the potential to cause toxic reactions if applied repeatedly and directly on children's skin. One offending chemical, he discovered, is diethyl toluamide (DEET), found in most over-the-counter insect repellents. It can cause a toxic encephalopathy if applied for as little as 3 nights in a row! Another California study links household pesticide use and leukemia in children.

The Case against Chlordane

Chlordane is a synthetic pesticide used to kill termites. It does a good job—so good, it's been the chemical of choice for professional exterminators for the

---

*Excerpted from *Silent Spring* by Rachel Carson. Copyright © 1962 by Rachel L. Carson. Reprinted by permission of Houghton Mifflin Company.

last 20 years. It's been used in more than 30 million houses in the United States. In Philadelphia alone, a home inspector estimates chlordane has been sprayed in three out of four houses.

It's now known that chlordane can make people very sick, depending on the length and concentration of exposure. Chlordane attacks the central nervous system, causing subtle changes in the way the brain works, changes that can affect moods, behavior, thoughts. Such poisoning occurred throughout the country in record numbers before mid-1987, when the manufacturer voluntarily quit making the chemical. In many cases, families literally abandoned their homes and their lifetime of savings because the houses they were living in were so badly contaminated and were making them sick.

Though the health hazards were known for some time, the EPA allowed continued use of the product because there was no effective alternative chemical available and because the EPA believed that when properly used, chlordane was not a hazard. Normally, chlordane is injected into the soil around and under the house. Such use meant that chlordane would never actually get *into* the house. Then, in the late 1970s and early 1980s, mistakes by workers were reported. In many instances, chlordane was accidentally pumped into basements or heating ducts, making people inside the houses very sick.

In 1987 a new study showed that, even when chlordane was "properly" applied, dangerous residues invariably seeped inside the houses, causing invisible air pollution that would not go away. In fact, when tested a year after chlordane was applied, many houses showed that fumes were two, three, sometimes four times higher than when the chemical was first applied. This led the EPA to outlaw inside use of chlordane in late 1987.

PEOPLE GET SICK   Once contaminated with chlordane, a house stays that way. The chemical gets absorbed by floors and walls, and toxic vapors keep gassing out. Even taking drastic steps to reduce levels of the poison doesn't work. You simply can't get rid of all of it. People inside the house are always breathing it, and it makes them sick.

A classic case study is the story of Larry and Kelly Purdle in Houston, Texas. Larry, Kelly, and their children experienced symptoms of chlordane poisoning for a year. They were sick to the stomach, were habitually nauseated, and had awful headaches every day that never seemed to go away. Perhaps the most frightening symptom, according to Larry Purdle, was the dramatic change in mood. Everyone in the family was irritable, anxious, wiped out. They simply couldn't function. Kelly, a housewife who stayed home much of the day, couldn't get dressed or cook. "I had this incredible feeling of exhaustion," she told NPR. "I was totally incapacitated. I felt like I was going crazy." The Purdles no longer live in their small, yellow house on Bluebonnet Street. The house now has large signs posted all around it proclaiming the residence unfit for human habitation.

Toxicologists say there is no way to absolutely prove that chlordane poisoned the Purdles. There's no foolproof blood test or anything like that. But they do know that chlordane attacks the central nervous system and short-circuits the chemical communication between cells. That can affect everything from muscle control to thinking to emotions.

Even though chlordane has long been a recognized danger, it took years before it was finally restricted. Why, if it was a recognized health threat, was the use of chlordane still allowed? According to U.S. law, the government has to indemnify manufacturers when it suddenly bans sale of a pesticide. This means that U.S. taxpayers pay the market price for all unsold stock, as well as for storage and disposal. The EPA has estimated that the potential indemnification cost of banning chlordane could be as high as $53 million.

IS YOUR HOUSE CONTAMINATED?   EPA studies show that approximately 90 percent of the houses treated with chlordane have detectable levels of the chemical in the air a year after treatment. These studies also show that houses built on slabs (on the surface of the ground) have lower levels than houses with basements or crawl spaces.

Basement rooms have the highest levels. Because chlordane has been found in the soil of treated areas 30 years or more after treatment, certain houses are more at risk: houses with air ducts located in or below slabs or in crawl spaces and houses with negative air pressure, causing chlordane fumes to get sucked into the house through cracks and leaks in the foundations.

If your house was treated for subterranean termites prior to 1981, it is likely that chlordane was used. Chlordane also may have been used in the interior to control other household insect pests, such as ants.

The best way to find out if your house is contaminated is to contact the pest control company that treated your house, the previous owner of your house, or its builder. Testing a house for pesticide levels can cost between $50 and $500, according to the EPA. To locate a testing laboratory, the EPA suggests calling the National Pesticides Telecommunications Network at 1-800-858-7378.

If chlordane is making you or anyone in your family ill, try fighting back. Many chlordane victims are, and they're winning. NPR reported that in Los Angeles, members of one unfortunate family won a $360,000 verdict after they got sick and abandoned their home. In Illinois, another family was awarded $600,000 after a medical specialist testified that a pest control company's chlordane job poisoned them, causing chronic illness and long-lasting damage to their immune systems. Both cases are under appeal.

To reduce the chance of prolonged exposure to pesticides, the EPA suggests increasing the circulation of clean air through the house; sealing foundation cracks and openings around pipes and drains where pesticides could seep in from treated soil outside; supplying outside air to clothes dryers and furnaces that now draw inside air; and sealing ducts in basements and crawl spaces.

Natural Remedies

The risk from pesticides stems both from the toxicity of the chemicals and the degree and duration of an individual's exposure. You cannot change the inherent toxicity of pesticide products, but you can keep your risks to a minimum by limiting your exposure.

The best remedy is to maintain your home so that it is unattractive to pests. Keep your house clean, especially in the kitchen and bathroom. Store food in containers that close tightly, wipe up crumbs and spills, and empty garbage cans frequently. Fix leaky faucets and eliminate all sources of standing water. Fill holes and cracks in the structure of your house so pests cannot get inside.

When getting rid of pests of all kinds, consider old-fashioned mechanical means first. Flyswatters and window screens may replace fly sprays. A well-aimed stream of water from a garden hose may replace garden sprays. Careful sanitation may replace cockroach and rodent pesticides. If these methods don't solve the problem, choose a low-tox, no-tox alternative before resorting to synthetic chemicals.

Don't waste your money on ultrasonic pest eliminators. These small electronic units claim to bombard your home with silent sound that turns roaches and other pests into nervous wrecks and makes them vacate the premises. *Consumer Reports* magazine (June 1983) found that pests seem to become conditioned to the sound quickly, so the devices have no observable effect. Don't use electrical devices, either, as a means of getting rid of flying insects. They're unsettlingly noisy, and the light attracts insects instead of repelling them.

It helps to remember that pests, too, have a reason for being. About 98 percent of all insects are harmless or beneficial to humanity. We should try to share our planet with them and live in harmony as best we can, but we don't necessarily need to share our *homes* with them. There is a host of things you can do to discourage insects. Here are a few tips:

ANTS

- Eliminate outdoor food and nesting sites. Make sure firewood and tree branches are not in contact with the house.
- Caulk common ant entry points such as windowsills, thresholds, baseboards, and so on.
- Keep ants out of the house by putting coffee grounds around doors and windows. Try planting peppermint at the entrances, or crush some mint leaves and leave them at the entrances.

BEETLES

- If beetles are getting into your food supply, put a bay leaf in a small cheesecloth bag in each container of cereal, flour, and other grain products; then store them in a cool cabinet or in the refrigerator.
- Carpet beetles should be stopped before they enter the house. Do not leave windows open in the spring unless they are covered with tight-fitting screens. Caulk all cracks in the siding or eaves, and screen

---

Homemade Roach Powder

To repel roaches, try this easy-to-make powder. The borax is the active ingredient—the roaches walk through it, then later ingest it and die. Keep the powder away from children and pets.

1 cup borax
½ cup flour
¼ cup confectioners' sugar
1 cup cornmeal

Mix all the ingredients and sprinkle the powder in all the dark, warm places that cockroaches love: under sinks and ranges, behind refrigerators, in cabinets and closets. Vacuum or sweep it up from time to time, and replace it with fresh powder.

---

attic vents. Seal all cracks along interior moldings and the openings around pipes and heating vents.

COCKROACHES

■ First eliminate or reduce their drinking water supply. When cockroach shelters are found, accessible areas can be vacuumed and washed.
■ Caulk or otherwise plug all small cracks around baseboards, wall shelves or cupboards, pipes, sinks, and bathroom fixtures.
■ Try boric acid to control roaches. It reportedly does a better job and at less cost than some highly touted synthetic pesticides.
■ Try repelling (not killing) roaches with a mixture of bay leaves and cucumbers. Or try the roach recipe given above.

FLEAS   (See chapter 12.)

FLIES

■ Sanitation is the key to fly control. Dispose of garbage, and clean garbage pails regularly. Sprinkle the inside of garbage pails with dry soap. Clean out and dispose of moist, uneaten pet food an hour after it is offered. If you leave fruit at room temperature, check fruit bowls daily and remove any fruit that is beginning to soften or overripen.
■ To keep flies out of the house, place sweet clover in bags made of mosquito netting (available at most large fabric stores), and hang them about the room.

■ Mix equal amounts of bay leaf pieces, coarsely ground cloves, broken eucalyptus leaves, and clover blossoms. Put this blend in small bags of mesh, mosquito netting, or other loosely woven material, and hang them just inside entrance doors.

■ Sweet basil and tansy are said to repel flies. Plant them near doorways, patios, and picnic areas. Or grow sweet basil in containers in the kitchen.

MICE

■ Plug up any holes where mice can get into the house.

■ Store food in containers, where mice cannot get at it.

■ Use the old-fashioned kind of mouse trap baited with cheese. Change the locations of traps every few days.

■ Try peanut butter sprinkled with a bit of cornmeal or oatmeal in a mouse trap.

MOSQUITOES

■ Eliminate all sources of stagnant water in your yard.

■ Keep mosquitoes out of the house by putting screens on all doors and windows. Use a yellow bug light outside entryways. Basil planted outside a window should keep them from entering.

■ Keep mosquitoes away from you by rubbing a bit of vinegar on exposed skin. Garlic will also repel them if you eat enough of it.

MOTHS

■ Instead of smelly mothballs, try herbal remedies. They are effective and leave woolens smelling good. Natural repellents include dried lavender, cedar chips, tobacco leaves, pennyroyal leaves and stems, and pyrethrum daisy flowers.

■ Make a simple sachet of dried southernwood (an herb, available at botanical centers and health food stores), and store it where you keep woolens. It helps to give sachets a little squeeze from time to time, to release a fresh burst of scent.

■ Herbal remedies will work only if the clothes are clean and stored in airtight containers that stay closed for periods of several days at a time. At least once a year, take everything out of the drawers and closets for a good airing. Unfold individual items, and give each a good shake; then hang them out in the sun and breeze for a few hours. Store them, then, with a fresh herbal sachet.

SILVERFISH

■ Silverfish feed on the starch of wallpaper paste and book bindings in environments with high humidity. Increase ventilation and reduce humidity in bathrooms and basements.

■ Replace old, peeling wallpaper. Store books in a dry location.

■ A silverfish trap can be made by placing strips of masking tape on the outside of a glass jar, from the rim to the base, to create a surface rough enough for the silverfish to climb. A bait of wheat flour, sugar, and chipped beef inside the jar will attract them, but once inside the jar, they will be unable to climb out. Place traps in areas where silverfish are found. Clean and rebait them each day.

TERMITES

■ Make sure soil around and under your home is well drained and that crawl spaces are dry and well ventilated.

■ Remove scrap wood, stumps, cardboard, firewood, and other sources of cellulose close to the house.

■ Fill voids and cracks in concrete or masonry with cement grout or coal tar. Wherever possible, remove soil within 18 inches of floor joists and 12 inches of girders. Replace any heavily damaged or rotted sills, joists, or flooring.

■ If you have a termite problem, try a nontoxic solution first. In *Nontoxic and Natural* (Jeremy Tarcher, 1984), author Debra Lynn Dadd recommends applying a heat lamp at 140°F for 10 minutes to a specific area you suspect is infested with termites. Or, use copper chromate, cryolite, or another nonvolatile insecticide. Keep the area very dry.

For information on safely getting rid of insects, contact the National Coalition against the Misuse of Pesticides, 530 7th Street SE, Washington, DC 20003; (202) 543-5450.

SAFE CHEMICAL DISPOSAL

The typical household does one of three things when it discards chemical products—dumps them down the drain, buries them, or throws them out with the garbage. "Out of sight, out of mind" is the way most homeowners usually operate. If something is no longer needed, we just throw it away.

Well, it's time to wake up to reality. There is no *away*. All of these methods pose threats to the quality of our air, our water, and our soil. At present, disposal of dangerous wastes is not being regulated by the EPA. So it's up to you, the consumer, to dispose of these wastes in an ecologically safe manner.

Realistically, with all the products available on the market, there is no way we can live in this day and age without creating hazardous waste. But we can reduce the health risks by cleaning up the environment and finding substitutes for hazardous products whenever possible.

Educate yourself on the types of products that are potentially dangerous. Substitute products that are less harmful. Find out the best methods for disposing of wastes if a household chemical product must be used.

An invaluable aid for action is the Hazardous Waste Wheel, available for $3.75 from the Environment Hazards Management Institute. This handy helper does two things: (1) identifies household products that may contribute to pollution in the community when improperly disposed of and (2) provides information on ways to reduce the amount of household hazardous chemical waste that is flushed down the drain, or discarded in the backyard or at the landfill. With a spin of the wheel, advice is obtained on safe selection of products, proper use of hazardous chemicals, and appropriate disposal of spent household hazardous wastes. To get a wheel, write Hazardous Waste Wheel, P.O. Box 283, 137 High Street, Portsmouth, NH 03801, or call (603) 436-3950.

A Few Rules

When throwing away trash and garbage, don't include any liquids, regardless of whether they are hazardous. Often they leak in the garbage truck and run out onto the street. If they are hazardous, they can burn workers or otherwise cause them harm. Solidify liquids instead, or if they don't pose a human or environmental hazard, empty them into the drain. To solidify a liquid, add absorbent material—soil, cat-box filler, disposable diapers, sawdust, paper towels, old rags—enough to soak up all excess liquid. Scoop it all into a plastic bag, and dispose of it with other household garbage.

Be careful of old products, especially herbicides and pesticides that may contain chemicals that are banned today. What do you do if you come across an old bag of insecticide containing DDT and you live in an area with no toxic-waste collection program? The best advice is to make sure the material is properly contained and continue to store it safely until some sort of toxic collection program is established in your community. Talk with your legislators about initiating such a program.

Never include household hazardous waste with weekly garbage. Look at the label. If it poses a danger to humans or the environment, dispose of it properly, following the suggestions below.

AUTOMOTIVE PRODUCTS   Most of these products are flammable and/or toxic and therefore present a hazard if mishandled or disposed of improperly:

Antifreeze: Do not pour used antifreeze on the ground or into a ditch. Use antifreeze according to directions, or donate it to others who can use it. Contact your local waste-water treatment plant to see if it accepts antifreeze. If not, take the antifreeze to a hazardous-waste collection center or to a licensed hazardous-waste disposal facility.
Degreasing fluids: These should be saved in a secure container and taken to a licensed hazardous-waste disposal facility.
Gasoline: Use up gasoline whenever possible. It's highly flammable and toxic and must be handled with extreme caution. Save amounts larger than a gallon or two, and gasoline containing lead or other hazardous contaminants, and take them to a hazardous-waste collection center or licensed hazardous-waste disposal facility. Gasoline

drained from small motors (lawn mowers, snowmobiles, boats, and so on) can be strained through cloth or paper coffee filters to remove impurities and stored for future use in tightly closed, well-labeled containers. Add dry gas to remove water. Consult your local fire department about storage precautions.

Old car batteries: Automobile batteries should be recycled, repaired, and reused. Acid and metals in old batteries pose a hazard due to their toxic and corrosive natures. Contact a local battery shop, listed in the yellow pages of the telephone book under "Batteries-Storage-Retail."

Used motor oil: Do not dump waste oil on the driveway, on the soil, into storm sewers, or down the drain or toilet. Used motor oil should be taken to an oil recycling center or to a gas station where it is collected, then taken to a reprocessing plant. Some communities have recycling programs for hazardous wastes like motor oil. Contact your county extension office for the location of oil collection sites in your area. Or call your local service station to find the nearest collection site, and be prepared to pay a small fee to drop off a few gallons of used oil.

Transmission fluid, kerosene, diesel fuel, brake fluid: These can be added to oil and recycled, as well, but only if the treatment facility near you can handle these fluids.

HOUSEHOLD CLEANERS   Cleaning products should be used up or donated, if possible. Otherwise, dispose of as outlined below:

Highly toxic or corrosive products: Drain cleaners, toilet-bowl cleaners, oven cleaners, mothballs, and other highly toxic or corrosive products should be taken to a hazardous-waste collection site or licensed hazardous-waste disposal facility.

Solvent-containing products: Furniture polishes, waxes, and other products containing solvents should be taken to a hazardous-waste collection site or licensed hazardous-waste disposal facility.

Water-soluble products: Small quantities (a cup or two) of less-toxic, water-soluble products like soaps and detergents can be poured down the drain with plenty of water. These products can also be wrapped securely and put in the trash. Liquids should be solidified first.

HOUSEHOLD PRODUCTS   Many common, everyday household items can be classified as hazardous waste. Take these special precautions when disposing of them:

Asbestos: A known human carcinogen, asbestos is harmful because the tiny fibers can be inhaled deep into the lungs. Nonfriable asbestos products are much less likely to cause health risks if left undisturbed rather than improperly removed. Leftover household items containing asbestos, such as ironing board covers, some hair dryers, and toasters, should be placed in heavy plastic bags and put in the trash. **Paints:** Save leaded paints and oil-based paints, and take them to a hazardous-waste collection center or disposal facility. Other paints should be used up or donated. Unusable water-based paints should be solidified. To do this, remove the lid and place the can in a well-ventilated area, preferably outside, that children and pets cannot reach. After the contents have solidified, replace the lid, wrap the can securely, and put it with the regular garbage. Most paints remain usable for many years if correctly stored according to directions and kept from freezing temperatures.

Used solvents: Paint thinners and furniture strippers can be recycled. They can also be filtered with a paper coffee filter or cheesecloth and reused in the home workshop. Or they can be taken to a reprocessing or treatment facility, a collection center, or licensed disposal facility. Allowing the solvents to evaporate outside is a highly controversial recommendation and not currently endorsed by most state health agencies.

Wood preservatives: These are similar to pesticides and should be disposed of in a similar manner. (See "Pesticides" on page 128.) Use them up or take them to a collection center or disposal facility.

PESTICIDES   There are many kinds of pesticides, each designed to kill a certain species of insect. All are highly toxic, and extreme care must be taken in their disposal:

- Follow the label directions for guidance on product (and container) disposal.
- To dispose of less than a full container of liquid pesticide, leave it in the original container, with the cap securely in place to prevent spills or leaks. Wrap the container in several layers of newspaper and tie them securely. Then place the package in a covered trash can for routine collection with municipal refuse (unless your municipality has other requirements).
- Wrap individual packages of dry pesticide formulations in several layers of newspaper, or place the package in a tight carton or bag, and tape or tie it closed. As with liquid formulations, place the package in a covered trash can for routine collection.
- Empty pesticide containers can be as hazardous as full ones because of residues remaining inside. It is unlikely that residues can be removed from empty containers, so never reuse these containers. Handle them as above.
- If you do not have a regular trash collection service, crush and then bury empty pesticide containers at least 18 inches deep in a place on your property away from water sources, where you grow food, or

where children may play. Do not puncture or burn a pressurized container. It could explode.

■ Do not burn pesticide boxes or sacks, either outdoors or in apartment incinerators, since this can create poisonous fumes or gases or cause an explosion.

■ Do not pour leftover pesticides down the sink or into the toilet. Chemicals in the pesticides could interfere with the operation of septic tanks or could pollute waterways, because many municipal waste-water treatment systems cannot remove all pesticide residues.

■ Rinsings and spent dips should be washed down your drain— never pour them onto the ground.

■ Puncture any nonpressurized containers to prevent reuse.

■ Watch for local "amnesty days" or opportunities to bring hazardous household wastes to properly equipped collection stations.

MISCELLANEOUS PRODUCTS   In addition, use care when disposing of these products:

Aerosol cans: These can explode. Check with local solid-waste officials. Only completely empty cans should be placed in the trash.
Ammunition: Don't throw it out with the trash! Contact your local fire or police department, sheriff, or state police for assistance with disposal.
Heating oil: Use up leftover oil, or take it to an oil reclamation facility. Heating oil is a significant factor in groundwater contamination from leaky underground storage tanks.
Smoke detectors: A smoke detector with an ionizing sensor (this type contains Americium 241) should be returned to the manufacturer or to the Nuclear Regulatory Commission for disposal.
Swimming pool chemicals: Use them up or donate them. Take undiluted pool chemicals to a collection center or licensed hazardous-waste disposal facility.

For more information about safe, ecological disposal, call your state office of the Department of Natural Resources, Hazardous Waste Division, or the cooperative extension service about problems and available services in your area. You can also contact the recycling, treatment, and disposal firms in your area to determine their willingness to accept household hazardous wastes. Your local health department can give you instructions on safe disposal in your area. Some communities have hazardous-waste cleanup days when toxins are gathered and segregated for safe disposal. If such a means of disposal is available to you, use it. These events usually run one day each year, so you may have to store the waste for a while.

You may also want to consider calling small businesses, such as photography labs, to see if they will take small amounts of related household waste to be recycled with their own.

Prescription: A Healthy Home Has . . .

. . . started a program of low-tox cleaning with homemade products. Here are a few other guidelines:

■ Get rid of aerosol sprays in the house. Many contain methylene chloride, a suspected carcinogen, which is dispersed into the air in large quantities when it is sprayed.

■ Clean up the home workshop and basement. Throw out half-empty cans of paints, solvents, and cleaners. Tighten the lids on those you keep, and turn the cans upside down. Clean up well after a project, and always ventilate the area thoroughly.

■ Follow strict rules when working with solvents. Be sure to follow the directions on the can, work in a well-ventilated area, and wear a respirator, if possible.

■ Cut down on pollution when cleaning the house. Think about replacing your portable vacuum cleaner with a central vacuum cleaning system, which carries dust into a main suction unit in the basement and has outlets in each room. Open windows while dusting and vacuuming, and use silicone-treated dustcloths, which hold the dust rather than resuspend it in the air.

■ Always protect your hands when using irritating cleansers. For those prone to dermatitis, vinyl gloves are reportedly better than rubber.

■ Limit the number of cleansers you keep in your house. You don't need different kinds of soap for every single thing you clean. Eliminate cosmetics you don't really need, or find natural alternatives for them.

■ Store pesticides safely, and keep the telephone number of the poison control center near the phone and on all pesticide bottles and on pesticide storage cabinets.

7

Furnishings

Imagine yourself on a winter afternoon with a pot of tea, a book, a reading light, and two or three huge pillows to lean back against. Now make yourself comfortable. Not in some way which you can show to other people, and say how much you like it. I mean so that you *really* like it, for *yourself*. You put the tea where you can reach it, but in a place where you can't possibly knock it over. You pull the light down, to shine on the book, but not too brightly, and so that you can't see the naked bulb. You put the cushions behind you, and place them, carefully, one by one, just where you want them, to support your back, your neck, your arms, so that you are supported comfortably, just as you want to sip your tea, and read, and dream.

That definition of comfort comes from Christopher Alexander, architect and author of A *Pattern Language* (Oxford University Press, 1977). It's a domestic atmosphere instantly recognizable for its ordinary, human qualities. Furnishings play a large part in this definition, but it's not a scene furnished to impress or be fashionable. Instead, it's highly personal. More than anything else, it *feels* good.

As we enter the 21st century, domestic comfort means a range of things: convenience, efficiency, leisure, ease, pleasure, domesticity, intimacy, privacy. You must define these abstract terms for yourself. It is, after all, *your* home. What does convenience mean to you? Is it the right tool at your fingertips while you're preparing a gourmet dinner or working in your shop? What is pleasure? Settling into your favorite chair with a good book, entertaining friends for dinner? Be true to yourself when answering these questions. Don't fall into the trap of adopting someone else's idea of comfort for your own. It's important to confuse comfort neither with decor, which is fashion, nor with behavior, which is the way the rooms are used. As Witold Rybczynski writes in his book *Home: A Short History of an Idea* (Viking Press, 1986), "Domestic well-being is too important to be left to experts. It is, as it has always been, the business of the family and the individual. We must rediscover for ourselves the mystery of comfort, for without it, our dwellings will indeed be machines instead of homes."

FURNISHINGS AND FINISHINGS

When furnishing your healthy home, adopt a philosophy of sparse and natural. The healthiest environment has hardwood floors, wool or cotton rugs, solid wood furniture put together without glue and upholstered with cotton batting, untreated cotton draperies or quilted opaque curtains to insulate windows, and walls painted to reflect available light.

Furniture

In the United States the standard for furniture is overstuffed chairs and sofas and soft, yielding mattresses. Though poor posture and back problems are endemic, we rarely link these health problems with our furniture. This may come as startling news, but it isn't necessary to slump in a sofa or hunch over a desk. Sitting cross-legged on the floor is good for you. So is sleeping on a firm surface. Here are a few pointers to consider in evaluating your furniture:

■ All furniture should provide a reasonable circulation of air. A 7-inch-thick mattress on a 7-inch-thick box spring does not allow air to circulate. Neither does an overstuffed sofa.
■ Seating should be designed to encourage a normal spinal curve to protect you from backache. Danish modern designs—solid wood

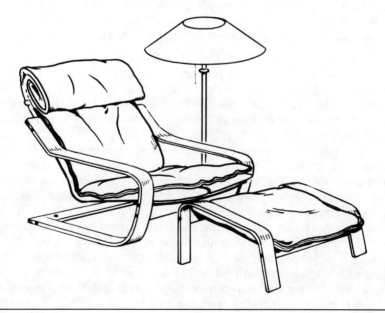

The Poem chair is a good example of ergonomic design. Its simple, flexible design supports and encourages the natural curve of the spine.

with simple lines—are good models to follow. Or take a look at "therapeutic" designs of chairs and stools. They may save much unnecessary pain and discomfort.

■ Try to avoid materials that produce asphyxiating fumes when they burn, such as foam rubber.

■ Avoid stuffings of synthetic fibers and cellulose padding.

■ Be sure that furniture is strong and free from protruding nails or splintering wood.

■ Eliminate all plastics. Plastic lampshades are taboo. Use cloth, glass, or metal shades.

■ Avoid furniture containing pressed wood.

■ Desks and kitchen counters must be at a reasonable height so you don't have to hunch over while using them.

Synthetic materials should be avoided whenever possible. Not only do they outgas, releasing molecules into the air, they can be a deadly hazard when they burn. Plastic, especially, has no place in the healthy home. Flames from burning plastic spread quickly, have extremely high temperatures, and produce large amounts of dense smoke. Ironically, plastic that's treated for flame retardancy will produce more smoke when forced to burn than untreated materials. Natural materials such as wood and cotton fibers also produce toxic combustion by-products but at a much slower rate than synthetic materials, allowing more time for occupants to escape before gases accumulate to lethal levels.

Wall and Floor Coverings

Pay special attention to what's on the walls and floors. These are huge surfaces and should not be covered with unstable materials that outgas into the air.

WALL COVERINGS   Nonpetroleum-based paint, like latex, is the best for a healthy home. Oil-based paints contain toxic organic solvents that tend to outgas over a long period of time.

If you choose to paper your walls, keep in mind that many wallpapers are treated with a fungicide, as are wallpaper adhesives. Check with the manufacturer before making a selection. All manufacturers are required to supply a materials safety data sheet, if requested, that lists the specific ingredients in the product.

When thinking about how to cover your walls, don't forget about covering the windows in the walls. The sun's rays coming through a window can release an odorless gas into the house from chemically unstable curtains. If you have polyester or fiberglass curtains or vinyl shades, consider replacing them with natural fiber curtains (cotton, linen, silk), wooden shutters, metal blinds, or homemade shades of rice paper or cloth.

FLOOR COVERINGS   It helps to make a distinction between those areas that get heavy traffic and those that get light traffic. Heavy-traffic areas will need hard-wearing, easy-to-clean floor surfaces—linoleum, wood, slate, brick, and so on. Floors in light traffic areas can be covered with materials that are less durable—like carpet or matting. Making this distinction is customary in Japan and the Soviet Union, where houses are divided into two zones: service areas (which are extensions of the street) and comfort areas (where you often must remove your shoes before entering).

Avoid factory-made wood parquet floors—they are likely to contain harmful adhesives. Likewise, sheet vinyl and rubber floors are likely to contain toxic chemicals, waxes, or adhesives that outgas and produce odors. These are particularly offensive to people who are chemically sensitive. Battleship linoleum (see appendix A), made from natural products with a burlap backing, is a good floor covering for kitchens and bathrooms. Doctors often recommend this to patients with allergies. Hardwood is another healthy floor covering in areas not subject to wetness—it has a natural "give" and doesn't hurt your back or legs when you stand on it for an extended period of time.

Wood, brick, and unglazed tile are healthy options for living areas, but they need to be sealed to prevent open pores from absorbing everything from dirt to water to cooking grease to chewing gum. Untreated, they turn gray, stain, and look flat. When finishing these floor surfaces, it's best to use paints, stains, and waxes made from plant ingredients. You can buy wood oil, beeswax, larch resin, and other products from companies like Livos Plant Chemistry, which imports products from West Germany (see appendix A).

Carpeted floors harbor more microorganisms than any other type of floor. This is the reason hard floors are recommended for hospitals. In a healthy home, rugs are preferable to carpet, especially old wool rugs (like orientals) that have not been chemically treated. However, handwoven area

---

Refinishing Hardwood Floors

A nontoxic method for refinishing hardwood floors is a dual procedure consisting of coating with a penetrating oil and then waxing. The result is a soft surface with a satin glow that requires some maintenance thoughout the years, with occasional waxing and buffing of areas getting heavier use. After about 3 to 5 years, remove the wax with soap and water, and re-oil and rewax the floor.

For a more durable coating requiring less maintenance, you may want to go with a urethane coating. Though urethanes contain strong solvents that emit extremely toxic fumes, the most hazardous time is during application and for a few days after. These products are flammable and require as much ventilation as possible during application. The use of urethanes may cause headaches, a general ill feeling, and allergies, so plan to be away from the house for a few days while the work is being done. The result is a strong and glossy surface that needs little maintenance and lasts for several years.

rugs—such as dhurries and kilims—are perfectly acceptable if they're untreated and made of natural fibers.

New carpet, especially when it comes directly from the factory, releases as many as 25 to 30 different chemicals into the air—many of them chlorinated hydrocarbons used as pesticides to control fungi, molds, insects, and rodents. That's why carpet stores smell the way they do. Most outgassing appears to occur in the first 3 months. Still, carpet has its advantages. A good carpet can cut noise levels and energy costs, besides covering flaws in the floor. If, after noting the health concerns, you still prefer carpet, get wool (a superior fiber, though somewhat costly) and try to find one that has not been subjected to a variety of chemical treatments. Ask the manufacturer. And be equally cautious about the padding. Get jute backing instead of rubber.

Be wary of "miracle fibers" touted by the carpet industry. Advertised to repel dirt and release soil easily, some are claimed not to mat, crush, show footprints or get smelly or shabby with ordinary wear. Find out what makes the carpet have those abilities. Remember—sparse and natural is the goal.

Think about installing a central vacuum cleaner with outlets in those rooms that are carpeted. This will greatly reduce the amount of dust stirred up on cleaning day.

Major Appliances

Latest research shows that low level electromagnetic radiation may be potentially harmful. Until more facts are in, it would be best to minimize the amount of electronic gadgets you have in your home. Make sure the ones you do have are unplugged when not in use, so they won't create a fire hazard. As for major appliances, be sure they are well maintained and operated safely.

MICROWAVE OVENS When microwave ovens were first introduced 20 years ago, there was some question about their safety. The latest models appear to be safe, as long as the door closes properly and the seals around the door are clean and undamaged.

KITCHEN RANGES Gourmet cooks insist on gas stoves because they like to be able to control the heat of the burner. Clinical ecologists, on the other hand, contend that gas ranges are a major source of pollution in the home. Gas is cheaper than electricity. If you prefer gas and no one in your house is sensitive to the fumes, be sure you have a ventilated range hood, vented *to the outside*, and adequate cross ventilation in the kitchen.

Though electric stoves have only a few basic settings, they are safer and cleaner to operate. When shopping for an electric range, choose the self-cleaning rather than the continuous-cleaning type. The latter type involves a chemical-laden coating that outgasses into your food and into the air in the kitchen.

DISHWASHERS Dishwashers often contain a hidden source of air pollution—tar-based insulation that outgasses whenever the appliance is used. KitchenAid dishwashers avoid the problem completely. They have only fiberglass insulation, porcelain interiors, and an optional cycle that prevents detergent buildup on the dishes. When buying a new dishwasher, check to see what kind of insulation it has.

REFRIGERATORS   Refrigerators may run quietly, but they don't run cheap. Chances are your refrigerator is spinning the electrical meter more than any other appliance in the house except the water heater. During its 15-to-20-year life span, the average refrigerator consumes more than $2,000 worth of electricity. If your refrigerator is more than 10 years old, consider investing in a new model. Newer refrigerators are designed to operate more efficiently than their energy-guzzling predecessors; they're also equipped with some features that were unheard-of even 5 years ago.

When shopping for a new refrigerator, pay close attention to the energy guide ratings posted prominently on the front of every model in the store. Compare the annual operating costs of various refrigerators, as well as their initial purchase prices. An efficient model may cost a little more at first, but in the long run, it's money well spent.

The simplest way to figure out how much it will cost to operate a given refrigerator over its entire lifetime is to multiply the big number on the energy guide label—the estimated annual operating cost of that particular model—by the number of years you expect to own the refrigerator. A typical 23-cubic-foot refrigerator-freezer, for example, might have an estimated annual operating cost of $124; after 19 years, that model would have consumed roughly $2,356 worth of electrical juice.

Conserving Energy

Consider the value of comparing energy savings. In 1987 the most efficient average-sized refrigerator was a no-nonsense model with an estimated annual operating cost of $63. On the other hand, the least efficient model in the same size range had an estimated annual operating cost of $101. For the 20-year life of the refrigerator, you could have saved $760 worth of electricity by purchasing the more energy-efficient model.

The Association of Home Appliance Manufacturers (AHAM) offers the following guidelines for rating energy conservation in appliances:

Water heaters: National appliance efficiency standards for water heaters will go into effect in 1990. There will be a standard for each storage tank size. Check the energy guide label on the heater for the estimated cost of operation. The higher the efficiency, the lower the operating cost.

Capacity of a water heater is an important consideration. The water heater should provide enough hot water at the busiest time of the day to suit your family's needs. For example, a household of two adults may never use more than 30 gallons of hot water in an hour, but a family of six may use as much as 60 gallons in a given hour.

Room air conditioners: Room air conditioners are rated by their energy efficiency ratios (EERs). The EER is obtained by dividing the cooling output by the power consumption. The higher the EER, the more efficient the air conditioner. The average new room air conditioner has an EER of about 8. You can consider any room air conditioner with an EER greater than 8.5 to be efficient, and any EER over 9.5 is very efficient. National standards for room air conditioners vary according to the unit's cooling capacity. The average minimum EER required by the 1990 standards will be about 8.6. Although units with higher EERs usually cost more, they save money in the long run because they use less electricity.

Central air conditioners: Central air conditioners are rated according to the seasonal energy efficiency ratio (SEER), the ratio of the cooling output to the power consumption. There are three efficiency classes: standard systems (commonly installed by builders) have SEERs around 8, better systems have SEERs around 10, and premium systems have SEERs above 12. The national appliance efficiency standard for split-system central air conditioners (the most common type) will take effect in 1992, requiring a minimum SEER of 10.

Central heat pumps: Central heat pumps provide both cooling in summer and heating in winter. The cooling performance of heat pumps, like central air conditioners, is rated by the SEER. Heating performance is measured by the heating season performance factor (HSPF), a ratio of the estimated seasonal heating output to the seasonal power consumption. The average heat pump has an HSPF between 6 and 7 and a SEER of 8.6. The national appliance efficiency standard for split-system heat pumps, which goes into effect in 1992, requires a minimum HSPF of 6.8 and a minimum SEER of 10.

Gas furnaces: Furnaces are rated by their annual fuel utilization efficiency (AFUE), a measure of overall seasonal performance. Gas furnaces manufactured in 1986 had an average AFUE of 74 percent. The national appliance efficiency standard for furnaces, which will take effect in 1992, will require that each furnace have an AFUE of at least 78 percent. High-efficiency *condensing* furnaces with AFUEs above 90 percent are now available from virtually all manufacturers.

Oil furnaces: The national standard for oil furnaces will be the same as that for gas furnaces: 78 percent AFUE beginning in 1992.

HEALTHY FURNISHINGS
ALL THROUGH THE HOUSE

The truly healthy home has healthy furnishings throughout. Use the following as a guide.

The Kitchen

In a healthy home the family shares in meal preparation and cleanup. To do this quickly and efficiently, you must have a kitchen that is large enough and laid out in a way that accommodates more than one person at a time. Major cooking centers—sink, stove, refrigerator—and centers for mixing, chopping, and serving all have adequate storage and at least 12 to 15 feet of free counter space. No one section of counter is less than 4 feet long. No two work centers are more than three or four steps (about 10 feet) apart.

ENSURING SANITARY FOOD   Having a healthy kitchen means storing and preparing food in a sanitary manner. Here are a few simple rules:

1. Buy perishable foods only in small quantities, and refrigerate them at once.
2. Refrigerator temperatures should be set at 45°F or below, and at 40°F at the highest if food is to be kept longer than usual.
3. Don't refreeze food that has thawed.
4. Never leave food on the table for any extended period after meals.
5. Store leftovers properly in shallow, covered containers. The more food surface that is exposed to the cold, the faster it will cool and ward off bacterial growth.
6. Store food in metal or glass containers.
7. Cook food in glass, stainless steel, or iron pots and pans. Stay away from Teflon and aluminum.
8. Frozen items should be thawed only if they're going to be used immediately. Food should be thawed in the refrigerator, not at room temperature.
9. Chemicals and synthetic household cleaners should never be stored where food is kept or prepared.
10. Grow your own food, organically, whenever possible. If you buy produce, peel or wash it with a stiff vegetable brush and soapy water to remove as much pesticide residue as possible.

STAY AWAY FROM PLASTICS   Since a healthy home avoids all known carcinogens, it is wise to stay away from all plastic that might come into contact with food. Vinyl chloride, a carcinogen, has been found to leach into foods and beverages stored in flexible plastic containers and wraps. Cooking oils, in particular, appear to harbor the carcinogen. Also avoid alcoholic beverages, milk and frozen vegetables packaged in plastic containers, as well as luncheon meats and cheese slices sold in packages with see-through, rigid tops on yellow bottoms.

THE QUESTION OF IRRADIATED FOOD   Nonionizing radiation is used, in some instances, to preserve food. It works—but is it safe? As the situation currently stands, irradiated food is not safe for many reasons: (1) the food cannot be eaten for 24 hours, to allow for radioactive decay; (2) irradiation requires chemical additives; (3) the procedure causes vitamin losses; and (4) there is little evidence presently available concerning the effects of irradiation

 If you see this symbol on food in your supermarket, beware! It means the food has been irradiated to preserve it. Many questions remain about the safety of irradiated food—pass it by in favor of fresh goods.

on additives, contaminants, pesticide residues, and packaging materials. Natural foods—grown and processed without synthetic chemicals or alteration—are still the healthiest.

GET THE LEAD OUT   The FDA estimates that 14 percent of the lead we ingest is brought to us in the soldering of the side seams of food cans. Because of findings they consider "disturbing," the FDA has proposed a reduction of lead amounting to 50 percent over the next 5 years. However, since quality of canned food is not the best, the occupants of a healthy home limit their use of canned goods; they concentrate, instead, on fresh, natural foods.

Lead is commonly found in improperly glazed pottery, too. Eating or drinking from such pottery can cause lead poisoning, especially if the lead is ingested little by little over a period of time. Most everyday dishes are not hazardous. Stoneware, porcelain, and fine china are almost always fired at high enough temperatures to bind the lead to the pottery, so it doesn't leach out. It's imported or custom pottery that usually poses the hazard. Here's how to protect yourself:

- Especially be cautious of items imported from Hong Kong, the People's Republic of China, and Mexico.
- When buying at a store, ask if a lab analysis has been done to determine lead and cadmium levels.
- Be cautious when buying abroad. If you do buy pottery from a roadside stand or private vendor, use it only for decorative purposes.
- Stop using pottery you believe is questionable. Acidic liquids— coffee, tea, juice, wine—and the routine cleaning by a dishwasher can speed the breakdown of glazes.
- Stop using pottery made before 1970, which is when new guidelines were adopted.

You can have pottery tested at a lab for about $60. To locate one near you, contact the American Council of Independent Laboratories, 1725 K Street NW, Washington, DC 20006; (202) 887-5872.

CABINETRY   Kitchen cabinets should be made of solid wood, metal, or exterior-grade plywood. Stay away from pressed wood—it can outgas formaldehyde and contaminate whatever you keep in the cabinets. If pressed wood is used, be sure it is adequately sealed (see chapter 5).

The Bedroom

We spend one-third of our lives in bed. That makes the bedroom the most important room in the house, and the bed the most important piece of furniture. Furnish this room with care. Provide adequate ventilation and good lighting (with a switch right inside the door), and paint the walls a harmonious color—something that makes you feel calm and peaceful. Here are a few basic rules to follow.

THE BED   Avoid beds made of pressed wood, especially when new. They out-gas formaldehyde, used as a binder, and can work to lower your immune system while you sleep. You should also avoid foam mattresses and pillows, if you can; they are petroleum products and give off toxic fumes when they burn. Likewise, avoid mattresses treated with chemicals; most sold in department stores have been sprayed with pesticides, fungicides, and flame retardants. You don't want to be breathing those vapors all night! A mattress made of natural fibers is the best, on a solid wood frame with a slatted base to ensure a healthy air flow. Cotton futons (not treated with chemicals) and solid wood, slatted knockdown frames are the best choice.

Bedding materials can exacerbate respiratory problems and provoke allergic reactions. Avoid polyester, a principal fiber in pillows, sheets, blankets, and mattresses; it's a plastic that releases fumes. Because it can't readily absorb perspiration, people sleeping under polyester blankets report being too cold in winter and too hot in summer. If you wake up in the middle of the night covered in sweat, switch to natural fiber bedding, and the problem will probably go away. Here are some other tips on healthy bedding:

- Quilts make good bedding, since they gather less dust than heavy blankets, but watch out that the filling isn't causing a problem (duck down, for instance, may cause allergies).
- Watch what kind of sheets you use. Permanent-press sheets are heavily treated with formaldehyde and require several washings to eliminate the health hazard. Flannel is a good choice for sheets. Normally untreated, its fluffy, air-filled texture also makes it more absorbent of perspiration and therefore warmer in winter, cooler in summer, and generally more comfortable.
- Babies and small children should have cots with sides. Don't give them pillows (to avoid smothering). If a child is restless, try using a fleecy underblanket for extra warmth and comfort.
- Until more is known about the health effects of electromagnetic radiation, keep electronic gadgets to a minimum in the bedroom. Remove electric blankets from the bed and clock radios from next to the head of the sleeper.

A healthy home does *not* have a water bed. Electromagnetic radiation from heaters in such beds have been linked to miscarriages in pregnant women and low fertility in males. Another drawback: The standard heater in a water bed uses about 125 kilowatt-hours of electricity per month—about the same as a large refrigerator. All the water beds in America together use an estimated 23 billion kilowatt-hours per year, equivalent to the output of four large power plants.

Prescription: A Healthy Home Has ...

... safe, healthy, and comfortable furnishings, including the following:

- an ambience that is sparse and natural
- hardwood, brick, or terrazzo floors, and floor coverings of wool or cotton with nonskid backings
- solid wood furniture that is nailed—not glued—together
- comfortable furniture that is ergonomic, meaning it encourages a normal spinal curve to protect against backache
- furniture padded with untreated cotton batting instead of foam rubber, synthetic, or cellulose padding
- a futon for a bed, with a solid wood, slatted base
- natural furnishings—wood, earthenware, hemp, wicker, burlap, wool, cotton, brass, copper, and iron—but no pottery with lead glazing
- untreated draperies of natural fibers, wood shutters, metal blinds, or shades made of rice paper or cloth
- safe, energy-efficient appliances, especially an energy-saving refrigerator
- a central vacuum cleaner, a vacuum with a water chamber, or a shop vac
- convenience and efficiency built into work areas, especially in the kitchen
- solid wood or metal cabinetry
- cookware that is glass, stainless steel, pottery without lead glazing, or iron, and no plastic dishes or food storage containers

8

The House and Yard

A house is more than a pile of bricks and mortar or a jumble of 2 × 4s and sheathing. It's a complex habitat, usually surrounded by a yard and garden, made up of interdependent systems: a skeleton, skin, pathways for heat circulation and waste removal, an architectural personality. Getting everything working together in a healthy manner is no mean feat. New houses are just as bad in this respect as old ones are. Where old houses often have overused, outdated systems that need repair, brand-new houses have lots of synthetic materials and chemical outgassing.

Here's what you need to know to update house systems to the point where they are healthy and serviceable for the 1990s.

BUILDING MATERIALS

The same high-power chemistry that makes modern building products perform so well also makes them potentially hazardous to our health. There's urea-formaldehyde in pressed wood, plasticizers and asbestos in vinyl flooring, volatile solvents (toluene, xylene, benzene) in paints and adhesives, and mildewcides and insecticides in paints, carpets, and caulks. Not only do these synthetic chemicals adversely affect the environment during their manufacture, but once inside your home, many of them outgas, gradually poisoning the air.

What's a modern American homeowner to do? Reject mass-produced building materials with their host of toxins. Substitute low-tox, no-tox products instead. They are available and, though they may cost more and require more upkeep, you'll have a cleaner, fresher, healthier environment.

The Nontoxic Approach

By now you're probably thinking it's impossible to build a truly nontoxic house in this day and age. Not so. Paul Bierman-Lytle, founder and president of

Masters Corporation in New Canaan, Connecticut, is doing just that. Paul is a carpenter and a graduate of Yale architectural school. In 1978 he founded Masters Corporation as a building-design firm for affluent people wanting craftsmanship and quality design in new homes or renovations. He does the design and has two teams of builders do the construction.

Around 1982, Paul became concerned when he noticed that his workers called in sick after working with certain building materials. After doing some research, Paul discovered what most of us now know—many building materials pose health hazards to people who live in the house, as well as to people who work with the materials during construction.

Being a conscientious and socially responsible type of guy, Paul set out to research toxicity and offer healthy alternatives. In experiments with different products, Paul observed that his builders felt noticeably better when they used no-tox and low-tox building materials. Gone was the fatigue, lack of motivation, low energy, and many days lost to illness and general discomfort. Stinging eyes, itchy skin, coughing, and headaches were significantly reduced.

In 1986, Paul created an adjunct to Masters Corporation—a mail-order and consulting business offering no-tox or low-tox substitutes for insulation, paint, finishes, and other unhealthy building materials. It was so successful, Paul made it company policy to build only "healthy" houses. Today, Paul is probably the nation's foremost authority on healthy construction.

SELECT HEALTHY PRODUCTS   Paul's approach to healthy building is two-fold: (1) Use the most inert and nontoxic materials possible and (2) provide good ventilation for living spaces. "We're looking for complete elimination of harmful products or materials in the houses we build," he says. "For us, the bottom line is quality, and if a material has even a little bit of something that's not good for you in it, that's not the top of the line to us."

Among the common materials that concern Bierman-Lytle and other designers and builders of healthy homes are the following:

> **Paints:** Bactericides and fungicides are added because most paints use cellulose thickeners, which are subject to bacterial attack. Many paints also have fungicides to resist mildew in areas of high humidity. If you're bothered by paint fumes, you'll have to find a manufacturer willing to custom-mix paint without chemicals. (See appendix A.)
>
> **Chemical solvents:** Solvents are added to paints to help them spread and dry properly. In some brands of oil paint, each gallon contains up to 2 quarts of solvent. Water-based paints contain only a fraction of the solvents found in oil paints. Breathing solvents while painting can cause dizziness, headache, nausea, and drowsiness. In a well-ventilated room, it takes a week for the fumes to completely dissipate.
>
> **Wood finishes:** Wood finishes and construction adhesives are often solvent-based and can be a problem to those who are sensitive to the chemicals. Switching to a water-based formulation is the best solution.

(continued on page 148)

A Guide to Building Materials and Furnishings

Material	Uses	Problems	Alternatives
Adhesives, glues, and mastics	Drywall, wallpaper, carpet backing	Many contain toxic hydrocarbon solvents that outgas.	Use epoxy adhesives, which are relatively nontoxic when fully cured. White glue (polyvinyl acetate) and carpenter's glue (yellow aliphatic resin) are safe when dry. Use alternative adhesives made from natural and nontoxic materials.
Carpets and rugs	Floor coverings	Both synthetic and natural carpets, together with backings and mats, can contain a host of chemicals used as stain repellents, biocides and fungicides. These may be applied during or after manufacture.	Consider a natural wood, tile, or polished concrete floor. Flagstone and brick are excellent in certain rooms. Old or handmade area rugs made of natural materials such as cotton or wool are usually toxin-free. Nylon is the most benign synthetic material. Use jute, not polyurethane, as a backing. Avoid using adhesives.
Countertops	Kitchen and bathroom surfaces	Plastic-laminated materials, such as Formica, are usually applied over a particleboard core, which gives off formaldehyde fumes.	When ordering countertops, make sure the laminate is applied to exterior-grade plywood and is sealed on both sides as described on page 147 for particleboard. Or use tile or Corian (a solid counter material made by DuPont). For safety's sake, a dust mask should be worn when drilling, sanding, or cutting this or any other potentially toxic material.
Drapes, furniture, upholstery fabrics	Decorative furnishings	These, more often than not, contain formaldehyde and a host of other chemicals. Because of their large, exposed surface areas and their close	Whenever possible, use untreated, natural materials such as cotton, wool, linen, or solid wood. When finishing a house or buying household products, keep in mind that hard plastics generally release fewer chemical fumes

Fiberglass batts, rigid foam panels, and blown-in celluose	Insulation	than soft plastics. Choose furniture made of solid wood (joined with wood or metal nails), metal, or natural materials such as bamboo, wicker, or rattan.
		Fiberglass insulation contains glass fibers that can irritate eyes, skin, and respiratory tract. Asphaltic coatings are used on some kraft-paper-faced fiberglass, and formaldehyde resins may be used as binders. Cellulose and rigid foam panels contain a variety of chemical compounds. Fortunately, these insulations (including fiberglass) seem to cause only minor, temporary irritation to most people.	Use a particle-filter dust mask during handling or installation of fiberglass or celluose insulation, and insist that an installer do likewise. Ventilate the house well after installation, and keep the fumes away from living areas with a vapor barrier. Make sure no insulation is exposed. Natural cork, with an R-value of about 4 per inch, is an expensive option. Another less expensive but hard-to-find alternative is Air Krete, a nontoxic, magnesium-oxide-based foam with an R-value of 3.9 per inch. (See appendix A.)
Gypsumboard	Interior walls, ceilings	There are none, for most of us. The material may contain some chemicals in the paper facing, but these affect only the most sensitive individuals. The joint compound, however, can irritate the respiratory tract if dry-sanded and may contain trace amounts of formaldehyde, asbestos, or other compounds.	Smooth and feather the edges of the joint compound with a wet sponge, or wet the material well before sanding. Dust masks help the wearer during dry sanding but won't help those who move back into the room and live with residual dust later on. Plaster, applied to metal or wood lath, is a good alternative, but competent plasterers are hard to find. Use low-tox drywall joint compounds such as Murco M-100 HiPo asbestos-free joint compound, Auro spackling paste and compound, Velo spackling compound, or Anavo oil-based spackle. (See appendix A.)

(continued)

A Guide to Building Materials and Furnishings—Continued

Material	Uses	Problems	Alternatives
Hardwood plywood	Decorative interior paneling; furniture and cabinetry veneers	This contains urea-formaldehyde resins, although in lower concentrations than in particleboard.	Remove it. Replace it with solid pine paneling or other wall finish material or seal all surfaces as described below for particleboard.
Paint stripper	Removal of paints, stains, and varnishes	Stripper contains a host of truly hazardous chemicals, including methylene chloride (a carcinogen), methanol, benzene (a suspected carcinogen), and toluene.	There is no safe way to strip paint. A combination of paint stripper and a heat gun appears to be the best way. Employ good cross ventilation (preferably with an exhaust fan in a wide open window), and wear gloves, goggles, and a respirator. You should cover lead paint or have it stripped by professionals only.
Paints, sealants, stains, and preservatives	Wood finishes	These may contain a variety of toxic solvents, mildewcides, fungicides, and other compounds.	Apply these only in well-ventilated areas that remain vacant and ventilate until all volatile solvents have evaporated and no odor is detected. Ventilation means you either do the work outdoors or use a large fan. Use an OSHA-approved mask to filter out vapors during application indoors. Or use special nontoxic finishes (see appendix A), or use no finishes at all.

Material	Common uses	Hazard	Recommendation
Particleboard (including chipboard, waferboard, composition board, and medium-density fiberboard)	Floor underlayment; roof and wall sheathing; shelving; core stock for plastic-laminated countertops, kitchen cupboards, and bathroom vanities; furniture framing; interior doors; stair treads; television and stereo housings	These contain urea-formaldehyde, which can give off fumes for years after manufacture.	Use pine boards or other solid wood wherever possible. Seal exposed (but not necessarily visible) surfaces of existing particleboard products, such as the bottom face of a laminated counter and the inside surfaces and edges of cupboards and vanities. Latex paint won't seal in vapors; use two coats of an alkyd-based paint (if you aren't sensitive to it), and ventilate the area thoroughly until it's dry. Other less common but more benign sealers are available. Use particleboard made without formaldehyde, such as Iso-Board.
Pressure-treated lumber and wood preservatives	Outdoor structures such as decks, porches, fences, outdoor furniture, and playground equipment	These contain fungicides and mildewcides, usually arsenic compounds, creosote, or penta.	Use naturally rot-resistant wood such as redwood, cedar, or cypress. Or use low-tox wood preservatives (see appendix A). Don't burn pressure-treated or other chemically treated wood. Wear a tight-fitting respirator or a high-quality dust mask when sawing pressure-treated wood.
Softwood plywood (meaning all common structural-grade plywoods)	Subflooring; wall and roof sheathing; some furniture, cabinets, and shelving	Interior-grade plywood contains urea-formaldehyde resins. Exterior-grade plywood contains phenol-formaldehyde resins, which are likely to produce less of the noxious fumes.	Seal exposed surfaces, as described above for particleboard. If you have to use plywood, use exterior grades.
Vinyl flooring	Floor covering, particularly in kitchens and bathrooms, usually laid on top of plywood subfloor	Plasticizers in vinyl flooring material outgas over time. Some contain asbestos. It is hazardous when drilled or sawed.	Use unglazed ceramic tile, hardwood, or some other natural material. Use hard vinyl tiles instead of soft (hard vinyl contains less plasticizer). Check to make sure the tile does not contain asbestos.

SOURCE: Adapted, with permission, from *Harrowsmith* magazine, September/October 1987.

Asbestos: Although banned as an insulation material in the 1970s, asbestos is still used in thousands of building products; among them are vinyl floor tiles and sheet flooring, siding, and wood stove insulation boards. In solid form, asbestos is not hazardous; but if it's sawed, drilled, sanded, or broken, invisible fibers can escape into the air. Once inhaled, they stay in the lungs and can cause respiratory illness and cancer. The best solution is to avoid using products that contain asbestos. If you're unsure what is in a product, ask the manufacturer for a materials data sheet. Manufacturers are required to have them available and are legally obligated to show them to you.

WHAT ABOUT A VAPOR BARRIER?   A metal vapor barrier, usually of light foil, is recommended instead of plastic. Place this on the inside of an exterior wall so fumes outgassing from treated wood, insulation, caulking, and electrical wires will be forced into the outdoor air, not into interior room spaces.

Foil-faced insulation may be used as an interior vapor barrier by stapling it to the studs and then sealing the seams with foil tape. Another approach is to use ⅛-inch foil-faced sheathing board as an interior vapor barrier.

HOUSE SYSTEMS

Like the human body, several systems operating together make up the total organism that is a house. Each of these systems needs to be functioning at an optimum level for the house to be healthy and health promoting.

Ventilation—Fresh Air Indoors

Do your windows drip condensation each winter? Does your upstairs feel like an oven on summer days? Can you still smell the liver and onions you had for dinner as you prepare for bedtime? If you answer yes to any of these questions, your home's ventilation system is not doing its job.

Excessive moisture, heat, and odors are all symptoms of indoor air pollution. Some pollutants, like cooking odors, are just unpleasant. But others, like combustion gases, can threaten your health. Unfortunately, tightening a house to save energy also concentrates pollutants by reducing the fresh air that would otherwise leak in through cracks and gaps all over the structure. The lack of adequate ventilation can cause a host of problems for you and your home:

Health problems: Accumulated pollutants lead to illnesses, from headaches to lung cancer.

Moisture damage: Water vapor can condense inside walls and ceilings, leading to mildew, peeling paint, and wood rot.

Structural damage: Summer sun can heat your attic to 150°F or more; without proper ventilation, this heat can cause roof shingles to deteriorate.

Higher energy costs: Inadequate attic ventilation also makes your air conditioner work harder.

The solution isn't to abandon energy conservation but to attack pollutants at their sources. With localized or whole-house ventilation, you can exhaust moist, contaminated air and bring fresh air in on its heels. You'll also help your furnace and air conditioner work more efficiently.

NATURAL VENTILATION   First, make sure your attic is well ventilated. You'll want to put vents both high in the ridge and low in the soffit. If that isn't possible, you can put vents in the gable ends. Soffit and ridge vents are made with different vent capacities, which are measured as *net free ventilation area* (NFVA). NFVA gives the ventilation area, in square inches, for a given vent. This figure is usually printed on the vent. To determine the vent size you need, figure on 1.5 square inches NFVA for every square foot of attic floor area. Finally, NFVA should be divided equally between intake and exhaust. In a conventional, gable-roofed house, allocate half the total NFVA to the ridge vent and 25 percent to soffit vents in each eave.

To encourage natural ventilation in the rooms of your house, open leeward windows (located opposite prevailing breezes) more than windward ones. This creates a negative-pressure zone as air moves through the interior space, causing more air to exhaust through leeward windows. This in turn helps to draw more fresh air into the room.

MECHANICAL VENTILATION   How much mechanical ventilation do you need? The rule of thumb for the *average* house is a fresh air supply in the range of 100 to 200 cubic feet per minute (CFM), depending on indoor air quality. Anything that creates stale or stuffy air—super-tight construction, heavy smoking indoors, or a fume-producing workshop, for example—puts an extra load on your mechanical ventilation system, regardless of the air that comes in naturally through doors, windows, cracks, and leaks.

To help your home breathe easier, choose one of the following mechanical ventilation systems:

- a network of localized exhaust fans—the least complex system
- a powerful ceiling-mounted whole-house exhaust fan
- a central ventilation system
- a heat recovery ventilator—a mechanical system that recovers heat from exhaust air

EXHAUST FANS   Exhaust fans in the kitchen and bathroom are a must in a healthy home. A kitchen range hood can expel heat, smoke, moisture, and odors—provided it sends the stale air outside. So-called recirculating range hoods don't really ventilate the kitchen; their carbon filters remove some odors, smoke, and grease, but they only recirculate moisture and combustion gases.

Your range's location and size determine the exhaust fan capacity. The Home Ventilating Institute (HVI) uses the formula of 40 CFM per foot of range width if it is installed against an outside wall and 50 CFM per foot if the range is on an interior wall or island. For example, a range 3 feet wide needs three times 40 or 50, which translates to a capacity of 120 or 150 CFM.

Bathroom fans help prevent moisture buildup that can lead to mildew and peeling paint. The HVI suggests that a bathroom fan provide at least eight air changes per hour (ACH). To find the fan capacity you need in CFM, multiply the square footage of the room by 1.1, assuming a standard 8-foot ceiling.

Venting stale air from kitchens and baths has three drawbacks: (1) You exhaust already-warm air in winter, wasting the energy it took to heat it, (2) use of exhaust fans can create negative pressure inside the house, thus creating a condition where radon and/or chlordane can be sucked up through the soil, and (3) negative pressure causes the potential for backdrafting of combustion appliances. There are measures you can take to balance air pressure, and the value of ridding the house of pollutants far outweighs the benefits of an extremely weathertight house.

WHOLE-HOUSE FANS   A whole-house fan is designed primarily to cool the house during summer by circulating air through all the rooms. A high-powered fan is installed in the ceiling, where it draws fresh air in through the windows and pushes stale air out through attic vents. It can lighten your air-conditioning load if you run the fan at night to cool the house and run the air conditioner only during the heat of the day. If the outside air temperature is usually below 85°F, a whole-house fan may eliminate the need for an air conditioner altogether.

Whole-house fans are priced in the $100 to $500 range and can be installed in a few hours. For a whole-house fan to work properly, it's important that the attic have large gable vents or continuous ridge and soffit vents to let the hot air escape. The fan is mounted above the ceiling joists, so you don't have to worry about the spacing between them.

To determine how powerful a fan you need (referred to as its *ventilation capacity*), HVI suggests multiplying your home's square footage—excluding garage, basement, and attic—by three. A sample house of 2,000 square feet would need a fan rated at about 6,000 CFM. You may need a more powerful fan if you live in a warm or humid climate.

Whole-house fans usually have thermostats that turn them on when attic air exceeds a preset temperature (typically 90°). Other options include a timer to run the fan at fixed times of day, an insulated cover to stop heat loss through the fan in winter, and a high-temperature safety switch to shut the fan off if the motor overheats.

A whole-house fan costs about $20 to $60 per year to operate, assuming an average of 6 hours of operation per day for 6 months of the year, with electricity costing 10 cents per kilowatt-hour.

As with localized ventilation, a whole-house exhaust fan can create negative pressure and cause backdrafting or spillage of combustion appliances. The tighter the house, the more dangerous this can be. For this reason, a very tight house requires a balanced system that includes both exhaust and intake of air.

CENTRAL VENTILATION SYSTEM   Many houses need mechanical ventilation more in winter than in summer because the windows are closed. A central ventilation system lets you regulate the intake of fresh air and the exhaust of stale air. If you are building a new, airtight house or have extensively caulked and weather-stripped your existing home, this type of system is ideal for you.

Central ventilation uses only a single exhaust fan, usually located in the attic. Ducts from the main sources of pollution (kitchens, baths, laundries, and workshops) lead to this fan, which discharges pollutants outside through the roof or a soffit.

In one central ventilation system, called *exhaust only* in the industry, only the exhaust is ducted and powered. Reduced pressure from the ducted air pulls fresh air in through bafflelike one-way intake ports. Unlike an open window, these through-the-wall passages keep out wind and rain. The ports are usually installed in bedrooms and living rooms, preferably where they won't create a draft. You need to leave inside doors ajar, use doors with louvers or transoms, or allow a space of half an inch or so under each door to let intake air circulate throughout the house.

Because cold air is always coming in, the cost of warming it is one drawback to exhaust-only systems (the fan itself is inexpensive to run). If your climate is cold enough and fuel is expensive enough, it makes economic sense to capture heat from the exhaust air and use it to warm the intake air. This is the idea behind the other type of central ventilation, heat-recovery ventilators.

HEAT-RECOVERY VENTILATORS (HRVS)   An HRV pays for itself most quickly (in saved heat) in a tight house in a northern climate. This system has all the advantages of the first type of central ventilation, but it overcomes the problem of cold intake air. When they were introduced about 7 years ago, HRVs were called air-to-air heat exchangers because they let the incoming and exhaust air exchange heat without mixing. Today's HRVs work the same way, but they're more efficient, extracting 50 to 80 percent of the heat from the exhaust air.

If you're thinking of buying an HRV, here are a few things to be aware of:

■ Choose a unit that supplies the minimum recommended ventilation rate of 150 CFM.
■ Make sure the manufacturer's ratings of heat-recovery efficiency and airflow capacity are certified by the HVI (in the United States) or the Ontario Research Foundation (in Canada).
■ For the most precise control of air flow, look for an HRV with separate blowers for intake and exhaust air.

It's possible to fine-tune an HRV's operating cycle to suit your life-style. Use a timer or a manual override switch to run the HRV when peak indoor pollution is generated—when you are preparing meals or entertaining, for example. And because air is brought in through only one opening and directed through a filter, an HRV helps clean the fresh air.

Although it's more expensive than other, equally effective ventilation systems, an HRV costs less to run because you save on heating. You'll also feel more comfortable in its preheated, draft-free air. In evaluating the cost-effectiveness of HRV models, remember that fuel costs and the severity of your climate are more important than small (up to 10 percent) differences in heat-recovery efficiency.

CONTEMPLATING THE CHOICE   When choosing a mechanical ventilation system, first consider fuel or energy costs in your area and whether you'll install the system in a new or existing home. Then decide the demands that variations in your climate will put on the system.

Localized ventilation through bathroom and kitchen exhaust fans, for example, is essential no matter where you live. Ductless central ventilation using a whole-house fan, however, is useful mainly to cool houses in hot weather because it relies on air brought in through open windows.

The two ducted types of central ventilation—central exhaust with wall ports and heat-recovery central ventilation—are designed for a house in a colder climate, where natural ventilation is not possible during much of the year. If radon is a problem, be sure to balance intake and exhaust of air so negative pressure is not created within the structure.

Most houses require 0.35 to 0.7 air changes per hour. Multiply the square footage of your living area by your ceiling height (typically 8 feet) and by the recommended ACH of 0.5. Divide that figure by 60 for your ventilation requirements in CFM.

Electricity

There's no justice when it comes to electricity prices. If you live in Seattle, you can buy the equivalent of a million Btus of the stuff for $5.80. Meanwhile, in New York City, utility customers shell out $43.28—seven times as much— for the same amount of electricity. Most areas of the country fall in between those extremes.

During the last decade, the price of electricity has climbed steadily, and there are good reasons to believe the price will stay on this upward path. It's fortunate that homeowners now have a powerful array of options to help them keep electric bills in check.

A good place to start is with energy-saving appliances, specifically the refrigerator. Over the 15-to-20-year life of a refrigerator, the owner will spend three times as much money running it as he or she spent to buy it. By replacing your old refrigerator with a new energy-efficient one, you will use 34 percent less energy to operate it. According to a 1987 study from Princeton University's Center for Energy and Environmental Studies and the World Resources Institute, the energy saved by just replacing the existing U.S. stock of refrigerator-freezers with the most efficient 17-cubic-foot frost-free units on the market would be equal to the output of about 18 large nuclear or coal-fired power plants!

ALUMINUM—HOT WIRING   Saving energy is just one consideration when it comes to electricity. Safety is another concern. What kind of wiring does your house have? If you have aluminum, or aluminum sheathed in copper, it is not a safe house.

Copper was scarce and expensive after World War II. To save money and keep up with demand, manufacturers of electrical wiring began to use aluminum as a substitute for copper conductors. Some aluminum wiring was used as early as 1947, and the practice was widespread by the 1960s. In 1966, the Underwriters Laboratories, a respected testing institute, gave the seal of approval to aluminum wiring, indicating that it could be used interchangeably with copper wiring.

But by the early 1970s, the use of aluminum wiring was linked with electrical fires in houses. Further study revealed that certain characteristics made aluminum a poor substitute for copper. The cheaper metal expands and contracts at a different rate than the steel or brass screws that are used at connection points on receptacles and switches. This, combined with corrosion, reduces conductivity. The result is overheating and (in the most extreme situations) sparking.

It's not difficult to check your house for aluminum wiring. Exposed cable in your basement, garage, or crawl space will be labeled AL or Aluminum. The wiring itself, once stripped of insulation, is silvery in color, rather than dark like copper. You might also have aluminum wiring that's sheathed in copper; this will have a silver core surrounded by darker copper.

If you do have aluminum wiring, there are straightforward ways to make your house safer. With the power turned off, remove the cover plates and unscrew the switches or receptacles from the outlet boxes. Then check the labeling on the base plates of these switches and receptacles. If the labels read either "CO/ALR" or "CU/AL," then they are designed to safely handle copper or aluminum wiring.

If a switch or receptacle doesn't carry an aluminum rating, you can simply replace it with one that does. Or you can splice insulated copper *pigtails* between the aluminum wiring and the receptacle or switch. Each splice should be sealed with antioxidation paste and capped with a wire nut. These supplies are available at most hardware stores and building or electrical supply outlets.

Plumbing

Check to see where your water comes from—is it supplied from the city main, a deep well, or a spring? If the supply is from a well, have the water tested for organics as well as for lead. If supply is from a city main, lead and chlorine are the major concerns. If from a spring, it will probably be necessary to drill a well.

To get the water from a well in the purest state, use a stainless steel submersible pump (no plastic components); an old-fashioned air pressure, galvanized-steel tank (no rubber bladder or plastic parts); and faucets and shower heads of copper and stainless steel (no Teflon or other plastic parts). Flush out the copper pipes thoroughly after installation.

Is the water main that's coming into the house made of lead? If so, it should be replaced to eliminate health hazards. Copper pipe is best, then brass, then galvanized iron.

Use a magnet to test for iron. Detect lead by scratching the pipe with a penknife to see if it's soft and silvery. If pipes are brass or copper, look for bluish green stains—they can indicate that the pipe doesn't have much life left in it.

Test to see if the solder is lead, too. Until recently, 50/50 solder (50 percent tin and 50 percent lead) was the most widely used solder for plumbing systems. Because some of this toxic lead can end up in the water, the federal Safe Drinking Water Act Amendment of 1986 banned lead-based solder for potable water supply systems. This applies to all new plumbing installations and all alterations to existing plumbing.

The best solder is both lead- and antimony-free. Check your local hardware store or plumbing supply company.

Plastic polyvinyl chloride (PVC) plumbing is a lot cheaper than copper and easier to work with. It's quick to install and resists corrosion. But it's not the healthy option. PVC pipe, by its very nature, contains a slew of organic chemicals—including aliphatic and aromatic hydrocarbons and phenolic compounds. To make matters worse, joints are seamed with a solvent-based glue. These organic chemicals leach into the water, though the PVC industry constantly downplays the dangers. Workers installing the pipe use solvents and glues that have been linked to lymphoma and birth defects in lab animals. One study showed an excess of several types of cancers among pipe fitters.

THE WATER HEATER   The most economical way to heat water is with a domestic solar hot water system, particularly if you now use electricity for this task. But in many areas of the country, there are not enough sunny days to make solar water heating a viable option without a backup system.

Electricity is about three times as expensive as natural gas or fuel oil on a heat-producing basis. A family of four paying 10 cents per kilowatt-hour for electricity will spend $8,200 for hot water over the estimated 13-year life of an electric water heater. The same family, using a high-efficiency gas water heater and paying 75 cents a therm for gas, would spend just $3,360, *a savings of more than $4,800.*

Though gas may be a desirable alternative, it is not efficient. Water that is heated but not used can account for up to *40 percent* of the total operating cost. One way to eliminate such waste is to get an integrated unit—one that supplies both space heating and hot water. Several highly efficient models are currently on the market (costing about $3,500), and technology is getting better all the time.

An integrated gas appliance is an especially good choice for new houses because it shrinks the mechanical systems to a single, efficient appliance that needs no chimney. An integrated system also makes sense as a retrofit, particularly if your old furnace and water heater are on their last legs or if you're anxious to replace your electric heating and hot water system with something less expensive.

For an investment of about $150 or less, you can lop 33 to 50 percent off your hot-water costs whether your heater is gas or electric. Here's how:

■ Turn down your water heater's thermostat to 120°F. (Note: If you use a dishwasher, your water temperature must be 140°F. Some dishwashers will heat the water to 140°F, so your house water can be turned down to 120°F.)

■ Spend about $8 to insulate the hot-water pipes from the water heater to the taps.

■ Install a pressure-reducing valve where your cold-water supply enters the house.

■ Wrap $10 worth of insulation around the water heater, unless you have a new, energy-efficient water heater.

■ Install low-flow shower heads, costing about $10 apiece.

■ Fit the faucets with aerators ($2 apiece).

■ Install a timer (about $35) to shut off the heater during times you don't need hot water.

■ Use cold water to wash your laundry. After showers and tub baths, your biggest hot-water user is your washing machine. By making the switch to washing in cold water, you'll save 12 to 25 hot gallons with every load.

In many communities the electric utility offers an off-peak rate, at about 40 percent of the normal rate, between the hours of 11:30 P.M. and 7:00 A.M. By connecting a timer to the electrical cable leading to the hot-water tank, you can heat water only when the rate is lower. You use about the same amount of electricity; it's just billed at a lower rate. To do this, a larger storage tank is required, but it pays for itself in a short time due to the lower electricity rates.

WATER-SAVING TOILETS   Toilets are responsible for 40 percent of the water usage in most households. With fresh water in short supply, that's a lot of water. You can significantly lower that amount by installing a new, water-saving toilet.

The old-fashioned toilet is a notorious water waster. With every flick of its handle, it flushes away 5 to 10 gallons. Today's water-saving toilets get more flushes to the gallon. The current industry standard defines a water-saving toilet as a unit that consumes 3.5 gallons of water or less per flush. Almost all toilets being manufactured today meet this standard.

The ultimate ecological toilet doesn't flush at all—it composts wastes. Culturally, most of us aren't ready for that improvement. We like toilets that flush. Even though they are notorious water wasters, they seem, well, more sanitary. But if you'd like to know more about composting toilets, contact Clivus Multrum, manufacturers of composting toilets for the home, at 21 Canal Street, Lawrence, MA 01840; (617) 794-1700.

WATER PRESSURE   The utility that supplies your water may be piping it to your house at a greater pressure than necessary. If too much water is forced through your faucets and shower heads, the water heater works overtime and you pay.

Find out what your water line pressure is from the water company. If you have your own well, there should be a pressure gauge near the pump or the pressure tank. If the pressure is above 45 pounds per square inch (psi), your water system could use a pressure-reducing valve. By lowering the pressure and thus the flow rate, you can save both hot and cold water. A pressure-reducing valve can be bought at a plumbing supply store for $20 to $35. You'll also need a pressure gauge (costing between $5 and $10), which you should install downstream from the pressure reducer.

What's the right pressure for your house? You can go as low as you like, until you feel the flow is inconveniently slow. Up to a point, the lower the pressure, the lower your monthly water bill and the less water your heater will have to heat. In some municipalities, the sewer bill is figured on gallons used, so you can reduce that cost as well. There are other benefits: Lower pressure extends the life of your water heater and minimizes "water hammer" problems (hammering sounds when faucets are turned on and off rapidly).

It's a good idea to leave some outside garden spigots at full pressure. If there's ever a fire, you'll want to be able to shoot water far and high.

Heating and Cooling

There are disadvantages to modern methods of thermostat-controlled heating and air conditioning. In addition to being expensive, heating and cooling systems can make air uncomfortably dry—provoking headaches, dry skin, and throat irritation.

A house with thermostatically controlled central heat usually uses one of three systems:

Hot water: Systems installed before World War II relied on convection and gravity to deliver hot water to radiators and were relatively inefficient. Most systems installed in the last 40 years use pumps, which are much more efficient, though more costly to install and repair. Heat is evenly distributed, balanced, and relatively high in humidity.

Steam: Generally found in houses built before World War II, steam systems don't need a pump because hot steam rises vigorously. This type of heat is clean, comfortable, and relatively high in humidity, but radiators tend to get waterlogged, which leads to noise and reduced heat output.

Forced air: Modern forced-air systems use fans and blowers to deliver heat through registers and baseboards. This is efficient, and it is easy to extend if an addition is built onto the house. Though warm air has a tendency to be dry, you can remedy the situation by adding a central humidifier to the furnace (about $200 installed). Such a furnace is also easily adapted for central air conditioning. Since hot air circulates dust, ducts and registers need to be cleaned periodically.

An alternative is radiant heat—heat from the sun or other hot sources such as a wood stove or radiant heat panels. Instead of heating the air, these raise the radiant temperature of a room's exposed surfaces (walls, furniture) as well as the contents (dogs and people) and make the space feel warmer. If a solar room is a larger remodeling than you want to handle, consider adding radiant panels, usually 3 by 5 feet in dimension, that attach to the ceiling or walls and run off electricity. One of the best uses of radiant heat is when you want comfort fast within a small space. For that reason, one of the medium-watt-density or lower-watt-density panels makes sense in a retrofit. First make sure that the ceiling above and the floor below are insulated, or you may increase your heat losses and still end up with a cold floor.

HEATING FUELS Paul Bierman-Lytle, architect and builder of healthy houses in New England, advocates a combination of solar gain, heat pumps and heat exchangers, and electricity for heating healthy houses. He rejects fossil fuels—gas, oil, kerosene, wood, coal—because they are not renewable energy sources and they pollute the air inside houses with deadly gases.

But most of us don't have the luxury of switching to the healthiest heating fuels available. We must live with what we've got, possibly updating and maintaining it so it's as healthy and inexpensive to operate as possible. Here's a rundown of the various types of heating fuels and what you can expect from them in a healthy home.

Oil In December 1976, heating oil was selling for 43 cents a gallon. Four years later, we were paying $1.22 a gallon. Such a roller coaster leaves the homeowner at the mercy of domestic and foreign supplies. All indicators show that prices will continue to be unstable. The message in all this seems clear: Efficient heating equipment and a well-insulated house are the best insurance against volatile prices.

There are thousands of oil-fired furnaces and boilers out there that are energy hogs. If you happen to own one of these clunkers, or even if your system is relatively efficient, there are a host of new cost-effective options worth considering. Compared to old oil-fired heating systems that lose half their heat up the chimney, modern boilers and furnaces are marvels of efficiency.

Natural Gas Though the price of natural gas has shot up more than the price of any other fuel in the last 10 years, gas is still less expensive than the competition. All things considered, natural gas shapes up as the homeowner's most economical bet for the future. Many a homeowner who heats with gas can save a lot of money by updating the furnace and boiler, a retrofit that can achieve more than 90 percent efficiency.

Technology in gas appliances has improved greatly in recent years. We now have the *pulse combustion* furnace (retailing for around $3,000) and *condensing* burners (retailing for $1,300 to $2,000). However, they can be noisier than other systems, so make sure the model you select has good sound control and is installed properly. When shopping for a condensing furnace or boiler, pay special attention to the warranty, particularly the section covering the heat exchanger, since that's the part most subject to corrosion.

Electricity   Clinical ecologists advocate all-electric houses for their chemically sensitive patients, but this is a decision you must make for yourself. Though electric heat is clean and efficient, it is the most expensive heat you can have, plus it increases reliance on nuclear power plants and creates a static charge in the house.

Heat pumps can help reduce high electric heat bills, and you can count on them to supply both space heating and air conditioning needs. But, because they depend on chlorofluorocarbons (CFCs), chemicals that are responsible for depleting Earth's ozone layer, heat pumps are not a socially responsible choice. In addition, heat pumps aren't a smart choice in really cold climates because as outdoor temperatures fall, their space-heating performance suffers.

Solar   Relying more on energy conservation and renewable energy and less on the planet's limited supply of fossil fuels is the most socially responsible way to heat your house. Even though our government is no longer supporting solar energy with tax credits, as it did in the late 1970s and early 1980s, solar heating is still a viable alternative economically.

The starting point for a passive solar house or sun-room is good southern exposure. Next, bear in mind that the best passive designs strike a subtle balance between insulation, thermal mass, and the amount of south glazing used. Think twice before using glass in roof sections of a passive solar space. Glass roofs can create overheating and night insulation problems.

Wood   Catalytic combustors and secondary combustion chambers make to-day's wood heaters cleaner burning and more efficient than ever before. In addition, today's stoves are safer, thanks to high-temperature chimneys, posi-tive-connect hookups (between the stove outlets and fireplace flues), better insulated wall pass-through systems for the stovepipes, and protective heat shields. Wood prices are historically stable, so you can depend on them year in and year out.

Routine Maintenance   Performing routine maintenance on furnaces and heating systems helps to cut down on air contamination, no matter what type of fuel the system uses. To cut down on dust, check the air filter often. If it's metal, remove and hose it off or scrub it once a month. If it's disposable, replace it every 2 months during the heating season. Place all-metal or cloth filters over duct openings to rooms. Have the furnace and ductwork vacuumed by a professional furnace-cleaning company once a year, just before heating season. Check for leaks, a cracked heat exchanger, or a blocked flue.

In his healthy houses, Bierman-Lytle isolates the furnace room from the rest of the house by building a ventilated stud wall that is both insulated and soundproofed.

COOLING SYSTEMS   In some areas of the country, cooling the house in summer costs more than heating it in winter. Because cooling systems can be a source of indoor air pollution and can be expensive besides, it's important to evaluate your cooling system and make it as efficient as possible.

Air Conditioning   A poorly maintained air conditioner can be a source of mold, dust, and disease-causing microorganisms. To prevent this condition, clean reservoirs regularly with detergent or a hydrogen peroxide solution. If you have a central unit, clean or replace the filters (usually located in the furnace) before the cooling season begins and periodically thereafter. Have the ductwork vacuumed regularly. If you have a room unit, clean the filter (located behind the air intake grille on the front) once a month during periods of heavy use. Vacuum dust and lint from the condenser and evaporator yearly. Have the system checked for leaks periodically.

Air conditioners recirculate indoor air, thereby lowering the rate of indoor-outdoor air exchange, so use them only when absolutely necessary. Fresh air is the best conditioner.

Natural Cooling   Before the days of air conditioning, homeowners relied on natural methods for keeping cool. These time-tested methods of cooling are just as valid today as they were years ago. Put principles of natural cooling to work in your home by following these tips:

- Install vents in attic gables so hot air can escape.
- Plant deciduous trees to shade the south side of the house in summer.
- Install overhangs, awnings, or trellises on the south and west sides to protect windows from the most intense sun.
- Add a screened-in porch on the south or west side to shield the interior of the house from intense sun.
- Install operable shutters to block heat.
- Keep windows slightly open on the north side to draw fresh air into the house.
- Design a recessed entry to protect living areas from wind and sun.
- Plant shrubs between the walkway and window to absorb heat reflected from the sidewalk.
- Replace dark-colored roof shingles with light-colored ones that reflect heat.
- Use the porch for social gatherings and sleeping in hot weather.

Though it takes attention several times a day, it is possible to cool the house with natural air currents. Here's how:

- Create a *stack effect* by opening windows in the basement or lower level to admit cool air and then opening clerestories, skylights, or dormer windows to exhaust warm air. This works best if the house has an open, central stairway.
- When possible, open windows low on the cool side of the house and high on the hot side of the house. For example, in the early

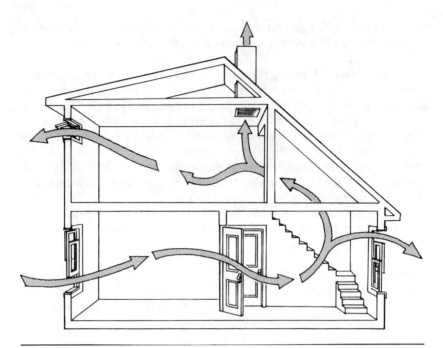

You can facilitate natural cooling just by opening a few doors and windows.

morning open windows low on the west side and high on the east side. In the afternoon, simply reverse the process.

■ Open windows across from each other or windows that can "see" each other. Windows opened opposite each other are three times more effective in creating a cross breeze.

■ Make sure trees and shrubs are trimmed so they do not block ventilation.

Saving Energy and Money   Save energy and money when heating and cooling by installing a setback thermostat with different set points for two or more periods, day and night. They're inexpensive and easy to install (requiring only a screwdriver). They range in complexity from a simple mechanical thermostat with a quartz clock and two daily set points, to an electronic thermostat with digital timing, many set points (for weekends and vacations), and override ability. Another way to save money is to be sure to close off rooms that are not needed during the heating or cooling seasons, and seal all potential air leakage areas in your house.

Be leery of filmlike materials that adhere to glass windows. Touted to reduce the sun's rays, these enable a house interior to stay cool in summer and warm in winter. While this material gives off no odor when cold, it has been found to emit a highly toxic and dangerous odorous gas when hot. It can produce violent headaches, ear pressure, and other severe reactions in chemically sensitive people.

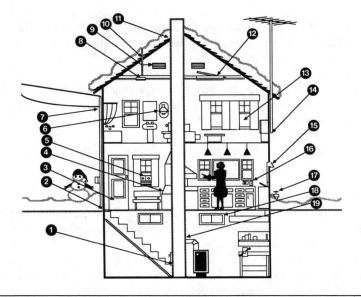

Don't let your expensively heated air fly out the window. Here's how to seal heat leaks.

1. Fireplace cleanout door: Seal around frame with furnace cement.

2. Sill plate: Push oversized piece of unfaced fiberglass insulation against inside of plate from basement and caulk it.

3. Outside door: Caulk, weather-strip, and install flexible threshold.

4. Fireplace: Stuff insulation into gap where fireplace meets wall and caulk it.

5. Room air conditioner: Caulk perimeter of in-wall unit; for a window unit, tape perimeter with duct tape.

6. Wall-mounted fixture: Turn off electricity, remove fixture, stuff gaps with unfaced fiberglass insulation, and reinstall fixture.

7. Electricity service cable: Stuff entry hole with unfaced fiberglass insulation, working from the inside, if possible; caulk it.

8. Recessed light fixture: Build box around appliance that projects above ceiling; insulate up to and over box.

9. Duct: In unheated areas, seal joints with caulk or duct tape; wrap ducts with foil-faced fiberglass insulation.

10. Plumbing vent: Place unfaced fiberglass insulation where vent passes through attic floor and roof.

11. Chimney: Place unfaced fiberglass insulation where chimney passes through attic floor and roof.

12. Attic door: Caulk, weather-strip, and install flexible threshold; treat this like an outside door.

13. Window: Caulk, use duct tape, and weather-strip.

14. TV antenna or cable entrance: Caulk.

15. Clothes dryer vent: Make sure damper is closed.

16. Electrical outlet and switch: Remove plate, install gasket, and replace plate.

17. Outside faucet: Seal with insulation and caulk.

18. Basement window: Caulk.

19. Furnace flue: If crack between flue and chimney is wide enough, stuff with unfaced fiberglass insulation; if not, seal with furnace cement.

CLIMATE   Temperature, humidity, and air quality make up the climate of a house. Each must be in proper balance to have a healthy system—both for the occupants and for the structure itself.

Temperature   It's easy to get used to overheating (or overcooling), making yourself vulnerable to colds and sore throats. In most cases, it's better to wrap up more warmly in winter and live in an environment with a lower background heat. Similarly, in summer it's best to get used to summer's temperatures, relieving them with fans and shade rather than artificial air conditioning. Generally speaking, optimum indoor temperature is 65° to 68°F.

Humidity   From a health standpoint, the optimum level of indoor relative humidity lies between 40 and 50 percent. It should not fall short of 30 percent and not go beyond 70 percent. This isn't easy to do. Hot, muggy climates have extreme humidity in summer, and cold, dry climates experience too little humidity in winter. A combination of forced-air heating systems and little ventilation can drop humidity levels to as low as 15 percent. Unless you live in an area blessed with constant 50 percent humidity, some moisture will usually have to be added or removed to maintain optimal indoor humidity.

How do you figure how much humidity you need? Take a look at this hypothetical example. Consider a 1,500-square-foot house with an air infiltration rate of about 6,000 cubic feet per hour (one-half air change per hour—a reasonable estimate). Let's assume that the outdoor air is at 30°F with 70 percent relative humidity. If you want the indoor air to be 68°F with 40 percent relative humidity, you'll have to add about 4 gallons of moisture per day. According to engineering statistics, the average family of four generates about 3 gallons of moisture per day through cooking, showering, and so on. So the net requirement from a humidifier would be about 1 gallon per day.

When shopping for a humidifier, get the ultrasonic, not the cool-mist, kind. It doesn't breed bacteria as readily. Though ultrasonic humidifiers are better than the cool-mist type, they may pose a risk if they're run with hard water. Minerals in the water form air-borne dust particles, small enough to be inhaled, as the mist emitted by the humidifier evaporates. EPA scientists have also expressed concern about using water containing lead, asbestos, and radon in humidifiers. If you have minerals in your water, you can buy a demineralization filter to remove unwanted particles. But no matter what kind you buy, make sure water doesn't sit in it for long and that it is cleaned daily with a cup of bleach per gallon of water. Then rinse the tank thoroughly with plain water before refilling.

Also, make sure the humidifier you select is the capacity you need. Most central humidifiers, which attach to the supply plenum of forced air systems, are more than adequate for the average house. Even the smallest units are capable of supplying up to a gallon of water per hour. Portable units vary considerably.

Anyone who is allergic to molds should not use a cool-mist or ultrasonic humidifier. Experts say that placing a clean pan of fresh water on a radiator or next to a forced-air heating register every day is the safest way to add moisture to indoor air.

Condensation Cures   New houses, and houses that have been tightened up to conserve energy, are the worst for harboring excess humidity. Vapor barriers, storm windows, weather stripping, and caulking all work to keep moisture inside. What can you do to remedy the problem?

The simplest way to prevent condensation problems is to keep the air inside your home at or below 40 percent relative humidity. Humidity meters are available at hardware and home center stores for under $10.

If the air is too moist, you can examine your family's habits to find out where the extra moisture is coming from and then remedy the situation. Running an exhaust fan or cracking open a window while bathing, cooking with pot lids on, and venting the clothes dryer outside are all small changes you can make to cut down on excess indoor moisture.

Uncovered crawl spaces may be the biggest source of excess moisture. Covering yours with 6-mil polyethylene, lapped at least 6 inches at the seams and along the walls, will prevent the moisture from wicking up into the house.

Another solution is to prevent the moisture that does get in the air from entering wall cavities. Plugging cracks, holes, and other openings in your interior walls helps cut down on the amount of air—and, therefore, moisture—passing into the wall. Painting inside walls with a vapor barrier paint also helps.

Get practical help with moisture, mildew, and condensation problems from the Conservation and Renewable Energy Inquiry and Referral Service, Box 8900, Silver Spring, MD 20907; 1-800-523-2929. Ask for their booklets on moisture control.

Clean Air   Ventilating alone may not get your house air clean enough. Fortunately, there are mechanical air cleaners on the market that help clear indoor air of pollutants, especially allergens such as pollen, dust, smoke, and animal fur. Although the models designed to sit on a desk or table are too small to be very useful, the larger units can remove as much as 75 percent of the particles floating in a 120-square-foot room in just half an hour. These units range in price from $100 to $450.

The basic component in nearly any air cleaner is a fan that draws in room air and propels it through one or more built-in cleaning mechanisms. These mechanisms may include a prefilter, an electrostatic precipitator (or a high-efficiency particulate filter), a negative-ion generator, and an activated-carbon filter.

A typical prefilter is simply a thin piece of foam that catches large airborne particles, such as lint, hair, dust, and even pollen. Like the prefilters in many vacuum cleaners, these swatches of foam are quickly soiled but easily cleaned.

Electrostatic precipitators (ESPs) have been used for decades in coal-fired power plants to capture fine ash particles from smokestack gases. Home air cleaners employ the same principle: An array of wire electrodes give incoming airborne particles a positive electrical charge. Downstream, negatively charged metal plates attract the particles, which cling to the plates. ESPs can be highly effective in removing particulates from the processed air, and they are easy to wash.

Air cleaners not equipped with ESPs typically use a high-efficiency particulate air (HEPA) filter instead. As room air passes through the HEPA filter, it captures small airborne particles in a dense web of fiberglass material.

Negative-ion generators—once hailed as cure-alls, then banned from the market as quackery—have made a comeback in home air cleaners. Many people claim using an ionizer makes them sleep well and feel better. Negative-ion generators counter the positive ions produced by air conditioning, central heating, tobacco smoke, and electrical equipment. An excess of positive ions—which occurs naturally in prestorm weather or with certain winds—may produce feelings of lethargy and depression, headaches, and respiratory problems.

Many newer air cleaners also contain filters filled with activated carbon to adsorb gaseous pollutants. Tests by *Rodale's Practical Homeowner* magazine showed that activated-carbon filters do remove such harmful gases as formaldehyde and nitrogen dioxide to varying degrees.

Of course, the cheapest, most natural air cleaners are houseplants. Many of them soak up air pollutants. (The spider plant is particularly effective.)

THE YARD

The plot of land on which your house sits is an integral part of the total home environment, as important in its own way as the electrical, plumbing, or any other building system. A healthy yard is free of debris. It has trees and shrubs, a grassy place where children can play, an outdoor living area for adults, a storage shed for paints and equipment, and a sunny spot for a garden.

Lawn Care

A healthy house does not use synthetic chemicals on the lawn. (Recent studies link the herbicide 2,4-D—perhaps the most ubiquitous chemical in lawn care products—to cancer.) Instead, natural methods are used.

There's no law that says your lawn has to be emerald green and weed free. If you're happy with it, that's all that counts. The most important step to a healthy lawn is to determine and respond to the nutritional needs of plants in your particular soil type. Soil tests done every few years will indicate nutrient and mineral deficiencies of nitrogen, phosphorus, and potash, to name a few. These tests can be performed by the cooperative extension service for a nominal fee. Once recognized, inadequate levels of nutrients can be supplemented by the correct mix of organic fertilizers.

Growing Your Own Food

Pesticides contaminating common American foods may be responsible for as many as *20,000 additional cancer cases a year,* according to a 1987 report by the U.S. National Academy of Sciences. That's as many cancer cases as is estimated to be caused by radon! Fifteen foods treated by a handful of pesticides pose the greatest risk of cancer. They are apples, beans, beef, carrots, chicken, corn, grapes, lettuce, tomatoes, oranges, peaches, pork, potatoes, soybeans, and wheat.

A good way to reduce your exposure to pesticide residues is to grow your own food. Even here, there are some things you may want to do to ensure that exposure is limited. Before converting land in an urban or suburban area to gardening, find out how the land was used previously. Choose a site that had limited (or no) chemical applications and where drift or runoff from your neighbor's activities will not result in unintended pesticide residues on your produce.

Generally, you'll need one-tenth of an acre for a family of four. If you don't have this much room, consider renting space in a community plot.

If you are taking over an existing garden plot, be aware that the soil may contain pesticide residues from previous gardening activities. These residues may remain in the soil for several years, depending on the persistence of the pesticides that were used. Rather than waiting for the residues to decline naturally over time, you may speed the process.

Plant an interim, nonfood crop like annual rye grass, clover, or alfalfa. Such crops, with their dense, fibrous root systems, will take up some of the lingering pesticide residues. Then discard the crops—don't work them back into the soil—and continue to alternate food crops with cover crops in the off season. During sunny periods, turn over the soil as often as every 2 to 3 days for a week or two. The sunlight will break down, or photodegrade, some of the pesticide residues.

Once you begin gardening, develop strategies that will reduce your need for pesticides while maintaining good crop yields:

- Concentrate on building your garden's soil, since healthy soil grows healthy plants. Feed the soil with compost, manure, and so on, to increase its capacity to support strong crops.
- Select seeds and seedlings from hardy, disease-resistant varieties. The resulting plants are less likely to need pesticides to flourish.
- Avoid monoculture gardening techniques. Instead, alternate rows of different kinds of plants to prevent significant pest problems from developing.
- Rotate your crops yearly to reduce plant susceptibility to overwintered pests.
- Become familiar with integrated pest management techniques so you can manage any pest outbreaks that occur without relying solely on pesticides.
- Mulch your garden with leaves, hay, grass clippings, shredded or chipped bark, or seaweed. Avoid sewage sludge to fertilize plants—it

may contain heavy metals and pesticides, both of which can leach into your soil. Newspapers make good mulch. Newsprint no longer contains the heavy metals it used to.

TEST SOIL FOR LEAD   Lead is a concern in garden soil. It's a good idea to have your garden soil tested for lead levels. You may be gardening in a high-risk area if any or all of the following conditions exist:

- Your house was built or painted before 1950, when leaded paint was used. Old lead paint continues to contaminate, even when painted over with lead-free paint (weathered chips fall into the soil or are scraped off before repainting).
- Your garden is near a major road, highway, overpass, or bridge.
- You live near a battery factory or metal smelter.
- You live near a large airport.
- There was once a building where your garden is.
- Your garden plot was once littered with garbage.
- A neighbor has lead-contaminated soil.
- Neighbors or family members have high levels of lead in their blood.
- There has been a local accident in which lead-containing substances were spilled.

Even if none of these conditions are true, your garden could still contain lead. A discarded window or door with lead paint or an old rat poison container can cause a lead hot spot in the garden. Also, the use of lead arsenate, a common pesticide for fruit trees, may have caused extensive and continuing contamination. The only way to really know how much lead is in your garden is to have the soil tested.

If you have high lead levels, the best thing to do is to bring in clean soil. Have the new soil tested first to make sure it is lead free. Be careful not to mix the new soil with the old. Fill your garden to a depth of 8 inches or more with new soil to ensure that the roots of vegetables will not reach the contaminated soil below.

GARDEN ORGANICALLY   If garden bugs are bothersome, consider battling them with natural insecticides derived from plants. A few of the most popular ones are pyrethrin, rotenone, ryania, sabadilla, and quassia. The latter may be the safest of all botanical insecticides. It is effective against soft-bodied pests, such as aphids and caterpillars, but does not harm bees, ladybugs, or other beneficial insects.

Aphids, mealybugs, scale, earwigs, rose slugs, white flies, and other insect pests can be controlled with a mild soap solution. Milky spore, a natural bacteria available in powdered form, will halt grub infestations. Weeds can, of course, be pulled by hand. And you can feed the grass yourself with a nonchemical fertilizer such as Lawn Restore (available at garden centers).

A HEALTHY HOME INSPECTION

Following is a checklist* to guide you in inspecting the structural and technical aspects of your house. This checklist is organized according to major elements of a house structure and its systems. Since houses vary with age, style, and geographical location, it is not feasible to cover all possible conditions. You may discover items that do not appear on the checklist. Add them to the list. Some items may not apply to your house. Ignore them. The important thing is to be as thorough as possible in your inspection.

For additional help with this inspection, consult your local agencies. The building department may offer assistance in checking for compliance with health and safety requirements of the building code. The fire department can inspect for fire hazards and suggest improvements for fire prevention and safety. Your public utility company may provide useful information on the maintenance of appliances and energy conservation. Be sure to understand, before you arrange for an inspection by a local governmental agency, whether the inspection results are advisory or whether you must correct all items found to be deficient within a limited amount of time.

Architects, engineers, and home inspection consultants also conduct inspections for a fee. Professional assistance is recommended when there are questions about structural problems for which the cause cannot be determined.

After completing the inspection, note the problem areas and list the repair and maintenance work the house needs. Organize the list according to the severity of the problem. Before repairing cosmetic defects, you should take care of the following:

1. Deficiencies and conditions that endanger the structure of your house, such as a leaking roof, decaying structural supports, or termite infestation
2. Fire hazards, such as faulty electrical wiring, worn insulation, or overloaded circuits
3. Hazardous conditions that can cause accidents, such as loose floor boards, weak railings, or decaying stair treads

Care should be taken to solve the cause of a problem and not simply treat the symptom. A crack can be patched, but it will reappear if the crack is caused by the settling of a foundation because of poor drainage around the house.

The solutions to most structural and mechanical problems are obvious. A structual post may have to be replaced. Additional electrical circuits may be required. A furnace may need to be serviced or replaced. Although you may be able to do some of this work yourself, you may need professional assistance to comply with building code requirements and deal with technical details.

*Adapted from *Home Renovation* by Francis D. K. Ching and Dale E. Miller, with permission. Copyright © 1983 by Van Nostrand Reinhold Company, Inc.

GENERAL OVERVIEW   Stand back and take a look at the exterior of your house:

- ☐ Are there signs of settling?
- ☐ Is the house level on its foundation?
- ☐ Does the roof ridge appear to sag?
- ☐ Does the chimney lean or tilt?
- ☐ Are there obvious signs of decay?
- ☐ Does groundwater collect around the foundation after a rain?
- ☐ Is the yard free of trash and overgrowth, particularly around the foundation?

EXTERIOR FOUNDATION AND BASEMENT WALLS   An unstable foundation is a severe problem for which professional help is needed:

- ☐ Is the foundation wall cracked? Small, hairline cracks may be okay. Large, open cracks may get worse. Active cracks can be determined only by observation over several months.
- ☐ Does the foundation tilt or lean?
- ☐ Does any masonry have loose or crumbling mortar?
- ☐ Is there proper drainage? Is ground sloped away from the foundation? Do downspouts channel water away from the house, to a dry well or drain well?
- ☐ Do basement window wells collect water? (Also see "Basements and Crawl Spaces" on page 169.)

EXTERIOR WALLS   Most problems are caused by moisture or insect damage:

- ☐ Is wood siding or trim warped or swollen?
- ☐ Are there any open joints in the siding?
- ☐ Is aluminum siding warped or dented?
- ☐ Are there signs of decay under windowsills?
- ☐ Are there signs of insect damage along the lower edge of the siding?
- ☐ Is any paint chipped, peeling, or blistered?
- ☐ Does masonry have cracks or loose mortar?

ROOFS   Roofs can be checked when dry, preferably within a day or two after a rain:

- ☐ Are there signs of wear indicating a need for replacement?
- ☐ Are composition shingles curled or losing their surface granules?
- ☐ Are wood shingles ragged, rotting, or broken?
- ☐ Is built-up roofing blistered, brittle, or soft in spots?
- ☐ Are joints around chimneys, dormers, or plumbing vents or along valleys cracked? Are there signs of leaking?
- ☐ Is roof flashing rusty, decayed, or loose fitting?
- ☐ Is the roof structure sound? Does it feel springy or spongy when walked on?

☐ Are soffit boards loose?
☐ Are there adequate vents along eave, ridge, and gable ends?
☐ Are gutters loose, corroded, or sagging?
☐ Are gutters clean and free of debris?
☐ Do gutters slope properly to downspouts? (Also see "Attics" on page 171.)

EXTERIOR DOORS   Doors should operate smoothly and be weathertight and secure:

☐ Are doors warped? Can you see daylight around or under them when closed?
☐ Are doors weather-stripped? Are joints around door frames caulked?
☐ Are any thresholds worn, weathered, or decayed?
☐ Is hardware secure and operating well?
☐ Do doors have deadbolt locksets for security?

WINDOWS   Windows should be weathertight:

☐ Are windows drafty when closed? Are they weather-stripped?
☐ Is caulking around window frames cracked?
☐ Does the glass fit securely in the sashes?
☐ Are there gaps in the glazing putty? Is the putty brittle?
☐ Are wood frames decayed?
☐ Do windows have security locks?
☐ Is at least one window in each bedroom operable and large enough to serve as an emergency fire exit?

PORCHES   Porches are exposed to weather and vulnerable to decay and insect damage:

☐ Is the porch pulling away from the house? Are stairs and railings secure?
☐ Do wood members and supports show signs of decay? Wood should not be in contact with the ground.
☐ Is there a porch light for safety?
☐ There should be no creosote-treated or pressure-treated wood in porches or decks.

BASEMENTS AND CRAWL SPACES   Basements are good areas to check for settlement cracks, groundwater leakage, the condition of floor joists, and problems with the mechanical and electrical systems:

☐ Are there signs of settling? Are there large, open, unaligned cracks in walls?
☐ Do basement walls bow inward?
☐ Do basement walls have damp spots or show scaling?
☐ Is any untreated wood in direct contact with soil?

☐ Has concrete been poured around untreated wood?
☐ Are there signs of decay or insect damage on wood posts, sill plates, beams, or joists?
☐ Is the crawl space well ventilated? Does it have an effective soil vapor barrier?

INTERIOR ROOMS   Interior surfaces deteriorate due to wear, structural distortion, and the presence of moisture:

☐ Are there signs of settling? Are there cracks in walls or ceilings? Cracks that increase in size or number may indicate settling in the house structure.
☐ Do floors feel springy or appear wavy or tilted? A marble placed on a floor will help indicate a sloping floor surface.
☐ Are concrete slabs badly cracked?
☐ Are there signs of moisture? Do walls or ceilings bulge or have water stains, especially below bathrooms or along exterior walls?
☐ Do hard-surface floors feel spongy?

KITCHENS   Check for watertightness around the sink and for fire safety:

☐ Are joints along the countertop and splashboard buckled or separated?
☐ Is sealer around the sink loose or cracked?
☐ Is the exhaust fan and filter clean and free of grease?
☐ Is a BC fire extinguisher handy in case of grease, flammable liquid, or electrical fires? (Also see "Plumbing Systems" on page 172.)

BATHROOMS   Check for water leaks, dampness, and mildew:

☐ Are there open joints in wall coverings or along the floor where water can seep through?
☐ Is caulking loose or missing around the tub, shower, or sink?
☐ Is any ceramic tile cracked or broken? Is any grout loose or crumbling?
☐ Is the bathroom adequately ventilated? (Also see "Electrical Systems" and "Plumbing Systems" on page 171 and page 172.)

STAIRWAYS   Stairs should be structurally sound and safe to traverse:

☐ Do stairs, railings, and supports feel sturdy?
☐ Does the framing around the stair opening show evidence of sagging?
☐ Do wood members show signs of decay?
☐ Are stairways safe? Are they too steep or narrow?
☐ Is there adequate headroom and clearance?
☐ Are there sturdy handrail supports?

☐ Is there a light and light switch at both the top and bottom of the stairs?
☐ Are there smoke detectors properly located at the top of the stairs leading to bedrooms?

FIREPLACES Check for proper operation, condition of masonry, and fire safety:

☐ Does the fireplace draw properly? The chimney should draw smoke from a lit newspaper at least within a minute.
☐ Is there a damper? Does it close tightly?
☐ Is any masonry cracked or loose? Is any mortar crumbling or missing?
☐ Is the flue lined? Is there a heavy coat of soot or creosote in the flue?
☐ Does the chimney have a rain cap?

ATTICS The attic is a good place to check for roof leakage and weakening of the roof structure:

☐ Are any rafters or sheathing sagging or loose?
☐ Are there signs of moisture leaking around the chimney, plumbing vents, skylights or along walls and valleys?
☐ Are there signs of dampness along the eave line or in the insulation?
☐ Is the attic space properly ventilated?
☐ Is there sufficient thermal insulation?

ELECTRICAL SYSTEMS Is the electrical system wired to meet your demands? Are there any safety hazards:

☐ Is the main electrical service panel large enough to handle house loads? A 100-amp minimum service is recommended for a three-bedroom house; a 200-amp service if there is electric heat.
☐ Are any circuits overloaded? Do any fuses blow or circuit breakers trip regularly? Do any lights dim or flicker when an appliance is turned on?
☐ Are there enough outlets in each room? Are they conveniently located? Rooms should have at least one outlet on each wall.
☐ The bathroom outlet should be protected by a ground-fault circuit interrupter (GFCI).
☐ Is any insulation on wiring, cords, or plugs worn, cracked, brittle, or split?
☐ Do all switches and outlets have protective plates?
☐ Are extension cords for appliances rated heavy duty?
☐ Are any extension cords used unsafely; for example, are they run under carpets or punctured by tacks?
☐ Is the electrical system properly grounded?

PLUMBING SYSTEMS   Check for leaks and for proper flow and drainage:

☐ Are there any signs of leaking? Are there signs of rust or crusting along pipes and fittings?

☐ Do any faucets leak?

☐ Do drains empty rapidly without bubbling?

☐ Is water flow adequate? Can two or three fixtures be turned on without noticeable loss of flow?

☐ Is there a hammering sound (called water hammer) when a faucet is turned on and off rapidly?

☐ Does the hot-water heater operate properly? Is the temperature setting too high? A setting of 120°F is usually sufficient (140°F if you have a dishwasher). Noise in hot-water pipes when the hot-water tap is turned on may indicate that the setting is too high.

☐ Is there sediment at the bottom of the hot-water tank?

☐ Is there a pressure relief valve installed on the hot-water tank?

☐ Do all fixtures have individual shut-off valves and functioning traps?

HEATING SYSTEMS   Check for safety and efficiency:

☐ Has the heating system's fuel or energy consumption increased over the last several years?

☐ Can you smell fumes from the furnace?

☐ Is heat distributed evenly through the house?

☐ Is the thermostat centrally located out of the way of drafts?

☐ Do supply register dampers operate properly?

☐ Are there dust coatings in the filters, air duct system, or outlets?

☐ Are flammable materials stored close to the furnace?

Prescription: A Healthy Home Has . . .

. . . a safe structure inside and out and healthy home systems, including the following:

- The floor plan is open, with lots of windows. The open plan lends itself to quick airing out of food odors, outgassing from new building materials, or any other episodic pollutants.
- Floors are sheathed in pine, and kiln-dried yellow pine is used for framing.
- Roofing materials should be slate, tile, or metal.
- Walls are as nontoxic as possible. Walls are especially critical surfaces due to the sheer area involved. The simplest and cleanest are bare plaster, perhaps covered with old-fashioned milk paint. Gypsum board (drywall or Sheetrock), the most commonly used interior wall and ceiling, is economical and convenient but not necessarily the best material from an ecological standpoint. Adhesives and joint compounds can outgas irritating fumes.
- Floors are covered with natural wood or unglazed ceramic tile. Parquet flooring is suspect because manufacturers frequently use a urea-formaldehyde resin to bond the many wood pieces to the tiles. No panel adhesives, carpet adhesives, or tile mastics should be used. The same goes for carpets, vinyl tile, and sheet flooring.
- Decay-resistant cedar or redwood is used in place of pressure-treated lumber in a porch or deck.
- The foundation is tightly sealed, both against radon gas penetration and against the moisture that can spawn mold, mildew, and fungus and can elevate formaldehyde levels.
- No common insulation materials are used. Rigid foam panels contain a variety of chemicals, some of which can be highly toxic when burned, and fiberglass and cellulose shed particles or fibers, that can be particularly hazardous to installers. Chemicals in the ink of shredded newsprint make cellulose insulation bothersome to some chemically sensitive people. Instead, a natural material should be used, such as plain, old-fashioned cork (which has an R-value of 4 per inch of thickness) or Air Krete, a foam insulation that is minerally based.

9

Light and Health

Interior lighting is an inexact science fraught with options and possibilities. When done well, it turns night into day for us, creates a positive mood, brightens our household tasks, and increases our sense of security. When done poorly, it can increase fatigue, ruin our mood, decrease performance, and bring on headache and eyestrain.

Light has a powerful effect on the human body. It influences every aspect of being—mind, body, emotions, and spirit. Richard J. Wurtman, professor of endocrinology at the Massachusetts Institute of Technology (MIT), goes so far as to say, "Light is *the most important environmental input* after food in controlling body function." Dr. Wurtman should know. He has been studying the effects of light on health for the past 20 years and is considered to be a leading expert in the field.

But what about artificial light? Is it as beneficial as daylight? Scientists in the field of photobiology say no, artificial light is not as healthy. In fact, in some cases it can even make you sick. As with everything pertaining to health, the more *natural* light is, the healthier it is.

WHAT IS LIGHT?

Natural and artificial light are very different forms of energy. Natural sunlight contains the full spectrum of electromagnetic wavelengths, complete with radio waves, microwaves, gamma and X rays, and visible light. Visible light is only a tiny part of that spectrum. It casts a rainbow of colors, from violet through blue, green, yellow, and orange to red. Beyond what our eyes see, sunlight carries the longer infrared wavelengths, as well as the shorter ultraviolet waves.

In short, sunlight provides the total electromagnetic spectrum of wavelengths in which all life has evolved on this planet. What's more, it contains them in a specific mixture—so much of this, so much of that.

Artificial light lacks many segments of the natural range, and it delivers an entirely different mix of spectral ingredients. Incandescent bulbs, for example, provide light primarily from the red part of the spectrum while minimizing or leaving out others. Cool-white fluorescent lamps, found in offices, factories, and schools, emphasize the yellow-green portion. Neither is a good source of ultraviolet or infrared wavelengths found in natural daylight. Artificial light is quite literally *not* the same as natural light.

We can even see the difference. Ever notice that the blue sweater you bought in a store is a different shade outdoors? That difference is the result of partial-spectrum artificial lighting influencing your visual clarity. Yet artificial lighting influences more than vision. Researchers are discovering it can effect subtle changes in living cells, as well.

Photobiology and John Ott

In the 1940s, a banker named John Ott traded in his pinstripes to do time-lapse photography of plant growth for Walt Disney films. While photographing the growth of pumpkins, Ott discovered that his photographic lights influenced plant reproduction. Female blossoms on pumpkin vines quickly shriveled up and died. When he changed lights, the male blossoms shriveled up and died.

This intrigued Ott. He began to change the lights deliberately to see what would happen. Then he undertook microscopic photography so he could see the changes occurring in the plant's cells. What he discovered was this: *Artificial lighting drastically alters the natural activity of cells.*

Ott eventually gave up photography to concentrate full time on the physical effects of light. Through experiments with plants and animals, he made many important discoveries, but because he is self-educated in the sciences (Ott has an honorary doctorate), some professional scientists doubt Ott's theories and many question his most recent findings. Nonetheless, Ott's experiments mark the beginning of the modern science of photobiology—the study of how light interacts with life. Its principal tenet, one many scientists now endorse, is that light, like food and water, is vital to a healthy existence. As with food and water, insufficient light—or the wrong kind—causes ill effects.

Since Ott's pioneering discoveries, scientific researchers have been studying the effects of light on humans. Though in its infancy, this research is already yielding insightful results:

- A host of 20th-century ailments can be directly attributed to artificial lighting—ailments such as fatigue, depression, decreased performance, diminished immunity, reduced physical fitness, and possibly impaired fertility.
- Exposure to artificial light, without a healthy balance of daylight, has been associated with hyperactivity, as well as changes in heart rate, blood pressure, electrical brain-wave patterns, hormonal secretions, and the body's natural cyclical rhythms.
- It's clear that many people suffering from periodic mental depression are unusually sensitive to light.

■ Early research with elderly people in nursing homes unearthed a hidden epidemic of vitamin D deficiency among people who don't get outdoors regularly. These studies found that indoor light, with its lack of ultraviolet radiation, significantly impairs the intestine's ability to absorb calcium, no matter what diet a patient is on. This results in tooth and bone loss and, if a fall should occur, bone fracture and crippling.

■ Fluorescent lights may be particularly harmful. Studies by the Food and Drug Administration (FDA) confirm that ultraviolet radiation from fluorescent lamps can increase the risk of nonmalignant skin cancer in certain people. Other researchers have tentatively linked malignant melanoma, a rare and dangerous form of skin cancer, to fluorescent lights. The flicker of fluorescent lamps is another problem. Though barely noticeable to the human eye, this flicker (at 60 times a second) is still perceived subconsciously and is suspected of sometimes contributing to irritation and headaches, eye strain and fatigue, and may even be a factor in triggering seizures in epileptics.

■ Newer lights, like the high-pressure sodium-vapor type (which are great energy savers but are spectrally limited), can cause eyestrain, headaches, nausea, and irritability. "These high-intensity lights put out a significant amount of ultraviolet radiation, especially if the globe is cracked or broken," says Morris Waxler, a research psychologist with the FDA's Center for Devices in Radiological Health. "If not fixed right away, hazardous levels of ultraviolet light can escape and poison the environment."

Without a doubt, certain biological responses in plants, animals, and humans are directly linked to specific wavelengths of light.

Natural Light

Sunlight is responsible for manufacturing vitamin D in the skin and for aiding absorption of calcium, which is vital for healthy nerves, bones, and teeth. Natural light is also responsible for boosting the body's resistance to respiratory diseases, as well as for synchronizing our biological clocks, telling us when to sleep and when to rise. These effects of natural light on human beings have been known for some time.

Scientists have recently made an exciting *new* discovery, however, that shows just how important light is for human health. This discovery links light with the very basis of physiological existence—activity of the endocrine system, which produces hormones. Here's how the physiological process works: Light enters the eye and hits the retina, triggering a message that passes along a nerve pathway to the pituitary and pineal glands buried deep in the brain. These glands control the production of hormones, thus influencing sexuality, fertility, and growth, as well as the whole range of human emotions.

The discovery that light influences hormone production is a tremendous breakthrough. Scientists have already discovered links between hormone levels and alcoholism, drug dependency, and certain mental disorders. Behavior, too, is strongly influenced by hormones.

This effect may well turn out to be the animal kingdom's equivalent of plant photosynthesis. Clearly, light is some kind of cellular food for both plants and animals. Whereas the cells of plants are influenced directly by light, humans are influenced in a more indirect manner—they take light in through their eyes, then it's passed into every cell of their bodies.

Malillumination and Light Stress

Until Thomas Edison invented the light bulb a century ago, people spent a lot more time working outdoors and, in the bargain, received large daily doses of natural, full-spectrum light. This regulated the body's internal clock, which regulates the cycles of rising and falling body temperatures, variations in body chemistry, and other natural changes that occur approximately once every 24 hours.

Nowadays, though, the average person spends from 75 to 90 percent of the day *indoors*, cut off from natural light. Ordinary room lighting is five to ten times dimmer than window light and much less intense than outdoor light, even in the shade. The smaller range of wavelengths found inside artificially lighted houses, offices, factories, schools, and shopping malls causes biochemical changes in the human body.

What's more, many of these buildings are built with tinted windows, cutting us off even further from the benefits of full-spectrum light. We often intentionally limit the quality of natural light we receive when we're outdoors by putting on sunglasses, applying suntan lotion, or driving in cars with tinted windshields. These block certain parts of the natural spectrum of light from entering our bodies.

As a result, people who spend most of their days indoors experience what John Ott calls *malillumination*, a condition similar to malnutrition. In his book *Light, Radiation, and You* (Devin-Adair, 1985), Ott expresses the belief that most artificial light lacks essential wavelengths in the same way that refined flour lacks certain vitamins and minerals. He claims that certain cells in the body can't function without those parts of the spectrum and that most indoor lighting promotes illness. Ott suspects malillumination causes disorders ranging from lack of vitality to lowered resistance to disease, and hyperactivity. He believes it can also lead to aggressive behavior, heart disease, and cancer.

In addition to malillumination, we often experience *light stress*, a condition similar to physical stress, as a result of artificially lighted environments. You experience light stress when, for example, you suddenly face an electric light switched on at 2:00A.M. In such a case the circadian rhythms of your body, conditioned by genetic wisdom to respond to sunrise and sunset, become desynchronized. In extreme situations, when this happens night after night, it can lead to depression as well as other physical and mental disorders.

MIT's Dr. Wurtman believes that wavelengths of light are like vitamins. He has maintained for years that most of us do not receive enough of the right kind of light for optimal health. Wurtman believes we are all unwitting subjects of a long-term experiment on the effects of artificial lighting on health. "This casual attitude

The Winter Blahs

Have you ever noticed how "blah" you feel after spending the entire day inside? That feeling isn't just psychological. It has its roots in the physiology of the human body.

That blah feeling is directly linked to melatonin, a powerful hormone that's released at night to induce sleep and modify other hormone secretions. Exposure to a bright light turns off production of melatonin during the day, so we have more energy and don't feel sleepy. Although artificial light can turn off the production of melatonin in animals, human beings need a much brighter light than that typically found in homes, offices, and schools.

Melatonin has been directly linked to seasonal affective disorder (SAD), a winter depression that begins in some people as soon as daylight savings time ends in the fall. It's believed that, with shorter days, many people do not get the bright light they need to shut off the production of melatonin. That makes them sleepy and sluggish all the time. Indeed, symptoms of SAD include oversleeping, overeating, a general slowing down of the body, and an inability to function normally. In some cases, this mild funk turns into a serious mental illness. Some people become almost incapacitated by it. They stop cooking meals, don't see their friends, and they may even become suicidal.

Though the best light for suppressing melatonin is daylight (the fresh light of morning does the trick quite nicely), artificial light can also turn off melatonin production if it's of significant brightness and duration. In studies conducted at the National Institute of Mental Health, 2 hours of bright artificial light at midday or 4 hours of natural evening light were as effective as 2 hours of natural morning light. These and other studies suggest that bright light may temporarily correct an as-yet-unidentified chemical imbalance in the brains of people with SAD.

So the next time you feel that familiar blah feeling, get outside and take a walk. Even sitting on the porch will do. Or you can sit inside in daylight coming through an open window. It doesn't matter if you're in the shade, as long as you're in light produced by the sun.

must change," he writes in *Scientific American* (July 1975). "Light is potentially too useful an agency of human health not to be more effectively examined and exploited."

Ultraviolet Light

Most artificial environments today expose people to unbalanced light sources, particularly unbalanced wavelengths of ultraviolet light. Incandescent light is almost completely lacking in ultraviolet wavelengths. The glass tubes of most fluorescent lighting fixtures absorb and screen out all but a narrow band of ultraviolet. Even window glass screens out 95 percent of ultraviolet light rays.

Ultraviolet, a much maligned and widely misunderstood form of light, is essential for good health. The fact that in large doses it causes sunburn, skin cancer, and maybe cataracts leads some people to believe it has no beneficial effects. Fact is, ultraviolet light—the full spectrum in small doses—is vital for a healthy human body. But it must be used judiciously. Too much ultraviolet, such as you get while sunbathing, can be damaging to the skin and eyes.

The full range of ultraviolet, as is found in sunlight, is vital to the functioning of a dozen different organs and glands. It's credited with lowering blood pressure and increasing brain activity. It reduces the incidence of colds and viral infections, improves physical fitness, increases work efficiency, and decreases fatigue.

But, like the full spectrum of visible light, you can't isolate part of the ultraviolet spectrum and screen out the rest for optimal health. In natural sunlight, it is the *interaction* of ultraviolet rays that produces beneficial biological changes in the human body. So, the real need in artificial lighting today centers on the full spectrum of light, including ultraviolet.

The Full-Spectrum Bulb

Clearly, the full spectrum of light is needed for good health. But evolution has brought us indoors, away from natural light. If we want to remain in good health while spending long periods of time in man-made environments, then man-made light sources will have to take nature's place and provide the radiant energy needed to sustain life.

Enter the full-spectrum light bulb. There are several currently on the market that claim to simulate the natural spectrum in both the ultraviolet and visible light ranges. Look for these at hardware stores, lighting centers, and natural food stores. (Also see appendix A.)

Most full-spectrum bulbs cost about $11 per bulb and fit into any standard fluorescent socket. At that price you may not want to furnish your whole house with full-spectrum bulbs, so try placing them in critical areas (like over your desk) to see if they improve the way you feel, especially in winter.

Although there has been some controversy surrounding the full-spectrum light bulb, many scientists recommend it. Among them is Dr. Wurtman, who firmly believes that the spectrum of indoor lighting should deviate as little as possible from the spectrum occurring outside.

DAYLIGHT

By far the healthiest light for people is natural sunlight. So it's important to use skylights and natural lighting through windows and glass doors whenever possible to allow the sun, rather than light bulbs, to light a healthy home. Daylight is more pleasing, more healthful, and *free*.

Like all things that fit into the natural plan, sunlight is extremely efficient—a double bonus for the homeowner. While energy emitted from an incandescent light bulb is roughly 90 percent heat and only about 10 percent light, energy from the sun is between 50 and 70 percent light.

But there are drawbacks to this free light. It's often accompanied by "hot spots" and more heat than you may want. Natural light also changes throughout the day, so you're not going to get a constant light in either color or penetration. These seeming disadvantages can easily be turned into advantages for you, the homeowner.

Sunlight versus Daylight

Sunlight and daylight are not the same thing. Sunlight is light direct from the sun that has not been scattered in the atmosphere. Because it contains infrared and ultraviolet light rays, sunlight can quickly cause overheating and rapid fading of fabrics unless precautions are taken.

Daylight, which includes both light from the sun and light from the sky, is much less drastic in its effects. Daylight is largely diffuse and is available for all windows, no matter what direction they face.

Studies show that most people prefer sunlight over daylight when given the choice. Why? Sunlight is valued for its warmth and therapeutic effects. It simply "makes you feel better." The negative aspects of sunlight—overheating and fading—can be easily overcome with ventilation and blinds.

Natural light is transient, changing colors and directions as the sun makes its daily trek across the sky. Seasons affect the journey of light, too. During the long, hot summer, for example, the sun rises in the northeast, arcs high in the sky, then sets again almost northwest. It's a different pathway in winter, when the sun stays much lower in the horizon. In winter the sun rises south-southeast and quickly sets south-southwest.

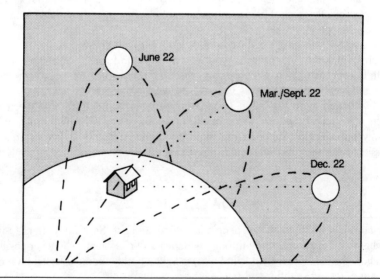

To make the most of the sunlight in your home, be aware of the seasonal path of the sun and how its light enters your windows at different times of the year.

You can use this geometry to stay more in tune with the natural rhythms of Earth. Pay attention this year to what window light does in your house. Watch how it penetrates deeply into a room during certain seasons and at different times of day. Experience its playfulness as well as its generosity. Analyze its color and character so you'll know how to use it.

COOL NORTH LIGHT   Daylight is characterized by the bluish, diffuse nature of north light. This is mostly indirect light reflected from the sky. Artists prefer it for its uniform, shadowless character. Skylights are excellent sources of daylight.

WARM SOUTH LIGHT   South light, more than light from any other direction, provides heat as well as illumination. At midday in winter, the sun shines with thermal intensity into south-facing windows. This south light is bright and direct, casting sharp interior shadows and maybe even causing glare.

Family gathering places—the family room, living room, playroom—are best located on the south side of the house where they can be warmed naturally by the sun and where people will be exposed to lots of natural sunlight coming through windows. The best use for south light is a passive solar space that helps heat your house in winter.

EAST LIGHT   Rooms on the east side of the house have direct light in the morning. Such light is cool in hue because much of its red wavelengths are absorbed into the moist morning atmosphere for warmth. It's best if your kitchen and breakfast room have east-facing windows; your bedroom, too. Greeting the fragile light of early morning is an inspiring way to begin the day if you're an early riser.

WEST LIGHT   Rooms on the west have direct light in late afternoon. This early evening light can be quite intense in both brightness and heat. Evening light has a warm pink, reddish, or orange hue—the exact color depends upon the density of the pollution in the atmosphere. Living rooms benefit from having a west-facing window to capture this warm light—it creates a relaxing atmosphere for winding down after a hard day. But be sure all west-facing windows have good, workable shades; otherwise, sunlight can cause overheating in summer.

Overcoming Daylighting Problems

Proper daylighting in a home is not an exact science. There's lots of latitude for getting the right light you need. But there are a few problems to conquer, including glare and overheating. In addition, there is a somewhat bewildering array of window glass available today.

GLAZING   In the name of energy efficiency, today's windows come in a parade of tints, each one proclaimed the best for a specific function. The only thing wrong with them is the spectrum of light they admit. As we have seen, the healthiest light contains the full spectrum of the sun. Tinted and low-emissivity glass block a wide range of that natural spectrum in the visible range, as well as in the infrared and ultraviolet light ranges. While ordinary window glass admits a fuller spectrum of visible light, it blocks as much as 95 percent of the ultraviolet range. We may be quite a few years from achieving the development of window glass that admits the full spectrum of the sun.

For now, the ideal situation is window glass that admits more ultraviolet light. At least one manufacturer is already marketing ultraviolet-transmitting (UVT) glass. It's expensive, though, and not readily available in all parts of the country. There is ultraviolet-transmitting plastic (Plexiglas and acrylic), too, that blocks only about 5 percent of the natural ultraviolet spectrum. These can be substituted for glass in windows and skylights, but they *may* pose another hazard—many plastics emit toxic fumes, especially when heated.

But Dr. Alfred V. Zamm, a clinical ecologist in Kingston, New York, says *soft* plastics emit toxic fumes when heated, *hard* plastics do not—and Plexiglas and acrylic windows are hard plastics.

FADING   Sunlight causes damage because it contains infrared and ultraviolet light rays in addition to visible light. Infrared light causes materials such as wood, rattan, and doré finishes to dehydrate, crack, and peel. Ultraviolet, at the other end of the light spectrum, causes fading.

Certain pigments are more apt to fade than others. Paint finishes, especially glossy ones, are not as susceptible as fabrics. Fiberglass, polyester, acrylic, and modacrylic are more resistant to fading than nylon, acetate, or rayon. Natural fibers—cotton, jute, sisal, wool, and silk—have poor resistance to damage caused by sunlight. A fabric is more fade-resistant when the fiber is thick, the weave is tight, the finish is shiny or bright, and the color is highly reflective. For all surfaces, the degree of fading is regulated by the kind and intensity of light and by the time of exposure.

OVERHEATING   Overheating can be easily remedied with proper ventilation. It's not difficult to place a small fan in a position so that it moves heat from one area to another, or to open windows to allow fresh breezes inside and stagnant house air out.

Window Layout

Windows bring light, air, and a view of the outdoors into a home. The best layout is for each room of the house to have windows on at least two sides. But all too often, windows don't perform as well as they could because the size, type, or placement of the windows is wrong for the room. When a room is too dark or too bright, or an inspiring view has been cramped by a window that's too small, it's time to rethink the window layout.

SIZE AND DIRECTION   The standard rule of thumb for sizing windows is that the window area of a room should equal one-tenth of the room's floor area. This standard overlooks the fact that the amount of light a window brings in varies, depending on the direction the window faces. Southern windows let in more light than north-facing windows, and they admit light for a longer period of time than windows facing any other direction. Windows facing east or west are about equal in the amount of light they provide.

PENETRATION OF LIGHT   Window shapes and configurations admit light in different ways:

Clerestories: These horizontal windows high in the wall reflect light off the ceiling and cast it deep into a room. Because the concentration of light is high in the room, the floor may seem dark by contrast.
Wide windows: In the middle of the wall, wide windows provide more even illumination.
Tall, narrow windows: These throw light equally on the ceiling and the floor, but the opposite wall is not uniformly brightened.
Windows on adjacent walls: In square rooms these give good penetration of daylight unless they are comparatively narrow and placed close to the corners of the room. They also reduce glare by lighting the area of wall surrounding the opposite window.
Bay windows: These fully illuminate the area of the bay, but not the rest of the room unless the bay is very high.
Large windows: Windows extending the full width of a wall distribute daylight more uniformly than windows separated by substantial wall areas, but they also create glare unless they are covered with blinds, screens, or overhangs.

You can reduce glare by minimizing the contrast between the window and the wall. A bright window in a dark-colored wall, for example, produces more glare than the same window in a light-colored wall. Small windows in a large wall surface also produce glare.

Skylights

Skylights are excellent sources of daylight. A properly placed skylight distributes *five times* as much daylight inside a house as does a sidewall window the same size.

Skylights must be used with caution, however, because they often lose more heat than they gain. They are also blamed for admitting too much direct sunlight, causing overheating, especially in summer. Both problems can be avoided. The key to getting the most from a skylight is to purchase one that is well built, orient it properly to the sun, install it well, and then use insulating shades to minimize unwanted heat loss or gain. It's best to limit the skylight area to approximately 5 percent of the total roof area. Keep in mind that skylights that lie flat against the roof are preferred over the bubble type because they don't disrupt the architectural profile of the house. Here are some location considerations:

North location: If your prime motivation is to gain even, natural lighting, locate your skylight on the north side of the house. Since the sun will never be directly overhead, you'll receive relatively even light all day without a lot of shadow and glare. Northern skylights are particularly suited to homes in the southern part of the country, where heat gain in summer is a problem.

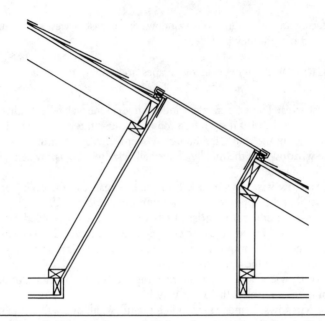

For maximum illumination from a skylight, splay the sides of the shaft so light will reflect off its sides and into the room below.

South location: If your goal is to gain heat and light, or if your house has any heat storing capability, install a skylight on the south or southeastern side of the house. Here, the sun will create a distinct path across the room as it moves from east to west. There may be more glare and shadow than there would be from a north-facing skylight, but this playful, directed light may be exactly what you want in some areas, like breakfast and family rooms.

Flat roof: Placing a skylight on a flat or almost-flat roof should be done with caution, particularly in southern areas of the United States. Summer heat gain can be intense unless precautions are taken to shade the skylight. In winter, a skylight on a flat roof won't bring in much heat, anyway, since the winter sun travels too low in the sky.

If you're looking for natural light and heat, choose a clear pane of glass in your skylight. With a clear pane, approximately 90 percent of the sun's heat and 92 percent of the light is transmitted. Colors in a room appear most natural when light enters though a clear or neutral gray pane. Translucent white panes give a bluish white hue to colors. Bronze panes make colors appear slightly warmer. UVT glass or plastic admits the fullest spectrum of light, but ultraviolet does fade furniture, carpets, and artwork.

Yet another consideration when choosing glazing is what you will see at night. When you look up at a white translucent skylight at night, you see the skylight. When you look through a clear, bronze, or neutral gray skylight, you see the sky.

Clerestories

Clerestories are long, horizontal windows placed high in a wall. They bring in a soft, nondirectional light that penetrates deep into a room without creating excessive brightness. Overhangs or horizontal louvers protect against heat gain through clerestories, just as they do on windows.

Clerestories are more energy efficient than skylights, and with clerestories it's easier to control glare, but they are definitely more difficult to add to a house. It often entails raising a ceiling and installing new beams. Such a remodeling has a drastic effect on the architecture of a house—clerestories must be carefully integrated with the overall design, or the house runs the risk of looking like an architectural nightmare. Orientation of clerestories is critical. North-facing windows with clear glazing admit the most light. South-facing windows must have some way of diffusing the intensity of direct sunlight, such as curtains or shades.

Reflectance

In large rooms, a high-reflectance ceiling is more important than high-reflectance walls because it reflects down into the middle of the room as well as into the corners. In small rooms, pale walls are often sufficient to maintain adequate distribution of light. In either case, a dark ceiling may cause the room to look gloomy, especially if sunlight comes into the room solely through side windows. In a room where window light enters obliquely, a pale floor is desirable, too.

Window details can have a significant effect on both the quantity and quality of light. Mullions, frames, heavy window supports, and small panes in doors or windows can obstruct up to 20 percent of the available light. Dirt accumulation can obstruct light, too, so it's a good idea to clean windows at least twice a year, inside and out.

Shades and Curtains

Shades, curtains, and draperies are an important part of any window plan. If you want as much light as possible, select light-colored window coverings. Hang them on either side of the window frame so that no part of the glass is covered up. Roller shades, venetian blinds, and shutters are better light savers than curtains. These can be rolled or neatly folded out of the way to admit light into the room.

ARTIFICIAL LIGHTING

After you've taken advantage of all the natural light you can in your home, you're still going to have to rely on artificial lighting at night and on gloomy days. To determine what's best for you, start by analyzing the lighting scheme you've already got; then study the options.

The biggest lighting mistake most people make is buying a fixture because it looks nice without first evaluating where it will go. It's easy to be captivated, but don't do it! Nine times out of ten, the light fixture you buy won't solve the problem at all. In fact, it may even make matters worse by giving you one more disparate element to work around. The first thing you should do is create a lighting scheme, *not* buy a light.

Analysis for a Lighting Scheme

What don't you like about the lighting in your house? How can it be improved? To cover all the details, use this checklist to analyze the lighting in your house, room by room:

Activities: What activities take place in the room—conversation, dining, sleeping, homework?

Attention-getting patterns and objects: (Note their locations.) Do they need special lighting? Do they compete with each other?

Color: What color are the walls, the ceiling, the floor, the furniture? Is the mood of the room warm or cool?

Daylight: What time of day is the room brightened? What is the color of light at that time of day? What part of the room is lit? (Include the direction the light comes from; whether it's from a window, door, skylight, or clerestory.)

Flexibility needs: Does the den need to double as a guest room? Is the dining room table also used as a desk?

Kind of light needed: Do you need ambient, task, or accent light; indirect or direct? Where should these be located?

Mood: What kind of mood are you striving for—lively or restful, productive or contemplative, for work or for rest, casual or formal, fun or serious, public or private?

Preferred light level: Do you prefer low, medium, or high light levels? How many watts or footcandles do you need?

Room proportions: What size is the room? (Include any nooks, crannies, sloping ceilings, or other peculiarities.)

Safety hazards: Are there hazards in the room or area that need special lighting attention—steps, wet locations, work areas, glare?

Special areas: What is the focal point of the room? What areas do you want to draw attention to? What areas do you want to make recede into the background?

Time of use: At what time of day is the room used—day or night, morning or afternoon? (List specific times, if possible.)

Traffic patterns: How does traffic move through the room? (Note stairs and hallways, as well.)

If you want a particular atmosphere and aren't sure how to get it, consult a lighting designer. These people are professional problem solvers and are wizards at working out complicated technical equations regarding the aesthetics of direction, reflection, contrast, and glare. Plus, they can often add that extra bit of magic—an interplay of light and shadow, perhaps—that makes your house special.

What Is Healthy Lighting?

Healthy lighting, by definition, is well balanced. That means there is good overall general lighting in the room so you can move about without fear of stumbling, and there is good task lighting, as well, giving you the brightness you need to do a job without straining your eyes. Don't skimp on either one!

In addition, healthy lighting promotes a positive mood. It's important to consider the kind of mood you want in a room. If it's a cocoon-type atmosphere you're after and the room is used mainly at night, you may want to paint the walls a dark color and brighten tabletops with intimate pools of golden light from shaded table and floor lamps. On the other hand, if you want a friendly gathering place, one used both during the day and at night, you'll want brighter walls and surfaces for a more extroverted, cheerful atmosphere.

Monotony and glare are *never* a part of healthy lighting. Monotony occurs when there is no focal point, when everything blends and blurs together, when all lighting in a room is the same degree of brightness. Beware of too much contrast, however. The eye should not have to cope with sudden great changes in light levels. You may need to create a buffer zone of transitional lighting, such as a darker hallway located off a bright living room, so the eye can adjust gradually.

Glare is uncomfortably bright light and occurs when light is reflected off a white, metallic, shiny, or glass surface; when it shines directly into someone's eyes; or when a light bulb is improperly shaded. Look for bright areas that cause you to blink, squint, or turn away. Avoid glare by reducing the strength of the troublesome light source, by installing a baffle or diffuser on the light, or by removing the source of glare. Pay attention to background surfaces. Are they contributing to glare? All-white walls may be responsible for making the room light too harsh.

The opposite of glare is light that is too dim. If you don't have enough light in a room, you can stumble and fall. Without enough light to do a job, you can overwork and strain your eyes. Inadequate lighting doesn't contribute to a job well done, either. If you don't have enough light to wash dinner dishes, for example, you won't be able to distinguish clean dishes from dirty ones. Dim light is downright dangerous when it comes to chopping, sawing, cutting, or shaving.

Consider installing a rheostat system in those places where you want to control the light. The light over the dining room table, for example, is a good candidate for a dimmer switch. With a dimmer you can have bright light to set the table and later to clear the dishes, but you can turn the light down for a more intimate atmosphere while eating. Socket dimmers that screw into table lamps (and that don't require rewiring) are available in most hardware stores. New kinds of track lighting come with a dimmer on each track fixture.

A WORD ABOUT BULBS   One of the first decisions you have to make when choosing light for your home is what type of light source to use. Your choices are basically limited to four kinds of bulbs—incandescent, fluorescent, halogen (a new, high-intensity incandescent), and full-spectrum. Any of the other high-intensity lights (high-pressure sodium, mercury vapor, and so forth) are inappropriate for use inside the home. Not only are they too bright, the weird spectrum of light often makes the human complexion look cadaverous.

Incandescent bulbs are usually preferred in the home because they give a pleasant, golden light, similar to that of the sun. Deluxe incandescent bulbs produce the most flattering light. Because incandescents produce more heat, they are not as efficient as fluorescent bulbs, but they cost less.

Fluorescent light provides good general room lighting as well as excellent task lighting, but before bringing them into your healthy home, consider the fact that the health effects of fluorescent lighting are still in question. Steer

Lighting Rules of Thumb

Keep these rules of thumb in mind when choosing lighting for your home:

■ Every room should have good, overall background lighting with a switch right inside the door.

■ A room with dark walls and floors will absorb light; one with light colors will reflect light. The darker room will require more light to achieve the same level of illumination as the lighter-colored one.

■ High light levels tend to create a sense of activity; low light levels induce an attitude of relaxation.

■ When integrating artificial lighting with daylighting, always use bulbs that produce light resembling the spectrum of daylight.

■ Avoid large fixtures in small spaces and small fixtures in large spaces.

■ If possible, all lampshades in a room should be at the same height.

■ For writing, right-handed people should have light coming from over the left shoulder; left-handers should have light coming from over the right shoulder.

■ Never place lights where they can get splashed by water. In potentially wet areas—bathrooms, garages, kitchens, and outdoors—install a ground-fault circuit interrupter (GFCI) receptacle to protect against electrical shock.

■ Always light stairs. Three-way switches are essential, with one at the top and one at the bottom of the stairs.

■ Lighting requirements change with age. A 30-to-40-year-old needs 17 percent more contrast to see an object as clearly as a 20-to-30-year-old. Those in the 60-to-70 age bracket need 2½ times as much contrast to see as well as the youngest group. The *quality* of light is a factor, too. Older people benefit from soft, diffused light that minimizes shadows.

clear of standard cool-white fluorescents for home use. They turn everything under them, including a peaches-and-cream complexion, a grim gray. Standard white bulbs aren't much better. The most flattering fluorescents are the soft-white or deluxe warm-white tubes now on the market. Though they cost a bit more, you'll appreciate the warmer tones of light.

Halogen lights are new to the home lighting scene. These are the small, bright bulbs used in modern, high-tech fixtures. They are desirable for their bright white light, which is closer to daylight than the other bulbs. A single 250-watt tungsten-halogen tube is powerful enough to provide indirect background lighting in an average-sized room, provided that walls and ceilings are white or pale colored. Although more expensive to buy and run, halogen bulbs last longer than incandescents. Disadvantages of halogen lights are the intense heat they give out, and the fact that special light sockets must be used. Standard domestic light sockets are unsuitable for many halogen bulbs. And, because the lights are very bright, they must be shielded with some kind of shade.

Perhaps the healthiest lights for home use are full-spectrum bulbs, designed to simulate the full spectrum of daylight while providing a bright, efficient, diffuse light. Full-spectrum bulbs fit into normal fluorescent sockets

Light Levels

Area	Pendants and Ceiling Lights	Recessed Fixtures	Wall Lights
Small room, under 150 sq ft	Three to five incandescent lamps for a total of 100 to 150 watts, or 35 to 60 fluorescent watts	Four 75-watt incandescent lamps, or 80 fluorescent watts	Four 50-watt incandescent reflector lamps, or 60 to 80 fluorescent watts
Medium room, 150 to 250 sq ft	Four to six 75-watt incandescent lamps for a total of 200 to 300 watts, or 60 to 80 fluorescent watts	Four 100-watt incandescent lamps, or 120 fluorescent watts	Five to eight 75-watt incandescent lamps, or 120 to 160 fluorescent watts
Large room, over 250 sq ft	One incandescent lamp per 125 sq ft for a total of at least 1 watt/sq ft, or ⅓ fluorescent watt/sq ft	From 2 to 3 incandescent watts/sq ft, or 160 to 200 fluorescent watts	One 75-watt incandescent reflector lamp per 25 sq ft for a total of 3 watts/sq ft, or 160 fluorescent watts

SOURCE: American Home Lighting Institute.

NOTE: The amount of light needed depends on the size of the room and the types of fixtures. Activity light from a fixture depends on how the light source is shielded and the type of bulb.

and can be purchased in many hardware stores and lighting centers (see appendix A).

Lighting Room by Room

Each room calls for different lighting according to the activities and functions performed there.

ENTRANCE   Outside, a light should welcome visitors, help ensure safety of the home, and provide sufficient illumination to find keys and locate the door lock. The style of the fitting should reflect the style and character of the house. Whatever kind of bulb you choose must be housed in a fitting for exterior use. Wall fixtures mounted at eye level, downlights recessed above the entrance, or ceiling fixtures are appropriate here.

Inside, the entrance is a place of transition. Eyes should be able to adapt from the dark night to indoor lighting and vice versa. Avoid excessive contrast. A dimmer switch may help. This is a place for practical lighting, so people can move around without fear of stumbling.

HALLWAY   Long, narrow passageways are difficult to light. Here are some tips:

- Plan even-spaced lighting here, and paint walls a pale color to efficiently spread the light.
- Track-mounted spots are a convenient way to solve the problem but can be overdone and unglamorous.
- Downlights as wall washers work well, lighting wall surfaces and making a small hallway seem bigger.
- Perimeter lighting, either recessed in coves or flush to the ceiling and wall, makes the ceiling "disappear" and adds a nice line.
- A set of wall-mounted lamps, like the geometric Italian kind, spaced at regular intervals create a sculptural lighting effect.

LIVING ROOM   Living room lights should be unobtrusive, yet accommodate a wide range of activity and moods—that's precisely why living rooms are so difficult to light. For such a versatile room, the lighting must be flexible in both quality and quantity, for people sitting alone or in groups. A mixture of background, local, and task lighting is called for.

Most people have an insufficient number of lights for a successful living room scheme. Even in a moderately sized room, a half dozen or more light sources are not necessarily excessive. For example, a room might have six recessed downlights, a pair of table lights, a concealed light inside a shelving unit, and an individual spot trained on a work of art.

Table and floor lamps are fine for around the periphery of the room or for punctuation in the center of the room. But don't run a cord underneath a rug—this is a fire hazard—and don't place a cord where someone is likely to trip over it.

Living room lighting can help secure your home, too. When you go out for the evening, use a time switch to turn lights on and off at programmed intervals, thus making the home seem occupied. An alternative, which requires no special wiring, is a plug-in timer for use with a table or floor light. This is available in both 24-hour and 7-day versions.

DINING ROOM   Lighting in a dining room should be a festive accompaniment to dining. As the focal point, the table should be the brightest spot in the room with a light directly above it. A dimmer switch can control the mood. Warm supplemental light should also be provided. Do this with wall sconces that spread soft, diffuse light or with localized lighting at a serving area or buffet.

To create a sense of intimacy while dining, lower the general room lighting and use a source of soft illumination between people to draw them together. Candles do this well.

FAMILY ROOM   In rooms where activities either take up the whole space or change from place to place within the room, use uniform background lighting along with localized lighting. This combination is the best way to reduce contrast between the activity area and other surfaces.

KITCHEN   Often the hardest-working room in a house, the kitchen can also be the hardest room to light. Most kitchens are plagued with two problems: (1) inadequate or too much overhead lighting and (2) not enough task lighting.

If you have a centrally located ceiling fixture and no task lights over your counter work areas, you will often be working in your own shadow. To remedy the situation, replace an old ceiling fixture with recessed or surface-mounted downlights. Supplement this background light with special task lighting at various work stations—sink, stove, chopping block, eating center.

Spotlights in a kitchen are less than ideal because they produce glare, harsh shadows, and reflections. Make judicious use of pendants over the table or island. This has a softening effect because it creates an intimate pool of light that caters well to noncooking activities.

If you have space between the top of the cupboards and the ceiling, you can attach bulbs in a soffit to bounce light off the ceiling and upper parts of walls for diffuse, indirect light throughout the room. If you're using tracks or other perimeter light, place them 18 to 24 inches out from the cabinet edge. The ceiling should be painted flat white.

Adding task lighting under the cabinet is a relatively easy procedure. Attach a strip light to the base of the cupboard above the counter, making the light two-thirds the length of the counter. Install the strip on the front of the cupboard, and shield it with a wooden batten or a cupboard door that drops below the bottom shelf. For countertops without cupboards over them, illumination can come from fixtures mounted on shelves or recessed in the ceiling, or pendants suspended from the ceiling.

Illuminate the critical sink area with a light mounted on the ceiling

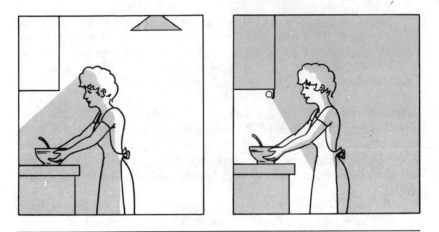

A ceiling light is not a good choice to illuminate a countertop, because it throws a shadow over the work area. A better choice is a light under the cabinet.

behind a cornice board, a pendant suspended from the ceiling, or recessed downlights spaced 15 inches apart. Center the lights over the sink.

The range hood may provide light for the stove and should accommodate the equivalent of at least two 60-watt bulbs; two 75-watt bulbs are preferred. If there is no hood, two 75-watt reflector downlights can be used on or in the ceiling over the front edge of the range top. Mount the two fixtures 18 to 24 inches apart.

LIBRARY OR OFFICE   A library or study is a place of quiet concentration, so lighting should be arranged to encourage maximum efficiency and comfort. Install a ceiling fixture to provide overall light in the room, and supplement it with floor or table lamps arranged to light specific work areas.

Ideally, your work surface should be about three times as bright as the rest of the room. You'll probably need about 200 watts of incandescent lighting or a 50/200/250-watt three-way bulb. To provide a glare-free and shadowless work surface, place a floor lamp slightly behind you and to your left or right, with the bottom edge of the lampshade at eye level. Position table lamps about 20 inches to the right or left of the focus of your activity, with the shade at eye level or slightly above.

BEDROOM   Lighting in a bedroom should be flexible, with the same mix as that in the living room. First, provide overall light to create a mood, and be sure it can be turned on and off from the door. For most bedrooms, this will be a fairly low level of light yet will throw light into the corners as well as into the center of the room. A pendant fitting may work if it doesn't get in the way. Downlights work well, too, but pay attention to how ceiling lights look from the bed—any glare can cause discomfort. Avoid spotlights in bedrooms unless they're low-voltage spots or recessed downlights. Consider installing a switching system that allows you to operate lights from the bed so you won't have to get up to turn them off when you're half asleep.

Here are guidelines for hard-to-light bedroom areas:

Dresser with a mirror above it: Place a pair of lamps about 3 feet apart on either side of the mirror, with the center of the shades at cheek height when you're standing at the dresser or sitting at the dressing table. If possible, place the mirror near a window. Light for a dressing table should be in front of your face, not behind it. Use a 100-watt soft-white bulb, or a 30/70/100-watt three-way bulb.

Full-length mirror: Light should illuminate the person, not the mirror. A fixture can go on the ceiling close to a wall and include a diffuser to soften shadows. Or place a fixture above the mirror or two fixtures on each side to illuminate the whole face.

Bedside: When you're choosing bedside lighting, it's best to have a plan that permits one person to read while another sleeps. Adjustable wall fixtures with opaque shades are good. Install these at the head of the bed so light can be directed away from the sleeping partner.

BATHROOM   The basic fitting for most bathrooms is a central ceiling fixture. Many small baths have only mirror lighting, which may be sufficient if properly done. For other bathroom areas, here are some ideas:

Sink: Theater lights are dramatic, yet practical here. These exposed, miniature bulbs eliminate shadow and glare.

Tub/Shower and Toilet: For safety, provide watertight, recessed ceiling lights over the shower or tub. If your bath has a separate toilet compartment, you need a light there, too—usually a 75-watt bulb.

Keep safety in mind when choosing and locating lights in the bathroom. Never position lights where they are likely to get splashed by a shower, and never handle an electrical appliance with wet, or even damp, hands.

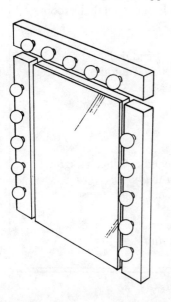

If you use your bathroom mirror for shaving or putting on makeup, theatrical lighting is ideal.

CLOSET   All closets 10 or more square feet in size should have lights. These can be recessed downlights with 25-watt bulbs or porcelain sockets mounted inside the closets. A good fixture for a heavily used closet is a strip light that's activated when the door is opened. For fire protection, any light in a closet must be mounted at least 18 inches from clothing or other stored items.

YARD   Doorways, porches, steps, and keyholes should be well lit. Avoid clear-glass fixtures and exposed high-watt bulbs—both cause troublesome glare. Instead, choose fixtures especially designed for exterior use.

Sockets for portable lights must be totally weatherproof. Shatterproof glass or plastic diffusers will help protect exterior lights against vandals. Tamperproof fittings, which can be dismantled only with special tools, are also available.

To be as glare free as possible, use low-wattage lamps or antiglare attachments. Low-voltage fixtures are well suited to outdoor use—they reduce the hazard of electrical shocks, and they're less costly to operate.

Never attempt to wire outdoor fixtures unless you know exactly what you're doing. There are many safety factors to consider, including the fact that underground cables must be buried a specified distance underground.

Prescription: A Healthy Home Has . . .

. . . good lighting. Here's what you need:

Daylighting

- lots of natural, unfiltered daylight entering through windows on at least two sides of every room
- window area in each room that equals at least one-tenth the room's floor area
- no problems with glare
- thermal shading on south-facing windows and skylights
- architectural integrity, even if skylights and clerestories have been added

Artificial Lighting

- safe lighting, indoors and out
- little or no fluorescent light
- a well-thought-out artificial lighting scheme using background lighting and task lighting in every room of the house
- uniform background lighting in all rooms of the house, with a switch right inside the door
- light that matches the mood and character of each room
- the age of the occupants taken into account

10

Color and Mood

Want to sell your house fast? Paint the exterior yellow. Would you like to shed a few pounds? Eat your meals off a blue plate. Troubled by insomnia? Try painting your bedroom walls violet. Strange as it may seem, a change of color just might do the trick because color has a distinct influence on mood, thought, and behavior.

Scientists have long known that color affects us psychologically. What they have recently discovered is that color affects us *physiologically*, as well. Warm colors are exciting in their effect—blood pressure increases, respiration rate and heartbeat speed up, brain activity and biorhythms increase. Cool colors have the reverse effect—blood pressure falls, heartbeat and breathing slow down, brain activity and biorhythms decrease. Since color surrounds us every minute of every day, it can have a profound effect on our lives. Like light (of which it is a part), color pervades and influences the entire human system—body, mind, emotions, and spirit.

It makes sense, then, to surround yourself with the colors that make you feel good. If you're jumpy and nervous much of the time, you don't want a home environment painted in reds and oranges. You'd *never* relax. Similarly, if you're melancholy and prone to be somewhat lazy, you don't want to be surrounded by serene blues or you'd never get motivated to do anything. It works together—the psychology and the physiology of the human machine.

THE LANGUAGE OF COLOR

The importance of color to the human psyche goes way back to the beginning of time, before language was developed. In that primitive era, color was *the first* language. People communicated using color to express emotion and to aid in the development of thought.

In the beginning, colors were assigned meaning according to where they were found in nature. Bright yellow, for example, was the color of sunlight;

thus it signified energy and incentive. Dark blue was the color of the nighttime sky, so it was associated with quiet and passivity—a time for sleep.

To primitive man and woman, activity took the form of hunting or being hunted, of attacking or being attacked. Red was the color for this activity—the color of blood and of passion. Self-preservation, on the other hand, was associated with the regenerative powers of the green plant world. Thus, green—the color of leaves, grass, and plants—stood for health. These four basic colors and their meanings persist throughout the world today. It's almost as if they were rooted in our genetic consciousness, a legacy of our primitive ancestors:

Red: excitement, passion
Blue: passivity, sleep
Green: health, self-preservation
Yellow: hope, incentive

What Is Color?

Color, in its simplest form, is vibrations of visible light. Natural sunlight carries the full spectrum of color—a glorious rainbow ranging from violet down through the spectrum of blue, green, yellow, orange, and red. You can see how this works by watching light filter through a prism. Crystals within the prism separate the wavelengths into individual bands of light, creating a dancing rainbow before your eyes.

Within this broad spectrum are four basic colors—red, yellow, blue, and green. Remaining colors are variations and combinations of these four basic hues. The basic colors are further divided into two groups—warm (red, yellow) and cool (blue, green). Each group causes a different physiological and psychological response.

Like light, when color enters our bodies through our eyes it releases energy that in turn affects the production of hormones. When we are exposed to red, adrenaline is released, preparing the body for action. Blue, on the other hand, has the reverse effect—11 different tranquilizing hormones are released into the body, slowing down the system and preparing it for sleep. Even people who are color-blind, and some who are visually blind, respond to these physiological effects. Psychologically, the effect is similar. Reds increase the appetite and stimulate creativity. Blues soothe and tranquilize the spirit.

THE SECRET OF WARM AND COOL COLORS   The dramatically different effects of warm and cool colors have been documented time and again in scientific studies. Among the discoveries are these:

■ Creative ideas emerge best in a room painted red. However, to develop and execute those ideas, the nurturing influence of green is needed.
■ Perception of time is influenced by color. Time seems to pass more slowly in a red room and more quickly in a blue or green room.
■ Perception of temperature is affected, too. We actually feel warmer in a red room and cooler in a blue room.

Try a Tranquilizing Dose of Baker-Miller Pink

To fully understand the physiological effects of color, consider the case of Baker-Miller pink. This intense shade of bubble gum pink has a distinct tranquilizing effect on the human body. Dr. Alexander Schauss, director of the Biosocial Research Institute in Tacoma, Washington, first discovered the effects of the color in personal experiments in 1978. Tests were then conducted at the U.S. Naval Correctional Center in Seattle, Washington.

Throughout a 3-month period, hostile youths brought to the center were placed in a detention cell painted with Baker-Miller pink. No matter how desperate their anger, the same pattern of behavior consistently emerged from each of the youths—*they became strikingly docile within 15 minutes*. In each case, the effect lingered about 30 minutes after their removal from the cell. The dramatic effect has since been substantiated in many other studies.

"It's important to understand that the effect of Baker-Miller pink is *physical*, not psychological or cultural," explains Dr. Schauss. "Even people who are color-blind respond to its calming influence. The eyes pick up color as waves of electromagnetic energy. When the pink band is detected, glands release certain hormones that slow the secretion of adrenaline. This, in turn, slows down the heart muscle. Even if a person tries to be angry or aggressive, he can't, because the heart muscle won't race that fast."

To date, scores of programs and institutions have used Baker-Miller pink to reduce violent or aggressive behavior in clients, patients, or inmates. Several municipalities are experimenting with the color to discourage people from defacing buildings and trains with graffiti, while football coaches are trying the color in visitors' dressing rooms in the hopes of debilitating their opponents.

■ Color preferences are apt to change with the weather. If it is hot, most people prefer cool blues. If the temperature is below 60°F, red is the first choice.

■ Color affects our desire for food. Bright, warm colors tend to stimulate digestion, while soft, cool colors retard it.

COLOR IN WESTERN CULTURE   In the United States, bold, attention-getting colors line the streets of every major city. What do you see when you walk down one of these major thoroughfares? A preponderance of *red*. Red and gold—the famous arches of MacDonalds. Red and white—the Colonel peddling chicken. Red and more red—the massive roof of Pizza Hut. The selection of red was not an accident: It's the most stimulating color to the appetite.

Color is big business in America today. Advertising agencies coast-to-coast know that color influences buying decisions. They've commissioned expensive scientific studies to probe the secrets of color. In addition to marketing products, color is used in other subtle ways to influence our moods and behavior in public places:

■ Many restaurants, snack bars, and fast-food joints employ combinations of red and orange in their decor to increase restlessness and appetite. These bright, warm colors are known to stimulate people to eat and move out quickly.

■ Cardiac units in some hospitals use a strong sky blue on the walls to ease patients' fears.

■ In state institutions, rooms painted peach, yellow, and blue are said to relax mentally retarded residents.

■ In the theater and in television studios, people waiting to go on stage relax in a "green room" to calm them.

■ In some factories, machinery is painted light blue or beige, instead of battleship gray, to inspire neatness and efficiency.

■ In England, London's Blackfriars Bridge was repainted blue in an attempt to reduce the number of people who committed suicide by jumping from it.

THE PSYCHOLOGY OF COLOR

Modern psychologists believe early childhood experience has much to do with our preferences for certain colors. For example, your fondness for pale blue may be traced back to a favorite aunt who wore that color when you were little. Unpleasant feelings about a color may be associated with a teacher you particularly disliked. Even though you don't consciously remember these incidents, they still influence you on a subconscious level and affect your color preferences.

Some theorists believe color preferences are a good indicator of personality type, though no two researchers seem to agree on what those indicators are. What appears to be certain, however, is that a person's preference for wearing bright or dull colors, and for warm or cool colors, says a lot about his or her personality. Extroverts and self-confident, outgoing people, for example, tend to favor bright, attention-getting colors. Introverts prefer colors that fade into the background. Generous, feeling personalities choose rich, warm colors—browns, crimson, golden yellow, burnt orange—while more aloof, wary, or reflective personalities favor cool colors—pale blues, grays, and some greens.

Carlton Wagner, founder of the Wagner Institute for Color Research in Santa Barbara, California, has studied color preferences and the psychological effects of color for the past 29 years. He finds that many factors influence our psychological response to color:

Sex: Whether you're male or female makes a difference in which colors you prefer.

Geographical location: Certain locations have conditioned responses to colors native to that location, such as associating soil with burnt red in Colorado.

Ethnic influences: Your ethnic background helps determine color preferences.

Age: Studies show that babies prefer primary red, a color that mirrors their intense emotional life. By the age of 5, this preference generally shifts to all primary colors. As we mature, we accept a wider range of colors and color combinations. By old age, the cycle completes itself—we again prefer primary colors.

Education and income: People of more limited educational background and income appreciate colors that are simple, while people with higher incomes and more sophistication tend to appreciate the more complex colors and color combinations.

How We Respond to Basic Colors

In his book *The Wagner System*, Carlton Wagner writes, "Though many color associations are highly individual, people have much in common in their learned responses. That is, people in similar social and economic circumstances share many of the same experiences and learn some of the same responses. Therefore, we are able to predict values certain groups of individuals place on certain colors."

Other color theorists agree. Manhattan interior designer Barbara Hauben-Ross says that, although colors affect people differently, there are many psychological commonalities. Another color expert, Faber Birren, author of more than 20 books on the subject, believes that color has a tremendous effect on the human psyche, triggering many common psychological prejudices and preferences.

CHOOSING COLORS FOR YOUR HOME

If the physical and psychological needs of people are to be well served, colors should not be chosen on whim or impulse. They should be chosen carefully to create a healthy, balanced emotional atmosphere. The best advice comes from Hauben-Ross, who advises keeping colors monochromatic and neutral in your house. "Do not do bright color schemes," she suggests. "Let color come from life, the people and the things you choose to bring home with you. Select a tint that is muted, and do as much as you can in that color, using it in various tones, values, and textures. This will give you a harmonious, flexible, and timeless environment."

If your soul craves bright color, provide it in throw pillows, afghans, art, and other accessories. Set against a neutral background, bright colors have more effect, similar to boldly colored flowers in a garden.

Rooms with little natural light should have light colors on the walls and in the furnishings, especially if people in the house suffer from annual bouts of the winter "blahs" (seasonal affective disorder). Light colors help spread diffuse background light by reflecting and bouncing what light there is, be it natural or artificial. Dark colors tend to soak up light.

Pay attention to the *quality* of light, too. It has a marked effect on color. The same color viewed in natural sunlight can look completely different under artificial lighting. Also, light that comes directly from a source, such as the sun or a light bulb, will make colors look different than they would under reflected light.

Generally, rooms with north and east window light need warm colors, rather than white or very light shades, on room surfaces. Yellows, apricots, and pinks warm up the soft bluish tone of northern light. Rooms facing south can be painted in darker colors, since south light is direct and intense, especially in summer. Dark colors will absorb the light, rather than bounce it around.

To have a recognizable effect, a color must be used in significant quantity. It's not good, however, to paint a room all one color. Most people feel uncomfortable in a room that's all one color, unless that color is white. It's best to provide some contrast when painting interiors, preferably by painting the walls and the trim in complementary colors. Exaggerated color contrasts should be avoided. These can be jarring. Here are some other color tips:

- The colors of the trim should be the same, or at least similar, throughout the house. This helps unify the house.
- White trim will make a wall color seem much brighter. On the other hand, buff or beige trim may flatten the wall color, so then you'd want to choose something slightly brighter and less gray for the walls.
- Strong, dramatic colors can be hard to live with. If you like them, use them in transient spaces—foyers, corridors, powder rooms.
- Dark colors in a softly lit room tend to get muddy and "fall apart." If you use a dark wall color, increase the room lighting so the color can be seen. And be prepared to be surrounded by dark, light-absorbing walls, rather than light, reflective ones.
- When picking a color in the paint store, put at least four identical sample chips together so you're looking at a larger mass.
- To be sure of getting the right color, buy as many as 5 pints of paint in colors that vary only slightly, and paint strips of the colors on the walls in three different places around the room. Let them dry for a full day, then study how they look in different types of light at different times of the day.
- A "warm" light, such as tungsten or candlelight, is preferred when matching colors in a room. These have less energy in the blue and more in the red range, thus creating a more comfortable, relaxed, and flattering atmosphere.
- Paint a bathroom all white. Most bathrooms are a hodgepodge—making everything white gives a chic, immaculate look.
- If your house has nice woodwork, paint it in varying shades of white to add architectural interest.

Pickle Your Floor

If you have hardwood flooring, you can really brighten the room by pickling the floor. Pickling differs from bleaching in that paint is used instead of bleach. Get ready, set, pickle:

1. Strip and sand the floor.
2. Coat it with clear (not orange) shellac thinned with an equal amount of denatured alcohol.
3. When it's dry, rub it smooth with 000-grade steel wool.
4. Brush out the dust with a dry paintbrush.
5. Brush an undiluted flat water-based white paint onto the surface, and then scrub and push it into the grain.
6. Let the pigment dry, and repeat until you have the look you want.
7. Seal the floor with varnish.

(Be sure to wear a cotton face mask and rubber gloves, and provide good ventilation. Avoid direct breathing of fumes.)

Creating a Healthy Emotional Atmosphere
All Through the House

Knowing which colors stimulate and excite and which depress and soothe can help in creating a positive, nurturing home environment. Some colors work wonders when used in just the right place. Here are some inside tips:

Blue: Bugs have preferences, too. Flies are turned off by pale colors, especially blue. For this reason, barn stalls and porch ceilings are often painted light blue to keep the flies away.

Brown: The red-browns are good interior colors for informal areas. People work efficiently and well in rooms painted a light brown.

Green: Green interiors are good for people who have been relocated. Studies show that people suffering from refugee disorder (with distresses such as eczema, diarrhea, and stomach upset) have fewer, less severe symptoms when placed in green environments.

Gray: Painting the walls of a home office or study blue-gray will create a calm, efficient, creative atmosphere.

Orange: This is a difficult color to live with. Instead of as a wall color, use it for accents in informal interiors—the den, family room, kitchen, rec room.

Pink: Think twice before painting your daughter's bedroom pink. Because it inhibits aggressive behavior, it may serve as yet another reinforcer of traditional female values.

Primary colors: Bright red, blue, and yellow, as well as green, are dramatic, full of energy, and have been known to increase self-esteem. Use these in kitchens, family rooms, and children's rooms. Do not use primary colors in rooms where you want to encourage rest and tranquility.

Red: This is a good color for an infant's nursery. Babies are attracted to red more than to any other color, and it stimulates early brain development.

Rose: To create a soft, warm, cheerful atmosphere, paint the walls of your living room a medium shade of rose. Gray is good for trim.

Yellow: Since yellow appears to increase anxiety and temper loss, it's not a good color for room interiors. However, yellow works well in transitional areas, such as hallways and mudrooms. Yellow is not a good color in the bathroom if the room is used for putting on makeup.

COLOR AND ILLUSION   Interior designers are masters of color. They've learned how to use it to create illusions of space and fool the eye. Here are ten of their basic tricks:

1. Dark or warm colors enclose a room. Light or cool colors open it up. If you want to make a small room appear bigger, paint it a light, cool color.

2. To visually lengthen a short passage, paint the walls a deep tone and keep the floor and ceiling light. To create the illusion of more length, place pictures along the wall in a horizontal line.

3. Deep or vivid shades are most effective in a passageway when it leads to a large, light area. The effect is that of a light at the end of a tunnel.

4. Open up a cramped space by lightening the color on the wall you want to expand. For example, if a sofa must be placed on a short wall, lighten both the wall behind it and the wall immediately opposite. The two remaining walls may be darkened to a medium or deeper tone. The same technique works for a narrow room. Paint the short walls a lighter color than the long walls.

5. To make a room appear less boxlike, paint one wall in a deeper tone than the other three walls.

6. Monochromatic and neutral schemes unify a small room and give it the illusion of greater size. Avoid large patterns in a small room— they visually crowd the space.

7. A ceiling will appear higher if it is painted white or a shade lighter than the walls. To visually raise a ceiling, use low-scale furniture and emphasize verticals within the space. A ceiling will appear lower if painted a darker color. Be careful of dark colors on the ceiling, however. This can create a disturbing effect.

8. To enlarge small windows, use shades the color of the walls. Mini-blinds and shutters with built-in vertical or horizontal lines are excellent expanders. Don't use heavy shades on small windows—as much light as possible should come through.

9. To visually enlarge the floor area, paint or finish the baseboard in the same manner as the floor.

10. If a room is cluttered or visually busy, simplify the color scheme and eliminate distracting patterns and textures. Paint details and distracting features the same color as the walls and ceiling. Avoid too many heights in furnishings.

Prescription: A Healthy Home Has . . .

. . . colors that have been chosen with great care to provide delight and harmony:

■ The personalities of the people who live in the house are complemented by its colors. Different temperaments respond to colors in different ways. Reds can be upsetting to people who are overactive or nervous, while they're stimulating to people who are melancholy or lazy. Similarly, blues are calming to the nervous and fearful but tend to depress the morose.

■ Colors elicit appropriate responses for their specific locations. As a general rule of thumb, bright, warm colors (red, orange, yellow) tend to spur outward activity and action. These are best used as accents in public areas of the house. Softer, cool colors (blues and greens) foster meditation, rest, and withdrawal from the outer world. These are best used in private areas of the house.

■ There are appetite-enhancing colors where food is served. Oranges and reds stimulate the appetite. (These are not a good choice if you're prone to overeating.)

■ Colors create a comfortable psychological temperature. Men react to temperature differently than women. Men find a room too warm about 5 degrees before women do. Similarly, women experience being cold in a room about 5 degrees before men do. Though it's difficult to put this knowledge to good use in rooms men and women share, such information can be useful when it comes to coloring rooms used exclusively by one or the other sex.

■ There are cheerful, harmonious colors throughout. As a general rule, deep tones are not good as wall colors. They absorb light instead of reflect it, creating a confining atmosphere. It's best to paint the walls a neutral tone and let color come from your favorite belongings and the people who populate the room.

■ Pay close attention to the colors in your home. If arguments seem to occur more frequently in one area than in another, it may be a response to color.

11

Sound versus Noise

Bells, buzzers, and vacuum cleaners; mixers, grinders, and garbage disposals; dogs barking, phones ringing, doors slamming, kids arguing. This domestic cacophony can lead to thumping headaches and jangled nerves.

Noise is America's most widespread nuisance. It's the leading cause of neighborhood dissatisfaction—surprisingly outranking crime, according to government studies. Urban traffic is by far the most pervasive outdoor residential noise source; airplane noise is a close second.

Life hasn't always been this noisy. Our early ancestors lived in harmony with the annual rhythms of Earth, its rivers, and forests. They trained themselves to be aware of the slight rustling of leaves, the deviation of a bird's call. A loud noise was often a danger signal, sending the heart racing in preparation for fight or flight. The human auditory system evolved to handle sound frequencies and levels necessary for survival in this natural world. It's no wonder that busy, high-tech noises of the 20th century have alarming health effects on humans!

Medical studies clearly identify noise as an important cause of physical and psychological stress, and stress has been directly linked with many of our common health problems. Coping with the increased levels of 20th century sound clearly aggravates the development of 20th century illnesses—heart disease, high blood pressure, stroke, hypertension, hearing loss, headaches, fatigue, and hostility. Many scientists believe that noise can alter physiological processes, including the functioning of the cardiovascular, endocrine, respiratory, and digestive systems. What's more, if we try to ignore the noise and dismiss our annoyance as the price we pay for living in the modern world, our stress becomes repressed, builds up, and creates more inner havoc. The answer is not to tune out noise, but to learn how to cope with and quiet it. A good place to begin is in the home.

WHAT IS NOISE?

Noise is unwanted sound. It's an intrusion on our privacy and a strain on our nerves. It can be a source of great frustration, especially if nothing can be done about it. Eventually, the ill effects of noise seep into each of our lives.

Noise interferes with conversation. In general, whenever you must raise your voice to be heard, background noise is too loud and should be avoided.

Noise hampers concentration and work efficiency. Noise reduces the accuracy of work rather than the total quantity, and it affects complex tasks more than simpler ones.

Noise interferes with sleep. Doctors and health researchers agree that there is an *absolute requirement* for rest and relaxation at regular intervals, to maintain adequate mental and physical health. Constant exposure to noise frustrates this requirement and affects well-being. If noise wakes you up at night, there's a good chance you can't return to the deepest, most restful level of sleep. So, even if you're disturbed only once in the night, quality of sleep is affected.

Noise causes accidents. Noise can lead to accidents by obscuring warning signals, and it can prevent rescue attempts by interfering with shouts for help.

How Sound Is Measured

Measuring sound is complicated by the fact that it has varying frequencies, varying levels of volume, varying durations, and varying times of occurrence —each with its own unit of measurement. To simplify matters, we will concern ourselves only with the two most common measurements—Hertz and decibels.

Frequencies are measured in Hertz, or Hz. Sounds at frequencies above 10,000 Hz (such as high-pitched hissing) are much more difficult for humans to hear, as are sounds at frequencies below about 100 Hz (such as low rumbling). Beyond human hearing there are ultrasounds and infrasounds, also measured on the Hertz scale. Dogs and birds can hear some high-pitched ultrasounds that humans cannot. Not many living beings can tolerate infrasounds, at the low end of the Hertz scale. These low rumbles beyond our hearing are extremely harmful and work on the body's internal organs to set up a vibration that can cause giddiness and nausea, even death. Powerful internal combustion engines often emit infrasounds.

Environmental sound is measured in decibels (db) to record its changing volume. Hearing begins at 0 db. Each increase by 10 units represents a tenfold increase; 20 units, a hundredfold increase (10×10), 30 units, a thousandfold increase ($10 \times 10 \times 10$), and so on. Thus, 100 db is 10 billion times as intense as 1 db.

For comparison, the rustle of leaves is rated at 10 db. A typical office has about 50 db, pneumatic drills put out about 80 db, a riveting machine blasts away at 110 db, and a jet takeoff heard from 200 feet away measures 120 db or greater. Noise above 70 db is harmful to hearing. Noise at 140 db is physically painful. The table below shows sound levels and their effects for some common 20th century noises.

The average person can safely tolerate lengthy exposure to 80 db, and some people can tolerate up to 100 db. A vacuum cleaner or a dishwasher may seem safe at around 70 db, but a lot depends on the size of the space in which the noise occurs and the length of exposure to it. According to occupational health and safety experts, the maximum safe exposure time at 85 db is 8 hours;

Sound Levels and Human Response

Sound Source	Noise Level (db)	Effect
Carrier deck jet operation Air-raid siren	140	Painfully loud, harmful to hearing
Jet takeoff (from 200 ft) Thunderclap	130	
Discotheque Auto horn (from 3 ft)	120	
Live rock band	110	
Garbage truck (close range)	100	
City traffic Heavy truck (from 50 ft)	90	Very annoying, possibly causing hearing damage after 8 hr
Alarm clock (from 3 feet) Hair dryer	80	Annoying, making telephone use difficult
Noisy restaurant Freeway traffic Man's voice (from 3 ft) Classroom interior	70	
Air-conditioning unit (from 20 ft) Conversational speech	60	Intrusive
Light auto traffic (from 100 ft)	50	Quiet
Living room interior Bedroom interior Quiet office interior	40	
Library interior Soft whisper (from 15 ft)	30	Very quiet
Broadcasting studio interior	20	
Rustle of leaves	10	Just audible
	0	Hearing begins

at 115 db it's only 15 minutes. Noise levels in a disco may reach between 100 and 120 db. Warnings to rock fans to turn down the volume might literally be falling on deaf ears.

HEALTH EFFECTS OF NOISE

Noise is a great biological stressor. It alone can transform a state of emotional ease into an anxious state of unease. Annoyance is usually the first response. It's an outward symptom of the stress building up inside. When added to the other stressors of daily life—unpaid bills, complicated relationships, a bad day at the office—the stress from noise can take its toll. Vulnerable mental and emotional ease shifts into dis-ease, impairing the body's ability to repair and restore itself.

Too much noise over a period of time can lead to hypertension, the most common chronic disease in America today, affecting over 15 percent of the adult population. It's a continuation of an old reflex—the fight or flight response—we inherited as a genetic legacy from our primitive ancestors. Because we can't put that reaction to the same uses our ancestors did, it gets bottled up inside. There's no outlet for the energy, so it turns inward, making us extremely tense.

When you are subjected to noise above the stress level, your heart starts to pound. The body shifts gears, responding automatically to the noise as a warning signal. Adrenaline is released into the bloodstream, blood pressure rises, breathing speeds up, blood vessels constrict, muscles tense. You cannot relax after the sound ceases because your body is geared up, ready for action. If you're frequently tensed, your body may be kept in a near-constant state of agitation. Consequently, you develop diseases of adaptation—ulcers, asthma, high blood pressure, headaches, colitis, insomnia, irritability, psychological disorders.

Some temperaments are more susceptible to the stresses of noise than others. Introverts, for example, are more aware of its intrusion than are extroverts. Empathetic, intelligent, and creative people seem to be more sensitive than people with "tougher" personalities. Elderly people and those who are going through physiological stress, such as rapid growth or illness, are especially vulnerable to noise. Children are noise sensitive, too. Many learning and reading impairments can be directly traced to noisy schools, play areas, and homes.

What's Your Day Like?

It's the cumulative noise level over a long period of time that is harmful. Take a look at your typical day and see how noisy it is.

Most of the noise that is *physically* harmful occurs outside the home, at work or at play. Factory workers often experience such noise levels with the ever-present whir of machinery in the background. The U.S. Occupational

Safety and Health Administration (OSHA) has set limits of 90 db for an 8-hour day (but as we've seen, 65 db triggers a stress response). The U.S. Environmental Protection Agency (EPA) maintains that daily noise exposure at these levels without regular periods of rest can cause permanent hearing damage.

Even those people tucked away in cozy offices are not immune to an overabundance of technological sound. Heating, cooling, and computer systems set up a low rumble in the basements of many large office buildings. On top of that, large work places often have "white noise" (a sound similar to that generated by a television station that has gone off the air) piped into the building. The continuous static is meant to provide a background sound so workers in open-plan offices cannot hear conversation in the cubicles next to them. Although not hazardous in itself, white noise adds to the cumulative total of environmental sound, and it is the total energy—sound level and duration—that enters the ear on a daily basis that is hazardous. You may begin to talk louder and strain, albeit imperceptibly, to hear. The higher background sound may increase your anxiety level, again almost imperceptibly. Check it by taking your blood pressure. That tells a more accurate stress story.

It's not as if we can walk out of the office or the factory and into an environment filled only with the sounds of bird songs and wind in the trees, either. Outside noise in the city generally exceeds 65 db. Traveling in automobiles exposes us to low-freqency noise levels between 100 and 120 db. Once home, if you use power tools, mow the yard, prepare meals using the blender and power mixer, or vacuum the carpet, the additional noise exposure heightens the risk of hearing impairment and chronic psychological stress. It's no wonder you have a headache at the end of the day!

Studies show that people who work in the midst of high noise levels during the day are more susceptible to frustration and aggravation after work. When the home is noisy, the tired and irritated worker may never be able to work out the day's accumulated stress. Then, even the innocuous sounds of children at play can become irritating noise. When that happens, the home is not a healthy one.

Protect against Hearing Loss

You can protect against hearing loss by avoiding noisy areas and limiting your noise exposure to intermittent or short periods of time. When engaged in a particularly noisy task, such as firing a gun, sawing lumber, or even mowing the yard, wear earplugs or earmuffs. Earmuffs offer the best protection. Make sure they're snug and airtight with a comfortable seal. When vacuuming or performing other noisy, routine tasks around the house, try listening to music through a set of headphones. This will help mask high-decibel task sound and won't leave you feeling as jittery and annoyed.

If eliminating the noise is impossible, try to lessen it or avoid it completely. Take refuge inside your quiet, healthy home. Lower your stress and relax.

HOW TO COPE WITH NOISE

To cope with noise, many people direct their anger and frustration inward, blaming themselves for being upset. These people are ripe for psychosomatic illness; they may become accident prone or suffer from migraine headaches and fatigue. Others direct their frustration outward, becoming argumentative, moody, and quarrelsome—they are difficult to live and work with. Still others deny the problem, considering themselves too tough for noise to bother them. These people, too, are prone to psychosomatic illness. But the vast majority of people cope with noise by taking sleeping pills, wearing earplugs, seeing doctors, keeping windows closed, spending less time outdoors, and complaining a lot.

   None of these is a positive way to cope with the problem. When possible, take action to eliminate the offending noise at its source. Speak up for your

---

Listen to Your House

Only by being completely aware of all sound and how it affects you will you be able to create the quiet, healthy home you seek. Evaluate the noises inside your house by using the criteria listed below. Does your house often have the following:

Noise that interferes with conversation: Not just overly loud noises interfere with conversation. Sounds that are at the same decibel level as the human voice will also make it difficult for your voice to be heard. You need definite contrast between background sound and speech to distinguish speech from noise.

Unexpected sounds: These take you by surprise, regardless of their intensity. Loud, unexpected noise, such as a dish breaking on a hard floor or the sudden blast of a firecracker, can practically unhinge even the most serene personality. In the quiet of night, the creak of a door can be overwhelmingly disturbing. Even the barely audible click of an electric blanket thermostat was once likened by Consumers Union to the "stomping of a robin on a lawn."

Intermittent sounds: The furnace going on and off is a good example. It can surprise you if you aren't expecting it. The more regular the sound, the more tolerant of it you become.

Sounds that threaten invasion of privacy: Nearby voices can be disturbing if you're trying to have a confidential conversation.

Intelligible sounds: Barely audible sounds can be immensely distracting, especially if you're trying to concentrate. You hear enough of them to pique your curiosity, yet not enough to know what is actually going on. Masking the sound with another, more controllable one, such as a radio on low volume, helps lessen the disturbance.

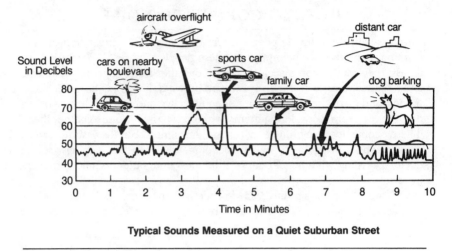

Typical Sounds Measured on a Quiet Suburban Street

Even a relatively quiet suburban street has its share of annoying sounds.

rights. Most communities have a law against disturbing the peace. If someone is creating *unreasonable* noise that disturbs your peace and quiet—such as a motorcycle racing up and down your street or a stereo blasting away at 3:00 A.M.—and asking them to quiet down doesn't help, a call to your local police department may do some good. If, however, the noise is caused by a business, and it goes on day after day or night after night, you may have a conflict of rights and may have to go to court to get it settled.

In most states, noise constitutes a nuisance in the legal sense if it is unreasonable as well as loud and intense enough to cause physical or psychological discomfort to ordinary people. This is a minimum standard. Some locales have stricter ordinances. Since there is not an absolute standard, each case is determined by its particular set of facts and circumstances.

A well-known noise nuisance case in Connecticut is a good example. In *O'Neil v. Carolina Freight Carriers Corporation,* a married couple who owned their home were able to prove that noise from a truck-loading terminal adjacent to their house was unreasonable. It caused them loss of sleep and prevented general enjoyment of their home. The court ruled that the truck terminal noises between 11:00 P.M. and 6:00 A.M. were unreasonable and that every property owner must make reasonable use of his or her land so as not to cause unnecessary annoyance to neighbors. The O'Neils won both an injunction to stop the business from operating during nighttime hours and financial damages for the harm caused them.

CREATING AN OASIS OF CALM
IN A NOISY, UPTIGHT WORLD

If we cannot find quiet elsewhere, at least we can make sure we find it in our homes. A healthy home is an oasis of calm, a place of regeneration. You can go a long way toward attaining that goal by controlling the noises you find

---

Achieving a Comfortable Silence

When New York designer John Saladino wanted to offer the gift of quiet to guests staying in his mountain retreat, he knew exactly what to do. Saladino covered nearly every surface in the guest bedroom with fabric. He upholstered the walls in cotton padding, then applied a cotton fabric over it. The table and sitting chair are covered with fabric, and a wool oriental carpet covers part of a finely woven wall-to-wall sisal rug. A quilt hangs over the bed.

The quiet, however, is not only acoustic. Saladino also calmed the room with tranquil colors. The wall covering is a faded periwinkle blue, and the wheat tone of the sisal is repeated in the oriental carpet. There are no abrupt changes in color—the tones blend quietly. Nor are there abrupt changes in the basic architectural elements of the room—the door has no molding and is upholstered in the same cotton-covered padding as the surrounding walls.

---

disturbing. Quieting a noisy house is not difficult. All it takes is an awareness of offending sounds, a rudimentary knowledge of basic construction techniques, and common sense.

Start by analyzing the sources of noise. You may find you don't have a serious problem at all—just a teenager's rock and roll music coming from the floor above. A carpet with padding may be all that's needed to solve that problem. If it's street sounds that bother you, the answer may be to add another pane of glass to windows on the street side. Adding bookshelves on the interior will help insulate against sound, too. Wherever the offending noise is coming from, there's a good chance a simple home improvement will quiet it.

Most neighborhood noises, including traffic and airplane noises, enter the house through exterior walls, doors, and windows. Reduce this transmission by tightening up the places noise can seep through. Doing so will give you an extra bonus—you'll get a more energy-efficient house in the bargain!

Solving the Problem of Exterior Noise

To retrofit a house for control of noise from the neighborhood, apply some of the following techniques.

INSULATE EXTERIOR WALLS   By insulating exterior walls, you'll create mass that absorbs sound. After the insulation is in place, check the walls for air leaks. If you find any, stuff the area with insulation and seal it with acoustic sealant.

If you can't find any air leaks, yet noise still bothers you, your best solution is to beef up the mass in the wall. Build another stud wall in front of it on the interior, and cover it with drywall or plaster. Or line the interior of the wall with bookshelves. Both of these solutions eat up square footage, so be prepared to sacrifice some interior space.

To further soundproof against exterior noise, insulate the attic roof and cover the interior side with sound board and/or drywall.

BEEF UP WINDOW GLAZING   Windows transmit a lot of sound. You have three choices here:

- Add a pane of glass, such as a storm window, to each window on the noisy side of the house. This will reduce street noise by 50 percent.
- Replace single-pane windows with double-pane ones, and make a tight seal with weather stripping and acoustic sealant.
- Purchase special noiseproof glazing available from some window manufacturers.

Hanging heavy draperies over the windows won't help shut out noise, since noise intrusion from the outside is mostly in the low to middle frequencies. Draperies have few acoustic values in this range. They will, however, absorb sound coming from within the room.

REPLACE DOORS   If exterior doors in your house are light or hollow cored, replace them with heavy, solid-cored doors. You'll be surprised how much noise this simple home improvement seals out.

LANDSCAPE WITH BUSHES, BERMS, OR FENCES   In general, noise control requires dense planting of considerable depth and height to achieve a reasonable amount of sound insulation. To block unwanted traffic sounds from your house, plant thick hedges, bushes, and trees on the side toward the road. Dense hedges at least 2 feet thick can reduce the noise level by 4 to 5 db. Viscous leaves also act as a general filter, trapping some of the dust stirred up by passing vehicles.

Earth berms help absorb sound between a noise source and the house, if you have the space. For further sound absorption, cover the mound with dense planting. A 6-foot earth berm topped with a dense hedge at least 4 feet high should reduce traffic noises by 8 db.

If your house is downwind from a factory or school yard, the best remedy is to plant a windbreak between the house and the noise. A tight evergreen or deciduous hedge will provide protection as far downwind as 20 times its height. So, a 9-foot-tall hedge can be planted as far as 180 feet from your house and still offer some protection from wind-borne noise.

Freestanding walls and tight fences covered with dense vines are also sound absorbing to some degree. But hard surfaces are not. If noise really bothers you, avoid placing brick, flagstone, or concrete between your house and a source of noise.

Solving the Problem of Interior Noise

When looking for ways to reduce noise within your house, first determine where the noise is coming from: within the room, outside of the room, or within the structure of the house itself. Once you've determined where the noise is coming from, you must then find a way to reduce each noise to a tolerable level.

Soundproofing a room may be as simple as sealing gaps around a door, or it may require rebuilding an entire wall or lowering a ceiling. To quiet the noise, there are three remedies:

- Muffle the noise as it seeps into the room.
- Contain it within a room so it doesn't leak out.
- Mask the noise with additional, controlled noise.

ABSORB SOUND WITHIN A ROOM   A good way to prevent noise from spreading to other parts of the house is to absorb it in the room where it originates. Do this with soft, porous surfaces. Heavy draperies, wall-to-wall carpeting, cork, and upholstered furnishings each go a long way toward soaking up sound to make a room quieter. Hard, slick surfaces—hardwood floors, plaster walls, glass windows—repel sound and tend to make a room noisy by bouncing sound around within it. A combination of hard and soft materials is the best solution acoustically.

CONTAIN NOISE WITHIN A ROOM   To contain noise within a room, add mass to the structure. Noise goes right through hollow doors, for example. Replace them with solid-cored doors, especially in bedrooms, baths, kitchens, and playrooms. Less expensive hollow-cored doors can be installed in quiet spots like closets and storage areas. To further contain sound, seal the bottoms of doors with sweep strips and seal all cracks with weather stripping.

Electrical receptacles placed back to back in a wall are another likely source of interior sound transmission. If you have back-to-back wall outlets in your house, make sure they are tightly installed. Add insulation around them if they're not. Ideally, outlets and switches should be at least 3 feet apart.

MASK NOISE   Mask noise with a constant, steady, controlled sound, such as a radio or a fan. This final solution is a rather clumsy one, since it adds to the background noise level.

If these quick and simple remedies don't work, you may need a more complicated renovation.

Reducing Noise within the Structure Itself

The structure of a house can be a willing conduit for the transmission of sound, but you *can* remedy noise seemingly built into the walls of a house.

HEATING DUCTS   If one heating duct is shared between two rooms, it provides an acoustic connection. The noise of airflow can be stopped by adding acoustic insulation inside the walls of the duct. One-inch-thick duct lining is good to use. (A nontoxic product is natural cork.)

WATER PIPES   Noisy water pipes are usually caused by water passing through narrow valves, faucets, and other tight spaces. When the water reaches such a spot, the velocity increases, causing noise and vibration that are transmitted through the pipes and into the walls where the pipes are supported. The walls act as a sounding board, radiating the noise. To solve the problem, use one of the following remedies:

> **Solution 1:** Where pipes are supported by walls, use an oversized pipe clamp and insert a gasket between the pipe and the clamp. Where pipes penetrate walls, the opening should be large enough to install a padding of insulation around the pipe. Finish the job by sealing off the padding, at the face of the wall, with an acoustic sealant.
>
> **Solution 2:** Reduce water pressure by installing a pressure regulator in the water pipe and maintaining a water pressure of less than 45 pounds per square inch (psi). Another approach is to insert a 3-foot-long piece of ¼-inch copper tubing between the water supply and an especially noisy faucet.

SQUEAKY FLOORS AND NOISY STAIRS   Though it's not high in comparative decibels, a squeaky floor can wake you from a sound sleep and be a source of continual irritation when you're trying to concentrate. Here are a couple of remedies:

> **Solution 1:** If the problem is created by loose or warped floorboards, try a squirt of mineral oil between the joints. If this doesn't work, drive a few ring-shanked nails through the wood to tighten up the floor.
>
> **Solution 2:** The problem may be caused by warped or bowed floor joists. You can remedy this only if the area underneath the room is unfinished, such as in an unfinished basement. Go into that room and check for gaps between the floor and joists. If you find one, butt a long, straight board up against the floor and nail it to the joists. If the squeak is caused by the floor's sagging between the joists, place a 2 × 8 in the space between joists, nailing through the joist into each end of the board.

Besides being noisy, bare wood stairs are an accident waiting to happen. Add rugs or carpeting for both safety and noise control. Carpet adds traction while muffling creaky boards and heavy footsteps.

Control Sound

Sound control is cumulative. The first steps you take will help a lot; subsequent steps will continue to help but with diminishing returns. Each of these building tips contributes in its own way, and each is most effective in a given frequency range. You don't have to do them all. A modest amount of work can go a long way toward attaining a comfortable silence day in and day out.

WALLS Here are several good ways to cut down on noise coming through walls:

■ Build two rows of 2 × 2 studs, separating them with a layer of sound board; then apply sound board and wall panels to both sides. This is the most expensive, but the most effective, treatment.
■ Build a double-stud wall. Though this is expensive, it makes a remarkable improvement in sound transmission. A double-stud wall

---

No-Tox Soundproofing Materials

The following nontoxic products (with manufacturers' addresses in appendix A) are specifically recommended for soundproofing a house:

Enkasonic: This polyester and nylon matting is designed as floor insulation to obstruct the passage of sound, especially in multiple-unit dwellings. It's easily installed—simply roll it out on top of the subfloor, then cover it with wallboard and finished flooring material.

Foil-Ray: A quilted foil wrap for insulation and soundproofing, Foil-Ray is good for wrapping noisy ducts and pipes to quiet them, and for lining cabinets, say under the sink. It can be used as a carpet pad as well as for insulation in walls, floors, and ceilings. Seal it with foil tape.

Marmoleum: A resilient vinyl flooring made entirely from natural products, Marmoleum has good acoustic properties.

Mineral Board: This formaldehyde-free wallboard is made of wood chips and bonded with an adhesive made from seawater. Eterboard is another natural-product wall panel made without synthetic chemicals. Both are nonflammable.

Sound-A-Sote: Designed specifically to deaden sound in walls, ceilings, and floors, Sound-A-Sote is a structural board made without asbestos or formaldehyde. Cover it with wall panels or wood.

There are also no-tox caulks and acoustic sealants available, though they may be somewhat difficult to find (see appendix A). If your budget doesn't allow a complete retrofit, spend your money on low-tox, no-tox insulation, wall panels, and ceiling tile—healthy materials that take up a lot of space and are spread over a large surface. Unhealthy building materials that cover massive areas are of the most concern.

is one in which there are two wall surfaces completely separated from each other. The stud supporting one panel of wallboard does not touch the opposite panel. In this way, when sound strikes one surface of the wall and makes it vibrate, the vibrations are not directly transferred through the studs to the other side. Instead, the air in the space between the wall vibrates, reducing the force of vibrations transmitted to the other side and serving as a sound barrier.

■ Use layers and different thicknesses of wall panels. Since different masses vibrate at different rates, several different masses of wall board vibrating at different rates tend to cancel each other out, reducing sound transmission through the wall.

■ Insert blankets of insulation between the studs.

■ Install sound-deadening board behind wall panels on the noisy side of the wall to reduce the effect of sound vibrations. Because the board is soft, it breaks up vibrations and doesn't transmit them.

■ Nail 1 × 2 furring strips across the studs parallel to the floor and cover them with wall panels.

■ Set wallboards in thick beads of panel adhesive, using as few nails as possible. The resilient adhesive provides a cushion to absorb vibration, and the tiny air gaps between the old and new wall facings act as sound traps. For further noise reduction, leave a ¼-inch space at both the top and bottom of the wallboard, fill each space with acoustic sealant, and then cover it with molding. This isolates the wall board and prevents noise transmission through cracks at the floor and ceiling.

CEILINGS AND FLOORS Here are ways to reduce noise coming through ceilings and floors:

■ Hang a new ceiling 4 to 12 inches from the existing one. Insulate the cavity, cover it with sound board, then finish it with wall panels.

■ Install sound board over the existing ceiling. If the existing surface is smooth and level, this can be done without furring strips.

■ If sound enters vertically through a ceiling, quiet the noise at its source by placing a carpet and a thick padding on the floor above. Or, cover the floor with sound board.

■ Tack furring strips to the ceiling, parallel to the ceiling joists. Then, nail resilient acoustic channels (or Z bars) to the furring at right angles to the joists. Space the channels 24 inches apart and fill the spaces with a thin blanket of insulation. Attach ½-inch wall panels or sound board to the channels, leaving ¼-inch gaps at the edges of adjacent walls; fill these gaps with acoustic sealant.

For a truly healthy house, don't hang a suspended ceiling of acoustic tile. Acoustic tile may aggravate illness in the chemically sensitive, and it probably adds to the overall level of formaldehyde in the house. Paul Bierman-Lytle is an architect of nontoxic houses and president of Masters Corporation, which sells low-tox building products. According to Bierman-Lytle, acoustic tile is suspected of containing fire-resistant chemicals, petrochemical solvents, and adhesives, including formaldehyde, which can outgas over time and emit harmful vapors into the air. It may also contain mineral fibers that aggravate airborne particulate pollution. If you're considering putting such tiles in your house, ask the manufacturer to show you a materials data safety sheet before you sign on the dotted line.

Good Workmanship Is Key

Effective soundproofing of walls, ceilings, or floors requires careful workmanship and strict adherence to four basic rules:

- Seal all cracks with caulking or acoustic sealant. A crack just ⅛-inch wide and 8 inches long can reduce the effectiveness of a soundproofed wall by as much as 10 percent.
- Do not make electrical and plumbing cutouts back to back in a wall. It's best to have at least one full stud cavity between them. Seal all openings.
- Work carefully and don't skip steps.
- Do not leave large gaps between the wallboard and the materials it butts up against. Inner layers must be installed as carefully as outer layers.

Make the most of your labor and materials. Remember that the denser a product, the better it stops sound. The most effective wall covering is ¾-inch plaster. Sound sealant should be applied in the intersection of walls and flooring. Wall panels should also be set into it. Most of the materials needed for soundproofing are sold at building supply stores, although special low-tox building materials may have to be ordered.

Lined draperies work well at absorbing sound coming from within the room. There are also special fabrics on the market made especially for sound control. For walls, fabric shirred on rods or stapled flat will absorb more sound than a coat of paint.

Retrofitting Room by Room

Take a walk through your house and assess how noisy each room is. Don't forget hallways and work zones. In these areas, cover the floors with carpeting or resilient flooring.

THE BATHROOM   Reduce noise from a ventilating fan by lining the duct with cork. When buying a fan, select a centrifugal model—they're quieter than the propeller type. Buy a properly sized fan for the size of the room and remember, you get what you pay for. Spend money on this item—it's worth it.

FURNACE OR LAUNDRY ROOM   Be sure walls and ceiling are well insulated. All doors should be solid cored. Place soft mats or rubber pads underneath

Appliances and Power Tools—the Worst Offenders

The best way to quiet the din of appliance noise is to buy quiet appliances in the first place. When shopping for a new household appliance, have the salesperson operate it for you before you buy so you can see how noisy it is. Check the label for a sound rating, and compare it to other appliances. If you cannot find an appliance that meets your need for quiet, write the manufacturer. Quiet appliances will not be produced unless there is consumer demand for them.

See the table below for noise ratings of the most common appliances and tools.

Noise Levels of Common Household Appliances

Appliance	Noise Level (db)
Air conditioner (window unit)	60 to 72
Chain saw	103 to 115
Clothes dryer	50 to 72
Electric drill	85 to 95
Electric saw	90 to 110
Electric shaver	45 to 75
Food blender	63 to 88
Garbage disposal	68 to 93
Hair dryer	60 to 80
Power lawn mower	80 to 95
Refrigerator	35 to 68
Router	85 to 100
Sander	85 to 105
Toilet	50 to 80
Vacuum cleaner	60 to 85
Washing machine	39 to 78

mechanical equipment, and glue cork tile to the walls behind noisy appliances, if necessary. If a blower motor is sending vibrations through the house, have it mounted on resilient rubber motor mounts.

LIVING AND FAMILY ROOMS   If you're using a window air conditioner, spend money and buy the best, quietest unit available. Then, isolate it from the wall with cork.

THE KITCHEN   To quiet appliances, apply the following techniques, as needed:

Dishwasher: There are two techniques you can apply here, but first make sure you have space larger than the machine itself to work in. Then, do one of two things: (1) put vibration-absorbing pads under the legs of the dishwasher, in place of the usual nonskid pads, or (2) pack the air space between the dishwasher and surrounding cabinets with cork.

Garbage disposal: First quiet the kitchen sink by coating the underside with a sound-deadening damping material. To reduce disposal noise, try fastening 1-inch-thick cork tile on the cabinet walls around the disposal.

Noisy ventilation fan: See "The Bathroom" on page 217.

Small appliances: Place can openers, blenders, and mixers on rubber or cork mats to isolate the vibrations.

THE GARAGE   If you have an attached garage, be sure adjacent walls and ceilings are well insulated. Close off any ducts leading from the garage to the house. Garages are best located next to public and noisy areas of the house, like the kitchen or family room.

TURN ON THE MUSIC

Music often repairs damage done by noise and other stressors. It can help lower blood pressure, relax tense muscles, promote rest, relieve troubled moods, enhance self-awareness, and generally readjust disturbed organic patterns in the body.

There's been an explosion in music research recently, creating a new vocation—music therapy—in which professionals use music to bring about self-repair, defuse stresses, and ease illness and pain. Here are some suggestions from therapists on which music to select for certain moods:

If you're severely tense or have insomnia: Try one of a number of sleep-inducing recordings on the market. Some use musical selections, others a medley of natural sounds. Stay away from vocals, and use the same music night after night to relax you.

To uplift the spirit: Try the music of flute, harp, electric piano, and/or bells.

For meditation: Nonvocal music with an easy rhythmic flow, maybe in a minor key, works best.

To relieve anxiety: Choose slow, regular rhythm; long, flowing melodies without strong musical accents and with a preponderance of strings such as harps, guitars, violins, and cellos.

If you're overtly angry or feeling violent: Play calming music. Stay away from brass instruments—they can be jangling and unsettling. Instead, choose music played by piano and strings.

Prescription: A Healthy Home Has . . .

. . . a quiet, peaceful environment. How does your house rate? Ask yourself these questions:

■ What are the noisiest rooms in the house? How are they separated from quiet zones? The ideal floor plan clusters noisy rooms—the kitchen, bathroom, playroom, music room, furnace, and laundry room—at one end of the house and quiet bedrooms at the other. Between this noisy zone and the bedroom area is a bridge of seminoisy rooms—hallways, family room, dining room. If your house is not laid out in this manner, take a look at where the offending noise is coming from. This will give you a better idea of what kind of home improvement is needed to quiet the noise.

■ Does your family have a special need for a soundproof room? If you have a teenager who plays the drums, or a youthful rock band that uses your basement occasionally for practice, you'll want more than the normal amount of soundproofing. Similarly, if there's a library or study in your house that's frequently in use, it should be well insulated from mundane household noises.

■ What are the normal sources of family entertainment? Count the noisy ways your family entertains itself—with radios, televisions, musical instruments. How do these sounds filter into quiet areas? If stereo or television noise is a bother, equip the sets with headphones or earphones. This can be done for a few dollars.

■ Are you aware of the accumulated background noise of appliances? Take a look at each of the appliances in your house. Does the furnace create a disturbance when it kicks on in winter? How about the vacuum cleaner—is it disturbing to others? (At 85 db, a vacuum produces almost as much noise as a subway train!) Look at low-level noise, too. The hum of a refrigerator alone can be enough to set your nerves on edge. Its resonance may make your stomach uncomfortable and trigger hunger, prompting you to raid the fridge.

12

Pets

A woman now in her 40s still vividly remembers the day, long ago, when her grandmother died. "I was 11 at the time, and my grandmother had always lived with us," the woman says. "I'm an only child, so I felt very close to her. When they called us from the hospital to tell us she was gone, I was devastated."

The girl went out to the backyard, where her pet cocker spaniel came running and jumping, ready to play. "But he immediately sensed that something was wrong," the woman recalls. "I sat down in the grass, and he snuggled beside me. I must have stayed there for an hour, and that dog never moved. He was my comfort."

Indeed, while no pet can comprehend such matters as a death in the family, dogs and cats can sense and share emotions. A pet is happy when you are happy, and sad when you are sad. A pet can be the perfect companion—a good, sympathetic listener who never talks back.

Studies reveal that a pet's companionship is so beneficial that it actually makes a positive contribution to physical health in the same way that other important aspects of our social environment do. We're beginning to understand the links between loneliness and death as well as the positive influence happiness and good morale have on wellness. That's why pets—those adoring creatures that banish loneliness, bring happiness, and bolster morale—can have a positive effect in a healthy home. A pet isn't a miracle drug that staves off heart disease, and it can't keep an obese owner from dropping dead. But the relationship you have with a pet (not merely its presence) brings a special and unique dimension to life.

Pets can actually help make sick people well. It follows, then, that they can also help keep healthy people healthy. In pets we have a creature to care for. At the very least, they provide companionship, pleasurable activity, and a source of constancy in our lives. Pets return us to play and laughter, act as a stimulus to exercise, are a comfort to touch, and are enjoyable to watch.

PETS AND HEALTH

In 1980 when Mount St. Helen's spewed forth its deadly volcanic ash, a photographer was able to film the helicopter rescue of an old man who lived on the mountain. Before entering the aircraft, the old man carefully placed his dog on the seat. It was an act of caring that shouted to the world the importance that the elderly gentleman placed on his dog.

Another, more common occurrence is illustrated in the story of a couple whose cat often wandered at night. They were distraught when the pet didn't show up on their doorstep one morning. They began a search that lasted 3 weeks, spending early mornings before work, evenings, and weekends until they found their pet—sick and undernourished. Then they watched their veterinarian's bills pour in as the animal was nursed back to health. And the only emotion the couple felt was joy—never resentment or anger.

In research at the University of Pennsylvania, Dr. Aaron Katcher studied the physiological effects of companion animal ownership. It had been known for some time that a dog's blood pressure drops when it is petted, presumably because the animal is gaining some comfort from being in a group situation. Interestingly, a human's blood pressure drops, too, when he or she strokes a pet.

The devotion and companionship of pets have caused residents of nursing homes to find new cause for living. In one case study, a woman who failed to communicate and remained curled in the fetal position was pulled out of her shell, albeit slowly, when given a cat. Today, she uses the cat as a means of striking up conversations, even with strangers.

In another study, at the University of Oklahoma, a group of recent widows who were pet owners seemed to adjust better to the death of a spouse—both physically and psychologically—than a group who didn't own pets. Dr. Hiroko Akiyama, who conducted the study, says "Non–pet owners, for example, had more persistent fears, headaches, and feelings of panic. They also tended to take more drugs than the pet owners."

In light of such studies, it comes as no surprise that a healthy home has healthy, happy pets with personalities that match up well with those in the family. A healthy home also provides the pet with healthy foods, takes care of parasites in an ecologically safe manner, and treats the animal with care and love.

What Pets Have to Offer

Good health is not the only reason it's nice to have a pet around the house:

Pets offer constancy. The world around us is always changing, and so are we. We are not animals of constancy, but pets are. They offer a bulwark of stability in our lives. A pet doesn't care if you nab the promotion, buy the new car, or join the country club. Animals are indifferent to our strivings. "They do not share our changing universe and they live in their own time," write Alan Beck and Dr. Aaron Katcher in their book *Between Pets and People* (Penguin

Books, 1985). "They remain themselves, unaffected by human progress or failure." That means your pet will always accept you for what you are, not for what you may someday become.

Pets provide stability. "A dog never grows up," writes Bruce Fogle in *Pets and Their People* (Viking Press, 1983). "We don't expect it to. We don't expect intellectual development, social concern, or moral acuity. It stays the same. It doesn't learn to read or write. It will never know the seven times table. It never learns to tie shoelaces. It never learns to talk or to ride a bicycle. We never allow it to take care of itself. It never learns shame. It is without original sin. It is a constant child, always subordinate to us in a parent/child way."

Pets offer "social" security. Studies show that, when accompanied by a pet, people have a greater feeling of security in public or social situations. Basically, a pet's presence provides us with an emotional security we might not enjoy if we were alone.

Peter Messent, an animal behaviorist in London, followed a particular veterinarian's clients along the street in Hyde Park and recorded the reactions of persons who passed by them. Then he had each client walk the same route with his or her dog. He found that when walking their dogs, the people had more social contacts than when they walked the same route unaccompanied by their pets. He also found that when they walked their dogs, the walk lasted longer.

Pets—at least dogs—give us praise. A dog is continually doling out its apparent love and appreciation. That's especially meaningful in times of stress for the owner. Then, the dog becomes even more important than usual.

Pets allow us to be intimate. Pets allow eye-to-eye contact, something that isn't always easy with another human. They also allow soft touch and quiet talk. In this way we form a bond with them that is more controllable and less threatening than human relationships. The human-to-animal bond can be warmer and less complicated. At times, you can enjoy perfect speechless communication.

DECIDING WHICH PET IS RIGHT FOR YOU

Generally, families who have pets also have children. A nationwide marketing survey found that 91 percent of dogs and 86 percent of cats live in families where children and young adults are present. That pets serve as a bridge between family members should come as no surprise. Often, two people within a family who have difficulty talking to each other can interact through or around a pet. Just as pets are used for therapy in nursing homes, they can also be used for marriage therapy. According to an article in the May 1987 issue of *Prevention* magazine, researchers at Indiana University asked 30 couples to discuss and attempt to resolve marital conflicts in sessions with and without their pet dogs. Afterward, the researchers concluded that the presence of the dog "was associated with changes in the emotional and physiological climate that are favorable for the process of marital conflict resolution."

Pets can also help transcend the gap between parent and child. One woman recalls that when she was a child, the only way she could approach her father was by first playing with his dog. Eventually, her dad would join in the fun and, ultimately, there was conversation.

Parents often will purchase a pet to soothe the feelings a youngster experiences when the family must move to a new location. The companionship the animal offers helps fill the void left by the loss of familiar surroundings and old friends.

The Choices

Deciding which animal would make the best pet for you and your family depends on personal interests, your living circumstances, and finances. Do you want a hunting dog, or would your family rather have a chatty parrot? Are your youngsters interested in raising 4-H rabbits, or would an aquarium full of tropical fish fit better in your home?

DOGS Dogs form the closest bonds with people, but they require time, space, training, and companionship. Though one breed is not necessarily better than another, it is important to get a breed that suits your personality. If you prefer a laid-back life-style, for instance, you probably won't enjoy the hyperactivity of an Irish setter. Similarly, if you enjoy quick intelligence in a dog, you may want to stay away from Afghan hounds. A good book that deals with dog psychology and the personalities of different breeds is *The Encyclopedia of American Dogs*, by Piero Scanziani (Bonanza Books, 1981).

Unless you're going to breed your dog, have it neutered. You won't have to go through the bother of heat (in a female) and spraying (in a male). It's a lot cleaner and a lot less hassle. You won't have other dogs prowling around the house, either.

Once you've settled on the breed for you, and you've adopted a puppy or a dog, it's important to see that proper socialization takes place. Take the dog to obedience school so it can learn some manners. A well-behaved dog is a happy dog and has a happier master. Some schools offer puppy classes (for the 2-month-old), but generally, training begins at 6 months. Lessons include how to come when called, sit, stay, drop, and heel. Look for obedience schools through newspaper ads or listings in the yellow pages of the phone book, or ask your veterinarian for a recommendation.

Ideally, the trainer should be the dog's master, because the dog will eventually pledge his allegiance to that person. However, some obedience schools discourage children from training, because there is the possibility that another dog in the class may turn on their dog, and children may not be able to handle the situation. In that case, says one trainer, the person who trains the dog can teach the child how to work with the dog once classes are over.

One last point: You *can* teach an old dog new tricks. Ten-year-old Fido can go through dog obedience classes just as well as a 6-month-old puppy. You can also teach old people new tricks. "Having an elderly person take a dog through the classes is excellent therapy . . . for the person," says one obedience school owner.

CATS   Cats are America's number one pet. There are some 23 million cat people in the United States, and they live in every setting imaginable—country, city, and in between. Cats are wonderful, independent companions, and often live to be as much as 15 years old.

Cats can be perfectly happy by themselves, a good point to remember if no one is home during the day. Plus, a litter box takes a big worry off a cat owner's mind.

If you want to raise, educate, and watch over a cat, get a cuddly kitten, but not one that is younger than 10 to 12 weeks, no matter how adorable. Younger kittens may have been weaned too early, they may not have been reliably litter trained, and worst of all, they may not be properly socialized. Such a kitten may grow up into a neurotic grouch or a timid misfit afraid of its own shadow.

If you don't have the time or patience for a playful kitten, consider adopting an older cat. Look for one that is healthy, stable, well-mannered, and loving. The best cat or kitten has been raised as a member of a human family. He or she knows and trusts people and is not shy or withdrawn.

Males are generally more affectionate than females, though you'll want to have a male neutered. An unaltered male will grow into a wandering tom whose mind roams elsewhere and who often gets into fights—not qualities to be found in a good pet. Females, too, should be spayed to prevent yowling, rolling, and carrying on during heat. An altered cat of either sex makes an excellent pet.

SMALL PETS   There are many small pets to choose from—mice, gerbils, hamsters, guinea pigs, birds, fish, and turtles and other reptiles (including snakes). Small pets are sometimes recommended for younger children, who enjoy watching their activity and learning the responsibility of caring for another living thing. They usually are less expensive to own, are less challenging to care for, and require less attention and less space than cats or dogs. Some don't live very long, and some, like parrots, live to be 40 or 50 years old. (If you want a parakeet that talks, choose a male. Females don't talk.)

EXOTIC ANIMALS   Quite simply, exotic animals don't do well in captivity and, consequently, don't make good companions. Most veterinarians will beg you to leave the poisonous snake, the leopard, the monkey, and the bear (and they've seen them all) to the care of a professional.

Some states prohibit possession of wildlife without a permit. If you have a question about whether your state has such laws, contact the office of the attorney general in your state capital.

Most laws that regulate possession of animals are city or town ordinances. Commonly, cities prohibit possession of "other than house pets" within city limits. For specific information, contact your city attorney.

If you keep a wild animal or an abnormally dangerous domestic animal, you will probably be held strictly liable for any damage it may cause to people or property.

Pets and Life-Style

Getting a pet that has a personality to fit your life-style and temperament is crucial for a harmonious house. A high-strung, nervous dog will probably not

Pet Choices to Match Your Life-Style

It's important that your pet fit in with your life-style. Different animals have different needs, some of which may be incompatible with yours. For example, a puppy needs to be fed three to four times daily; must be taken outside every few hours, especially in the morning, after each meal, and before bed; requires close supervision; and must interact with its owner most of the day. A kitten (under 6 months old) also needs to be fed three to four times daily, requires close supervision, and must interact with its owner most of the day.

On the other hand, an adult dog or an adult cat can be without constant supervision, since it has already gone through the socialization stage; and an adult dog is already house-broken, so it can wait 8 hours for a walk. An adult cat can be left alone for longer periods. Two dogs or two cats can keep each other company while the owner is away. (A dog-cat combination also sometimes works.)

There are other small animals that make good pets and require much less care and supervision—birds, fish, gerbils, and hamsters can provide companionship and pleasure to those who want to be pet owners but have limited time available or have a very hectic household. Check the table below to find the pet most suitable to your life-style.

Life-Style	Puppy	Kitten	Adult Dog	Adult Cat	Other
Single person or couple in apartment or house and working much more than 8 hr each day				■	■
Single person or couple in apartment or house and at least one working a normal 8-hr day			■*	■	■
Single person or couple in apartment or house and at least one person home all day	■*	■	■*	■	■
Young couple in apartment or house and expecting a child					■†
Young couple in apartment or house with very small children			■*	■	■
Couple in apartment or house with older children and at least one person home all day	■*	■	■*	■	■

SOURCE: The Anti-Cruelty Society.

* Not all breeds function well in apartments.

† This is, of course, unless you already own a cat or dog.

be as happy with an active family as it might be with a quiet, retired couple. A person who isn't home much should probably forgo adopting a frolicking, curious kitten that needs lots of love and attention; such a person should consider an older, more mellow feline that is perfectly happy to while away the hours in an empty apartment or house. Take a look at the table on page 226 for suggestions on matching pets to your life-style.

KEEPING PETS HEALTHY

Just as you take care of your own health, you need to take care of your pet's health. Your duties vary, depending upon what kind of animal you have, but there are some general guidelines to follow for dogs and some cats:

- Clip toenails monthly.
- Brush the coat at least two or three times a week.
- Provide *daily* exercise.
- Begin vaccinations when the pet is 6 to 8 weeks old. There will also be an annual vaccine that covers a number of diseases. Rabies vaccinations vary according to local laws.

Keep in mind that small female dogs first go into heat between 5 and 6 months of age; larger female dogs between 8 and 9 months. Discuss this with your veterinarian ahead of time so you'll know what to watch for and how to deal with it.

Making your own pet food is preferable to buying commercial pet foods. However, if you don't want to cook for your pet, be sure that what you buy does not contain food coloring, slaughterhouse by-products, preservatives, sugar or sweeteners, or artificial flavorings. Avoid generic pet food. Once you've taken away the cost for marketing and distribution of generic food, there's very little money left for good nutrition and protein.

Housebreaking

Can anything loom more darkly than the prospect of housebreaking a pet? Probably not, but the process does not have to be a long and difficult one. Try this procedure for dogs:

- Teach your puppy to come, sit, or respond to some other command at least twice a day, to begin instilling discipline.
- Feed the puppy at the same time every day, 7 days a week. Offer no tidbits or snacks.
- Establish only one toilet area and take the puppy there after meals, water, sleep, excitement, or play. Stand by your pet, and offer lots of praise whenever it urinates or defecates in the toilet area.
- When you discover an accident (and be assured, you will), don't make a big fuss. At the most, comment by the tone of your voice that you aren't pleased with what you see. (When a pet wets the rug, vinegar will kill the odor and prevent staining, as long as you get to it

right away. First, absorb as much moisture as you can with dry paper towels. Then, mix 2 cups of white vinegar in a gallon of cold water. Apply the vinegar mixture to the spot with a clean cloth or paper towel, and gently blot the stain. Vinegar may bleach some dark, sensitive colors, so try it in an inconspicuous area first.)

■ When you leave home or go to bed at night, put the puppy in a good-sized cage. Take away drinking water at night and when the puppy is left alone.

Cats need to be housebroken, too, but not to such a great extent. Remember these tips:

■ Feed the cat at the same time every day, and don't offer tidbits or snacks.

Household Dangers for Pets

Protect your pet from these common, around-the-house hazards:

Antifreeze: Keep antifreeze containers tightly sealed, wiped clean, and out of reach of your cat or dog. Wipe up any puddles of it in your garage or around your car. Some animals, especially cats, love the taste of antifreeze and will eagerly lick up this lethal liquid.

Carriers: Molded plastic pet carriers are okay in cool weather, but when it's hot, heat can build up inside a carrier and cause your pet to have heatstroke, a potentially fatal condition.

Chocolate: Though most cats don't like it, dogs do. This is a hazard because many dogs can't handle the stimulants contained in chocolate. A dog that has overdosed on chocolate will have a bloody stool and suffer dehydration. Consult a vet immediately.

Collars: Check your growing pet's collar for fit every week. Many pets have slowly strangled from collars put on when they were small and not enlarged as they grew.

Houseplants: Some houseplants, such as poinsettias and philodendrons, are toxic if eaten. Check with your veterinarian for a listing of common house and garden plants that are dangerous to your pet.

Milk: Though kittens and puppies like and need milk, adult dogs and cats lack an enzyme needed to digest it. If you want to give your pet the nutrition of milk, gradually introduce it into the diet, watching carefully for signs of diarrhea.

Pickup trucks: Don't drive with an animal in the back of an open pickup truck. Many accidents and pet deaths are caused this way.

Windowsills: It's not safe for a pet to sit on a windowsill at an open window several stories above the ground. Many animals have been injured and killed by falls.

■ When you first bring home a new cat or kitten, keep it confined to one room for a day or two so it gets used to its surroundings. Then move the litter box to its permanent place, and take the cat or kitten to the box several times during that day to make sure it knows where the box is.

■ Buy or make a scratching post for your clawed pet, and encourage its use by sprinkling some catnip on it or at its base. If you catch your pet scratching at furniture or draperies, spritz the animal with water from a plant spray bottle. If you have fine furniture that you absolutely don't want the animal near, close off that room as best you can.

■ If you have a house full of plants, be sure to keep them out of reach of your cat, or you may come home to chewed-off leaves. You may want to hang your plants or keep them in a closed room, then leave one plant on a windowsill or other accessible place for the cat. If the cat has a plant of its own to chew on, it will most likely ignore yours. (Make sure the plant is not poisonous.)

■ Give your kitten or cat a bed of its own. While you may find it cute or comforting to have your pet sleep on your bed, you may soon be annoyed at its kneading or at the cat hair that gets left behind. To encourage your pet to sleep elsewhere, give it cozy surroundings, such as a box or basket with a soft blanket, cushion, or carpet scrap in it.

The Human Psyche and Its Effect on Animals

It's obvious that pets have an effect on their owners. Pets require time, attention, and most importantly, love. Being the care giver brings out the best in an owner. But did you ever wonder about care givers having an effect on their pets? Amazing as that may sound, it's true. The human psyche does have an effect on animals and, specifically, on animal health. It's common for itchy dogs to have itchy owners or for overweight pets to have overweight owners. Veterinarians report that a client with a cough or a sinus problem may well have an owner with a similar cough or sinus problem.

Animals further react to the human psyche by developing problems when there are emotional tensions between family members. In her book *What the Animals Tell Me* (Harper & Row, 1982), Beatrice Lydecker cites a case of a dachshund that chewed and scratched at herself every time her owners argued.

Finally—and this should come as no surprise if you already own a dog or cat—pets often get sick shortly after an upsetting change in the household. If your family goes on vacation or if there's a divorce, a new baby, or a death, it's not unlikely that your pet will react. After all, such situations mean a loss of attention for your pet.

Not every health problem your pet experiences is a result of that human-to-animal bond. But because so many are, you need to consider that *you* might be a part of the problem. What can you do about it? And how can you help your pet to remain healthy? In their book *Natural Health for Dogs and Cats*

(Rodale Press, 1982), Dr. Richard Pitcairn and Susan Hubble Pitcairn suggest a list of questions for you to consider as a good starting point:

1. Is my pet's health problem similar to one I have now or have had in the past?

2. Did I ever worry that my animal would get the very problem it has?

3. Is my animal similar to me? In what ways? Why did I choose this particular type of animal?

4. Does my pet seem especially upset when there are emotional tensions or conflicts in the household?

5. With regard to my animal's illness, what mental images, concerns, or attitudes typically go through my mind? Is it possible that I may be "broadcasting" images to my pet?

6. Did a major change occur or did something upsetting happen immediately before this animal first began showing symptoms?

7. Whenever this animal shows a symptom, do I give it any special attention, either positive or negative?

8. Do I get anything out of my pet's illness? Do I enjoy taking care of it?

If you've answered yes to two or more questions, consider yourself a possible negative health influence. The Pitcairns suggest that if you answered yes to questions 6, 7, or 8, you may be reinforcing your pet's symptoms. If that's the case, you need to stop giving the pet special attention for its symptoms. For example, don't coddle the animal every time it coughs. Rather, provide overall good health care.

If you answered yes to questions 1 through 5, the problem may be with your attitude. "More than anything," the Pitcairns say, "simply understand that the way you think and act has its effect in the world, including your pet's world."

Controlling Fleas

Have you ever wondered why some dogs and cats have severe flea problems, while others are hardly bothered by the little pests? Parasites—and that includes fleas—are most attracted to weak, unhealthy, or very young animals. The presence of parasites can result from (1) inbreeding of purebreds; (2) the increasingly high level of pollutants in our environment; or (3) the shortcomings of most commercial pet foods, which leave pets with varying degrees of vulnerability due to poor nutrition.

If your pet appears to have a flea problem, its immune system is probably not functioning properly. So you need to not only get rid of the problem but also strengthen the animal. Before you begin treatment, make sure the problem really is fleas. Don't assume that an itchy animal has fleas or that all insects on your pet are fleas. Look for hard, shiny, dark brown insects that are slightly smaller than a pinhead. Fleas spend 90 percent of their lives off the animal and only hop aboard for a blood meal. Unfortunately, that can be as many as 20 times an hour. Look for fleas over the rump or around the neck and ears. If fleas are present, you'll almost always be able to find flea "exhaust" or excrement—tiny black specks that turn brownish red on wet tissue paper. Comb your pet over white paper, and if you see on the paper what appears to be black pepper, it's flea excrement.

The first line of defense against fleas is keeping your pet as healthy as possible. This means paying careful attention to diet, exercise, and grooming.

DIET AND DIETARY SUPPLEMENTS   Dr. Jeffrey Levy, president of the California Holistic Veterinary Medical Association, strongly recommends a "homemade diet of fresh wholesome foods, which must be nutritionally complete and balanced for your pet's breed, age, and physical condition." Here are some dietary tips:

- Add raw, chopped garlic, garlic oil, or garlic powder to the daily diet (one clove for a cat, one to three cloves for a dog). Mix it into meat or cheese, or make a thin paste of it and pour it down the animal's throat with a squirt bottle.
- Add 5 milligrams of thiamine (vitamin B_1) to the food daily, or crush a 50-milligram thiamine tablet into 10 teaspoons of brewer's yeast and mix 1 to 3 teaspoons with the animal's regular food daily.
- Add raw and cooked greens, liver, and dried apricots to your pet's diet. They are reported to be excellent preventive medicines.
- Put ½ teaspoon cider vinegar in your cat's water dish for 3 days.

EXERCISE   A good, brisk walk in the fresh air and sunshine helps maintain your pet's muscle tone, good circulation, and proper elimination of metabolic wastes.

GROOMING   Regular brushing or combing (best done outside) helps the skin and coat, especially for long-haired animals whose fur becomes matted easily. If your cat has fleas, use a flea comb to catch the pests.

If, despite your best efforts, your pet should get a good case of fleas, don't despair. Try some of these remedies:

- Use an herbal flea collar. You can find them in most pet shops. Don't use chemical flea collars, dips, or sprays. They're strong enough to kill an invading flea force, so did you ever consider what they may do to your pet? Some contain phosphate insecticides—spin-offs from research on nerve gas warfare. They work by paralyzing an insect's nervous system, but they also present a risk of heart and respiratory depression, allergies, damage to the nervous system, and in extreme cases, death for your pet.
- Use eucalyptus oil on the skin or hair. Herbal powders are even easier to use, and most contain pyrethrin flowers or diatomaceous earth. Apply the products outdoors daily until the fleas are gone. After that, use them two to four times a month for the rest of the flea season.

■ Provide 1 to 4 teaspoons of brewer's yeast daily, depending on your pet's body weight. This will cause your pet to give off an odor that supposedly keeps fleas away, though you won't smell anything. Crushed garlic and/or brewer's yeast are very effective, but smelly, repellents if applied directly to the skin or hair. Repeat the application every few days.

■ Use a natural flea shampoo. There are various classes of insecticides, one or more of which may be contained in commercial pet shampoos. Fatal poisonings have resulted from either improper or excessive use of some of these products. So be on the safe side—use only natural products. Work the shampoo into a thick lather, then leave it on your pet for 15 minutes to drown the fleas. Be careful not to let small puppies or kittens become chilled or overheated, and don't bathe them more than once a week.

■ Add one lemon, sliced and including the peel, to 1 pint of boiling water. Steep it overnight. Strain the liquid and spray it on the skin and coat daily. This will heal the skin and repel insects.

■ Add ¼ to ½ teaspoon pennyroyal or citronella oil to your regular dog or cat shampoo. Always follow with a cream rinse or oil. (The oils are available at health food stores.) Pennyroyal can cause miscarriages; *avoid* using it if either you or your animal is pregnant.

HOUSEHOLD FLEA CONTROL   Remove existing flea eggs and larvae by frequent, thorough vacuuming of all pet bedding and any carpeting, furniture, and so forth that the pet may have been on. Remember, though, a vacuum-cleaner bag can be a reservoir of fleas, so it's important to change the bag after each cleaning session. You can kill the fleas, as well as the eggs and larvae, by putting the vacuum-cleaner bag in a plastic bag and leaving it in the freezer overnight. Or pour some flea powder into the bag before using the vacuum. A clean environment is the ultimate control, since it's in carpeting, furniture, and so forth—not *on* household pets—that fleas breed and hatch.

You can also try sprinkling garlic powder, brewer's yeast, or diatomaceous earth onto the carpeting, the furniture, and the animal's sleeping areas. (Diatomaceous earth is a natural substance mined from old seabeds. Be sure to buy an unprocessed brand because the kind sold for use in swimming-pool filters is harmful if inhaled.)

If your dog spends most of the time in a doghouse, place fresh pine needles in the house or under the dog's bed pad. Or salt the crevices of the doghouse.

Fight fleas that bite you or other members of the family by taking daily doses of vitamin B_1. While you're at it, give some to your flea-ridden pet. Sometimes it helps, sometimes it doesn't—but it's always worth a try. Once you've been bitten, treat bites with calamine lotion.

Prescription: A Healthy Home Has . . .

. . . owners who care about their pets' health and well-being, and who follow these simple rules:

■ Protect animals from road and traffic dangers. At least 1 million dogs and cats are killed annually in this country by traffic accidents. But traffic is not the only danger posed for your pet. Because pets live close to the ground, they are vulnerable to the heavier air pollutants (such as lead and carbon monoxide) and to asbestos dust that is shed from brake linings. Furthermore, dogs who ride in the back of pickup trucks can be seriously injured if they fall. They are also exposed to excessive car exhaust. Finally, it is easy for an animal left in a hot, sealed car—even for a short time—to suffer heatstroke.

■ Keep garbage cans and wastebaskets well sealed. Pets love to prowl through the leftovers for a bite to eat—and they often get sick after doing so, because the discarded food has become spoiled or tainted.

■ Store household chemicals out of reach. Pets, like youngsters, are curious and will eat or otherwise absorb almost any toxic household product they can get to. Veterinarians are constantly seeing anti-freeze poisoning, partly because the antifreeze tastes sweet and pets are tempted to lap up the spills. Keep containers sealed and out of reach. Clean up spills at once. Minimize (or avoid) the use of harsh floor cleaners.

■ Be aware of obvious physical dangers. Keep electrical cords away from puppies, who are constantly in search of something to chew. Before closing a door on the refrigerator, oven, or clothes dryer, make sure the cat did not crawl inside. If you live in a high-rise apartment, do not let kitty nap at open windows or on outside sills. For chewing, provide pet toys rather than newspapers, books, plastic toys, or even balls of yarn. Finally, make sure you are around when a child decides to play with the pet. Sometimes, without meaning to, a youngster can get too rough.

■ Keep your pets well groomed. Brush them regularly, preferably outdoors, especially if someone in the family has allergies. If you have ever ruffled up an animal's fur in the light of a sunbeam coming through a nearby window, you have undoubtedly noticed all that airborne fluff. But the most allergenic component of that material is so small that you can't even see it with the naked eye. That is why brushing outdoors, with your face upwind, helps.

■ Train your pet. Be sure that any pets in the house can be quickly

(continued)

brought under control at all times. Dogs should be taken to obedience school.

■ Neuter your dogs and cats. There are so many dogs and cats in the world who have no owners, it is a shame to allow more to be brought into the world unless you are a breeder with a market for your animals.

■ Know where your pet is at all times. Never abandon an animal that has been your pet. That amounts to extreme cruelty. Similarly, if you see an abandoned pet on the street, leave it alone. Eventually, it may find its way home. If not, call local animal authorities to take care of it.

13

Safety

It was nearing 2:00 A.M. when Ron Mason became aware that the grandfather clock was no longer chiming. Though drowsy from the late hour and from reading in bed, he got up to rewind the large clock. Normally the act of pulling the chains that lift the 12-pound weights is a simple procedure. Not so this time. Ron recalls what happened: "As the canister containing the weights got within about 6 inches of the top, the eyebolt came unscrewed, breaking the canister and propelling four 7-inch pieces of lead, sharp as knives and each weighing about 4 pounds. They came crashing down on my bare foot, leaving two gashes in my big toe. I jumped around for about 10 minutes trying to relieve the pain."

Though Ron's is not a common story, the moral is. Your home may be your castle, but it's also where you're most likely to cut your hand, break your leg, hit your head, or bloody your toe. Every year one in three Americans ends up in a doctor's office or hospital because of an injury. The statistics—33.2 injuries per 100 people—show that accidents are inevitable, and a large share of them occur at home.

Certain types of injuries are more likely to occur at home than anywhere else. If you break a bone, for example, you probably broke it at home. More than half of all cuts and bruises occur at home, as do 47 percent of broken shins and forearms and 50 percent of cuts, bruises, and open wounds. This wouldn't be so bad except that many of these injuries are disabling. The National Safety Council reports that more disabling injuries occur in the home than in any other place.

Carelessness accounts for an estimated 70 percent of all home accidents. This means that in 1985 alone, *2,170,000 accidents* could have been prevented if people were simply more cautious. Why is this figure so high? There's a good chance it's cultural. We're simply in too big a hurry, we believe that accidents are acts of fate, and we perform potentially dangerous tasks when in the wrong state of mind.

235

Safety awareness is an inherent element in any healthy home. It comes easily to some people, not so easily to others. It may take some exercising, but it's well worth the effort. Once safety awareness is developed and practiced in the home daily, it becomes an easy task to instill in children. Knowing the hazards, practicing prevention, and passing knowledge onto the next generation—that's what a healthy home is all about.

SAFETY AWARENESS

What can you do to prevent accidents at home? The first step is developing a safety awareness that is with you all the time:

Take your time. People in a hurry have more accidents. Whenever you're about to embark on a task, slow down. Think it through. What are the dangers? What shape is your equipment in? Does anything need to be repaired? If so, do that first. If you don't have time to do the job thoroughly and well, save it for another day.

Assess the hazards realistically. Why go into a potentially dangerous task with blinders on? Take off those rose-colored glasses. Your safety is up to you and you alone. If you get hurt, chances are it's your fault—no one else's. Most accidents are preventable. Adopt that attitude from the outset, and keep it uppermost in your mind.

Cultivate safety daily. Don't use power tools, knives, or ladders or work with glass when you're angry, tired, or have had a few beers. If you're tired after a hard day at work, sit down, put your feet up, and relax for a few minutes before fixing dinner or performing other routine tasks. Don't do anything but relax when you're sleepy. Not only will you be safer, you'll soon find you have a better quality of life.

Think! Pay attention, plan, use your mind. For example, if you get a slight shock while using your toaster, don't use it again as if nothing happened. You don't need to be an electrician to know that something is amiss. Take the toaster to the repair shop. Don't wait for the shock to become more severe.

FALLS: THE NUMBER ONE CAUSE OF ACCIDENTS

Falls are the number one cause of accidents in the home. They can be severely disabling, even deadly. Thirty percent of accidental deaths in the home are attributed to falls. Misplaced scatter rugs, slippery floors, dimmed lights, electrical cords stretched across corridors, and objects left on stairs are common culprits. Older people are the most vulnerable. More than 80 percent of the people killed by falls each year are over the age of 65.

You must first find hazards before you can eliminate them. Check floors in your house for slippery areas. Look for obstacles that can make you trip. Be aware of hazards that can appear unexpectedly. The National Safety Council advises specific awareness when it comes to these conditions:

Slippery floors: Don't wax floors to a slippery luster—safety is vastly more important than aesthetics. Scatter rugs can slide, taking you with them. Give a small rug a nonskid backing with abrasive strips or foam rubber. Never use a scatter rug at the top or bottom of a stairway. A carpet or rug that doesn't lie flat can catch your foot and make you stumble. Smooth out wrinkles and folds, and tack down loose edges. Repair frayed edges and rips. When buying a new rug or carpet, pass up those long, thick piles. They won't give you firm footing. Instead, choose a short, dense pile and install it over a good-quality, medium-thick pad.

Crowded traffic lanes: Keep traffic lanes free. People should be able to walk through rooms without detouring around furniture. People should be able to move through doorways and halls without squeezing past obstacles. Areas between bedrooms and bathrooms should always be clear.

Outdoor conditions: Check your yard and other outdoor areas for hazards. Patch broken walks and driveways, and fill in lawn and garden holes. Put away garden tools and hoses, and get rid of rocks, loose boards, and other obstacles that can make people stumble. Clear wet leaves and snow from walkways, steps, and porches, and sprinkle icy patches with salt. Provide doormats at entrances so people can wipe snow and mud from their shoes, and not track it onto your floors.

Poor lighting: Darkness can turn any room into an obstacle course. Shadows can hide hazards. Reduce the risk of injury with plenty of good, strong light. Install light switches near doorways so you never need to walk through a dark room to turn on a light. A lamp that's easily reached from your bed will help you avoid nighttime falls. Night-lights in the bathroom and hall add to your safety.

Avoid Injury

Take the necessary precautions to avoid injury. Start by wearing the right shoes. Always wear footwear with soles and heels that provide good traction—don't walk around in stocking feet. Replace boots or galoshes when soles and heels are worn smooth, so you don't slip on wet or icy surfaces.

Be careful when you carry bulky packages. Make sure your path is clear. Hold laundry baskets, trays, and large bundles to one side so they don't block your view.

Store frequently used items within easy reach. Use a sturdy step stool to reach high shelves. Never stand on a chair; it can tip or slide. When you use a step stool or stepladder, be sure it's not too short for the job. Set it up on a firm, level base that's free of clutter. Make certain it's fully open and that side braces are locked. Face the steps when you climb. Don't stand on top of a step stool or climb beyond the second step from the top on a stepladder. Always keep your body between the rails.

Knowing how to fall can help you avoid serious injury. When you feel yourself falling, it's only natural to tense up, resist, and put out a straight arm to take the shock. Ironically, you're much more likely to get hurt this way. Instead, relax and go limp. Try to roll as you fall, to reduce the impact. Bend your arms so you can ease yourself down.

FIRE: THE SCARIEST HAZARD

Although hotel fires receive the most notoriety, the majority of fire deaths and injuries occur at home. To have a healthy house free of fire hazards, you need to do two things: (1) Exercise fire prevention and (2) make a plan so that everyone in the house knows what to do if a fire occurs.

Fire Prevention

The first rule of fire prevention is caution—don't start the fire that kills you. It's a bit simplistic, but nevertheless important. Beware of hazardous situations and remedy them immediately.

Begin by taking a close look at your heating system. Keep your furnace and heating system in good working order. Have it professionally inspected every 2 years. If you have an oil burner, have it checked each year. Check the chimney and flue pipes to be sure that masonry separations are intact and there is no contact with wood house framing.

Portable heaters accounted for 103,000 house fires in 1985, many of them fatal. When using a space heater, follow these rules:

- Be sure your gas or fuel-burning space heater is properly vented, unless the unit is specifically designed to be unvented. In that case, make certain that a door or window is opened slightly in the room in which the unit is operating.
- Use only an electric space heater that has a tip-over shutoff switch and protective grilles around heating elements.
- Use only extension cords that match the electrical requirements of electric space heaters.
- Never put a portable electric heater in a bathroom or near a sink.
- To protect against carbon monoxide poisoning, purchase space heaters with oxygen-depletion shutoff systems.

To prevent kitchen fires, the simplest suggestion is to keep your kitchen clean. Grease will burst into flame when heated to its ignition point, so clean the areas where grease collects—the stove hood and venting system, the broiler, and any drain pans.

Use pot holders and turn pot handles away from the front of the range so they won't be dropped or knocked over. *Don't* leave food cooking while you become engrossed in a TV show or a phone conversation. Use a timer. Check for combustible materials, like curtains or a paper-covered shelf, near the burners..

Follow these instructions in case of a grease fire:

In a pan on the stove: (1) Put a lid over the pan to cut off air; (2) turn off the burner; and (3) never carry the pan from the stove, or you may fan the flame.

In the oven or broiler: (1) Close the oven or broiler door and (2) turn off the burner.

Are Your Circuits Overloaded?

To find out whether your electrical circuits are overloaded, map out the separate circuits in your house. Turn on a ceiling fixture and lamp in each room. Then trip a single breaker or disconnect one fuse. In most houses the lights in one or more rooms will go out, thus locating a circuit. Mark each circuit separately at the service panel.

Once you have located a circuit, test each wall outlet and switch to see to which circuit it belongs. Identify potential overloads by making a hand-drawn map of this entire system and then making an amperage chart for each circuit. Here's how to calculate amperage:

1. For lighting and wall receptacles, multiply 3 watts by every square foot of floor space served by the circuit. (For example, in a 12-by-14-foot room you have 168 square feet; times 3 watts equals 504.)
2. Then add the wattage for each appliance on that circuit. (To find the wattage of an appliance, consult the owner's manual or read the wattage from a plate on the appliance itself.) So, if on our hypothetical circuit there is an iron at 1,000 watts and a space heater at 1,250 watts, there are 2,754 watts (504 + 1,000 + 1,250) on that circuit.
3. Now divide the total watts (2,754) by the effective voltage of that circuit. In most cases, that will be 120. If the circuit is for large appliances, like an air conditioner, it will be a 240-volt line. If our hypothetical circuit has 120 volts, then 2,754 divided by 120 is 23. This is the amperage for that circuit. Compare this number to the fuse or the number on that circuit at the service panel. If the circuit is for 15 or 20 amps, it is overloaded. If it's for 30 amps, you're all right. You should have some margin for safety because many appliances use a surge of electricity when starting up. Thus 30 amps on a 30-amp circuit is too close for comfort.

For a more detailed analysis of this calculation process, plus a chart of estimated amperage for most appliances, consult *The Reader's Digest Home Improvements Manual* (Reader's Digest Association, 1982).

ELECTRICAL FIRES   Electrical wiring should be professionally installed according to applicable building code standards. The dollars you save by a do-it-yourself wiring job are not worth the potential harm from an electrical fire.

Overloaded circuits are the number one cause of domestic fires. The first step toward electrical fire prevention is to be sure that you have adequate circuits for what you're running.

Replace blown fuses only with those of the correct amperage. Changing a fuse to a higher number will not increase the electrical capacity for that circuit, because the wire gauge, not the fuse, determines the current-carrying capacity of a circuit. By changing to a higher number, you invalidate the safety-valve function of the fuse; an overload will overheat the wires rather than blow the fuse. This is likely to result in the insulation being burned off the wire, causing dangerous sparks and (if not caught in time) a fire.

Wiring isn't the only source of electrical hazards. Major appliances, such as televisions, need to be checked, too. Televisions generate a lot of heat, so they need air around them. Don't place a TV tightly in a bookcase or flat against a wall. Don't get in the habit of falling asleep with the TV on; it can overheat and may explode.

If you have an old "instant on" TV (the TV set is always warm), plug it into a outlet controlled by a wall switch and turn the power source off at night. Manufacturers ceased making these in the 1970s because they are a fire hazard.

FIRES CAUSED BY SMOKING   Smoking causes many fire deaths among smokers and innocent victims alike. Because smoking is so antithetical to health, the occupants of a healthy home never allow smoking within its walls. If you are going to allow overnight guests to smoke, you must *demand* that they absolutely do not smoke in bed. It's best if you can confine smoking to an area outside the house altogether; and at the very least, forbid it in the bedrooms. If you smoke, the first step toward health is to quit smoking. Rules for "safe" smoking do not apply to a healthy home.

OTHER HOUSEHOLD FIRES   In addition to safety checks on heating systems and major appliances, you should also be aware of some common household products that are potential fire hazards:

Aerosols: Aerosols can explode if punctured or left close to heat or fire. The propellant used in some aerosols is propane gas, which is extremely flammable. Moreover, some of the chemicals in the can may be flammable in a liquid state. Spraying some hair sprays, for example, produces a mist of liquid and gas, both flammable. If done near a heat source, such as a hair dryer or kitchen range, the result could be disastrous. Best advice is to avoid aerosols altogether.

Gasoline-powered equipment: Lawn mowers, chain saws, and other gasoline-powered equipment present fire hazards both in their use and in the storage of the gasoline. Never refuel this equipment while it is still running, or even while the engine is off but still hot. Gasoline spilled onto a hot engine will instantly vaporize and can burst into flame, which can in turn run up to the gas can you're holding and explode in flames. Even when done properly, fueling and refueling should be done outdoors rather than in the garage or storage shed. Store gasoline in its original container away from the house, preferably in a detached garage.

Christmas paraphernalia: Electrical and other burning accidents have ruined many a Christmas. If you buy a live tree each year, make sure it's fresh (no dropping needles) and keep it in water in a sturdy stand away from all heat sources. Don't leave tree lights on when the tree is unattended, and don't leave small children unattended around Christmas trees or burning candles. After the holiday, throw your tree away or put it outside and hang bird food from its branches. Don't burn it in the fireplace! Don't put flammable decorations on the mantel or above any other heat source. If you buy an artificial tree, be sure the label says it's a fire retardant.

LIGHTNING   A house standing alone is a prime target for a lightning strike. If you have lots of electrical storms in your area and your house is located on a high, exposed site, you may want to install a lightning rod on the roof. A lightning rod will intercept electrical charges before they strike a building and will divert them to the ground.

A lightning rod won't protect you from injury caused by lightning striking a telephone wire while you're talking on the phone. This is not uncommon, according to an article in the June 23, 1986 *Medical Journal of Australia*. Two Australian doctors tell the story of a 31-year-old man who was thrown against a wall, temporarily paralyzed, and subjected to mild hearing loss from the jolt he received when he was struck by lightning through the telephone.

"Customers are encouraged not to have telephones installed near wet areas, electrical appliances, and other fixtures that are conductive to the ground," the physicians noted. The lightning victim in the article was sitting on a stool with his leg touching a dishwasher when his conversation was shockingly interrupted.

Fire Safety

A house fire can be a killer in less than 3 minutes. The owners of a healthy home avoid destruction and death by fire. They have a fire escape plan, which incorporates the use of smoke detectors and fire extinguishers, well placed throughout the house.

FIRE ESCAPE PLAN   Don't plan to make a plan—do it now! Get some graph paper, and draw a floor plan for each floor in your house. Include all apertures

—windows, doors, skylights, and so on—even old openings that have been painted or nailed shut. Include heat sources—furnaces, stoves, hot water heaters, and so on. Mark a primary escape route from each room in green pen. Include a secondary escape route marked in yellow. Mark blocked windows, doors, and other dead-end routes in red. The locations of all fire extinguishers should be marked, so your family can learn them through drilling. Leave a copy of the plan by the main telephone, and bring it to the attention of baby-sitters and overnight guests.

Gather the family together to study and practice implementing the plan. No joking—make sure the kids take this seriously. Discuss the plan to see if any adjustments should be made. If you find that certain windows are stuck, plan around them. Ideally, all windows open easily enough that even small children can open them if they have to. As you analyze secondary escape routes, you may find there's no easy jump to the ground from a particular window or roof. Place either chain or rope ladders near these points. The best ladders are those with spacers holding the ladder away from the house.

As you discuss the plan with young children, don't overload them. Concentrate on escape routes from their bedrooms. Make sure the plan includes a specific neighbor's house at which to regroup. Not only will this diminish concern on the family's part, it will save fire fighters extra work and possible injury; they won't have to enter the house to look for someone who is really out but not in sight.

With the plan finalized, it's time to drill and drill again. Have some scheduled and unscheduled drills. Have everyone learn the following escape tips:

Feel a door before you open it. Feel it at the top and on the knob. If it's hot, don't open it—look for a secondary route.

Crawl on your hands and knees. This keeps your head at just the right height—below most of the smoke and carbon monoxide (since heat rises) and above the dense toxic gases that settle near the floor.

Keep a damp cloth over your nose and mouth, if possible. This filters out most of the deadly smoke. Remember, over 80 percent of fire deaths are from smoke inhalation.

Don't run. Running fans the flames. If your clothing does catch fire, roll over to smother the flames.

Don't delay in escaping; once out, don't reenter for anything. Don't take time to save your favorite teddy bear, your great-grand-ma's clock, your stamp collection, or even your pet dog or cat. This same principal applies after you're out—don't reenter for *anything!*

SMOKE DETECTORS Seventy-four percent of U.S. houses have smoke de-tectors, according to a Louis Harris poll. Yet, only one in four reported house fires occurs in a house with a detector. That means that 75 percent of the fires are in 25 percent of the houses.

If you don't have smoke detectors in your house, get them now! There

Burning Plastics Emit Toxic Smoke

Smoke—not flames—is the primary killer in a fire. This is not new. What is new, however, is the *kind* of smoke that fires are generating these days. It's much more toxic than it used to be. Smoke inhalation is responsible for at least 80 percent of fire fatalities today. People die from smoke and gas inhalation before the flames even reach them.

Synthetic materials appear to be responsible for the higher levels of smoke toxicity. According to a Washington fire safety group, synthetic materials, mostly plastics, "burn twice as fast, twice as hot, and give off up to 500 times as much toxic gas as more conventional materials."

In one hotel fire in which ten people died, deadly gases from burning synthetics "contributed to most, if not all," of the deaths, according to a study by the Foundation for Fire Safety. In that study it was found that hydrogen cyanide gas resulted from the combustion of polyurethane carpet padding, nylon carpet and blankets, and polyurethane cushions on upholstered furniture. Hydrogen chloride gas came from burning polyvinyl chloride wall coverings.

Synthetics are also found in modern building materials. Some insulations contain rigid or flexible foams that emit dense, black smoke and toxic gases when they burn. Plastic conduit, or PVC pipe, is another culprit. This tube, composed mostly of polyvinyl chloride (PVC), is used to enclose electrical wiring, plumbing, and gas lines. PVC plumbing has been implicated—controversially—in some of the 83 deaths in the MGM Grand Hotel fire in Las Vegas in 1980.

Though the U.S. Consumer Product Safety Commission has set mandatory flammability standards for some products, few codes, standards, or laws address smoke toxicity. State and local regulations concerning smoke toxicity of building materials go largely unenforced. It's a new and controversial area, involving huge economic stakes, with the issues clouded by corporate maneuverings and rhetoric.

What can you, the homeowner, do about it? Analyze the materials in your house: both the furnishings and the building materials. Whenever plastics or other synthetics are found, think about replacing them with a more natural material. When remodeling or adding on, study your options and find out how materials burn. Practice fire prevention. Install smoke detectors and fire extinguishers, and develop a plan of action in case fire breaks out.

are three types to choose from. One belongs in a healthy home, the other two do not.

Ionization smoke detectors: These contain approximately 1 microcurie of americium 241, a radioactive material that is distributed under license from the U.S. Nuclear Regulatory Commission (NRC). Americium 241 causes the air that moves through a small chamber within the detector to become electrically conductive. When smoke particles enter the chamber, the current flow is reduced and a warning buzzer sounds. These detectors react to a small amount of smoke, smaller than that perceived by the human eye.

Photoelectric detectors: These use a chamber and a beam of light that, when deflected by smoke particles, sounds the warning buzzer. These detectors react more quickly to smoldering fires.

Combination photoelectric/ionization detectors: These employ both methods of detection.

All types are available in battery-operated models (using a single 9-volt battery) or in models suitable for connection to your house's 110-volt AC circuit. The overall cost and simplicity of the battery-operated units makes them preferable. Moreover, they will continue to operate even if your electricity is temporarily interrupted. The only real caution is that you should make sure the batteries are replaced once a year. Nearly all units will make an intermittent chirping sound when the batteries get low.

The photoelectric detector is the smoke detector of choice for a healthy home. Who wants even a tiny amount of man-made radioactive material in their house? Even though the NRC says the ionization type is perfectly safe, there is no reason to believe that is true. Common sense says that if a small beam of light will do as well or better than americium 241, why compound your exposure to radioactivity? Furthermore, product tests in both *Consumer Reports* and *New Shelter* magazines found that, generally, the photoelectric type responds more quickly to fire than does the ionization type.

The problem is simply this: Several recent field surveys found the photoelectric type to be unavailable in many localities. If you find this true in your area, ask for and special-order photoelectric units. (Your hardware store or building center should be able to help you.) Dealers won't stock them unless there is sufficient demand. Or send for units through the mail (see appendix A). They cost around $30 (ionization types cost between $7 and $20; combinations are priced around $25).

If you already have an ionization smoke detector, there's only one good way to dispose of it. Mail it back to the manufacturer or to the NRC with a note explaining why you are doing so. The NRC used to require that spent ionization units be returned to the NRC for disposal. That requirement was deleted from the Code of Federal Regulations in January 1981, and now printing on packages of ionization detectors includes this statement: "The purchaser is exempt from any regulatory requirements." Thus, we're free to keep the americium 241 in our closets if we want to; throw it into the trash; or, if we'll take the time, return it to the manufacturer or the NRC. (See appendix B for how to obtain the addresses of regional NRC offices.)

Because smoke rises, the best location for smoke detectors is on the ceiling or high on an inside wall just below the ceiling. Install at least one on each level of the house, always having one between sleeping areas and the rest of the house. As a general guideline, on the first floor the detector should be placed on the ceiling at the base of the staircase or in the living room. For basements, at the bottom of the stairway is best.

FIRE EXTINGUISHERS   If fire breaks out, you're going to have to quickly decide whether to fight it or flee. If you decide to fight, always keep your back to the door so you can escape if the fire begins to spread.

Deciding whether a fire is extinguishable or not can be a tough call. As a general guideline, a fire started by an electrical appliance would be difficult for you to extinguish. The same is true with a wall fire due to electrical wiring. These kinds of fires often smolder deep within the wiring and are difficult to get to. On the other hand, with a good homemade fire extinguisher, you'll probably be able to put out a grease fire in a skillet or a fire in a trash can. Throw baking soda (*not* water) onto a grease fire, or cover it with a lid, and turn off the flame. A trash-can fire can also be put out with a lid of some kind. Any flat object, like a cookie sheet or a large pan, will smother the fire by

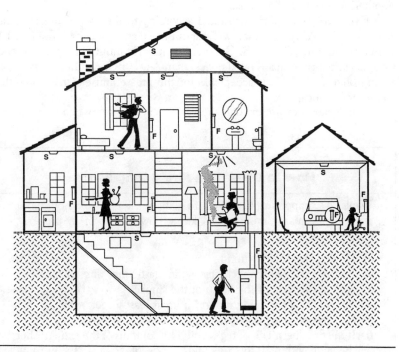

Keep your home safe—be sure there are fire extinguishers and smoke alarms placed throughout the house. F = fire extinguisher; S = smoke alarm.

cutting off its oxygen. If you have any doubt about your ability to put out the fire, close the door on it, warn others, and go elsewhere to call the fire department.

The best method of extinguishing a house fire is by using a fire extinguisher. What kind? That depends on the type of fire. There are three kinds of fires:

Class A fires: fueled by wood, paper, rubber, and most plastics
Class B fires: fueled by flammable liquids such as oil, gasoline, paint, or grease
Class C fires: ignited by live electrical equipment like televisions, radios, and other appliances

A multipurpose extinguisher is marked for all three types—ABC—and is effective against all three types of fires. This extinguisher is filled with a dry chemical called monoammonium phosphate, which interrupts the chemical chain reaction of fire and, with ordinary combustibles, smothers the fire.

Also on the market is an extinguisher filled with sodium bicarbonate, or baking soda. This will extinguish class B and C fires, but it will not work on wood, paper, and fabric found in class A fires. The advantage of the ABC extinguisher is obvious, but it's not foolproof. For example, it won't completely extinguish a deep upholstery fire. Further action is needed, such as smothering it outside the house.

Fire extinguishers are also rated according to the size of fire they can extinguish. A 2A, 10BC rating will put out twice as big a class A fire as a 1A, 10BC extinguisher. The U.S. General Services Administration recommends a house extinguisher that is rated no less than 2A, 10BC. Around the stove, an extinguisher rated 5BC is acceptable for the grease and electrical fires that commonly erupt there.

The location of fire extinguishers is critical because, when a fire erupts,

---

How to Operate a Fire Extinguisher

While it's important to have fire extinguishers throughout your home, it's equally important to know how to use them properly. Here's how:

1. Have a clear exit in mind.
2. Remove the safety mechanism (the plastic pin, ring, or tape).
3. Aim at the base of the fire, not the smoke.
4. Spray with a sweeping motion from at least 5 feet away.
5. Use several short bursts rather than a steady stream.
6. If the fire doesn't go out, get out! The contents of the extinguisher will be gone within 10 to 25 seconds. If possible, remove the burning material from the building. Then call the fire department.

you won't have time to go looking for one. Every house is different, but here are a few general guidelines:

- Keep an extingisher near an outside door, not in a dead-end corner where you could be trapped.
- Hang the kitchen extinguisher so you don't have to reach across stove-top flames to get it. Other places to consider include the bedrooms, the garage, and workshop areas. Easy access is key.

ELECTRICAL SHOCK: A DANGER IN EVERY HOME

Water and electricity don't mix. You've probably heard this a thousand times. Don't forget it. Teach it to your kids. It's an important rule of home safety. A common misconception is that it takes a large jolt of electricity to upset the heart's rhythm, while in fact, about one-third of an ampere—barely enough to light a light bulb—is enough to kill.

In spite of advances in product design, electrocutions still occur. The U.S. Consumer Product Safety Commission estimates that 600 people die yearly by electrocution around the home. A typical case is the man who died when his hair dryer fell into the bathtub with him. Dozens of people have died this way, many of them children and teenagers.

Where does the combination of water and electricity occur in your home? The kitchen, bathroom, laundry room, and patio/deck/porch are standard areas. What are the chances someone in your house can get electrocuted in these areas? Check them out. Does an obvious hazard exist? If so, fix it. Remove radios, hair dryers, and other appliances from the bathroom. Make sure everyone in the house knows not to operate the clothes washer if the floor is damp, particularly if the floor is made of concrete. Post a sign.

Take Precautions

Advances in electrical safety—like the three-wire ground system, the polarized plug, and double insulation—have decreased the amount of accidents involving water and electricity. But the danger is still there, and carelessness is usually the cause. It's up to you to be responsible for safety.

When you buy an appliance that will be used in wet areas, be sure to read the instructions that come with it. Follow those instructions to the letter, and see that others in the house know the dangers. Pay special attention to hair dryers, as they account for 60 percent of all bathtub electrocutions. Don't leave them plugged in when not in use. Even with the switch off, a plugged-in dryer still carries a current.

In the kitchen, it's a good idea to develop the habit of working one-handed. For instance, don't touch the toaster, mixer, or coffee maker with one hand while you turn on the faucet with the other. Also get into the habit of disconnecting appliance cords at wall outlets—not at the appliance. A cord

---

The Ground-Fault Circuit Interrupter

The ground-fault circuit interrupter, or GFCI, is a relatively new device that shuts off electrical current if a leak occurs. The *National Electrical Code* requires that all receptacles in lighting circuits in potentially wet areas—such as bathrooms, garages, and yards—be protected by a GFCI against electrical shock.

A GFCI monitors how much electricity goes into an appliance and how much comes out. If there's a leak—a ground fault—and less electricity comes out than went in, the GFCI cuts the power within $\frac{1}{40}$ of a second—30 times faster than a heartbeat! A GFCI can detect leakage levels far below those that would trip a circuit breaker or blow a fuse, and thus prevent fatal shock.

GFCIs can be installed in place of standard receptacles by anyone with electrical know-how. The built-in receptacle type is the most practical for residential use. Many homeowners are installing GFCIs in kitchen, laundry, and workshop circuits, although they are not yet required there by most local codes.

---

removed from an appliance and left plugged into an outlet is energized and could be deadly if it falls into a sink full of water.

Keep spills wiped up in the laundry room. And be wary of a flooded basement. Don't venture into one unless you are positive the water is not in contact with a source of electricity.

POISONS: THE TOXIC DISABLERS

Every year, 5 to 10 million household poisonings are reported in the United States. Ninety percent of these are accidental. Ten individuals a day are killed by accidental poisonings, according to the National Safety Council. Children represent 64 percent of all reported cases. But it's adults, more than children, who die. More than three-fourths of accidental poisoning deaths happen to people aged 25 or older.

Cleaning substances, plants, and pain remedies are the worst culprits. A report by the National Clearinghouse for Poison Control Centers revealed that in 1981 more than 17,000 cases of poisoning were attributed solely to cleaning and polishing agents. But pesticides pose a real health hazard, too. They are the second most frequent cause of poisoning in young children, following medicines.

What can you do to make your home safe from poisonings? Prevention is the best cure. Go through all cabinets and drawers in your house periodically and weed out the toxic substances. These include disinfectants, ammonia, insecticides, bleaches, mothballs, kerosene, paint thinners, prescription drugs, cosmetics, detergents, and acids as well as a host of other substances. Dispose of those you no longer need, in an ecologically safe manner. (See chapter 6 for information on disposal.) Analyze the toxicity of those you keep. Store high-tox substances under lock and key in a cool, dry place where children and pets cannot find them.

Keep the telephone number of your local poison control center posted near each telephone, and don't hesitate to use it. If you think you or another family member has ingested a poisonous substance, call. The person answering the phone will be able to tell you whether or not there is a hazard, will tell you what action to take next, and if necessary, will relay information to a hospital and/or to emergency personnel.

Prescription: A Healthy Home Has ...

... safety built into every area of the house. How does your house rate?

Kitchen

■ You need a stepladder to reach things on topmost shelves. A cheap, wobbly ladder is worse than no ladder at all.

■ Knives should be carefully sheathed and out of reach of children. Store them in a knife block or secure rack away from the edge of the work surface—not loose in drawers. When knives are washed, immediately dry them and put them away.

■ Exhaust fans piped to the outside carry off fumes, unwanted grease, heat, and moisture. Moisture vapor and heat can be vented by a wall or ceiling-mounted exhaust fan near the range. Grease and smoke must be filtered by a ventilating hood over the range top. Grease that collects in a hood's filter can be a fire hazard and also reduce the efficiency of the unit. The filter should be cleaned regularly, at intervals specified by the manufacturer.

■ Have a burn remedy close at hand. An aloe vera plant growing in a pot on the windowsill is best.

■ Keep a box of baking soda near the stove, to put out grease fires.

■ A fire extinguisher should be handy to douse any kitchen fires.

■ Store cleaning products and toxic substances under lock and key in a cabinet or pantry.

■ You need both general room lighting and specific task lighting over work surfaces for food preparation, cooking, and cleanup.

(continued)

Prescription: A Healthy Home Has ... —*Continued*

Bathroom

■ A ground-fault circuit interrupter (GFCI) should replace any standard electrical outlet.

■ A ventilation fan should be located close to the shower or bathtub, and it should be switched independently of the light fixtures. If the fan is installed within a tub or shower enclosure, it should be UL (safety code) listed for the location and installed on a GFCI branch circuit.

■ Floors and tubs should have nonslip, textured surfaces.

■ Have a minimum of sharp corners. Countertops and shower doors should have rounded edges to reduce the risk of injury.

■ Supervise very young, elderly, or sick people while they're in the tub.

■ Hot radiators or heaters should be covered or mounted so that they do not cause burns.

■ Medicine cabinets shouldn't contain dangerous drugs or toxic chemicals. The moist, warm, humid environment of a bathroom can affect the stability of many drugs. Medicines should be kept in a cool, dry cabinet that can be locked, and cleaning products should be located elsewhere in the house.

■ Lowered the hot-water temperature. It should be no higher than 130°F. Avoid burns in the shower by using a thermostatically controlled mixer faucet that maintains a predetermined temperature throughout the shower.

Living Area

■ Leave room to move around without tripping over objects or furniture. Keep toys out of the middle of the floor.

■ A wire screen across the mouth of a fireplace keeps sparks from flying into the living area. Andirons should be placed to prevent logs from rolling out into the room when the fire shifts.

■ Chimneys of fireplaces should be cleaned at least once a year to prevent chimney fires.

Bedroom

■ Leave clear paths from the doors to the beds. Many people are hurt in bedroom falls when these pathways are obstructed.

■ Remove slippery rugs.

■ There should be overall general room lighting, with switches right inside the doors.

(continued)

Prescription: A Healthy Home Has ... —*Continued*

■ Light the closets, especially if they are 10 or more square feet in size.

■ Stable shelves in a closet prevent items placed on them from falling down and keep things neat and organized..

Stairs and Hallways

■ Install good lighting. Three-way switches are essential, with one at the top and one at the bottom of the stairs. There should also be one at either end of a long hallway.

■ Carpeting or other flooring material should be firmly fastened down to prevent trips and falls.

■ Stairs should have sturdy handrails.

Workshop

■ A GFCI breaks electrical current in an emergency.

■ Keep the floor clean, without obstructions. All sawdust should be promptly swept up—it makes the floor slippery.

■ File instructions for all power tools readily at hand.

■ Protect yourself from the blades of sharp tools—hatchets, saws, drawknives— with blade guards. You can make them from pieces of a garden hose cut to fit. Slit the side of the hose, and fit it over the sharp edge.

■ Keep lids tight on all glues, paints, solvents, and household cleaners. These can be ignited, especially in unventilated rooms, by flames from the hot-water heater or furnace pilot. When instructions say to use manufacturers' products only in well-ventilated areas, open the windows wide.

■ You need good overall room lighting, with task lighting that's not too bright. Your work surface should be only about three times brighter than the rest of the room.

■ Minimize electrical cords. If you group power tools in the center of a work area, consider installing overhead outlets. Install plenty of outlets over workbenches, too. One outlet every 3 feet is considered ideal.

Garage

■ You should have an operable reverse switch if the garage door is automatic. If your automatic door opener lacks such a switch, call a garage door company and have the system fixed so it's safe.

(continued)

Prescription: A Healthy Home Has ... —*Continued*

Garage—*continued*

- Build organization into storage areas. Regularly clean out unwanted items and unused chemicals, and tidy up the rest.
- Store flammable products in a fire-resistant chemical bin or all-metal dustbin.

Yard

- Maintain play equipment for children. Check children's slides, swings, bicycles, and other outdoor play equipment annually for rusty chains, bent or loose bars, and general instability.
- Keep your walks and driveways in good repair.
- Keep litter—especially nails, broken glass, tin cans, splintered wood, and other dangers to bare feet—out of your yard.
- All outdoor electrical circuits should be protected by a GFCI.
- Nonslip decks and patios prevent accidents.

14

Security

Barbara's Christmas present from husband Jim was a week's vacation at a health spa, but before that week had barely started, they both got a whole lot more than they bargained for. "Jim came home from work that first night after I left," Barbara recalls. "He was walking into the house through the garage when he noticed that another door, leading to the backyard, had been ripped out of the wall."

Although it had never happened to them before, Jim knew that they had been burglarized. The realization was sickening. Sometime that day, a burglar had decided to help himself to some of the treasures Barbara and Jim had acquired over the years. To do that, he knocked a pane out of the back door and reached through to unlock the dead bolt. It was obviously then that he discovered that the couple had a sophisticated dead bolt that couldn't be opened from inside or out without a key. With the dead bolt no longer an option, he used a crowbar on the wall until the door came off.

Once inside, he opened the front door so he would have two exits; then he toured all three floors of the house, carefully making his selections, which included a VCR, a small color television, Barbara's good wool coat, and a shotgun.

Barbara and Jim never got their belongings back, and their uninvited visitor was never apprehended. "But we learned that a good burglar can pop a door with a crowbar in 3 or 4 seconds," Barbara says. The couple now has metal front and back doors installed in metal frames. Each door has a floor bolt, a dead bolt with extralong locks, and peepholes.

Even with those precautions, Barbara is realistic enough to know they can be burglarized again. "The police told us burglars sometimes wait 2 to 3 months so their victims can get things replaced. Then they'll hit you again," she says. "We'll take what security precautions we can, but I won't live in fear. We'll just have to be more careful."

PROTECTING AGAINST INTRUSION

Not only did Barbara and Jim have a dead-bolt lock on their door, but they had one so sophisticated it required a key to be unlocked from the inside as well as out. Still, that was not enough to deter a burglar.

Fact is, unless you're willing to hire armed guards to protect the premises, you can't guarantee that your house will be totally secure. According to the latest available U.S. Federal Bureau of Investigation (FBI) figures, 542,775 robberies and 3,241,410 burglaries occurred nationwide in 1986. That's not even the whole story; a U.S. Justice Department study indicates that only one out of three crimes is ever reported.

Still, having a house that's unattractive to burglars is not just a matter of luck. There are steps you can take that will—at the very least—discourage intruders. For starters, rate your house by answering the following questions:

1. Are your windows designed to keep intruders out? Twist latches on double-hung windows may be pried open without even breaking the glass. Keyed locks, on the other hand, have large screws that bolt one window sash to the other and take a special key to unscrew.

2. Can your basement windows be easily jimmied? If so, fasten them with screws or locks. You might also consider metal bars inside or outside on those windows. You can get them for $10 to $15 per window at a hardware store.

3. Do you have dead-bolt locks on your doors, or are they spring-bolt locks that can be opened easily with a plastic credit card?

4. How solid are your doors? A burglar can put a fist or foot through a hollow or fragile door. That's not possible with solid-cored doors that are at least 1¾ inches thick.

5. Are windows and doors kept locked, especially when you're away from the house? (More than half of the burglaries in 1986 were easily accomplished because the thief simply came in through an unlocked door or window.)

6. Is your garage door always shut? If you have an electric garage door opener, place a padlock in the door's track and unplug the door openers during vacation. If it's an old-fashioned door, keep it locked with a padlock.

7. What would it take to force entry into your house? Look around. Pretend you're the burglar. You may be amazed at how easy it is to gain entry without a front door key! Many police or sheriff's departments will do a security check of your house. Specially trained officers can show you places where a burglar could enter. They'll give you a list of recommendations to make your home safer. Check with your local law enforcement agency. The effort could cost you nothing but save you lots!

8. How long would your current locks and alarm systems delay a thief?

9. Is your home easy to see through surrounding trees and shrubbery, or from a nearby road?

10. How well do you know your closest neighbor? And how well does that neighbor know you? That means understanding a person's routine well enough to notice when something may be amiss.

11. If there is a picture window on the main floor of your house, do you have something valuable sitting in front of it? That's an invitation to a burglar.

12. Do you depend on wide-angle peepholes rather than door chains? A door chain usually won't hold up against a strong kick.

13. Is there a phone by your bed for emergencies? (You can have your phone programmed to dial the police automatically at the push of a button.)

14. If you live alone, are you listed by an initial and last name in the phone book? As far as a visible listing on the mailbox is concerned, there should be no name given at all—whether or not you live by yourself.

15. Have you taken the time to record all the serial numbers, purchase dates, and prices of your expensive items? If so, keep the list in a safety-deposit box at the bank. In case of burglary, this list may well be a valuable assist in recovering your belongings.

Use Light as a Deterrence

Burglars don't like to be in the spotlight, whether it's trained on the porch, in the yard, or at any of the entrances to your house or garage. On the other hand, you don't want your property to look like the aurora borealis all through the night, either.

The kind of outdoor lighting you install depends upon both the surroundings (a bright urban or suburban setting requires less than a dark rural one) and the area to be lighted. It's best to illuminate as large an area as possible with a low level of light. Light up large walls, driveways, and paved ground surfaces, creating a background that will make intruders uncomfortable. There are several kinds of outdoor lighting systems to consider.

THE SECURITY LIGHT CONTROL   This infrared heat detector can be connected to existing lighting. When a person passes near it, the light is activated. "The beauty of this device," says locksmith David Swearingen, "is that it comes on only when needed, and it makes an intruder think that someone in the house has spotted him. It's better to use this device instead of leaving your porch light on. To most burglars, a lighted porch is like a neon sign announcing 'The residents are out—will return later.' Keep all your security lighting out of reach, and protected from breakage."

AUTOMATIC OUTDOOR LIGHTING   This turns itself on by a photosensor when daylight gets dim. When the sun begins to rise the next morning, the lights switch off. One drawback of the photosensor is that it can't distinguish between a cloudy, rainy day and sunset. That means your outdoor lighting could come on during the middle of a dreary day. However, you can install a wall switch inside your house to override the sensor signal. Some switches allow you to turn the lights off at bedtime, even though it's still dark outside.

THE TIME CLOCK　A time clock activates and deactivates outdoor lights at predetermined times and days. Unless your clock will automatically compensate for daylight saving time, you'll have to do some adjusting twice a year. (Incidentally, a time clock uses more energy than a photosensor, even a photosensor with an override switch.)

As far as outdoor lights on the house itself, you should have two lantern-type lights on each side of the front door. That way, if the bulb in one lantern burns out, you'll still have a front light on. One wall lantern on the lock side of other entry doors is sufficient, as is one wall lantern centered above the garage door. Install sufficient post lights to ensure that your walkways, fence gates, driveway entrances, and steps have adequate illumination.

Indoor lighting is important, especially when you're not at home. The best deterrence to a burglar is to put lights on timers in several rooms of your house. Then set the timers to go on and off at various intervals. For example, you might have a kitchen light come on early in the evening, then one in the family room, and finally, a couple in the bedrooms.

PROTECTING THE PERIMETER

A yard with smart perimeter protection may discourage a potential burglar from even approaching. After all, the further out you can keep an intruder, the more visible he or she will be to passersby.

Good perimeter protection begins with a relatively accessible view of your house from the street and from neighboring houses. That doesn't mean you need to go out and chop down your favorite old oak tree, but some well-planned pruning may make the landscaping work for you.

Begin that planning process by going outside at night and walking around. Notice which entrances are shrouded from sight by trees or shrubs and which areas of the house and yard would provide excellent protection for a burglar. Once you've determined your problems, prune away. Keep bushes and hedges well trimmed, probably to around the 3-foot level. According to a study at the University of Utah, a low, living wall provides a psychological barrier, even if it can't physically exclude anyone intending to burglarize the house.

Cut off low branches from both the trees in the yard and the ones nearer to the house. (This will also make mowing much easier.) Make sure no trees give a burglar easy access to a second-floor window; cut away any strong branches close to the house.

You may want to consider installing a lighting system around the house foundation and/or on the patio. Outdoor lights that are low to the ground look attractive from the street yet provide enough illumination to make a burglar's access to a house more difficult.

The best perimeter protection is a fenced-in yard with lockable gates. Cast iron is the best type of fence for security purposes. It provides no place for the criminal to hide, as a wooden fence does. And unlike a chain link fence, it's not easy to climb. But the cast-iron fence does have one drawback: It could conceivably cost more than your house!

Use Common Sense

When it comes to security, the commonsense approach is always best. The best crime-prevention device ever invented is a good neighbor. When neighbors band together to look out for each other, the crime rate often goes down, according to the Law Enforcement Assistance Administration. In fact, a study

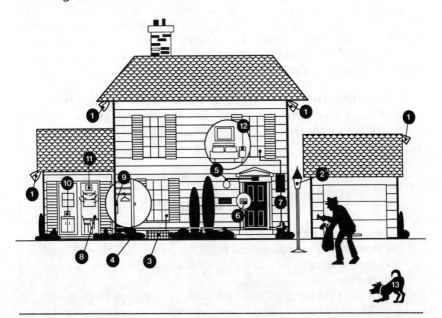

From simple outside lights to sophisticated electronic alarms, there's a security system to fit every budget.

1. Floodlights
2. Supplemental lampposts
3. Accordion grate on basement window
4. Shrubs trimmed below window
5. Motion-sensing automatic light
6. Solid doors with dead-bolt locks
7. Perimeter alarm linking points of entry
8. Reinforced patio door with sensor
9. Electronic alarm system control panel
10. Motion or heat detectors
11. Lights and appliances on timers
12. Bedside "panic" alarm
13. Dog

of 30 suburbs and towns by the U.S. Bureau of Justice indicated that, without exception, there was a substantial drop in property crime rates shortly after neighborhood crime-watch programs had been started.

It's easy to organize a neighborhood or block crime-watch program. First, contact your local law enforcement agency. Then invite your neighbors in to discuss the crime problem and how to combat it. Ask your police or sheriff's department to send an officer to the meeting, to offer tips on home security, self-protection, and what to report to police.

At the meeting, exchange work schedules, home and business telephone numbers, and addresses. Keep these near your telephone so you can use them if you need to report a crime.

Choose one person or several individuals who are at home during the day to be responsible for crime-watch activities. Then make arrangements to watch each other's houses and properties and to be on the lookout for suspicious activities or persons. Also be sure to make arrangements for keeping an eye on the homes of neighbors away on vacation. Some neighbors form block clubs that meet regularly to discuss community issues and security techniques. (See appendix B for the address of the National Crime Prevention Council for information on the Neighborhood Watch program.)

OPERATION IDENTIFICATION   Another commonsense approach that serves as a deterrence to burglars is Operation Identification. That's where you mark your property so you will be able to identify things if they're stolen and

---

Going on Vacation?

It's one thing to get yourself and your family ready for a vacation. But the smart traveler also takes time to get the house ready, as well. And that means doing a lot more than unplugging the coffee pot and watering the plants.

A mistake people often make is to hide away the common signs of daily life while they're gone. When there are no garbage cans by the street on trash pickup days, when there's no newspaper tossed on the front porch every morning, when there's never a car parked in the driveway, the message to a cunning observer is all too clear: Nobody's home.

To avoid this pitfall, follow these tips to make your house look occupied when it really isn't:

■ Leave the garden rake leaning against the side of the house. You might even want to leave the garden hose in the backyard. However, lock up any tools and ladders that a thief could use to break in.

(continued)

Going on Vacation?—*Continued*

■ If you think the weather will call for it, use an appliance timer to run your air conditioner (fan only) on a periodic basis.

■ Tell a trustworthy neighbor where you're going, but ask that person not to tell others you're away. Explain your security system, and leave your vacation phone number. Have that person check the house daily.

■ Some experts suggest you cancel all predictable deliveries and have your neighbor collect the unexpected ones. Others will tell you not to stop newspaper and mail delivery. Instead, give a house key to a neighbor and ask that person to come over daily and bring the mail and paper into the house. If you don't know your paper carrier, it's best that he or she does not know you are away.

■ Leave a locked car in your driveway or invite your neighbor to park there while you're out of town. Nothing can discourage a would-be burglar more than the thought that someone's home.

■ If you park your car at the airport, remove mail and other documents showing your address.

■ Use timers liberally inside the house. Timers are readily available in hardware stores. Simple, unsophisticated units cost around $12. Use timers with lamps, radios, and television sets. Keep the radio and television volume normal. The noise should be enough to discourage anyone who is prowling around outside the house.

■ Keep the lawn mowed. Tall grass is a telling sign that no one is home. Make arrangements to have it mowed as needed, and total up the bill when you return.

■ Leave drapes and shades partially open. Criminals figure that people at home like sunlight.

■ Turn down the phone bell so a burglar won't hear a phone ring that goes unanswered. If your telephone is hooked up to an answering machine, simply ask the callers to leave phone numbers and names so you can get right back to them. Never, never leave a recorded message that tells people you're away.

■ Put cash, jewelry, and important papers in a safety-deposit box. Never leave jewelry hidden in your bedroom. That's the first place a burglar will look.

Tell the police or local law enforcement agency that you'll be gone. Provide them with dates of departure and return, an address where you can be reached, the phone number and address of the person who'll be watching your house, and a description of the car you'll be leaving in the driveway. As they make periodic swings by your house, they'll be on the lookout for anything unusual.

recovered. The best way to mark goods is with an electric engraving pen (you may be able to borrow one from a local law enforcement agency) or with an inexpensive diamond-tipped marking pen. They're for sale in most hardware and department stores.

Next, ask your local police or sheriff's department what identification number is recommended in your state (usually your Social Security number), and engrave this number on all your valuable possessions—bicycles, lawn mowers, snowblowers, televisions, radios, stereos, VCRs, computers, printers, typewriters, golf clubs, appliances, tools. Mark any portable item you think a burglar might want to steal and sell.

Once that is accomplished, photograph unmarkable items such as china, silver, or jewelry. Finally, draw up an inventory of household goods, including the serial numbers of television sets, appliances, and so on. Put the inventory, along with the photographs, in a safety-deposit box. If you are burglarized, this list will be invaluable to both the police and your insurance company.

Be sure to let would-be burglars know what you've done by putting Operation Identification stickers (available from many local law enforcement agencies) on a front window, front door, and any other places where they will have clear visibility.

GUARD DOGS   Is man's best friend also a home's best protection? Could be. A trained attack dog will scare off all but the most determined intruder. But the animal will also require a fenced-in yard and a leash because the dog will, in all probability, be too large and high-strung to be cooped up all day.

To be on the safe side, never bring a guard dog into a house when small children are present. A youngster's sudden movements and spontaneous behavior may be all it takes to trigger a violent reaction. The dog might never knowingly harm a child, but it has been trained to attack and can't always differentiate the fine lines of behavior.

Posting one of those "Beware of Dog" signs on your property may not be such a good idea, either. If the dog nips someone, the sign could be used as evidence against you, indicating that you knew the dog was violent.

So, unless you want to make your home into a fortress, a small to medium-sized dog with a large bark is probably one of the best and least expensive security devices you can purchase. But before you run out and buy one, you must understand the pluses and minuses of dog ownership. (See Chapter 12.)

The main reason people *should* get a dog is for companionship. The animal ideally will become part of the family and will require much more attention than an alarm system. If the only reason you're considering buying a dog is for protection, you'll do everyone a favor if you shop around for a security system instead.

Using Weapons for Self-Defense

Whether you choose to use a weapon to protect your belongings is a personal decision that only you can make. Give this decision careful thought, considering the legal ramifications as well as how calmly you believe you will act under duress. Here's some information that may help:

Mace and tear gas: Both chemicals are available in small hand-held containers, but whether it's legal to use them depends upon the laws in your state. It's downright illegal in New York, for example, while in Pennsylvania you can buy mace in gas stations and convenience stores. In some states you must attend a 1-day seminar and obtain a permit before you can carry these chemicals. (If you're caught without a permit, it could result in a felony conviction.) Check with your local police department or state attorney general's office to find out the law in your state.

For either spray to be effective, you have to aim it directly into the eyes of your assailant at close range. The chances of your having the mace or tear gas in your possession and being positioned so you can accurately hit a burglar are minimal. Furthermore, if you haven't learned any other means of self-defense, it's possible your attacker can wrest the canister away, then use it on you.

Guns: Think twice about using guns as a means of making your house more secure. A lot of people who buy guns for protection don't know how to use them properly. Too many accidents occur when the gun's owner takes aim at a would-be burglar only to end up shooting a family member who decided to head for a midnight snack in the kitchen. Or the burglar ends up shooting the homeowner with the homeowner's own gun. Granted, you have a constitutional right to bear arms, but you also have a responsibility to know how to handle those arms.

If you decide to purchase a handgun for protection, contact local authorities to find out whether it needs to be registered. Consider taking a course in handgun safety, too.

ON BEING A VICTIM

Taking all the precautions in the world won't guarantee that a burglar won't strike. If you suspect someone you don't know has been in your house, don't go in. Instead, run to a neighbor's house and call the police immediately. Then wait outside for officers to arrive.

If you confront a burglar in your home, don't try to stop him or her. Says one man who used to be a burglar, "My anxiety level was certainly high [when burglarizing a house]. I hoped to God that I wasn't going to confront somebody. If you confront somebody, they could hurt you, or they might force you to hurt them. If anybody was around, I split."

According to a recent U.S. Justice Department survey, 13 percent of the time that a burglary occurs, someone is at home. And 30 percent of those encounters end in violence. Three-fifths of the rapes and one-third of the assaults that occur at home are committed during burglaries, the survey showed.

Some say that compliance is the best way to defuse potential violence. Other experts, however, suggest that you run to a neighbor and call the police from there, if that's possible. A former burglar offers a novel approach: "If you wake up to the sounds of a burglar in the house, don't go tiptoeing around," he suggests. "Sit up and shout, 'There's somebody in the house. You get the shotgun, I'll call the police.'"

And finally, once a burglary has occurred, don't touch anything. Again, call the police immediately. Every minute you wait delays the chances of officials catching the criminal.

SECURITY SYSTEMS

Deciding what level of security you want for your house will depend upon several things: how much value you place on your possessions, the type of neighborhood you live in, and how much you are willing to spend.

You can purchase everything from bars for the windows to infrared detectors to radio-controlled alarm systems with sophisticated microprocessor technology. No matter what you ultimately choose, you'll be purchasing either a system that simply provides physical security or an electronic system that tells you that an intrusion has occurred or that one is occurring.

Good physical security begins with hardware. There are three considerations when shopping for the right hardware to protect your house:

Quality construction: Steel and solid brass are much stronger than alloys and plastic.

The finish: If something is poorly finished, it was also probably poorly constructed and—you can bet on this—will perform poorly.

The price: Buy the best you can afford to match your needs. "Price really does dictate quality," says Mike Cutler, a director of Associated Locksmiths of America.

The Secure Door

Hollow-cored or paneled doors provide little security, no matter what type of lock you put on them. Look for doors that are solid-cored wood (at least 1¾ inches thick) or steel. Your door should fit its frame tightly, with no more than ⅛ inch of clearance between the door and frame. If there is an unacceptable gap, you may want to consider getting a new door. If that option is too expensive, you can bolt a sturdy metal strip to the existing door edge. You can also reinforce points of stress, such as the hinges and strike plate, with either wood shims or spacers.

Doors with glass panels are a lot like windows—very inviting for a would-be thief who knows that it takes only a few seconds to break the glass and undo the lock. You can either replace the door with a solid-cored windowless one or install a decorative grille over the glass. However, be sure to use special, nonremovable screws when attaching the grille.

HINGES Most door hinges are on the inside, safe from a burglar's tools. But if your door swings out, those hinges and pins will be easy to remove. Once that's accomplished, a burglar can easily take the door out of the frame. Remedy that by replacing the standard hinge pins with nonremovable ones. Or install security studs: Remove the middle screw on each side of each existing hinge plate, and insert a metal pin or headless screw on one side of each plate. When the door is closed, the end of each pin will fit into the opposite hole. That way, even if the hinge pins are removed, the door will remain "bolted" to the frame.

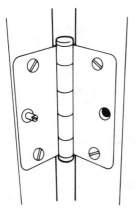

Security studs keep the door in the frame.

KEY-IN-KNOB LOCK WITH DEAD LATCH The most common door lock features doorknobs inside and out, with a small lock cylinder in the outside knob into which a key is inserted. It's an inexpensive lock with a big drawback: It's the easiest to break. All a thief needs is a heavy object to break off the entire outer knob and lock. That exposes the inner mechanism, which can then be easily unlocked.

Furthermore, the bolt in that lock is usually of a spring-latch design, beveled on one side. When the door closes, it automatically retracts, then springs back into place. A simple credit card can be used to push back the bolt, which consequently opens the door.

Some spring latches have a dead latch featuring a small plunger along the beveled latch. While this does make it more difficult to unlock, security is still low.

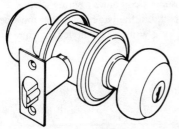

A key-in-knob lockset like this won't stop a burglar.

DEAD BOLT   Ideally, you should have a dead-bolt lock—separate from the lock on your doorknob—on every entrance door, including the garage. The dead bolt provides good protection because when you turn the key, the lock mechanism slides a strong metal bolt from the door into a metal box (called a strike plate) on the frame. The bolt should project an inch or more into the strike plate. The stronger models feature hardened metal or contain sawproof steel rods. Some also have thick metal collars around the lock cylinders.

The connecting screws that hold the lock together should go on the inside of the door, and the strike plate should be attached to the door frame with screws that are at least 3 inches long.

A tubular dead bolt slides horizontally into the door when you turn a key outside or a thumb knob inside. A double-cylinder dead bolt lock works only with a key, both inside and out. While this provides more security, you must remember to keep the inside key near the lock when you're home (but not close enough that it can be reached through a glass panel). In case of an emergency, you'd need to use the key to get out of the house.

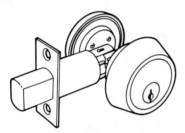

A dead bolt offers good security, especially the double-cylinder type that can be unlocked only with a key from either side.

Before installing a double-cylinder dead bolt, however, check with your local law enforcement agency or housing officials. Some communities place restrictions on its use.

Interconnected locksets or double-security locksets combine the spring latch and double-cylinder dead bolt. With this setup, a full turn of the inside knob retracts both the latch and the bolt to allow for quick emergency exits.

MORTISE LOCK   The mortise lock is cut into a large rectangular cavity in the edge of the door (the mortise) and combines a spring latch and dead bolt. It's a

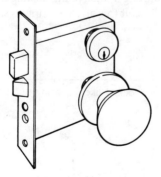

A mortise lock combines a spring latch with a dead bolt, but the large cavity that must be cut out for it weakens the door's structure.

convenient design, but it results in a weakened door structure. Furthermore, these locks can be expensive.

RIM LOCK   The rim lock is mounted on the inside of the door near its edge (the rim). A locking device on the door fits into a plate on the frame. When you turn the key, strong metal bars join the two parts of the lock, much like a hinge pin holds two leaves of a hinge together.

Most rim locks mount with ordinary wood screws, which can be torn out easily. Replace them with extra-long screws for the lock and strike plate, or use machine screws that go through the door and fasten with nuts.

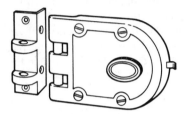

A rim lock installed with screws that go at least halfway through the door will keep burglars at bay.

FOX DOUBLE-BAR LOCK   This lock provides maximum security but little aesthetic value. It mounts in the center of the door on the inside. Keys enter the lock cylinder through a small hole on the outside or the lock can be activated from the inside. The lock throws two strong steel bars into strikes in both door jambs.

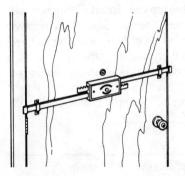

The Fox double-bar lock isn't much to look at, but it does the job.

PADLOCK   Padlocks are typically used for garages, sheds, and workshops. A good, sturdy padlock won't release the key until the padlock is locked. Look for one that is in a rugged laminated case with a ⅜-inch shackle that can resist smashings. There are also double-locking designs that can prevent the shackle from being pried away from its case.

No matter what type of padlock you purchase, it'll only be as strong as the hasp it's mounted on. The hasp should be secured with bolts that are mounted on a metal plate and concealed when the padlock is in place.

The Patio Door

Sliding glass patio doors, and most of the lock systems that come with them, provide feeble protection. It's a good idea to add a security bar that adjusts to fit into the door's track, blocking it from sliding open.

Some bars come equipped with a light and alarm system. Homemade wooden boards or broomsticks at least an inch thick work in the same manner, although they obviously don't provide the added protection that a light and alarm system offer.

It is possible for someone to lift a sliding glass door off its tracks. It's also possible to foil that plan by adjusting the rollers so the door can't be pushed up far enough. You can also insert screws along the upper track of the door, leaving enough room for the door to slide but not enough space to lift the door out. Or drill a hole and insert a nail through the inside frame and partway through the metal frame on the door itself. You'll have to remove the nail when you want to open the door, but it won't be removable from outside the house.

The Secure Window

While most people spend a lot of time securing their doors, they often neglect to secure their windows. Yet, an unsecured window—even one that isn't easily reached from ground level—is an open invitation to a burglar.

NAIL/BOLT WINDOW LOCK   The most effective way to secure double-hung wood windows is with a nail/bolt lock that you install yourself. Close the window, and drill a single $3/16$-inch hole slightly downward through both the top rail of the bottom sash and the bottom rail of the top sash. Insert a 20-penny nail or eyebolt to "lock" the window. The window can't be opened until you remove the nail or eyebolt. You can also make a second set of holes with the window partly open, so you can have ventilation without inviting burglars.

There are ready-made copies of this lock in hardware stores. Some use lag screws instead of nails, thereby providing even more strength.

Sliding aluminum windows present more of a security challenge than do

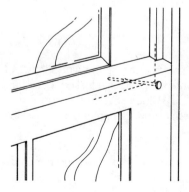

The most effective way to secure double-hung wood windows is with a lock you make yourself with a 10-penny nail or a bolt.

windows with wood frames. Sometimes, patio-door-type pin locks will work on the windows. There is also hardware available that clamps onto the rail or the track on which the window slides.

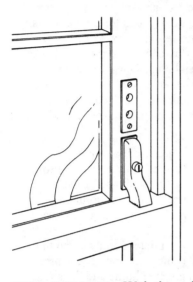

A ready-made alternative to the nail/bolt window lock is a keyed sash lock made of aluminum.

KEYED SASH LOCK   With this style, a short aluminum bar at the bottom of the upper sash keeps the bottom sash from moving. A small, keyed lock cylinder holds the bar in place. You'll need to keep the keys away from the windows, but make sure everyone in your family knows where to find them in case of emergency. Again, check with your local law enforcement agency or housing officials to see if there are any restrictions on installing these locks.

GRATES OR GRILLES   If you live in an especially vulnerable area, consider installing grates or grilles on your street-level windows. Make sure they have a quick-release feature for emergency exits.

Burglar Bars, Bolts, and Chains

How's the security at your house? Does keeping burglars out keep you in? This is a hazard during fire.

Burglar bars are fine *if* they can be released and opened from the inside, and *if* everyone in the house knows where the keys are (close to the bars) and how to work them. Key-operated dead bolts provide good protection *if* these same precautions are taken. Lock bars on sliding patio doors are wise *if* they can be removed quickly. Don't protect against one hazard only to create another.

Electronic Security Systems

Today, only 1 of every 11 houses has a burglar alarm system. Considering that virtually every business has some sort of electronic security, you may question why homeowners haven't followed the same route.

One reason is that the security devices developed for businesses simply don't adapt to a homeowner's needs. They're expensive to install, because they require running wires through walls to connect sensors with central controllers, and they provide only one operational choice: on or off.

But now there is an increasing number of electronic security systems being offered for the homeowner. These can be simple or complex, relatively inexpensive or costly. Since there are so many options involved, consider these points before investing in anything:

- A local system is designed to send a signal from a sensory device directly to a light system or to a bell or a siren. When your sensory device detects an intruder, the bell or siren goes off and/or the lights in the house automatically turn on. Since most neighborhood burglars are not professionals, this activity is generally sufficient to scare them away.

- A local alarm can be combined with a central reporting alarm that is constantly monitored by an alarm company. Once the sensory device is tripped, the lights and sounds go on at home and the alarm company notifies the police department. In most cases, you'll be charged for installation of the central reporting alarm system as well as for monthly service charges. Don't buy or lease a system from any company not offering a contract for continued maintenance service.

- A sticker, prominently displayed, that notifies would-be burglars that you have an alarm system is generally sufficient to discourage an intruder.

Before making a purchase, you need to consider your family's living patterns and how an alarm system will interact with your household activity. For example, if you have young children who are constantly going in and out of the door, an individualized alarm on each door would be a nuisance. But if you live alone, that might be just what you need.

No matter what purchase you ultimately make, the system will include a sensor, control panel, and alarm. You can purchase alarm systems that have all three components in one self-contained unit, or you can get a system where each part is separate. Either can be a do-it-yourself installation project.

The sensor, or detector, receives the warning. This is what the intruder must trip for an alarm to be activated. Simple sensors operate on a magnetic connection. If that's broken, an alarm will go off. A more advanced sensor is the passive infrared type, which responds to body heat. However, it will also respond to a room heater or sunlight.

An ultrasonic sensor fills the room with high-frequency sound waves, then monitors the echo for any changes. The change is intended to indicate movements made by an intruder. But air pressure around the sensor will change (such as when a window or door is opened) and could trip the alarm.

The newest sensors on the market contain devices that respond to a combination of passive infrared and ultrasonic or microwave modes. An alarm will sound only when both sensors agree that someone is in the room. While this is still not foolproof, it does eliminate a lot of false alarms.

The control panel, or receiver, reads the message from the sensor that there's an intruder. The alarm is activated once the control panel has received the message. The alarm can be a bell with a limited range and little direction, making it good for densely populated areas. Since the bell is on the outside of the house, you should enclose it in a cabinet with a tamper switch that will automatically trip the alarm if the cabinet is pried away from the wall.

A siren alarm is more expensive but louder, making it good for suburban areas. Like the bell, the siren is on the outside of the house and should be enclosed in a tamperproof cabinet.

A third type of alarm sends silent messages via intercom or telephone lines to a neighbor or a security company.

ALL-IN-ONE UNITS   If you opt to install the alarm system yourself, begin by securing the windows and doors. In most instances, that's where the burglar gains entry. Your best option for a window will be small, preferably concealed, magnetic switch. This device has a switch and a mating magnet. When the window is closed, the two halves are in contact and the switch is closed. If the window is opened, the switch is opened and an alarm sounds.

If the window is large enough for a burglar to cut a hole in and climb through, install a glass-breakage detector instead of magnetic switches.

The all-in-one door alarm works basically the same way as the window device. But in this situation, you'll want an alarm that's easy to turn on and off. Otherwise, it will sound every time anybody goes in or out of the house. Good systems come with keys to easily turn off the alarms.

Some self-contained security units respond to changes in air pressure or sound waves. These can cover an entire room, in contrast to the more simple versions that merely tell you if someone is tampering with a locked window or door.

SEPARATE COMPONENTS   An alarm system with separate components features intrusion sensors on windows and doors that are hooked up to a control panel by either a hard-wire or wireless system. While the hard-wire system is much less expensive, it takes longer to install. You'll need to solder all connections and return the wires from each sensor to the control.

With a wireless system, you won't have to send a wire from each sensor to the control panel, because radio frequencies do the communicating for you. Simply install a battery-powered sensor in each window and door; then set up the receiver in an out-of-the-way spot.

A good wireless system has the following features:

Immunity from radio interference: As much as 92 percent of all alarms triggered by home security systems are false. Most occur because the occupant trips the system and either doesn't know how or forgets to deactivate it before the alarm sounds. Another cause is equipment malfunction that occurs because the owner doesn't maintain the system adequately. And finally, there are so many radio signals already in a house—from the television to the garage door opener—that those signals may trip a sensor.

According to David Petraglia, an independent home security consultant, the most stable system sends a computerized *data word*, consisting of 8 to 20 bits of information, to signal alarms. The receiver will respond only if it receives the exact signal it expects. That alleviates a lot of false alarms.

Supervision: Each sensor will occasionally "check in" with the receiver. If a battery is low, a maintenance signal will alert you. Also, if you're home when the alarm sounds, you'll be able to look at the control panel and know just which sensor was activated.

Concealment: If burglars can see your sensors, they'll know exactly which windows and doors are protected. You need sensors that contain their own transmitters and are small enough to fit into the frames. While systems such as this may sound complicated, the truth is that they're getting easier and easier to use.

Whether you put in a hard-wire or a wireless system, you'll want to consider where the alarm is going to sound and who is going to hear it. The local alarm, which sounds on the spot, needs to be effective enough to surprise the burglar and alert neighbors as well as the people inside your house.

The automatic dialer sends a prerecorded message or some type of signal via the telephone. It can be directed to a neighbor or a relative, but that will do little good if no one is home on the receiving end. That's why you should consider a monitoring service provided by most alarm companies. They'll provide 24-hour digital monitoring of your system through the phone lines. Then you *know* someone will respond, whether you're home or not. No matter where the telephone message goes, however, you'll need to check with your local telephone company before installation for rules and regulations.

If doing it yourself doesn't appeal to you, there are plenty of systems on the market you can have installed, all the way up to a complete home control unit that not only provides you with security but also takes care of the lights, radio, television, pool heater, and other electrical devices. As a rule, these systems are hard wired.

The high end of all this high-tech security protection is the TV camera system. Miniature cameras, each weighing 6 to 7 ounces and featuring built-in microphones and motion detectors, sell for between $600 and $1,000.

POINTS TO REMEMBER   Lest you begin to think that alarm systems will bring you 100 percent security, there are several points to remember:

■ Remote alarm devices are too slow for the crack burglar. By the time a security company contacts the police department and the dispatcher gets a patrol car to your house, enough time may have elapsed for the burglar to get in, take what he or she wants, and leave.

- Electronic systems are expensive. Consider that a security contract for your house could cost upward of $2,000.
- Central-monitored house systems rely on telephone lines to communicate to the monitoring station. If phone lines are cut, your system is useless.

ECONOMIC SECURITY: HOME INSURANCE

Insurance is an important element in a healthy home. It's not as complex as you might think. Who needs homeowner's insurance? Everyone! A lot of people who rent apartments or houses operate under the assumption that they will be covered under the owner's insurance policy. That may prove to be a costly assumption when an electrical fire destroys your furniture and clothes or when a break-in occurs and you lose your stereo. Renters should have insurance for their furnishings and personal property.

If you live in a condominium, there's a policy adapted to the peculiarities of owning both private and communal property. If you own your own house, you'll probably want an all-risk policy that covers both dwelling and personal property, although bare-bones policies are available from some companies. There are three basic areas that should be covered in your homeowner's policy.

The Dwelling

Your dwelling, including garage and other outbuildings, should be insured against the endless catastrophies (*perils*) listed in actuarial tables. There are two ways this can be done. You can either name the perils against which you're insuring or buy *all-risk* coverage that protects you against all risks except those named as exclusions. This all-risk coverage is by far the most popular today, and it is preferable because the burden is on the insurance company to prove that the loss was not covered, rather than on the homeowner to prove that it was.

Perils that are commonly excluded from an all-risk policy include earthquakes, floods, wars, nuclear accidents, and normal wear and tear. When you determine what is excluded, you need to then ask whether you need additional coverage and to see if it is available. For example, if you live in a floodplain, you'll want special coverage (called a *rider*) against flood damage. This is generally available, but it will cost more. If you live on an earthquake fault line, you'll want an earthquake rider. If you live next to a nuclear power plant, you may want coverage against nuclear accidents, but you won't find a company that will issue that rider. Similarly, there is no commonly available coverage against war or normal wear and tear.

The next question to ask is how much coverage should you have on the dwelling. You'll want your policy to cover at least 80 percent of the replacement cost. In fact, most companies require this much coverage for them to pay your full loss. The theory is that even if the dwelling is destroyed, the land and foundation remaining will be roughly 20 percent of the total value. The trap here is that this *80 percent coinsurance clause* is more than just a rough guess as to how much insurance you should have; it determines how much of your loss will get paid under the policy. The way it works is this: Say you have a house with a replacement cost of $100,000, but it is insured for only $60,000 (60 percent of its value). If you have a $10,000 fire loss, the insurance will cover only $7,500 of that loss. The calculation is that $60,000 is 75 percent of the $80,000 coverage that you should have had. Thus, 75 percent of the loss will be paid. By contrast, if you had the full $80,000 of insurance, the full $10,000 loss would be paid under most policies.

Two additional points: First, the prior discussion refers to *replacement-cost* insurance. Make sure you have this. You'd hate to lose a 100-year-old, $100,000 house only to find out that your coverage was for *depreciated value*, which might be $50,000 or even less. Second, don't get caught in the underinsurance trap. Underinsurance is seldom intentional. It comes about because real estate values have significantly outpaced inflation over the past 30 years, and people often have houses of greater value than they think. An *automatic inflation escalator clause* should be written into your policy. This will certainly help keep your coverage close to replacement cost. However, if your house is in a rapidly appreciating real estate market, or if you've added major improvements, check with your insurance company to be sure you have enough coverage.

Personal Property

A homeowner's policy covers not only the dwelling but its contents as well. A deductible clause is common, and you'll want to decide how much you can handle. Generally, the additional cost in going from a $250 deductible to a $100 deductible is small.

An even more important decision is whether you want *replacement-cost* insurance or *fair-market-value* (depreciated-value) coverage. Once you've been a victim of a fire or a theft, you'll become a convert to replacement-cost insurance. For example, say a break-in to your garage nets thieves a 12-year-old power mower. The mower cost $180 in 1977; it's beat up but it still cuts the grass every week or so. At a garage sale you might get $30 for it; this is its depreciated value and all you will get with fair-market-value insurance. However, the same model new costs $400 in 1989; with replacement-cost insurance, you'll be covered for this amount. Apply this same analysis to anything else that might be taken, and you'll see that the difference in coverage could be substantial. The deductible amount will be subtracted from the total loss, not from each item.

The other major concern is to make sure you actually cover all the things you own. Under most policies, for example, furs, guns, jewels, stamps, coins, and silverware either are not covered or are covered up to a low maximum of $500 or less. If you simply assume that you have coverage for your $5,000 stamp collection and it's stolen or destroyed in a fire, you'll likely be out the entire value. For these items you'll need a special rider, and it is likely you'll need an appraisal of the items before the rider will be written. This will involve some time and expense but may be well worth it.

Another issue to discuss with your insurance company is coverage off the premises. For example, theft of personal property from a car is a common problem. Be sure you're covered. It is not uncommon for certain items—such as computers—to be covered at home but not elsewhere. Other, more common items, such as clothing, will likely be covered even if in a vacation cottage or a college student's dorm room. Be sure that your policy is tailored to your needs.

Personal Liability

The third major area of coverage under your homeowner's policy should be for bodily injury or property damage for which you or a member of your family may be legally responsible. This will generally cover not only accidents on your property but also injury to someone while you're playing golf, for example.

You may also want to consider an *umbrella* policy. This is generally available when you have your homeowner's and automobile insurance with the same company, and it is issued to insure you where the other insurance leaves off. Coverage here is not only for accidents but also for such unwelcome occurrences as a libel or slander judgment or a judgment for wrongful prosecution.

Contact your insurance company for information on a number of other areas of possible coverage, such as these:

- loss of use, if you're forced to move while repairs are made to your house
- credit card and forgery losses
- medical payments to others under your liability coverage
- debris removal
- damage to trees, shrubs, and other plants
- damage from power losses, water, and spills of paint or chemicals

Complete coverage provides the peace of mind needed for a healthy home.

Prescription: A Healthy Home Has . . .

. . . a well-thought-out security plan:

- Have separate key chains for car and house keys.
- Develop a telephone routine, for the kids as well as the adults, and get it down pat. No one should be giving out unnecessary information to strangers. It's especially important that youngsters not let a caller know when they're home alone.
- Enforce strict rules about who's allowed to come through the front door. Any stranger—and that includes a police officer—should provide proper identification. Remember, even the police cannot enter your house without a search warrant. If you're in doubt about the legitimacy of the stranger at the front door, ask to see proof of identification or call the place that person claims to represent.
- Make sure your house numbers are clearly visible from the street, day or night. That makes it easier (and consequently quicker) for law enforcement agencies to find you. Use 6-inch-high numbers made of reflective materials, or use black numbers against a white background. Avoid script letters; they're hard to read. If your house is back from the road, put the numbers at the driveway entrance. If you live on a corner, be sure the numbers face the street listed as your address.
- Think about what should appear in the newspaper. Don't include your address in a classified ad. Make sure social event and vacation write-ups run *after* the event. If there's a death in the family, have a friend stay at the house during the funeral.
- Use a safe storage place for money, jewelry, and credit cards. There's no need to have a lot of cash around the house. Keep jewelry in a home safe or vault or even in a bank safety-deposit box.
- Carry the proper amount and type of homeowner's insurance.

15

A Possible Future

There's absolutely nothing standing in the way of you and a healthy home. It's an attainable goal requiring the following:

- **Commitment:** all the way along the process
- **Control:** of your actions and buying behavior
- **Challenge:** to obtain a worthy goal

Think positively! Anticipate change as a new opportunity, not a possible threat. Negative thinking is the biggest trap. You *can* make a difference. Take it one step at a time, and work diligently toward improvement. When a problem stands in your way, remove it, or simply go around it. Don't distance yourself from the problem and pretend it's not there. This negative type of coping strategy can make you lose sight of your original goal—to have a healthy home. Don't expect things to change overnight—it's a gradual process, with little steps made every day.

A TEN-STEP PLAN

Develop a sense of priorities. Get a plan. Write it down so you can check off steps you've completed, getting a sense of accomplishment as you move on down the list. Here's a sample ten-step program to get you started on the road to a healthy home:

1. Give your house a health audit, using the checklist in chapter 2. That way you'll know where the problems are so you can begin to solve them.
2. Test for radon. If there is a problem, take the necessary steps to correct it. (See chapter 5.)
3. Find out what's in your water. If you have a well, have the water tested. If it's a municipal system, call your water company and ask to

see a list of the contaminants that are routinely found in the water. If there are pollutants in your water, install the appropriate home treatment device as described in chapter 4.

4. Don't allow smoking in your home.

5. If you have frayed asbestos anywhere in the house, see that it is either encapsulated or professionally removed.

6. Mix your own cleaning solutions using natural or low-tox ingredients. (See chapter 6). Then give your house a thorough cleaning, following the guidelines in chapter 6.

7. Analyze your house for technical and structural problems using the checklist found at the end of chapter 8. Remedy any problems you find, using low-tox and no-tox building materials.

8. Install an exhaust ventilation fan, directly vented to the outside, in both the kitchen and the bathroom.

9. Install photoelectric smoke detectors and fire extinguishers on each floor of your house, and see that each entry door is equipped with a dead-bolt lock and a peephole.

10. Be an energy-conscious homeowner. Buy only energy-efficient appliances. Tighten up the house for air leaks, and employ energy-saving techniques whenever possible.

Become an Ecologically-Minded Consumer

As we approach the 1990s, American society has two choices: to barter its health for modern conveniences and stop worrying about all this, or to begin ridding the environment of chemicals that cause cancer and immune disorders, and threaten the very planet itself. As Michael H. Brown suggests in *The Toxic Cloud*, "We must move toward a policy by which no company is allowed to make or use any compound until the firm proves that it can either dissassemble that compound into harmless, natural compounds—destroy it completely with no toxic residues—or proves that the compound has absolutely no health repercussions whatsoever. Those compounds that fail the test but already exist must be gradually phased out if not outright withdrawn."

You can play a major role in this development simply by becoming an ecologically minded consumer. Take the following steps:

■ **Decrease your use of synthetics.** When making decisions about your healthy home, always try the natural solution first. If it doesn't work to your satisfaction, try a low-tox alternative. Anything above low-tox is chemical warfare.

■ **Wean yourself from plastics.** This is a difficult challenge, considering the sheer ubiquity of the product. Not only does their manufacture require the use of nonrenewable petrochemicals, but plastics take longer than steel to break down in a landfill. A plastic toy may last longer than the pyramids! When burned, plastics form some of the most toxic gases known—dioxin, furans, hydrochloric acid—that hang around in the air for days. Start by not purchasing plastic bags. Or simply wash and reuse the plastic bags you have—an action that, if performed by every American, would decrease plastic production by 50 percent.

■ **Boycott aluminum.** It doesn't biodegrade at all. When there is nothing left of Earth, there will still be aluminum, plastic, and cockroaches.

■ **Boycott products from manufacturers that are known polluters.** Hold them responsible for their pollution. Since the bottom line is what most American manufacturers understand best, the most effective way to make your opinions known is to simply not buy their products. Make do with something else. Be creative. It's not that difficult to do, and it's fun.

■ **Stay informed.** Subscribe to a good, reliable newspaper that regularly reports on health, toxins, and environmental issues. Be discerning when you read or listen to news reports. Much of the information we get is veiled public relations from self-serving interests whose main reason for being is the bottom line, not the good of society.

Reduce the Amount of Garbage You Produce

Americans are the biggest consumers in the history of the world. In garbage alone, we throw out 4 pounds per person per day. That amounts to 11 pounds of garbage per day for the average American family—enough to fill the New Orleans Superdome, floor to ceiling, twice a day. But that is just our personal waste. There is 20 times more waste in the manufacture of what we throw away.

We pay $4 billion a year to collect and dispose of all this trash. That's more money than the entire budget of the U.S. Environmental Protection Agency. And disposal doesn't solve the problem. Garbage pollutes our air and waterways, takes up space, and uses our natural resources.

What can we do to reduce the amount of garbage we produce? Quite a bit, really. As with all problems generated within the home, the solution is up to those within it.

BE PICKY   If you don't buy an item in the first place, it won't become garbage later on. Think about your life-style, and buy only what you need and use. Buy things separately, if you can, not packaged. Packaging is often unnecessary and greatly increases the garbage dilemma.

Pay attention to how things are packaged. Paper and cardboard are biodegradable. Plastic and aluminum foil are not. Don't buy those products that add unnecessarily to solid waste. This includes those handy plastic bags, which you probably don't need, anyway.

Carry this philosophy through to other areas of your life—clothing, appliances, furnishings, and so on. Every time you pull out your wallet to pay for something, think twice. Do you really need it?

Avoid buying highly toxic and hazardous products. Consider buying the least toxic product available. Natural is best.

Avoid buying aerosols. For one, they are expensive. Some contain hazardous propellants, and the pressurized cans can explode when heated, crushed, or punctured. Consider buying paste, liquid, and spray-pump products instead.

REUSE   Buy only what you need. Buy cooperatively to reduce waste. Share leftovers with neighbors, friends, relatives, public service organizations and institutions, hospitals, group homes, schools, community organizations, churches—anyone who can get some good out of it.

Make sure you get the maximum use out of the things you buy. If the mayonnaise is all gone, for example, don't throw out the jar. Use it to store something else, like nails in the workshop or vegetable oil in the pantry. Unusable clothing can be made into rags—that way you won't need paper towels.

Don't buy things with built-in obsolescence. Doing so only fosters the use-it-up, throw-it-away philosophy that is gradually destroying Earth.

RECYCLE   Think about how you can put to use what you're tempted to throw away. Can someone else still get use out of it? Used clothing and furniture can be donated to Goodwill, Disabled Veterans, or similar organizations. Or they can be sold at a local flea market. Take excess paper bags, glass jars, and egg cartons to your local food co-op. They can always use such items. Separate out your aluminum cans, and sell them for scrap. Food scraps can go into a compost pile to fertilize your garden next spring. That way, this year's food waste creates next year's vegetables. Raked leaves can also go into the compost. Is there a neighborhood recycling co-op in your area? They often collect trash for sale or reuse.

Toxic Torts

If either you or a member of your family is being or has been harmed in some of the ways described in this book, you may want to consider taking legal action. The ensuing lawsuit could be broadly categorized as a *toxic tort*. A tort is a civil wrong, other than a breach of contract, for which the law will provide a remedy. A good synonym for *toxic* is *poisonous*. Thus, a toxic tort would be a poisoning (in a very broad sense) of a person that legally gives rise to a civil remedy.

What remedy? That depends on the case. For example, if the plaintiff can prove that her late husband's death was caused by regular exposure to frayed asbestos in their basement, her legal remedy could be monetary damages. If, as another example, a plaintiff's air is being polluted by a neighboring smelting operation, the legal remedy may be to enjoin (stop) the smelting operation.   *(continued)*

Toxic Torts—*Continued*

The legal tort theories upon which a plaintiff-homeowner can proceed are varied. They include: (1) negligence, (2) nuisance or trespass, (3) ultrahazardous activity, and (4) products liability. A few examples may help draw some lines.

You would probably pursue a negligence theory if you hired someone to lay new gas lines into your house and they leaked, thus causing harm to you or someone in your house. If, on the other hand, you purchased a new gas-fired hot-water heater and it leaked gas and caused the same harm, you would perhaps proceed under a products liability theory.

If a manufacturing firm established a new plant on your side of town and it began emitting toxic smoke that was both annoying and harmful, you could pursue a nuisance or trespass theory to either enjoin the operation of the plant or to recover damages for the personal and economic harm the defendant caused. Moreover, certain activities are considered so abnormally dangerous that the person responsible for them can be held *strictly liable* for any harm caused (which means there is no defense). Thus, this same toxic smoke emission could have come from such *ultrahazardous* activity for which the defendant would be strictly liable.

You should also be aware of the procedural device called a class action suit. In the example of the manufacturing plant emitting smoke on your side of town, it would not be feasible for everyone in town to join together as plaintiffs in a single lawsuit. But, if one homeowner brought the suit on behalf of all the homeowners who were affected by the toxic smoke, that would be an efficient way, from both the court's and the plaintiff's perspective, to resolve the dispute. Thus, a lawyer for either you or another homeowner might have suggested a class action suit.

One final point is the question of how to finance a lawsuit. First, find a lawyer you trust. Second, make the financial arrangements with that lawyer from the outset. In most tort cases, lawyers will represent you for a *contingent fee*, which means the lawyer will get paid by taking a percentage—usually 25 to 40 percent—of what you recover. If you lose, the lawyer will lose, too. If you're seeking an injunction, however, there will be no monetary recovery and the lawyer will want to be paid a fixed dollar amount or an hourly fee. In class action suits, the plaintiff class can usually recover attorney's fees from the defendant if the plaintiff class wins.

Don't be afraid to become a plaintiff in a homeowner lawsuit. It's being a defendant that's no fun.

Many communities have mandatory recycling—residents sort their garbage before haulers pick it up. Aluminum, cardboard, paper, and leaf waste are the items usually separated.

Remember, there is a limit to the ecological disturbance our planet can withstand. You don't have to buy more to be happy or successful. It's time for a change in thinking. Don't continue to contribute to the problem.

MAINTAIN A POSITIVE ATTITUDE

Emotions have a lot to do with good health. A good attitude laced with frequent laughter is the key to a happy, healthy, pain-free life. A negative outlook, on the other hand, has a negative effect on the body, breaking down its immunological defenses and weakening it in its struggle against disease.

Studies show that laughter and compassion can turn on the switches of even the most negative person. This turnaround has a marked positive affect on the body, making it stronger and more able to fight disease. To those who dispute that (and some empirical scientists still do), there is the unrefutable argument that laughter and a positive attitude improve quality of life. Isn't that enough?

Since the home is the seat of our emotional life, it should be a positive, close to hassle-free environment that provides comfort, encouragement, stimulation, and regeneration. Such a happy home is certainly a healthy one.

Minimize Stress

You can't have a healthy home if you're constantly stressed out, late for appointments, unorganized, with relationships and life in general in disarray. It's hard to have a positive impact if you aren't feeling mentally sharp and well rested, if you don't respect yourself or those you live and work with. In these hectic times, you need to have integrity and self-esteem to be physically, mentally, and emotionally fit.

To help get you started on a routine program of well-rounded fitness, Helen Nearing, who with her husband, Scott, authored the landmark *Living the Good Life* (Schocken, 1970), offers the following ten tips on destressing your life:

1. Do the best you can, whatever arises.
2. Be at peace with yourself.
3. Find a job you enjoy.
4. Live in simple conditions: housing, food, clothing. Get rid of clutter.
5. Contact nature every day. Feel the earth under your feet.
6. Take physical exercise through hard work, gardening, or walking.
7. Don't worry. Live one day at a time.
8. Share something every day with someone. If you live alone, write someone, give something away, help someone else somehow.

9. Take time to wonder at life and the world. See some humor in life where you can.

10. Be kind to the creatures, and observe the one life in all things.

WHERE ARE WE HEADING?

As we approach the turn of another century, our houses are no longer healthy places to be. Our air, water, and consumer products contain many dangerous substances that change our moods, affect our cells, leave us depressed much of the time, and contribute to slow thinking. If it doesn't add up to serious disease in later life, it does add up to decreased quality of life—a life where we simply are not reaching our full potential for health and happiness.

You can always get off this crazy merry-go-round. A simple, natural home environment is a safe home environment. Avoid as many alien chemicals as possible. Simplify! You don't need different kinds of soap or cleansers for every single thing you clean. Cut back your use of unnecessary, expensive, energy-draining appliances like electric knives, electric can openers, trash compacters, air conditioners, and dishwashers. Eliminate cosmetics you don't really need, or find natural alternatives for them.

Keep it simple, and you'll be helping to make your home a healthful, regenerative place to be. A healthy, happy home can be heaven on Earth.

Appendix A

Products and Services

AIR CLEANERS
Bionaire Corp.
565A Commerce St.
Franklin Lakes, NJ 07417

Honeywell, Inc.
1985 N. Douglas Dr.
Golden Valley, MN 55422

North American Phillips
Consumer Products Div.
P.O. Box 10166
Stamford, CT 06904

BEDDING
The Company Store
500 Company Store Rd.
La Crosse, WI 54601
*Offers down comforters, cotton
bedding.*

Futons & Furnishings
Dona Designs
825 Northlake Dr.
Richardson, TX 75080
*Organic cotton products; no
pesticides, herbicides, defoliants, or
flame retardants.*

FULL-SPECTRUM LIGHTS
Duro-Test
2321 Kennedy Blvd.
North Bergen, NJ 07047
Maker of Vita-Lite.

Environmental Systems
204 Pitney Rd.
Lancaster, PA 17601
Maker of Ott-Lites.

GTE Products Corp.
Sylvania Lighting Center
100 Endicott St.
Danvers, MA 01923

North American Philips Lighting
  Corp.
P.O. Box 6800
Somerset, NJ 08875

FURNITURE AND FURNISHINGS
Masters Corp.
P.O. Box 514
New Canaan, CT 06840
Offers natural upholstery fabrics.

Rabbit Systems
100 Wilshire Blvd.
Santa Monica, CA 90401
*Maker of VCR Rabbit (also
available from Radio Shack stores).*

HEAT-RECOVERY VENTILATORS
AQ Plus
P.O. Box 5205
New Castle, PA 16105

Enermatrix, Inc.
P.O. Box 466
Fargo, ND 58107

Nutone
Madison & Red Bank Rds.
Cincinnati, OH 45227

HOUSEHOLD PRODUCTS
Granny's Old Fashioned Products
P.O. Box 256
Arcadia, CA 91006
*Send self-addressed stamped
envelope for information.*

Necessary Trading Co.
694 Salem Ave.
New Castle, VA 24127
Offers natural pest controls.

Rexair, Inc.
900 Tower Dr.
Suite 700
Troy, MI 48007
*Maker of Rainbow, water-based
vacuum.*

Scovill
NuTone Div.
Madison & Red Bank Rds.
Cincinnati, OH 45227
Maker of whole-house vacuums.

**INDOOR AIR POLLUTION
  MONITORS AND CONTROLS**
Air Chek, Inc.
P.O. Box 2000
Arden, NC 28704
*Offers radon detectors; charcoal and
water samplers from $11.95.*

Air Quality Research Institute
Grayson St.
Berkeley, CA 94710
*Offers formaldehyde monitors: $48
per kit, including analysis; $18 per
kit for customer performing own
analysis.*

At Ease
Sun Nuclear Corp.
415-C Pinea Ct.
Melbourne, FL 32940
*Offers continuous radon monitor
with alarm.*

bdc Electronics, Inc.
P.O. Box 4996
Midland, TX 79704
Offers carbon monoxide sensors.

Bio-Tech Systems
P.O. Box 25380
Chicago, IL 60625
*Manufactures special covers that
keep firm seals between dust mites
and bed mattresses.*

Direct Safety Co.
P.O. Box 50050
Phoenix, AZ 85076
*Offers safety clothing and
respirators for asbestos removal.*

Enkadrain
Akzo Industrial Systems Company
1 N. Pack Sq.
P.O. Box 7249
Asheville, NC 28802
*Offers subgrade surface venting for
radon.*

Glenwood Laboratories
3 Science Rd.
Glenwood, IL 60425
Provides radon testing.

Infiltec
P.O. Box 1125
Waynesboro, VA 22980
Makers of radon detectors.

Quantum Group, Inc.
11211 Sorrento Valley Rd., St. D
San Diego, CA 92121
Sells carbon monoxide sensors.

Radon Detection Services, Inc.
P.O. Box 419
Ringoes, NJ 08551
Offers radon mitigation fans.

The Radon Project
P.O. Box 90069
Pittsburgh, PA 15224
Offers radon testing.

Radon Testing Corp. of America
12 W. Main St.
Elmsford, NY 10523

Threshold Technical Products
7225 Edington Dr.
Cincinnati, OH 45249
Maker of home radiation detector.

Track Etch
Terradex Corp.
460 N. Wiget Ln.
Walnut Creek, CA 94598
Offers radon detectors for $25.

**LOW-TOX, NO-TOX BUILDING
    MATERIALS AND SYSTEMS**
AFM Enterprises, Inc.
1140 Stacy Ct.
Riverside, CA 92507
*Makers of Dyno Flex and Dyno
Seal adhesives; Carpet Guard floor
covering.*

Bangor Cork Corp., Inc.
P.O. Box 125
Pen Argyl, PA 18072
*Maker of battleship linoleum (made
from natural materials).*

Clivus Multrum
21 Canal St.
Lawrence, MA 01840
Maker of composting toilets.

Glascrete, Inc.
1900 Norris Rd.
Bakersfield, CA 93308
*Maker of Wonderboard, concrete-
and-fiberglass-mesh wallboard.*

Homasote Co.
Box 7240
West Trenton, NJ 08628-0240
*Maker of Homasote 440 Carpet
Board.*

Livos Plant Chemistry
614 Agua Fria St.
Santa Fe, NM 87501
*Maker of Linami Cork Adhesive,
Children's Paper Glue, Bilo floor
wax.*

Masters Corp.
P.O. Box 514
New Canaan, CT 06840
*Distributor of Biofa brand
adhesives; ISO Flock, Air Krete,
and Insulation Cork insulation
materials; Marmoleum resilient
flooring.*

Plywood Assoc.
1825 Michael Faraday Dr.
Reston, VA 22090
*Provides information on low-
formaldehyde wood products and
emission testing methods.*

MUSIC
Effective Learning Systems, Inc.
5221 Edina Industrial Blvd.
Edina, MN 55435
Offers tapes for improving self-image, relaxation, weight control, taking charge of your life, and managing stress.

PAINTS, STAINS, AND FINISHES
AFM Enterprises, Inc.
1140 Stacy Ct.
Riverside, CA 92507
Maker of Safecoat paint.

Livos Plant Chemistry
614 Agua Fria St.
Santa Fe, NM 87501
Maker of fungicide-free and biocide-free paint.

The Old Fashioned Milk Paint Co.
P.O. Box 222
Groton, MA 01450
Maker of casein-based milk paint.

Pace Chem Industries
779 S. LaGrange Ave.
Newbury Park, CA 91320
Maker of fungicide-free and biocide-free paint.

William Zinsser & Co., Inc.
39 Belmont Dr.
Somerset, NJ 08873
Maker of alcohol-based primer and shellac.

PET PRODUCTS
Very Healthy Enterprises
P.O. Box 4728
Inglewood, CA 90309
Offers vitamins and minerals for pets.

SAFETY PRODUCTS
BRK Electronics
780 McLure Rd.
Aurora, IL 60504
Maker of First Alert Model SA202 photoelectric smoke detector.

SECURITY SYSTEMS
Radio Shack
Check yellow pages of phone book for store near you. Offers Duofone Sensor Alert, which will keep track of conditions at home while you're not there. In event of trouble, system will dial preprogrammed telephone numbers with voice-synthesized alert message. System monitors indoor temperature, electrical outages, burglar or smoke alarm signals.

SETBACK THERMOSTATS
Quad Six, Inc.
3753 Plaza Dr.
Ann Arbor, MI 48108.

SOUNDPROOFING
Akzo Industrial Systems Co.
1 N. Pack Sq.
P.O. Box 7249
Asheville, NC 28802
Maker of Enkasonic, polyester and nylon matting designed as wall, ceiling, and floor insulation to obstruct passage of sound.

ESI Energy Saver Imports
2150 W. 6th Ave., Unit E
P.O. Box 387
Broomfield, CO 80020
Maker of Foil-Ray, quilted foil wrap with many insulation and soundproofing uses.

Homosote Co.
Box 7240
West Trenton, NJ 08628-0240
Maker of Sound-A-Sote, structural board made without asbestos or formaldehyde.

ULTRASONIC HUMIDIFIERS
Brookstone
Vose Farm Rd.
Peterborough, NH 03458
Maker of Corona UF-40.

UVT GLASS
CYRO Industries
P.O. Box 950
Arlington, NJ 07856
Maker of UVT Acrylite.

Rohm & Haas
Independence Mall West
Philadelphia, PA 19105
UVT Plexiglas, ultraviolet-transmitting plastic for windows, is available through distributors throughout United States.

Schott America
Glass & Scientific Products, Inc.
3 Odell Plaza
Yonkers, NY 10701
Distributor of ultraviolet-transmitting window glass.

WALL FINISHES
Livos Plant Chemistry
614 Agua Fria St.
Santa Fe, NM 87501
Maker of Anavo oil-based spackle, Velo spackling compound, Lavo wallpaper paste.

Masters Corp.
P.O. Box 514
New Canaan, CT 06840
Offers Auro spackling paste and compound; Auro wallpaper adhesive; pine wall sheathing; Mineral Board and Eterboard, formaldehyde-free wall panels.

Murco Wall Products, Inc.
300 N.E. 21st St.
Fort Worth, TX 76106
Maker of Murco M-100 HiPo joint compound; Murco M-100 HiPo asbestos-free drying type compound.

WATER POLLUTION MONITORS AND CONTROLS
EPS
P.O. Box 191
Concord, CA 94522
Maker of all-stainless-steel water filters.

Hydromek, Inc.
4527-H San Fernando Rd.
Glendale, CA 91204
Simple kit for testing drinking water for lead levels, for $10.95 and up.

National Testing Labs, Inc.
6151 Wilson Mills Rd.
Cleveland, OH 44143

Water Quality Assoc.
4151 Naperville Rd.
Lisle, IL 60532
Provides information on suppliers and dealers of water treatment devices.

Water Test Corp.
33 S. Commercial St.
Manchester, NH 03108

WOOD PRODUCTS
AFM Enterprises, Inc.
1140 Stacy Ct.
Riverside, CA 92507
Maker of AFM Water Seal.

DeGraco Coatings
Valspar Corp.
200 Sayre St.
Rockford, IL 61101
Maker of particleboard sealer.

Denny Sales Corp.
3500 Gateway Dr.
Pompano Beach, FL 33069
Maker of Dennyfoil, used as vapor barrier.

Fabulon Group
P.O. Box 1505
Buffalo, NY 14240
Maker of Crystal Fabulon, durable varnish.

Livos Plant Chemistry
614 Agua Fria St.
Santa Fe, NM 87501
Maker of Aravi-Borax wood preservative, Donnos Wood-Pitch Impregnation.

Masters Corp.
P.O. Box 514
New Canaan, CT 06840
Distributor of Auro clear wood sealer, Auro particleboard fume sealer.

Pace Chem Industries
779 S. LaGrange Ave.
Newbury Park, CA 91320
Maker of clear finish for wood products that acts as sealer to block out harmful fumes.

Appendix B

Resources

289

COLOR AND MOOD
Alexander Schauss, Director
The Biosocial Institute
1529 Commerce St.
Tacoma, WA 98402
Research with Baker-Miller Pink

The Wagner Institute for Color
   Research
111 W. Valerio St.
Santa Barbara, CA 93101

COMBUSTION BY-PRODUCTS
The Gas Research Institute
1331 Pennsylvania Ave. NW
Suite 730 North
Washington, DC 20004
*Provides information on latest
technology research, as well as
correct venting of appliances.*

COMMUNITY ACTION
Citizens for a Better Environment
Suite 523
33 E. Congress St.
Chicago, IL 60605

Institute for Local Self-Reliance
2425 18th St. NW
Washington, DC 20009
*Nonprofit organization deals with
issues such as energy, recycling,
housing, health care.*

Natural Resources Defense Council
122 E. 42nd St.
New York, NY 10168
1-800-648-NRDC
*Nonprofit organization dedicated to
protecting and improving quality of
human environment.*

CONSUMER PRODUCTS
Consumer Product Safety
   Commission (CPSC)
Washington, DC 20207
1-800-638-2772
(In Maryland, 1-800-492-8363)
*If you suspect household product is
hazardous, write to or call CPSC.
However, CPSC does not regulate
pesticides, foods, drugs, cosmetics,
or personal-hygiene products.*

Environmental Protection Agency
401 M Street SW
Washington, DC 20460
(202) 755-0707
*Regulates manufacture and use of
pesticides, foods, drugs, cosmetics,
and personal-hygiene products and
has jurisdiction over all air and
water pollution and hazardous
waste.*

Golden Empire Health
   Planning Center
2100 21st St.
Sacramento, CA 95818
*Offers booklet "Making the Switch:
Alternatives to Using Toxic
Chemicals in the Home" for $5.50.*

CORPORATE RESPONSIBILITY
Council on Economic Priorities
30 Irving Pl.
New York, NY 10003
Publishes book Rating America's
Corporate Conscience.

EPA REGIONAL OFFICES
Public Information Center
Environmental Protection Agency
West Tower Lobby, North Gallery
401 M St. SW
Washington, DC 20460
(202) 755-0717
There are 10 regional offices. To find location nearest you, call or write.

FORMALDEHYDE
Consumer Federation of America
1424 16th St. NW
Suite 604
Washington, DC 20036
Send self-addressed stamped envelope for copy of booklet "Formaldehyde: Everything You Wanted to Know But Were Afraid to Ask."

FURNISHINGS AND FINISHINGS
The American Council
   for an Energy-Efficient Economy
1001 Connecticut Ave. NW
Suite 535
Washington, DC 20036
For latest update on energy-efficient appliances, ask for copy of "The Most Energy-Efficient Appliances."

The Assoc. of Home Appliance
   Manufacturers (AHAM)
20 N. Wacker Dr.
Chicago, IL 60606
(312) 984-5800
Publishes various booklets for consumers about appliances, including annual "Consumer Selection Guide for Refrigerators and Freezers."

Consumer Product
   Safety Commission (CPSC)
Washington, DC 20207
1-800-638-2772
(In Maryland, 1-800-492-8363)
Ask for CPSC "Bulletin," which tells what's in household appliances (such as asbestos in some hair dryers and toasters).

INDOOR AIR POLLUTION
Air Pollution Control Assoc.
P.O. Box 2861
Pittsburgh, PA 15230

The American Academy
   of Allergy & Immunology
611 E. Wells St.
Milwaukee, WI 53202
Provides information on allergens.

The American Council
   of Independent Laboratories
1725 K St. NW
Washington, DC 20006
Provides information on local testing laboratories.

National Cancer Institute
1-800-638-6694

National Pesticides
   Telecommunications Network
Texas Tech Pesticide Laboratory
P.O. Box 2031
San Benito, TX 78586
Provides information on wood preservatives, mildewcides, insecticides.

Toxic Substances Information Line
1-800-648-6732

LIGHT AND HEALTH
Mark Zitelman
SunBox Co., Inc.
1132 Taft St.
Rockville, MD 20850
Source for full-spectrum lighting.

MOISTURE
Department of Energy
P.O. Box 8900
Silver Spring, MD 20907
Offers booklet "Moisture Control in Homes."

MUSIC
National Assoc.
   for Music Therapy, Inc.
505 11th St. SE
Washington, DC 20003

NOISE
Office of Noise Control
California Dept. of Health Services
2151 Berkeley Way
Berkeley, CA 94704
Offers catalog of sound transmission class (STC) ratings for wall and floor/ceiling assemblies.

PESTICIDES
Distribution Center
7 Research Park
Cornell University
Ithaca, NY 14850
"Guide to Safe Pest Management around the Home" available for $3.90 postpaid.

National Coalition against
   the Misuse of Pesticides
530 7th St. SE
Washington, DC 20003

National Pesticides
   Telecommunications Network
Texas Tech Pesticide Laboratory
P.O. Box 2031
San Benito, TX 78586
Provides information on wood preservatives, mildewcides, insecticides.

Pesticide information also available from county agent (U.S. Department of Agriculture Extension Service), regional office of U.S. EPA, regional office of U.S. FDA (for tolerances and pesticide residues on food), and closest U.S. OSHA office or state occupational safety office (for protective clothing and safety gear).

PETS
Delta Society
P.O. Box 1080
Renton, WA 98057
(206) 226-7357

RADON
Call state health department and ask for office dealing with radiation.
    EPA offers four radon publications: "A Citizen's Guide to Radon: What It Is and What to Do About It," "Radon Reduction Methods: A Homeowner's Guide," "Radon Reduction Techniques for Detached Houses, Technical Guidance," and "Radon in Drinking Water." Call or write to local office. (See "EPA Regional Offices" in this appendix.)

SAFETY

Center for Occupational Hazards
5 Beekman St.
New York, NY 10038

Direct Safety Co.
7815 S. 46th St.
Phoenix, AZ 85044

Lab Safety Supply
P.O. Box 1368
Janesville, WI 53547
(608) 754-2345
*Provides information on safety
equipment for do-it-yourselfers.*

Lightning Protection Institute
P.O. Box 406
Harvard, IL 60033
*Send 50 cents and self-addressed
stamped, business-sized envelope for
brochure "Lightning Protection for
Home, Property, and Family."*

National Fire Protection Assoc.
Batterymarch Park
Quincy, MA 02269

National Safety Council
444 N. Michigan Ave.
Chicago, IL 60611

Nuclear Regulatory Commission
   (NRC)
1717 H St. NW
Washington, DC 20555
(202) 492-7715
*Mail ionizing smoke detectors back
to manufacturer or to regional NRC
office. Call national office listed
above for address, phone number of
regional NRC office.*

SECURITY

Enterpress Partners
P.O. Box 7097
Redlands, CA 92374
*Offers workbook that simplifies the
complex job of making inventory of
everything you own—all you do is
fill in blanks.*

National Crime Prevention Council
733 15th St. NW
Suite 540
Washington, DC 20005

Security Equipment Industry Assoc.
2800 28th St., Suite 101
Santa Monica, CA 90405

TOBACCO SMOKE

Office of Smoking & Health
Parklawn Bldg., Room 158
Rockville, MD 20857
*Single copies of the Surgeon
General's "Report on Smoking and
Health" are available.*

TOXINS

Chemical Manufacturers Assoc.
Chemical Referral Center
1-800-262-8200

Consumer Federation of America
Consumer Information Service
1424 16th St. NW
Suite 604
Washington, DC 20036

Emergency Planning &
   Community Right to Know
   Hotline
1-800-535-0202
(In Washington, DC, and Alaska,
   202-479-2449)
*Responds to questions concerning
community preparedness for
chemical accidents.*

Fund for Renewable Energy
  & the Environment
1001 Connecticut Ave. NW
Suite 719
Washington, DC 20036
Offers "The State of the States"
brochure, which details what states
are doing to protect public health
and air, soil, and water.

National Campaign
  Against Toxic Hazards
Henry S. Cole
317 Pennsylvania Ave. SE
Washington, DC 20003
Offers copies of EPA study
providing complete state-by-state
listing of accidents and toxic spills;
available for $25.

VENTILATION
Superintendent of Documents
U.S. Government Printing Office
Washington, DC 20402
Booklet "Heat Recovery Ventilation
for Housing" available for $2.25.

WASTE DISPOSAL
Enterprise for Education
1320A Santa Monica Mall
Santa Monica, CA 90401
"Hazardous Wastes from Homes,"
excellent booklet describing common
household hazardous wastes and
how to dispose of them, available
for $4.25.

Golden Empire
  Health Planning Center
2100 21st St.
Sacramento, CA 95818
(916) 448-8246
Book Household Hazardous Waste:
Solving the Disposal Dilemma *can*
be ordered for $15. Contains
information on how to set up
household hazardous-waste disposal
program in your community.

WATER
Clean Water Action Project
317 Pennsylvania Ave. SE
Washington, DC 20003

Safe Drinking Water Hotline
Environmental Protection Agency
1-800-426-4791

Bibliography

Aeppel, Timothy. "Controlling Pests without Poisons." *Christian Science Monitor*, 22 July 1987, 3.

———. "Safe Pesticides Polluting Environment." *Christian Science Monitor*, 20 July 1987, 1.

———. "Third World Grows Addicted to Pesticides." *Christian Science Monitor*, 21 July 1987, 3.

Alexander, Christopher. *A Pattern Language*. New York: Oxford University Press, 1977.

Alvarez, Mark. "Carpeting Cleanup." *Rodale's Practical Homeowner*, February 1987, 31.

———. "Healthy Building." *Rodale's Practical Homeowner*, February 1987, 30–35.

American Council for an Energy Efficient Economy. "The Most Energy-Efficient Appliances." Washington, D.C.: American Council for an Energy Efficient Economy, 1987.

American Lung Association. "Air Pollution in Your Home?" New York: American Lung Association, 1987.

Andrews, Steve. "Asbestos: Can You Live with It?" *Rodale's Practical Homeowner*, September 1986, 12-14.

"Are You Allergic to Your Air Conditioning?" *Rodale's Allergy Relief Newsletter*, June 1987.

Beck, Alan, and Aaron Katcher. *Between Pets and People*. New York: Penguin Books, 1985.

Begley, S. "How Clean Is Clean?" *Newsweek*, 4 January 1988.

Best, Don. "Home Heating Options." *Rodale's Practical Homeowner,* October 1986, 67–79.

Birren, Faber. *Light, Color, and Environment.* New York: Van Nostrand Reinhold Co., 1986.

Boyce, P. R. *Human Factors in Lighting.* London: Applied Science Publishers, 1981.

Brobeck, Stephen, and Anne C. Averyt. *The Product Safety Book.* New York: E. P. Dutton, 1983.

Brown, Michael H. *The Toxic Cloud.* New York: Harper & Row Publishers, 1987.

Canine, Craig. "Beyond the Icebox." *Rodale's New Shelter,* March 1986, 16–21.

———. "Clearing the Air." *Rodale's New Shelter,* January 1986, 64–67.

Carson, Rachel. *Silent Spring.* Boston: Houghton Mifflin Co., 1962.

"Chemical Group Is Up in Arms over Trend of Product Bans." *Indoor Pollution News,* 19 May 1988.

Ching, Francis D. K., and Dale E. Miller. *Home Renovation.* New York: Van Nostrand Reinhold Co., 1983.

"Chlordane Consumer Information," Washington, D.C.: United States Environmental Protection Agency Office of Pesticides and Toxic Substances, 1987.

Claybrook, Joan. *Retreat from Safety.* New York: Pantheon Books, 1984.

Dadd, Debra Lynn. *Nontoxic and Natural: A Guide for Consumers.* Los Angeles: Jeremy P. Tarcher, 1984.

———. *The Nontoxic Home.* Los Angeles: Jeremy P. Tarcher, 1986.

de Chardin, Teilhard. *The Phenomenon of Man.* New York: Harper & Row Publishers, 1959.

Department of Rural Sociology, Cornell University. "National Statistical Assessment of Rural Water Conditions." Washington, D.C.: Environmental Protection Agency, 1984.

De Smidt, Gene. "Soundproofing a Music Studio." *Fine Homebuilding,* October/November 1986, 60–63.

"Dust Mites: A Microscopic Monster You Can Tame." *Rodale's Allergy Relief Newsletter,* September 1986.

Ecology Center of Ann Arbor. *Michigan Household Hazardous Substance Handbook.* Ann Arbor, Mich.: Ecology Center of Ann Arbor, 1986.

Eiseman, Leatrice. *Alive with Color.* Washington: Acropolis Books, 1983.

Evans, C. L. "High Pressure Sodium Study." Fort Worth, Tex. Fort Worth Independent School District, 1977.

Fogle, Bruce. *Pets and Their People*. New York: Viking Press, 1983.

Fossel, Peter V. "The Pollution Within." *Country Journal*, September 1987, 44–49.

————. "Sick Home Blues." *Harrowsmith*, September/October 1987, 46–55.

Garbage. Baltimore: Great American Radio Conspiracy, 1986. Sound recording.

Gilliatt, Mary, and Douglas Baker. *Lighting Your Home*. New York: Pantheon Books, 1979.

Giovannini, Joseph. "Intangible but Attainable." *New York Times Magazine*, 12 April 1987, 34–37.

Greenfield, Ellen J. *House Dangerous*. New York: Vintage Books, 1987.

Harper, Joan. *The Healthy Cat and Dog Cook Book*. Richland Center, Wis.: Pet Press, 1984.

Herriott, James. *All Things Wise and Wonderful*. New York: St. Martin's Press, 1977.

Hodges, Ralph. "The High End: Sound Decor." *Stereo Review*, December 1986, 200.

"Home Safety Quiz." *Rodale's New Shelter*, November/December 1985, 78–80.

Housemending Resources: The Journal of the Housing Resource Center, Winter 1986–1987, 5.

Hunter, Linda Mason. "Fighting Fungus." *Rodale's Practical Homeowner*, December 1987, 16–17.

————. "Getting the Lead Out." *Rodale's Practical Homeowner*, December 1986, 18–20.

————. "Let the Sunshine In." *Rodale's Practical Homeowner*, March 1987, 14–15.

————. "The Right Light in the Right Place." *Rodale's Practical Homeowner*, December 1988, 34–40.

————. "Safe at Home: A Guide to Common Toxic Household Cleaners." *Rodale's Practical Homeowner*, October 1986, 14–16.

Illich, Ivan. *Tools for Conviviality*. New York: Harper & Row Publishers, 1973.

Johnson, G. Timothy, and Stephen Goldfinger, eds. *The Harvard Medical School Health Letter Book*. New York: Warner Books, 1981.

Kansas Rural Center. "Is Your Water Safe to Drink?" Whiting, Ks.: Kansas Rural Center, 1986.

King, Jonathan. *Troubled Water*. Emmaus, Pa.: Rodale Press, 1985.

Klein, Larry. "Speaker Placement: Understanding the Fundamentals of Room Acoustics." *Stereo Review*, September 1986, 61–63.

Kull, Kathie. "Fresh Air Indoors." *Rodale's Practical Homeowner*, September 1988, 45–49.

————. "Home Security Report." *Rodale's Practical Homeowner*, June 1987, 26–37.

Lafavore, Michael. *Radon: The Invisible Threat*. Emmaus, Pa.: Rodale Press, 1987.

————. "The Radon Report." *Rodale's New Shelter*, January 1986, 29–35.

"Long Distance Lightning." *Men's Health*, April 1987, 2.

McClintock, Mike. *Home Sense*. New York: Charles Scribner's Sons, 1986.

Makower, Joel. *Office Hazards*. Washington: Tilden Press, 1981.

Mander, Jerry. *Four Arguments for the Elimination of Television*. New York: Quill, 1978.

Marshall, Eliot. "Immune Systrem Theories on Trial." *Science*, 19 December 1986.

Mueller, William. "Dark Waters." *Harrowsmith*, November/December 1987, 69–79.

National Testing Laboratories. "Your Drinking Water—How Bad Is It?" Cleveland, Ohio: National Testing Laboratories, 1985.

Nisson, Ned. "Health and Humidity." *Rodale's New Shelter*, April 1986, 12–15.

Ott, John N. *Health and Light*. Old Greenwich, Conn.: Devin-Adair Co., 1973.

Pfeiffer, Guy O., and Casimir M. Nikel. *Household Environment and Chronic Illness*. Springfield, Ill.: Charles C. Thomas Publisher, 1980.

Pitcairn, Richard H., and Susan Hubble Pitcairn. *Dr. Pitcairn's Complete Guide to Natural Health for Dogs & Cats*. Emmaus, Pa.: Rodale Press, 1982.

Practical Homeowner Institute. *Safe and Secure—Home Security Guide Book*. Emmaus, Pa.: Practical Homeowner Institute, 1987.

Preuss, Peter, et al. "Predicting Ozone Pollution." *EPA Journal*, June 1987.

Raloff, Janet. "Noise Can Be Hazardous to Our Health." *Science News*, 5 June 1982, 8.

Reader's Digest Home Improvements Manual. Pleasantville, N.Y.: Reader's Digest Association 1982.

Rose, Carol. "Aging U.S. Nuclear-Production Plants Pose New Radiation Dangers." *The Des Moines Register*, 12 February 1987, A13.

Rybczynski, Witold. *Home: A Short History of an Idea*. New York: Viking Press, 1986.

Schwartz, Joel, and Ronnie Levin. "Dealing with the Dangers of Lead." *EPA Journal*, April 1987, 6–8.

"Securing the Home and Keeping Burglars At Bay." *New York Times*, 10 July 1986, C1.

Shakman, Robert A. *Where You Live May Be Hazardous to Your Health*. New York: Stein and Day Publishers, 1979.

Shaw, Webb. "New Research Rekindles Fiberglass Health Issue." *Roofing/Siding/Insulation*, May 1987.

Smith, Fran Kellogg, and Frederick J. Bertolone. *Bringing Interiors to Light*. New York: Whitney Library of Design, 1986.

"Sound Resistant Walls." *Practical Homeowner*, October 1987, 56.

"State of Battle on Pollution." *New York Times*, 28 February 1988, A50.

Sullivan, Thomas F. P. "Environmental Law Fundamentals and the Common Law." In *Environmental Law Handbook*. 9th ed. Rockville, Md.: Government Institutes, 1987.

Swearingen, David. "Old House Security." *Old House Journal*, November/December 1986, 429–433.

Thomas, Lee M, et al. "Pesticides and the Consumer" *EPA Journal*, May 1987.

Toffler, Alvin. *The Third Wave*. New York: William Morrow and Co., 1980.

Turiel, Isaac. *Indoor Air Quality and Human Health*. Stanford, Calif.: Stanford University Press, 1985.

U.S. Consumer Product Safety Commission. "What You Should Know about Home Safety Fires." Washington, 1983.

U.S. Consumer Product Safety Commission. "What You Should Know about Smoke Detectors." Washington, 1985.

U.S. Environmental Protection Agency. Office of Pesticides and Toxic Substances. "Chlordane Consumer Information." Washington, 1987.

U.S. Environmental Protection Agency. *Radon Reduction Methods, a Homeowner's Guide*. 2d ed. Washington, 1987.

Wagner, Carlton. *The Wagner System*. Torrance, Calif.: Wagner Institute for Color Research, 1985.

"Warning: Pottery Can Be Dangerous." *Woman's Day*, 1 June, 1987, 26.

Wasserman, Harvey. "Downwind from Disaster: The Story of Three-Mile Island." *Harrowsmith*, May/June 1987, 41–54.

Worldwatch Institute. *State of the World 1988, a Worldwatch Institute Report on Progress toward a Sustainable Society*. New York: W. W. Norton & Co., 1988.

Wurtman, Richard J. "The Effects of Light on the Human Body." *Scientific American*, July 1975, 69–77.

Zamm, Alfred V. *Why Your House May Endanger Your Health*. New York: Simon and Schuster, 1980.

Index

Page references in *italic* indicate tables. **Boldface** references indicate illustrations.

301

About the Author

LINDA MASON HUNTER has held numerous editorial positions at newspapers and magazines, including the *Des Moines Register* and *Better Homes and Gardens Remodeling Ideas*. She resides in Des Moines, Iowa, where she lives and works in a house built in 1910. Located on a quiet, tree-lined boulevard, it's a healthy home, with plenty of sunshine and fresh air, hardwood floors, and plaster walls. She shares it with her husband, children, and two dogs.